Pioneer's Progress

ALVIN JOHNSON

Pioneer's
Progress

AN AUTOBIOGRAPHY BY

Alvin Johnson

NEW YORK · The Viking Press · MCMLII

Copyright 1952 by Alvin Johnson

First published by The Viking Press in September 1952

Published on the same day in the Dominion of Canada
by The Macmillan Company of Canada Limited

Printed in U.S.A. by the Vail-Ballou Press, Inc.

To my wife Edith Henry Johnson, pioneer's daughter, bearer of the spirit that thrust resolutely westward from the New England coast and won a continent for the mightiest republic in history.

Contents

Preface

SOMEWHERE in the Southwest I was once privileged to stand hours and days, watching engineers bore a deep well. They were very deliberate, for the well was undertaken as an exploration. Each core brought up was expertly examined for what it might reveal as to possible wealth in the depths. I did not understand what it was in a core that made the engineers' faces light up or take on a gray hue of disappointment. But the cores were to me an exciting manuscript of world history. I saw stratum upon quiet stratum, with occasional intrusions of pebbles from some unknown source, uninteresting to the engineers but setting up in me speculations as to the topography and floods of a million years ago. The well went through an area of ancient settlement; there were human artifacts, shards, charred stones that the engineers would not look at; but they made me dream.

There were cores with the stratification all topsy-turvy; some earth forces from distances more or less great had exerted their shattering influence. A dozen cores testified to a lava flow. And below it was black sand, heavy as cast iron—eighty per cent iron, the engineers said. Below that was a fine-grained stone, made of diatom skeletons, a good abrasive; but the billions and billions of diatoms had each had a microscopic bit of carbohydrate, which under the pressure of thousands of feet of sand and stone dripped, dripped microscopic droplets of oil into the underlying salt sea sand.

The real world is made up, apparently, of symbols for man to read, as if man were anything in the vast drama of cosmic forces. My well is a symbol to me, arrogantly anthropocentric child of earth.

What is this account I have given of my life but a well through human life, sunk through the strata of three-quarters of a century? What I present are the cores. They exhibit strata, often with pebbles of uncertain provenance, and with occasional artifacts.

I would give much for the opportunity to study a hundred such

successions of cores. Then perhaps I might be in a position to understand my times. And understanding one's times is an essential part
of a civilized standard of living.

But I return to my own well-digging. The cores bring up the spread
of American settlement over the prairie, the hopes of the soil, the
disillusions of an era of declining prices, the rise of class feeling and
radicalism in politics. These were strata of relatively quiet times, to
be slightly distorted by the minor seismic disturbance of Kiplingesque
imperialism.

Again they exhibit the laying down of level strata of clays and
sand, all to be shattered and uptilted by the terrific upheaval of the
First World War. Then they record the slow work of depositing sands
and clays, destined to be cracked and confused by the Second World
War. Finally they exhibit a period of daily quakes in the struggle
of ideologies and chicaneries, bold assertions and abject fears.

Such are the main geologic forces revealed by the cores of the well
sunk through the three-quarters of a century of my life under the
sun. But as in Tertiary times, when the sea roared in over the land
and roared out again, and mountains sank under the sea and other
mountains burst up toward the sky out of the stagnant swamps, our
human progenitors dodged the falling cliffs and the feet of the mighty
beasts of the plains and continued anxiously their quest for security,
so I, with hundreds of millions of other human beings, have gone on
with life, experiencing the eager thrill of dawn and not too deeply
discouraged by the gathering darkness of night.

Pioneer's Progress

ONE

Mostly Hearsay

DECEMBER 18, 1874, was remembered for many years in northeastern Nebraska as the date of one of the worst drifting snowstorms on record. That was the day I chose to be born, without benefit of the medical profession, since the doctor, who lived fourteen miles away, could not possibly get through the drifts. I have kept myself fairly aloof from the profession ever since, though deeply respecting it.

I arrived in a snug room. The light came dimly through frosted panes and was supplemented by a tallow candle, for in those days kerosene lamps occasionally blew up and set the house on fire—a risk my parents did not choose for me on my first day. My oldest sister, Jane, after one glance at me, went off to the girls' bedroom and cried bitterly. Why did our family have to have such awfully homely babies? My mother didn't accept the appraisal, and anyway, her dreams for me did not turn on my looks.

My father walked back and forth in the room with his quick, noiseless Indian tread. What he felt could not be known, for he was bearded up to the eyes, and eyes under a lofty, smooth brow are not revealing. Two years earlier, when the birth of my sister Edith was expected, he had said to my Uncle George, "I'd give two thousand dollars to have it a boy." When my birth was expected he said, "I'd give twenty-five hundred to have it a boy." It wasn't that boys had gone up in his estimation. He was a responsible man who never said he'd give what he didn't have. He had estimated all his possessions at two thousand dollars two years earlier. But land had gone up.

There was another person, my mother's father, who sat by my mother's bedside, repeatedly passing his long sensitive fingers over my head. "This boy," he declared, "will be a philosopher. He will lift our branch of the Bille family to its rightful place."

The prophecy entered into my mother's plans and dreams for me.

It became the more firmly fixed because my grandfather died shortly after. I was destined to be a scholar, without any reservations for the possibility that my natural bent might take another direction.

I have never been convinced that I was constituted for a life of scholarship. I have always been too restless for the patient, painstaking work of the scholar, nor have I yearned for scholastic reputation or been much thrilled by scholastic honors. I have hungered too persistently for action. I think I should have liked best to follow the pattern of my father's family—sailor, soldier, pioneer. But a child is helpless in the mesh of family expectations.

For the next three years the voice of hearsay is all but silent. I am alleged to have been of little trouble, preferring to manage my own affairs to having them managed for me. My sisters would sometimes seize me and rock me, singing "Rock me to sleep, Mother," in their flutelike voices. I did not protest, although the last thing I ever wanted to do was to go to sleep.

What I liked best was to go off by myself on exploring expeditions. From the house the ground sloped down abruptly to a little stream, known as the "crick." Usually the water was crystal clear, rippling over many-colored gravel, or pausing in deep pools where tiny fishes kept themselves in regular ranks against the current. I loved those fishes. The first experience I ever had of the tragedy of life was the sight of a dozen fishes on the kitchen table, inert, their eyes glassy. I had never heard of death; but here was the thing itself, unnamed, tragic. I went down to the creek and wept bitterly.

I had an inkling that my exploring was not approved, and I was happiest if I could complete an expedition and be at home again before my mother and sisters set up a hubbub around the house, calling "Alvin!" I dimly recall a lot of admonitions and warnings, which I considered useless but inevitable. Yet I found that the perils I disbelieved could be real. On one of my excursions a huge turkey gobbler, with no provocation, bore right down on me, ruffling his feathers until he seemed bigger to me than any ostrich to an adult, and poured out the most outrageous and terrifying noise I had ever heard. I fled sobbing to the house and would not be comforted until my father promised that I should help to eat that gobbler on Christmas.

My biggest fright came on a visit to the horse pen. I crawled through the fence and walked around in a forest of immense horse legs, entirely confident that no horse would hurt a child. But a humorous horse lowered his great muzzle at the back of my neck and snorted, his hot breath puffing out my shirt like a balloon. It was some time before even the comfort of my mother's arms could stop my shrieking mechanism from going on of itself.

In those first three years I can't remember how any of my family looked to me. But I do remember my father's hands, so strong and protecting. Our house had been visited by scarlet fever, and as I lay in bed, burning with fever, my father brought in two newborn lambs, one all white, the other entirely black. I have a vivid picture of the little creatures lying in my father's two hands, their heads bobbing on their thin necks, their agate eyes staring piteously, their hoofs not so large as my father's fingernails.

And that was the time my ears were opened to music. All my family sang at their work. My father hummed old Jutland folk airs, my mother the old airs of the Danish islands, my sisters American folk songs and hymns. I too sang, in a thin monotone I regarded as very fine. Once during my convalescence my sister Jane sat by my bed and sang an air I suddenly realized was sweet. I have never heard that air sung again except by myself, and I don't know what its name is, but it remains in my memory.

Not long afterward I was awakened from my early sleep by the most entrancing music coming up the stairway. As I later understood, the youth of the neighborhood had organized a "surprise party" for our house. The music drew me out of my bed and to the head of the stairs, where I saw three fiddlers seated on the landing, making magic sounds with instruments I had never heard of. I was drawn down one step and then another, until I was crouching among the fiddlers' huge feet. The music paused; people were laughing, and one of my sisters ran up the steps, caught me up, and carried me back to bed. Almost faint with bliss, I still listened to the music.

As my third birthday drew near, a momentous change came over my life. I was taken out of the pleasant world of the illiterate to engage in a lifelong struggle with the printed word.

In my neighborhood children began to attend school at five. My sister Edith, my constant companion and playmate, was soon to be five, and I discovered my mother was teaching her to read. Teaching Edith to read and leaving me out! I made an awful scene. In vain my mother sought to soothe me by promising to teach me when I should be two years older. I felt that age was a wholly irrelevant matter. In all our games and expeditions I had assumed that I was the leader. When we played at keeping house I was papa, Edith mamma. I made long, authoritative speeches to her, in the rhythm and sounds of Danish, which I did not understand, and she replied in the tones of sweet reasonableness my mother used. For Edith to be taught reading while I was left out was simply an outrage.

My mother thought to get out of the difficulty by giving me a lesson she hoped would bore and discourage me. It did not. There was something immensely exciting in seeing how words I knew could issue out of the groups of little marks on the page, and I became passionate about the exercise. There were, to be sure, many words I could not understand, but I could pronounce them, and that was sufficient achievement.

When I did begin school, at almost five, I balked at being put through the childishness of the First Reader. The teacher good-naturedly let me try the Second Reader, which I had gone over again and again. I appealed for a place in the Third Reader class, but the teacher assured me that nobody could be in the Third Reader before he reached a certain height, eighteen inches over my head. I was disappointed, but knew I couldn't buck the laws of nature.

I was not approved by the neighborhood. My mother received grave warnings that if she did not keep me away from books I would grow up "brain-broke," our local term for insane. But my mother said that so long as I ate well and played ardently, a bit of reading wouldn't hurt me.

TWO

My Father

M Y FATHER was born in 1827, on a little farm near the North Sea coast of Denmark. Since time immemorial the farm was known as Dejrup or Deyrup, a name that was attached to the owner and his family by right. Hence my father was christened Jens Jensen Deyrup. When he came to America in 1849, the immigration officer declared that there was no such name as Deyrup: John Johnson was name enough for him. My father was satisfied. What was an Old World name in the New World that lay before him?

My sister Edith and I are the last of the immigration-office line of Johnsons. My brother and all our children have reverted to the family name.

The farm Deyrup was held under a peculiar but rational tenure. Not the eldest, but the youngest son inherited it. The older son or sons went to sea, inheriting the family fishing schooner. The youngest son had to work the farm and take care of the parents in their old age.

My father's father was the younger of two sons, a big mercurial man with the sea in his blood. He worked the farm well but with much groaning. His elder brother was an impassioned admirer of Napoleon and joined the Danish cavalry contingent in Napoleon's Moscow campaign. Returning half crippled and with his constitution badly impaired, he was no longer fit for the sea. And so, to my grandfather's great delight, he proposed to exchange the boat for the farm. My grandfather had some twenty years exactly to his taste, rolling around the North Sea and the North Atlantic. When a terrible storm fell upon the Danish fishing fleet off the Orkneys, my grandfather's craft was one of the many that went down. My father became an orphan at the age of six. His widowed mother had three other children to bring up and had to indenture her two sons to farmers in the back country. My father became the child slave of a hard-drinking and violent farmer, who nevertheless had sense of fairness enough to liberate him at fifteen.

He set off to see the little world of the Cimbrian peninsula—Jutland, Schleswig, and Holstein. For three years he roamed from village to village, working on farms when he could find no better jobs, but preferring service as helper to carpenters, masons, blacksmiths, harnessmakers, learning what he could of these handicrafts. He learned a lot. No New England Colonial carpenter could better hew a log square or mortise it into position. Nobody could more deftly split a great granite boulder to two smooth faces, just by tap, tap, tapping with a light hammer, creating straight lines of intolerable stress in the apparently adamantine stone. Danish handicraft still had the instincts of the Old Stone Age. Nobody could more competently beat out the blunted edge of a heated ax and retemper it to taste. Indeed, my father was never able to resist the temptation to learn new trades. In America he learned from the Indians how to make a container of wilted marsh grass woven with split kinnikinnick withes, which would hold water as long as any ceramic. In his fifties, when he was laid up with a broken leg, he learned my mother's art of knitting complicated patterns and improved on them.

The English craftsman, with his genius for making two jobs grow where one would suffice, foisted upon the ignorant literati the formula, "Jack of all trades, master of none." The corresponding Scandinavian formula was, "Jack of only one trade, professional time-waster."

No statement is so simple that it won't bear an illustration, and I want to digress to illustrate the Scandinavian way. Many years ago I visited Iowa City. My host, Clark F. Ansley, dean of the University of Iowa, noting that as usual I badly needed a haircut, took me to his barbershop, where a quick-eyed Swede lifted the superfluous hair off my head as deftly as an Indian would have lifted my scalp.

As we came away my host said, "I hope you took a good look at that Swede. He came to this city as a carpenter. The city was booming, building houses everywhere, and this Swede soon got the reputation of a carpenter worth two or three. The slump began, overtaking a lot of houses without chimneypieces finished. This Swede asserted that his real trade was bricklaying and setting tiles, and he did the best work ever seen here. Times grew worse; no more building even to finish, but after every boom plastering cracks and falls off. He declared that his real trade was that of plasterer. So he'd pull off a fraud of plaster and in a wink replace it with plaster that lasted like marble. But he was too good: he finished everything people could pay for. Then the Swede declared that in the old country he was a barber and set up a shop.

As whiskers grow even faster in a depression, he had plenty of work.

"Iowa City had imported from Switzerland a magnificent town clock whose only fault was that it struck rising time at four minutes after one at night. The city had twice paid for experts from Chicago, but the clock remained unreliable as ever. The city council decided that the clock should not be wound, but the hands should be set at the hour when everybody ought to go to work.

"One day the Swede, coming from his barbershop, said, 'Ay tink Ay fix him, if somebody give me ladder and two dollars.' The ladder was found, and the two dollars. The Swede went up, opened up the works, made an adjustment here, another there, set and wound the clock, and came down.

" 'Here's the two dollars,' said a councilman.

" 'No,' said the Swede. 'You give me two dollar for Christmas, if he work.'

"That's the clock," said my host. "Set your watch by it. It's four years since our barber fixed it."

To get back to my father—he never meant to be a Jack-of-all-trades. He meant to come to America, which, in the 1840s, was said to be a land of unlimited opportunities, where a man who started with nothing could acquire land that would make a barony in Denmark. He knew well that strong, capable hands could make a living anywhere. And he cultivated his hands.

It was terribly difficult to get together the money for passage to America, with farm wages two dollars a month for a seasoned laborer and the pay of a carpenter's helper fifty cents a month and keep. From time to time my father would accumulate a riksdaler, equivalent to our American silver dollar, and tuck it into his hollow belt. He accumulated also the Low German language and the High German, and a vivid sense of the stupidity of letting silly differences in language set men apart. There was a great jangle then about Schleswig-Holstein, ruled by the absolute Duke who was at the same time absolute King of Denmark. There were fools talking war between the good folk of languages not very different. War, everybody's ruin: war, rich man's quarrel and poor man's fight.

My father had a good job with a shoemaker in Kiel and learned how to put a shoe together. But a dollar and a half a month was little and the cost of living high. Wages were better in Copenhagen. My father set out on foot, stopping at farms to earn his food and bed. Being young and lithe and bright-eyed, and having an irresistible way with horses, he promptly got a job in Copenhagen as coachman of a snobbish school for enormously rich young ladies, most exquisite little fools, shepherded by most forbidding duennas who carried their charges around the city for calls that might last hours, while the coachman in his furs and the horses in their blankets slept peacefully. What the horses did when they got back to the stable I don't know. But my father, having slept all afternoon, was awake as an owl at night. He took an additional job as night watchman for a jewelry store, adding three dollars and keep to his three dollars from the young ladies' school, and tucked all six into his belt.

But the first Schleswig-Holstein war broke out. It was a sickening business, my father's friends of North Germany coming to murder and burn among his own Danish people. He was under age, and no draft applied to residents of Copenhagen, but Danes were enlisting, and he was a Dane. He volunteered. For several years he marched up and down Schleswig and Holstein, boiling with rage about the wanton destruction of war. I don't know what he experienced. Once when he was dressing I asked him where he had gotten those enormous white scars on his shoulder and hip and leg. Oh, those were German bullets in the Schleswig-Holstein war. What battles? I asked eagerly.

"All battles are idiotic. Best to forget them." That was all he would say.

My father must have acquitted himself well, for after the war and the annexation to Denmark of Schleswig-Holstein he was drafted for a six-year term as a drill sergeant and sent down into Holstein to help make good Danes out of German conscripts. He was instructed strictly to use only the Danish language with them. If they did not obey orders given in Danish, he was to swat them over the cheek with the flat of his sword.

Such unreason was revolting to him. He would get his squad together early in the morning and tell them in German what the Danish orders meant. For this he was reported and severely reprimanded.

What shocked him most was the attempt to use religion as a nationalizing agent. The government sent leather-lunged preachers to roar forth interminable sermons to congregations that could not understand a word. My father had to bring his squad to church and see that they appeared attentive through the three-hour tirade. He envied them their inability to understand the tedious orthodoxy of the sermons.

The thought of six years of that kind of life was intolerable. My father made up his mind to slip away at the first opportunity and get off to America. He would desert: what of it? In peacetime it would be easy to replace a drill sergeant. He had riksdalers enough in his belt to pay his passage if ever he could get out of Denmark.

On his first furlough he went down to the German border, hoping to cross at some unguarded point. But the border was closely watched, to restrain Holsteiners from fleeing Danish sovereignty.

A Jewish peddler came along the highway, bent under an enormous pack. An idea struck my father. He approached the Jew and asked him why he didn't have a man to carry his pack.

"Because since this damned war wages are outrageous."

My father offered to carry the pack for nothing, down to Hamburg, if the Jew could pass him through the border.

"No," said the Jew. "I will pay you wages, but prewar wages."

My father shouldered the pack and got by the guards without a question.

Trudging along the highway to Hamburg, my father had hours of the most entertaining and instructive conversation, in a lingua franca made up of Danish, Low German, High German, with some expressive words from other languages thrown in by the Jew, who had traveled all through northern Europe. My father found that the Jew agreed with his views on war, aristocracy, officialdom, and preachers. When the Jew halted to sell a few kerchiefs or knives or beads, he explained with delicious humor the tricks of the trade. My father became very fond of him. Prosemitism was so firmly fixed in his blood by this experience that it became, apparently, a transmissible acquired characteristic, which runs undiluted into the fourth generation.

When they reached Hamburg the Jew insisted on paying my father postwar wages. Learning from another peddler that there was a British sailing ship in the harbor, picking up belated refugees from the abortive German Revolution of 1848, the Jew led my father down to the docks and foisted him on the British agent, who couldn't tell a Dane from a German. No question was asked as to whether my father had money for passage, and, indeed, the ship was in the middle of the Atlantic before the purser busied himself to find out whether his passengers could pay or not. My father exhibited the tale of riksdalers in his belt. The purser took half of them, saying my father would need the rest when he got among the sharks that populated America.

After leaving Hamburg, the ship docked at Queenstown, Ireland (Cobh), to take on a mass of Irish fleeing from famine. While the captain and crew treated the German refugees, including my father, with consideration, they treated the Irish, packed in the hold, like beasts a grade lower than pigs. During the fifty-seven days from Queenstown to New York, the store of water became foul, green with slime and stinking like a marsh. For the Germans the drinking water was boiled; for the Irish it was served raw, with strings of slime hanging from the cup to the floor. The Germans were fed on potatoes and bully beef, with lime juice to prevent scurvy. The Irish were supplied with oatmeal, ground with the husk, that stuck in your throat if you weren't a horse. If a storm came up the sailors would go down among the Irish and swat with a rope-end any Irishman they were drafting to work the pumps or haul in sail.

My father tried to get the Germans to join him in a protest against the mistreatment of the Irish. All he got for his pains was a great roar of German laughter. Irish were born to be walked over. Maybe they were human and maybe not.

In fifty-seven days my father had a lot of time to wander around the ship, and he spent many hours among the Irish, trying his few English words on them, but mostly communicating by friendly glances with anxious mothers clutching to their almost bare ribs wizened babies clad only in filthy diapers; with young fellows, bow-legged and stunted to half-man size, but blithe as a spring morning, singing clattering Irish airs and staging quarrels that looked mortal but ended in warm embraces.

These Irish were visibly and audibly Catholic. In Denmark you might hear the charge, "You might have gone crazy or Katolsk." My father felt that but for the Catholic religion these poor people, in starvation and unimaginable filth, would simply have died. Throughout his life he had a tender feeling for Catholics.

Just off the boat he set out to see the great city of New York, extending way up to Canal Street and even beyond. He had not gone a block before a glib fellow fell upon him, insisting, in international pidgin English, that he enroll in the Democratic party. Another block, and he stopped to watch a worn but energetic woman selling cabbages to the Irish who pushed their thumbs into the cabbages and yelled that they were worth only half the price. Being, as he thought, an expert on the Irish, he took his place beside the woman and bullied the customers as they expected to be bullied. The woman liked him, and before her stock was sold she invited him to come and work for her on her farm in Maspeth, near Brooklyn.

He was bent on going west, but it was already October; better to wait for the spring. He agreed to work for the woman, at six dollars a month and keep, until April.

She was a good and valiant woman, a widow with two small children, full of hope because she could grow infinite cabbages, and the Irish, cabbage-eaters, were coming in on every ship. There was a good piece of ground on the edge of Brooklyn. It could be had for five hundred dollars, and she was prepared to lend my father the money to buy it. They would both raise cabbages, and my father would fight their price out of the Irish. But he had not come to America to sell cabbages. In April he bade his patroness good-by and set off for the West.

The railroads had not yet gone through to Chicago. My father went by steamboat up the Hudson, by canal boat to Buffalo, by steamboat to Detroit, by another steamboat to the village of Milwaukee, and by stage to the village of Madison, state capital of Wisconsin, and as yet not much else. There he fell in with a number of young foreigners—German, Norwegian, Danish, Swedish, Dutch. As he could handle all their languages, as well as English after a fashion, he assumed a position of leadership and negotiated contracts for the group to excavate basements and do other jobs around new buildings. He needed to accumulate a little money to buy a team of horses, wagon and plow, in order to realize his plan of a farm of his own. At the same time he acquired a wife, a lovely Norwegian girl, sister of one of his associates. She was deeply religious, but, my father used to say, religion never hurt a woman very much.

His brother-in-law urged him to settle in the vicinity of Chicago. He visited the place but decided against it. The land was sandy and barren. As nearly as I can judge, the site available was part of the land now occupied by the University of Chicago.

I sometimes twitted my father for passing up two opportunities to become a landed millionaire, once in Brooklyn and again in Chicago. He would remark complacently that although there had been things in life he wanted but failed to get, there had been none he missed out on merely for lack of money. One thing he had got, he said, was a son as indifferent to money as he had been, and for that he was content.

The land he selected was a quarter-section of broken, partly wooded land in western Wisconsin. It was cut through by a small stream, fed by living springs. It had a good block of oak timber, much cedar, and a limestone outcrop. At that time science had very little to say about soils, and what it did say was unknown to my father. Oak trees, limestone, and living springs appealed to his instinct. I'd have chosen the same land today, knowing that where oak trees thrive the ground is rich in potash, and that soils made up largely of disintegrated limestone are rich in phosphate and have enough iodine for the sound growth of children's bodies.

He built a house, hewing all the timbers with his own hands, and cleared enough ground for fields of wheat and oats and corn. His plan of life was simple but laborious. In the open months he worked his farm. In the long winters he worked in the pine forests farther north, to earn a little money to equip his farm better. Soon a daughter, Jane, was born, then Helen, and then a son, Julius, whom my father welcomed, as would any pioneer. But Julius died the next winter, when my father was away in the pineries. A third daughter was born, whom my father named Julia and to whom he transferred all the love he had for his son. Julia was followed by Mary, who was a babe in arms when my father volunteered for the Civil War.

He still detested war, but he felt that if Secession won there would be two countries here instead of one, with standing armies, inevitable misunderstandings, and a war in every generation, as in the European countries.

After some months of training my father's regiment was built into Grant's army and participated in the Battle of Shiloh, where the opposing armies drew up two ranks deep and shot it out with frightful loss of life—an incident in the education of the refractory human material of Ulysses S. Grant. Later the regiment played its part under Sherman in the siege of Vicksburg, and after the fall of the city proceeded by forced marches to Chattanooga.

From Chattanooga my father's regiment marched to the attack on Atlanta, then through Georgia to the sea, laying waste the food bin of the Confederacy. My father hated the destruction of innocent citizens' property, but to the end of his life he revered the memory of Sherman. For Sherman, though ruthless in the destruction of property, hated to destroy life. If he could keep the Confederates on the run by flanking their positions he did so, although he could have forced a battle and destroyed them.

My father was filled with indignation when he heard that Grant was admired in the South while Sherman was detested. Grant was ruthless of men's lives, the lives of his own soldiers as well as those of the enemy. Sherman never threw away a life if he could help it. But you can still see the marks of Sherman's property destruction in Georgia.

Who knows where to look among the tangled bushes and honeysuckle for the graves of the boys in blue and gray who fell in the useless Battle of the Wilderness? Property has a longer memory than life.

My father was always reticent about his battle experience. Once a visiting corporal from his company said to me, "Say, Bub, did you know your dad was one of our best sharpshooters? Did he ever tell you how he picked off a general?"

My father interrupted him. "Killing a man is murder. You've got to do it in war, but it had better be forgotten."

After the collapse of the Confederacy my father's regiment formed part of a group of divisions held on the Ohio River. Probably Washington couldn't surmount the bookkeeping entailed in mustering them out. But Army gossip had it that the government was preparing to put the French out of Mexico, if they did not leave of their own accord. Also, the gossip suggested that the Confederate veterans would be invited to join in this foreign war and that perhaps Lee would be associated in the high command with Grant and Sherman, thus reconciling the former enemies.

At this time the Indian authorities were preparing to move the Winnebago Indians from northern Wisconsin to a new reservation in Nebraska. After the Minnesota massacre in 1864 the State of Minnesota had passed a law forbidding Indians to cross the state except under military escort. A single soldier would fulfill the definition of military escort. Few soldiers were ready to jump at an opportunity to march another six hundred miles, even through a peaceful land, but my father volunteered for the post of escort and was sent to Wisconsin, with a week's furlough for visiting his family.

He found his wife near death from tuberculosis. Her rare letters had given no inkling of illness. She had prayed for him incessantly and, to support her prayers, had given to the Lutheran Church every dollar of his soldier's pay, which he had sent her regularly with nothing reserved for himself. She had also mortgaged the farm for all it was worth, to help build a new church. My father's home was nothing but a shell.

"Poor woman," he said, "she thought by giving to the church she might keep me from being killed in battle. I hadn't a word of blame for her. But that preacher, fat fool, who took the bread out of the mouths of a sick woman and her little children, and even the roof from over their heads—it was lucky I didn't meet him before I went off to the Indians. We both would have had something to regret."

The expedition with the Indians was uneventful. They were headed by an intelligent old chief, who spoke a little English and kept better discipline than any Army command. My father rode a cavalry horse, and the chief and a few other old men had ponies. But the great majority of them—men, women, and children—made the six hundred miles on foot, using the unwearying Indian step that subordinates the heel and grasps the footing as with hands. My father adopted it and found that he could walk forty miles in a day without excessive weariness.

One incident impressed my father strongly. The chief came to him and, struggling with English, informed him that a woman had to fall out to have a baby. My father proposed to halt the expedition. No, the young boys would make trouble, sneak up to the rare settlers' farms and steal, if they weren't kept moving. Then, my father said, a wise old woman would have to stay with the expectant mother. No, that would be unnecessary; the woman would go by herself into the willows by the stream and take care of her own affairs. My father yielded, and the woman, wrapped in her blanket, trudged toward the stream and disappeared in the willows. The expedition moved on at its rate of twenty-five miles a day.

The third morning, as they were breaking camp, the woman appeared, with a baby in a sort of package on her back. The baby's head bobbed around, its bright eyes seeming to take in the whole tribe and the vast stretches of prairie. Not a complaint from the mother or a whimper from the baby in the next three hundred miles.

When my father got back to his home his wife was dead. He attended the funeral service. The potbellied preacher who had skinned her out of house and home preached an eloquent sermon on the virtues of the deceased—how she had fed her own children on skim milk in order to sell a little butter to get money for the church, how she had given all her husband's war pay to the church and raised money on mortgage for the wonderful new building.

My father, being bearded up to the eyes, was just able to conceal his anger. He made no scene. He went back to his farm, laid waste by the Lutheran Church, not visibly but as efficiently as Sherman had laid Georgia waste. However, the church had overlooked his team of two fine horses and a two-year-old colt whose price would pay the funeral expenses. The church had also overlooked the cows that had been giving skim milk for the children and butter for the church. These he sold.

Whatever was left to him he liquidated, to equip a prairie schooner, as we called the covered wagon, to take his little orphan daughters and himself far to the southwest, away from the bitter Wisconsin cold and the more bitter Lutheran Church, away from the Norwegian language and the abominable idea of a Little Norway in America.

The season was too advanced: he had to wait for spring and the hardening of the prairie surfaces. The spring came early in 1866, and in late April he set off in his covered wagon, which was packed with provisions, seeds, and tools. His four little daughters—Jane was eleven, Helen nine, Julia six, Mary four—sat on feather-stuffed gunny bags atop the barrels of meat and bags of beans. Beside him on the front seat he kept his trusty Civil War muzzle-loading rifle, in case a deer crossed his path, or a brigand.

There are a lot of rivers to cross between Dunn County, Wisconsin, and the southwest. There were no bridges and, except on the Mississippi and on the Missouri at Sioux City, no ferries. But in Sherman's army you learned how to cross rivers. You take down the canvas cover of the wagon, in case there should be gusts of wind. You tie the wagon box to the running gears and drive into the river in God's name. Horses can swim, though they may not know it, and a wagon is nearly all wood and will float if not too heavily loaded. You keep tight hold on the lines, and either by your own muscular exertion or the differential thrusting of the horses' hoofs you get nearer and nearer to the other side. You watch the banks, and when you are abreast of a gentle slope you draw in and roar at the horses, who make a mighty effort and pull you up on dry land. You get off and put your arm round their necks and your cheek against theirs. "Oh, my beloved horses, you did it again!"

The horses like that. Who doesn't like appreciation?

The Floyd River in northwest Iowa is an alternation of the smile of nature and the wrath of God. It may weave gently in and out among sandbars dotted with willows that bow their heads downstream and meet fate with pliability, or it may become a great roaring flood a mile wide, carrying uprooted trees and farmsteads in its boiling muddy water. My father had to cross it. Why not? Horses can't drown if you manage them. Wagons not too heavily loaded can't sink if you don't let them overturn. The river was flush with its banks. Somewhere on the other side you could drive up on terra firma.

As he prepared to drive into the river, two Indian women, Winnebagos, who had hidden when the tribe left but who now were bent on joining it, indicated by signs that they wanted to ride with my father across the river. He didn't want more weight. But those Indian women were very skinny, maybe a hundred pounds each. The wagon could stand it. Anyway, my father was incapable of turning down a woman trying desperately to get to her people.

He drove into the river. The current carried him down and down, but he had got out to midstream, where the ripples of muddy water stormed along, two feet high. The wagon spun around. The little girls shrieked, "Julia! Julia!" for Julia had fallen off into the horrible flood. Sweet little six-year-old Julia, apple of my father's eye! Let his hand falter, and the horses would tangle up, the wagon overturn, and the whole family perish together.

Out of the corner of his eye he saw a woman's head bob up in the stream a hundred yards below—one of the Indian women, and she had little Julia's head on her shoulder. My father let the wagon float down, and the Indian woman came on board, with Julia, destined to live to a ripe old age and go to her God on the firm land, with a rich harvest of fine children and good works.

As my father drove up on the south bank the two Indian women slipped off. My father never saw them again. Safe across the river, he set up camp, built a fire, cooked food, and assured his little daughters there was no such river ahead of them to cross, not even if they went all the way to Mexico.

A comrade from Sherman's army who had also crossed the river came to him. "My horses are old cripples. I couldn't bring my goods over. Your team are wonderful young horses. Let me borrow them to get my goods across." How can you refuse an army comrade? My father, with misgivings, loaned him his team. The man got across all right, but in coming back he mismanaged and drowned one of my father's horses.

So there my father was, with a two-horse wagon and one horse. No use talking about going farther. The remaining horse was a mare, due to foal in a month. Till the colt grew up, my father had no traction.

He borrowed another horse, crossed the Missouri by ferry at Sioux City, and drove through the level bottom with grass eight feet high. He followed a big stream and then a small confluent, found a bit of broken ground with a clear stream fed by living springs, with a stand of oak wood, the last to be encountered before the Rocky Mountains, a thousand miles west.

That land he took for his homestead. Sweet land to me, for there I was born.

THREE

My Mother

M Y MOTHER was born in 1844, in a little peasant village in the island of Fyn, Denmark, near the shore of the Belt. On both sides her parents were of families that had come down in the world. Her father, Anders Pedersen Bille, was the son of a cultivated gentleman, an intense Francophile and worshiper of Napoleon. All his fortune was invested in Napoleonic bonds, and when Napoleon was shipped off to St. Helena he shot himself. His ideal and his fortune had turned ashes together; life was insupportable.

Anders Pedersen Bille was fourteen at the time, and a cadet in the most snobbish military school in Denmark. His fate fell into the hands of an uncle, who had envied and hated his more brilliant brother. He had the eager and aspiring Anders apprenticed to a blacksmith, then regarded as the coarsest and most laborious of trades. The boy never saw his uncle again.

Anders was a skillful craftsman, though discontented and unsteady, and he wandered from city to city, practicing his craft. A job in Odense brought him into the neighborhood of my grandmother, whom he married after a short and violent courtship.

My grandmother's family had come down a generation earlier. Her grandfather was the son of a tyrannical aristocrat who, in a rage over the youth's determination to marry a girl of a lower class, put him in the army with orders to break his will. In the course of a beating with this object in view, the army broke his back and returned him on a stretcher. In time he recovered, a hunchback. The father's conscience could not abide his presence, so he was sent to Paris, where he lived for many years, spending his money too freely, as a hunchback who would take a place in society nevertheless. He had some success and could count among his friends Diderot and d'Alembert. He deeply admired Turgot and Mirabeau, and he was an avid reader of Voltaire. When the French Revolution degenerated toward the Terror, he returned to Denmark to live on a small annuity and to marry the woman for whom he had had his back broken.

He lived to be one hundred and six years old. To the last he was the domineering head of the family, feared by his son who earned his bread as gardener on a noble estate, by his granddaughter—my mother's mother—and especially by my mother in her childhood. But he had good hours when he would talk fascinatingly about the beautiful France of the *ancien régime*.

My grandparents' marriage was not at first happy. My grandfather could not forget that he was born into the minor aristocracy and put on airs wholly inappropriate to a blacksmith. My grandmother hated the aristocracy with more than a peasant's hatred. My grandfather spoke the standard Danish of Copenhagen. My grandmother insisted on speaking the peasant dialect of Fyn, which my grandfather could barely understand and detested thoroughly. Their bickering blossomed into war over the christening of my mother. My grandmother would have none of the aristocratic name Bille. She insisted on the simple surname Pedersen. To my grandfather this was an outrage to his daughter and himself.

The local religious authority was Provost Foens, scion of an aristocratic family. He vetoed absolutely the dropping of the name Bille. Who could know whether in the course of time an inheritance might not come to the family? My grandmother retired from the contest. My mother was christened Edel Maria Katrina Bille, after the great ladies in the family history. She had to suffer severely at the hands of her peasant schoolmates for the aristocratic pretensions of her name.

The bickerings and quarrels became increasingly bitter, and not long after the christening my grandfather packed his kit of tools and went off, wandering as far as Spain and Italy. He had become a skillful craftsman in fine iron work and sometimes found employment in noble cathedrals where ancient iron work had too much rusted away. Finally he returned to his wife, tamed, his craftsman fires banked down to the uses of the domestic hearth. Instead of intricate grill work, the common jobs of a peasant community—shoeing horses, beating out the blunt edges of plowshares, making nails at a profit of half a cent an hour—became his lot.

In the barn and sheds of his son's farm in Nebraska, where he passed his last years, I saw as a child many pieces of delicate iron work. They had all become rust before I realized that they were beautiful. The only piece that proved useful was a bold stencil of my father's name, for marking his grain sacks to keep the dusty miller from adding to his wealth by the exchange of decrepit sacks for sound ones.

While my grandfather was traveling, his wife had to take a place as a maid in a prosperous peasant family, some distance away. My mother was placed with her maternal grandparents and saw little of her mother during the eight years her father was away. She was treated very kindly: even the terrible old hunchback would unbend occasionally and tell her a story of old France. Her grandmother was a repository of folk tales and folk songs, going far back into the Middle Ages.

My mother remained in her grandmother's house long after her father's return. It was hard for him to earn bread for his wife and the three sons who came in quick succession. They were all christened by the name of Bille and, like my mother, had to run the gantlet of quips and sneers from their peasant schoolmates.

Provost Foens kept an eye on the family, asserting that they were not destined to remain in the peasant class. He loaned my mother books and encouraged her to write poetry, and occasionally found her a friendly publisher. If only she were a boy, he said, he would put her through the university. But he would see to it that her oldest brother, George, should have the benefit of a university education and training for the law.

As next best to university education, Provost Foens found a position for my mother as secretary to Bishop Melby in Odense, a liberal and a devoted friend of the great Bishop Grundtvig, who was then revolving his plans for an expansion from within of Danish life through folk schools and cooperatives. In the first months my mother won much appreciation for her ability to write, but Bishop Melby wished her to change her literary objectives. Instead of taking her inspiration from folk myth and folk poetry, he wanted her to throw her talent into the promotion of the new Danish democracy: peasant education, cooperation, a liberalized Lutheran religion. My mother was fully aware of the significance of the Grundtvig movement, and she would have applied to it her writing skill if she could. But her temperament was not right for political propaganda. The bishop would set her themes she honestly tried to execute, but there was no spirit in her writing. She would tear it up, to the great disappointment of her employer. My mother came to the painful conclusion that she was a failure. There appeared to be no place for the kind of writing she could do; and she was not good at the kind of writing that was urgently needed.

One of her aunts had gone with her husband to America, and they had taken a homestead about a mile from my father's. Like all immigrants of the time, they wrote home glowing accounts of America, its freedom from class distinctions, its boundless opportunity. They invited my mother to visit them and assured her that she would easily learn the language and launch herself upon a literary career with chances of brilliant success.

My mother had no illusions about embarking on a literary career in a foreign language, but she despaired of any success, however modest, in Denmark, and the idea of a new life in a great new country appealed to her.

She arrived in Nebraska in late October of 1867. She saw a landscape of long, low hills of clayey earth, recently swept by prairie fire and exhibiting a black Dantesque hideousness. At long intervals in the valleys little farmhouses cropped up in their isolation, mostly two- or three-room frame shacks, often one-room houses built of blocks of prairie sod, with sod roofs supported by willow poles and covered with dead grass, adorned by gaunt stalks of wild sunflower. Her hosts were very enthusiastic about the future of the country; but what my mother saw was the present—a pioneer country with no place for anything but manual labor.

Here she became acquainted with my father. He held a position of prestige among the Danish settlers, having had a longer experience of America and as a veteran of the Civil War. He was a personable man with a gift for exciting narrative, a resolute man fearing nothing. He had been twice married and was keeping house with four little girls by his first wife and one by his second. He needed a wife and wasted no time in convincing my mother that her career lay with him.

It was not a love match, as my mother told me after his death, but it was a match of mutual respect. She realized that it would be difficult to be a mother to five stepdaughters who had for years run the house, after a fashion. She knew that if America was a land of opportunity, opportunity was slow in materializing. It would not come to her, but if she should have children she meant to see that they had a chance in the world.

She was not a woman to make a plaything for herself out of a child. From my earliest memory she took me seriously, conversed with me on matters supposed wrongly to be over a child's head. She had a wealth of stories, which she would tell me as I sat on a stool beside her while she milked.

On almost all matters my mother and I had the same point of view. There were rare exceptions. Whenever I expressed enthusiasm for farm life and its possibilities, my mother would douse my ardor with cold water. She did not want me to stay on the farm. I'd wear myself out prematurely with hard work, she said, and be an old man when professional men of the same age were in their prime. In my adolescent years she added another item to the disadvantages of the farm. A farmer has to have a wife: there is no thrift in a bachelor farm. Where would I find a wife? I'd be limited to the country girls, all ignorant, some frightfully dull, others silly. In the end my chief business would be the bringing up of a houseful of children inevitably inferior.

My mother was a staunch believer in selective breeding for man as well as animals. I would maintain that the differences among men as among animals were chiefly due to environment. She would ask me how I accounted for the superior intelligence of the Indian pony. We had a halfbreed Indian pony who had more good sense in her shapely little head than a dozen horses of standard breed. My mother's explanation was that the Indian ponies were Spanish horses practically run wild, horses with a strong Arabian strain. And on the human level, how did it happen that the Bille family had managed to keep their name on the books of history for more than a thousand years?

I thought to counter her argument by the observation that in every generation the Billes had to mate with outsiders and that the blood of the original Billes must have run thin. That might be, my mother agreed; but as far back as records were extant, the Billes had mated not for money or rank but for ability. They had not limited themselves to the local belles but had taken wives often from Sweden, Germany, Holland, and even England.

My mother was an uncompromising feminist. As a child I was strong for women's rights, but as I began to feel the oats of adolescence I developed misgivings about women's suffrage. I found an essay by Herbert Spencer which set forth, with great philosophic authority, that man's fundamental characteristic is reason while woman's is emotion. Did we want our legislation and our legal system to develop in an orderly fashion, becoming more rational generation by generation, as indeed had been the actual political progress of Europe since the suppression of feudal anarchy, or did we want the whole system of political life to sweep back and forth on the tides of emotion?

At thirteen that looked to me like a convincing argument. I tried it on my mother. It was her principle to entertain any argument and refute it calmly. She tried to dispose calmly of Spencer, but there was a sharper note in her voice, a gleam in her eye, which caught my father's attention.

"Alvin," he said, "all this is very interesting, but you and I have to go out and set that post."

What post? I thought. I knew none needing to be set, but of course I'd have to go with my father.

Out of ear's reach of the house my father came to the point. "It's no use, Alvin, arguing with your mother against women's suffrage. It makes her hot. I don't know anything about that Spencer fellow. He may know what he is talking about or he may be a damn fool. But you have to recognize this. Your mother's got brains. She has more brains than I have or you will ever have. And isn't it a shame that she isn't allowed to vote while those Blyburg bums, who can't sign their own names, can vote—and sell their votes for two dollars each?

"Some say that if women get the vote the preachers will have more to say in politics. And some say if the women get into politics and read and talk about the same things men do, the preachers won't have so much to say to women. I don't know. But if I get a chance I'll vote for women's suffrage."

I reread Spencer's essay the next day and came to the conclusion that the great philosopher was after all a damn fool, a conviction that rests with me to this day.

FOUR

The Home

THE farm home was totally the product of my father's handicraft and energy. The Old House, the first structure, was built by my father without help from anyone. While his four little girls, the eldest eleven, kept house in the tent made out of the cover of the prairie schooner, my father felled trees, hewed them square and mortised them together for the frame or split and smoothed them for the floors. The New House, built when I was five, was of stones from a quarry my father opened in the hillside, and of beams hewn by himself. Lumber and shingles for interior and roof were available by that time.

Indeed, my father had even surveyed the homestead for himself. He found one stone set by a government survey. Guided by the North Star, he ran a line a quarter-mile north, two other quarter-mile lines at right angles to the first, and connected their ends. Our line fences were set according to this homemade survey. Later they proved somewhat askew, because the North Star isn't quite due north.

The best part of our fields had been covered by a tangled thicket of wild plum. My father had grubbed out the plum trees, many of them six inches in diameter and with hard imperishable roots. Twenty years later I would plow up some of those roots if I set the plow deep.

Man cherishes the work of his own hands. My father loved the farm, but he hated the climate of northeastern Nebraska, with its bitter winter, its winds often approaching tornado velocity; often in summer like a breath from a furnace, rolling the corn blades like cigarette wrappers; droughts and flash floods.

We children loved the farm. As it was then, before the high prices of wheat and corn wrecked the landscape, the place was very charming, with its rich fields and meadows, its grassy uplands, its timber lot fast growing into cool density under my father's Old World conservation practices. Now the uplands are all under plow. The timber is gone except for a few mangy oaks that give meager shade to pasturing calves. The springs that fed the brook disappeared with the plowing of the grassy uplands, which used to catch the water of heavy rainstorms that percolated deep through the ground. Instead of a brook there is now a dry run, disfigured with the rubbish left on down-bending trees by the flash floods. Instead of the hundreds of species of flowering plants in the woods and along the stream, there is a continuous mass of marihuana sown by the birds, and useless except as provender for the vast flocks of migratory birds sweeping down from the North in autumn. The New House is now only a heap of rubble.

The family constellation, to employ the inappropriate Adlerian concept, consisted of father and mother, four sisters by my father's first wife, one by his second wife, and a daughter and three sons by my mother. But there can't be a constellation of shooting stars. Not one of us, not even my father and mother, expected to remain long on that farm. When the children had flown the nest, the parents meant to go to California, as indeed they did in the end. The half-sisters got jobs in the Indian Service. The Winnebago Agency was only seven miles away and the Omaha Agency about ten miles. These served as introduction to the Service; after a few years employees were likely to be transferred to the greater masses of Indians in the Dakotas and Wisconsin. My sister Edith set out on a schoolteaching career and hoped to shift from city to city. But she settled in Sioux City, twenty miles from home, until she made up her mind to study medicine. My brothers and I dreamed of Oregon. A confluent of the Oregon Trail passed through my father's farm, and I never saw a file of prairie schooners passing through without a yearning to go along with them. Indeed, when I was eight I slipped into a prairie-schooner camp beside a bridge on my father's land. I heard talk of the time it would take to get to the Pathfinder Canyon, the easy route along the Sweetwater, the rough going from the Tetons to the Snake River. The campers invited me to stow away with them, and I regretted that my parents were so kind I couldn't leave them. I have traversed much of that lovely route since—and felt deeply moved by nostalgia for the bright childish dream of adventure.

Counter to my childish wanderlust was my mother's determination that her four children should all enter professional pursuits and orient themselves toward the East instead of the West. She did not argue, she assumed; and a vital assumption can't be refuted.

On the farm there can be none of the jealousies, complexes, inferiorities, and superiorities that make up the stock-in-trade of the Viennese school of psychologists. The arrival of a little brother or sister does not put the next older child's nose out of joint. The farm child is not his mother's plaything, for the farm wife has no time to play. There is no property or position to inherit, to bedevil the relations between siblings. I was four when my brother John arrived, and I remember distinctly how set up I felt over this addition to the family. At first he was very unresponsive to my advances, but before long he gave me his first smile. I loved him very much. When he was two Harry arrived, and John and I were wholly for him. To the day of his untimely death John and I loved each other intensely, although we had many a temperamental clash. I never had any clash with Harry, from the day of his birth to the present time, when he serves the State of California as a Superior Court judge.

My father was absolute monarch of the family group. We were all afraid of him, with the exception of my mother and my sister Edith. But no Oedipus complex could root itself under farm conditions. However absorbed in each other young farm husband and wife might be in the honeymoon stage, by the time the first baby can crawl and play, caresses have given way to ceaseless toil, indoors and out, and to mostly monosyllabic conversation. The budding child intelligence sees no amorous privilege from which he might like to oust his father. Later, he probably sides with his mother in family rows, but that is another story.

My father exercised his authority with the minimum of means. A few words, or even a look of disapproval, passed for a scolding and cast the sinner down utterly.

For protection against cattle thieves and other marauders my father kept a Civil War rifle in the corner behind his chair. Eight years of army service had trained him to sleep with his ears on guard. Sometimes I would awaken in the night at the sound of his tiptoeing steps as he made his way to the dark stairs and to the corner where he kept his rifle. The door would open and close; my heart would beat noisily. Later the door would open—who? My heart would stand still. I'd hear his steps to the corner; I'd hear him set down his rifle with a military groundarms. I could sleep again.

That rifle, not the sheriff or the courts, meant law and order to me. I loved to put my hand on it when nobody was looking. And one time, when my parents had driven to town, taking my sister Edith and leaving me in charge of the house, I got the rifle out, put on a per-cussion cap, and, aiming at trees across the brook, pulled the trigger. Instantly I was flat on my back with an awful pain in my shoulder. For a few minutes I was convinced I had somehow shot myself. But I soon recovered and put the rifle back in its place. My father would probably not pick it up for months, and then he would conclude that it had not been loaded.

Returning, he sniffed the air. "Alvin, have there been hunters around?"

No, I hadn't seen any.

He went into the living room, sniffed again, picked up the rifle, sniffed at its muzzle, and turned his eyes on me. "Alvin—ts-ts-ts." That is all he ever said about it. It was enough.

My father was heavily bearded in dark brown up to the cheekbones. Above forthright eyes and a high white brow he had a mass of lighter brown wavy hair. I have since come to realize how effective that kind of make-up is for the head of a household. All weaknesses, doubts, irresolutions written on the mobile features are hidden by the beard. Brow and unflinching eyes are always consistently resolute.

No one could possibly be as resolute as my father always appeared. Even the horses were confident that he knew what he was about. If I tried to drive out of the field with too heavy a load of hay and the horses thought they couldn't pull it and refused to try, my father had only to go up to them, pat their necks, and talk to them in his even voice. At his command they would make a mighty effort and get the wagon moving forward.

One time when my father and I were driving home from the city, we found that a bridge we had to cross was a foot deep in water from a flash flood. My father calculated that the flood had not been going long enough to wash out the earthen approaches to the bridge and we could still cross. The frightened horses looked around appealingly; did they have to breast that roaring flood? My father talked to them calmly and gave the command; the horses plunged ahead in God's name.

My father had a span of beautiful horses, brought up by his own hand, five and seven years old, just in their youthful prime. Under a sultry storm-threatening sky we were straining every nerve to get the wheat into the stack. A succession of rains, with the wheat standing in shocks, might ruin it. We had no time for the customary noon recess; we tied the team, still hitched to the hayrack, to the corner post of a shed, put a box of oats before each horse, and rushed to the house to wolf down our midday meal. We had hardly sat down when we heard a terrible commotion from the sheds. We rushed over, only to see the horses galloping down the field with the hayrack careening behind them. Beating around at the flies, they had pulled down the corner post of the shed; the shed roof had fallen heavily on their heads and necks, knocking them into a frenzy.

I ran as fast as I could, for the horses were heading for a forty-foot precipice. Over they went, wagon and all. When my father came up he could look down on two dead horses and a smashed wagon and hayrack.

My father surveyed the scene. I thought he would at least groan, for those horses had been his love and his pride. No. His face did not change.

"Alvin," he said, "run over to the pasture and bring in the colt and the old mare. I'll fix up the old wagon and we'll go ahead with the stacking."

The old mare had been a pensioner for years, the colt had barely been broken. We put them into odds and ends of harness, got back into the field, and hauled wheat till sundown, when my father finished it off in a beautiful stack capable of shedding any deluge.

That night it rained in torrents, and the next day. Between showers we got the harness off the dead horses, pulled our wagon, now three-wheeled, away from them, and spaded down great slabs of earth from the precipice to bury them deep. We could not let the coyotes tear the carcasses of our faithful horses.

When the burying was done my father leaned on his spade and reflected. "Things will often go wrong with you, Alvin. It can't hurt you, if you don't lose your courage."

I can't refrain from adding one more bit to this picture of my father. Since his death, a third of a century ago, whenever I go to sleep in grave perplexity my father comes to me in a dream. I'm driving a car down a steep street; the brakes do not hold; at the bottom there is a crazy tangle of traffic, and my uncontrolled speed is accelerating. Suddenly I am aware of my father seated beside me. He is huge; he towers a yard above my head; his shoulders are a yard wide; his beard, still dark brown, floats out over his mighty chest. He says nothing. We both know that he is dead. But all my perplexities are gone when I awaken in the morning. All right, I say to myself, I will go ahead in God's name. And I get credit for resolution because I'd dreamed of my father's beard.

I cannot give so definite a picture of my mother, although I was much closer to her; indeed, we were companions in all our ideas and hopes, rather than parent and child. We were companions, too, in our intellectual interests.

Through her associations with Bishop Melby and the influence of the great Grundtvig, my mother had been steeped in the theological controversies raging in Denmark. The Grundtvig position was not far from our Unitarianism and was anathema to the ruling Lutheran dogmatists. My mother was deeply interested in what our meager literature could tell us of the Transcendentalists and of the attempts going on in England to reconcile religion and science, even if the outcome was Spencer's idea to claim all that is knowable for science, leaving only the unknowable to religion. For years I read aloud to my mother while she worked. Thus I read to her Mrs. Humphrey Ward's *Robert Elsmere,* and many long discussions we had about it.

This religious liberalism set up a barrier between my mother and her four older stepdaughters, who had imbibed orthodox religion from their poor mother who wasted away with tuberculosis. Jane and Helen, the older sisters, were of mercurial temperament, and while sincerely professing religion bothered little about it. Julia, the third stepdaughter, was seriously religious but too shy to intrude her beliefs on the rest of us. Mary, the youngest, was the most purely, intensely religious person I have ever known.

She was a sweet and lovely girl, but sad, often crying for hours about our father, who detested preachers and held most religious doctrine to be hypocrisy. She also tried timidly to draw my mother toward the true faith, my mother's faith being inadequate, in her eyes, for salvation. She had a little hope in us small children. In the Sunday School romances, which composed the only literature she read, were instances of little children who won strong-hearted sceptical parents to the true faith. Why should not little Alvin be such a Christian hero?

It was Mary who first taught me to pray. Praying could be done only if, before getting into bed, you got down on your bare knees on the cold floor and recited:

> "Now I lay me down to sleep
> I pray the Lord my soul to keep.
> If I should die before I wake,
> I pray the Lord my soul to take."

I must have been very little when that prayer was put into my mouth, for I misinterpreted it badly, to the damage of my conception of the Lord. I thought that if I did not get down on my knees and pray that prayer, the Lord would come in the night with a butcher knife and take my soul, whatever it was, out of me, as my mother took the entrails out of a chicken on the kitchen table.

By the time I was a big boy of six the horror had gone out of that prayer, and Mary was teaching me to pray in words of my own composition, for my father and mother, my little brothers and my sisters. But she wanted me particularly to pray for my father, pray that he might see the light. She cried, and when I wanted to know why, she said our father was in terrible danger; if he should die suddenly he would surely be cast into the everlasting fire.

My father to be cast into everlasting fire! My father, source of law and right, protection, and whatever we needed to live by? I was shocked. I asked my mother about it.

"Do you think your father would put even a cat into the hot stove? God who is all goodness and kindness would not put even the worst of men into everlasting fire. Certainly not a good man like your father."

I reflected much on things that were said, even by people as lovely as Mary, that were simply not true. Mary had made a freethinker of me.

About this time my stepsisters began to leave home. Jane, Helen, and Julia got their jobs at the Indian Agencies; Mary went off to normal school to prepare herself for teaching. They would come home for brief vacations, with toys and caresses for the little children, new recipes for pies and cakes, new songs, fascinating stories of little Indians. I was crazy about those sisters.

As for my younger brothers, I felt myself a sort of vice-father to them. This would have been the case in any event, for I was four years older than the one, six years older than the other; and in that stage of life four years is equivalent to a generation later. But a peculiar circumstance heightened my sense of responsibility.

When I was seven my father fell gravely ill with pneumonia. I observed the gloomy face of the doctor as he left the sick room, and I was filled with foreboding. My father, who did not usually want to see his children when he was sick, sent for me.

"Alvin," he said in a whisper, "the doctor says I will die before morning. If my hour has struck, the doctor is right. If it hasn't struck, the doctor is wrong. But if I die you are the man of the house. You will do your best to take care of your mother and Edith and, most of all, of your little brothers. They are the most helpless. The older girls can take care of themselves. That is all. Now I want to sleep."

I left the room, crying bitterly. But I felt that I had been elevated to the position of head of the house; if my father recovered, vice-head. I felt that I was my brothers' keeper—a feeling that has been with me through life, with the concept of brotherhood expanded to include anyone needing help that I could give.

My parents had still a third of a century to live, half of the years in Palo Alto, California, where they could enjoy sea air as fresh and soothing as the Gulf Stream winds that breathe over Denmark.

FIVE

The Neighborhood

IT WAS a country of recent settlement when I was a child. There were a few families that had come at the time of the Kansas-Nebraska struggle, intending to help hold the region against the Slave Power, without getting too close to the firing line. There was an old fellow who had set out from Maine in an oxcart to try his luck at California gold. He found the gold diggings packed with pistol-carrying ruffians and turned back for Maine. In our vicinity one of his oxen died, and he had to settle down.

Most of the settlers came with a rush at the close of the Civil War. There was a thick sprinkling of veterans, who had learned to hate work in the confusion of campaigning over the South. There was one man who had fought in the Confederate Army. My father stood up for him against the taunts of the Union veterans. What was wrong in fighting for one's own state? As my father had a better military record than most, and looked dangerous besides, Wigle was let alone. There was a man who had escaped the penitentiary in Sweden for poaching, that is, killing a deer that was destroying his garden, and eating it. Lindstrom, to my boyish way of thinking, was grand. He was blithe as a bird, singing Swedish lays in a rich baritone, dancing like a wild dream. He carried a big knife to settle accounts with any other Swede who dared to throw in his face his near-penitentiary record.

Lindstrom had a whole repertory of crafts: stone masonry and bricklaying, carpentry, furniture making. He was quick as lightning at farm work. Binding sheaves in my father's field, he did exactly three times the work of the next best man. But, alas, he had a wife twenty years older than himself, no doubt fair once but now a hag burning with jealousy. I once saw her face pressed against the window-pane, surveying the room where my father and two of my sisters were playing euchre with Lindstrom. I heard her hoarse admonition and saw the joy on his face turn to bitter anger.

He ran away finally. America is large, and what was the use of abiding in the one spot that was hell? The hag remained with us, to make all the trouble she could by carrying tales.

We also had our local idiot. Gyp was an ape man—long arms ending in crooked fingers, sparse bristly hair all over his face, rolling eyes. His lower lip hung away from teeth sown broadcast. His only flight of speech was in the words, "Pass the 'lasses, hah!" Gyp's parents were very religious and regarded him as a cross laid on their backs by God—therefore to be endured in humbleness of spirit.

His passion was for adolescent girls, and if he saw one passing on the road he would utter a sound, half growl and half obscene laughter, and start to pursue her. Nobody bothered about that. He was club-footed, and any girl could outrun him. As for the girls, they could pose as heroines if they had been chased by Gyp. None of them, so far as I know, developed neuroses. They couldn't, for the word neurosis had not reached us.

There was a philosopher from a German university, Winkhaus, held by the other settlers to be brain-broke. From a promising academic career he was dumped upon an inappreciative America by the abortive Revolution of 1848. He was deeply absorbed in the implications of a mathematical formula he had worked out, which proved to his satisfaction that time, space, matter, and the causal nexus were all different manifestations of the same thing, capable of expression in a single equation. He had the books of Kant and Hegel, Schopenhauer and Feuerbach, and could tell you precisely where each philosopher went wrong or fell short. The time he should have given to cultivating his corn or getting in his hay he spent in scribbling on the margins of his books or in the composition of a monumental treatise. His worried wife and daughters made shift to live on the scanty product of his weedy fields. A good husband and father he was, they said; pity that he was brain-broke.

For our cornfed, humor-hungry farmers Winkhaus was a godsend. He was used to haze new settlers. An old settler would gravely advise a new one that if ever he drove by on the road past the Winkhaus farm, he should shout to Winkhaus and invite him to ride to town. Winkhaus would drop his ax or hoe or milk pail and run to the road. Aboard the wagon he'd plunge into time, space, matter, and the causal nexus, or into the errors of Fichte or Schelling. His host's eyes would begin to start from his head: what in the world had he taken on himself? In town he'd inquire, "Who the hell is that old fellow with his cowsaul nexous?" The laughter would run in concentric waves through the community.

My Uncle George, the only other educated man in the community, maintained that Winkhaus was no more brain-broke than any other German philosopher; that, in fact, he was a philosopher of powerful and original ideas. My uncle wanted me to cultivate Winkhaus. But I had enough to do in struggling with my nickname, Professor Frog, conferred on me for my long legs and my zeal for knowledge. I didn't want to be associated with brain-brokes.

Many years later, after the death of Winkhaus, I tried to get hold of his manuscript and his books annotated on the margins, but the family had burned them. Nobody, they said, could make head or tail out of the manuscript, and as for the books, he had ruined them by scribbling on them. "Poor Pa. He was a nice man; pity he was brain-broke."

There were two clusters of Danish settlement: one, a group of relations from my mother's island, Fyn, industrious and retiring folk, concealing their thought in a dialect not even my father could understand; the other, a group of émigrés from Schleswig, which had been annexed to Prussia and was therefore intolerable for Danes. They seemed a race apart, huge, noisy men, eager for a fight but dominated by their wives, who were prevailingly little.

There was a Little Deutschland of Germans who hated Bismarck but loved beer and a high voltage cheese, which they made by maturing it in jars at the center of a heap of green grass, whose fermentation would keep it warm for weeks. The result was something that made Limburger pap for babes and sucklings.

There was a community composed of new immigrants from the Emerald Isle, the men Paddies with snub noses and long upper lips, the women thin and crooked. On Nebraska food their boys were growing tall and handsome and irresistibly charming, their girls graceful and bright-eyed, proving the old German principle, *"Man ist was man isst."* Too bad the pun can't be reproduced in English. But one is what one eats.

There was a colony of real Americans who originated in "York State"; good solid farmers, God-fearing men who kept their religion in their great hearts and raised hell with nobody about his beliefs or lack of beliefs. There was an inset of settlers who claimed origin in Old Virginny, who had moved westward by generation stages. For several generations they had moved through malaria country, and the men were born tired. The Nebraska winds are intolerable to the anopheles, and malaria could not survive among us. But the malaria psychology is good for two generations, if not three. The only man among them who amounted to anything was the illegitimate son of one of the faithful wives of the tribe. He was industrious, steady, ambitious. He set up in business as a cattle feeder and proved the wisest and most skillful in the trade, made money, married a choice girl out of the rising upper class, got elected to a county office, and would sooner or later have been in Congress. But, alas, he got "inflammation of the bowels"—appendicitis, then fatal—and died.

Our sardonic neighbor Holsworth was moved by his career to philosophize: "Funny thing about the Long Tails"—the local name for this group from the Southland—"they are the only tribe I've ever heard of where the children born in wedlock are bastards, and the strays are an ornament to the state."

It was a discordant community. The Protestants disliked and distrusted the Irish—they were dominated by the priest, and the priest took his orders from Rome. My father regarded all that as nonsense. He had seen the priest, a tall, grave man, standing outside the door of the saloon, saying nothing, but making it impossible for any Irishman to go beyond a single glass. He almost made a Protestant out of the saloonkeeper, whose business was shrinking to a mere trickle. My father used to say he'd give all the preachers in the county for that one priest. As for orders from the Pope, the Pope had his own job to do, way off in Italy.

The chief butt of old American dislike was the Dane. He was taking over the damn country. He lived on what the pigs wouldn't eat. He was unspeakably gross in his disgusting broken speech.

At that time native American speech in the presence of women was highly refined. It was an insult to pure womanhood to say at dinner that you preferred the leg of a chicken. Refined folk said "limb." You could not use the word stallion; you said "horse," with a peculiar intonation. But above all you could not use the word bull. If a neighbor precipitately climbed your barbed-wire garden fence and appeared with long rips in his shirt and pants he complained, "Your gentleman cow chased me. Like to of killed me."

And suppose you told a Dane it wasn't decent to use such words. His reply was, "Dat's Pjank" (nonsense). Now listen to that word Pjank. Is that a language?

There was a graver indictment of the Danes. Around the threshing machine, no women being present, it was the rule to express every obscenity known to man. The Danes did not contribute to the bawdy talk; therefore they must be deep in some kind of secret sin. For sound men talk bawdy.

I first encountered the prejudice against the Danes when, at four, I was taken by my sisters to visit the school. A tall girl of ten, named Hattie, took me by the hand and led me around. I was in a daze; for the first time in my life I experienced a sense of overwhelming beauty, Hattie's eyes, "nut brown pools of Paradise."

A big girl, Bertha, came up. "Hattie! Take your hand away from that nasty little Dane. He isn't fit to touch your hand."

Hattie squeezed my hand, let her lovely eyes shine upon me, and moved away.

I hadn't known that I was a Dane—only Alvin, a man child. Nasty? I looked at my hands. They were clean. Apparently that big girl didn't like me. But I remembered Hattie's wonderful eyes. I never got another good look at them, but two or three years later I saw just such two beautiful eyes in a calf, and I named it Hattie.

In this community my family lived in individualistic isolation. We were on speaking terms with a wide range of people, but of fast family friends we had few. My three uncles, particularly Uncle George Bille, stood first. William Holsworth, an exceedingly brilliant man, who could make a more effective speech than any I have ever heard except from William Jennings Bryan, was my father's closest friend; his sons, Charlie and Willie, were mine. Uncle Jesse Wigle, the ex-Confederate, illiterate, but a repository of the sweetest folk songs, stood high with us. Dibble, a man who had got his tongue inextricably tied through a medical course, in which he had to observe major operations without anesthetics or antiseptics, and had fled from the ghastly profession to the prairie, was our wisest friend, though we saw him seldom.

My friends among boys of my own age were few. I had no enemies to reproach me with my Danish origin, and that was because I had a redoubtable protector in Charlie Holsworth. He was six years older, and why he bothered to defend me I never could make out. No boy could twit or bully me without a fierce look from Charlie.

He had inherited his father's brilliant mind and had drawn from somewhere in the past a blazing hot temper. When his temper was stirred he went berserk; even a grown man was no match for him. People regarded him as a potential killer, for in a fight he would use a stick of wood or a stone, if he could lay hand on it, and knock his enemy cold. But to me he was always gentle. He would flatter me by discussing serious problems on equal terms.

One time when Charlie was sixteen I was plunged into deep distress over him. Rumor reached us that his father, then a deeply frustrated man, had come home drunk and Charlie had hit him with a handspike, knocking him unconscious. My father and I hastened to the Holsworth house. Holsworth was still unconscious after two hours. In about an hour the doctor arrived. After examining the patient he said that there was small chance that he would regain consciousness. Fortunately the doctor was wrong.

The official story of the family was that Holsworth had come home crazy drunk and had attacked his wife. Charlie had struck his father in defense of his mother. My father and I knew that this account was false. Holsworth was mild as a lamb when he was drunk—the drunker the milder. But we accepted the story. At least there was no hanging in it.

Later Charlie told me all about it. A self-binder had been delivered, all dismembered and boxed, with directions in fine print for putting it together. Charlie had worked desperately to set up the machine, under a blazing sun, in heat of at least 130 degrees. If he could set it up he could get into the field for at least a few hours before dark. The wheat was overripe and the heads were beginning to shatter.

Charlie had got the machine set up, he thought. But here was a piece of wood a yard long and three inches wide, with holes for bolts at either end. Where the devil did that piece go? Was it necessary to take the whole machine apart to fit it in?

Just then Holsworth drove up from town, where he had been drinking up the substance of Charlie's hard labor. He staggered to Charlie's side. "Y' can't put that machine together (hic), Charlie. Y' ain't got brains enough." Charlie hit him with the piece of wood in his hand. Holsworth went down as if struck with a poleax.

That evening, while Holsworth's life was feebly flickering, one of his friends got together a meeting of a dozen of Holsworth's cronies and proposed to lynch Charlie. "They'd have done it right then," Charlie asserted, "before my old man was dead or alive again. You know what stopped them? Your dad.

"Your dad said there was not one of them cared for Holsworth the way he did. But killing me wouldn't bring him back to life; it would just ruin the family. He said I never intended to kill the old man; it was like an accident. And they better take the story of the attack on Ma, whether it was so or not.

"Your dad don't talk much, but when he does they listen. But you know, Alvin, I think what stopped them was the idea that your dad would have been there with his rifle to stand by me. By God, he would have, and you know it."

By the time I was twenty-two my family had moved away from the neighborhood. For nearly fifty years I didn't see Charlie. Then I visited my old post-office town of Homer. I found Charlie living comfortably in a spick-and-span house, with a cheerful wife and a grandchild or two. He greeted me as if we had parted only a day before.

"What do you say to running out to see the old places?" he asked. I was eager to do so.

He stopped the car on a hill crest overlooking my father's farm. "See that big cornfield over there? Somewhere there was the house where you were born, but you couldn't find the place. You see the course of the old creek? Not a drop of water except when there's a flood. You had the best spring in the country, same coolness summer and winter. Remember how we used to douse our heads in the heat of the day and feel like April or May? The spring is gone. Look at what's left of the timber. Your dad would never cut down a straight tree or let a big tree fall on young trees. It was pretty.

"Everything goes, Alvin. Everything but friends, and the oldest are the best." He put his hand on mine. "I'm considerable over seventy and you ain't far from it. We ain't here for long. But somehow I think we'll get together on the other side."

SIX

Education

WITH gratitude I acknowledge that my early schooling interfered very little with my education.

Our school district was small—three miles square. Half the settlers were homesteaders who refused to "prove up"—that is, go through with the final formalities making them owners in fee simple. So long as they did not "prove up" they were tax exempt. The school depended on the tax-paying capacity of the other half of the settlers, most of them very poor. As a consequence the school was in operation for only three months, December through February. The teacher was paid only twenty-five dollars a month—an income of seventy-five dollars for the year. The teachers were prevailingly those who had failed elsewhere or were just beginning. The beginners were as a rule sixteen years old, young girls who had little more education than their pupils.

We expected to learn nothing in school, and we were not disappointed. The teacher tried hard to make us write according to the Spencerian copybook, do simple arithmetic, read aloud, spell, learn the geography of New England. We always began with Maine and were mostly through Connecticut when the first of March appeared and we closed our books for nine months of successful forgetting.

The real function of the school was social. Children who saw each other rarely the rest of the year had the opportunity of playing together in the recesses, wrestling, occasionally fighting, and whispering together while the teacher was occupied with the class that was reciting. The big boys and girls occupied themselves mainly with flirting. And one boy of eighteen or another would cast sheep's eyes on the sixteen-year-old teacher and by some deliberate act of disobedience court the conventional punishment of being kept after school, alone with the teacher. The small boys and girls looked forward impatiently to the time they could enter the flirtation game. In the meantime they were storing up points from the frank discussions of older pupils of

their sex and were learning the meaning of cryptic words and phrases
that could cross the sex line.

As in the days of the *Hoosier Schoolmaster,* the community demanded of the school just one thing, that the children should learn
to spell. We had spelling exercises twice a day, and Friday afternoons
we were drawn up in two lines, to "spell down." On rare occasions
our school might join with other schools, and the adult community as
well, for a grand "spelling down." It was exciting to see an old bearded
fellow vanquished by a skinny little girl or long-legged boy.

Spelling fascinated me. When I had raced through my own spelling
book I borrowed the spelling books of other children, for we had
no such thing as uniformity in textbooks. Most of the children who
weren't dunces got something of a thrill out of spelling. It was a game.
I do not know how German and Italian children can acquire an interest in words, under their systems of phonetic spelling. They have
nothing to correspond with "Bill Wright, the mill wright, can't write
'rite' right."

Of course the meaning of many of the words I spelled was unknown
to me. But an enterprising local dealer offered a Webster's Unabridged
Dictionary as a premium with ten spools of barbed wire. My father did
not need ten spools, but they would come in handy later. He loaded
them up and thrust the huge volume into my arms. How many an hour
I spent tracking down meanings and the origins of words! I had
already been introduced to evolutionary thinking. Here was a new field
of development, selection, adaptation.

Another ceremony of the school was "speaking pieces." At first I got
on very well. My memory was good even for the "Evil Influence of
Skepticism."

> "Ah me, the laureled wreath that murder rears,
>   Blood nursed and watered with the widow's tears,
>   Seems not so foul, so tainted nor so dread
>   As waves the nightshade round the skeptic's head."

When at last I saw that the laureled wreath stood for Napoleon and
the skeptic for just such "freethinkers" as abounded in our own community, I presented my discovery to the teacher, who cried indignantly
that I always thought I was smarter than the teacher.

One day I had to recite a piece of moral propaganda:

> " 'I'll never use tobacco, No!
>   It is a filthy weed.

I'll never use tobacco, No!'
Said little Johnny Reed."

As I finished the stanza I saw the big boys on the back benches roll their eyes, purse up their lips, and squirt an arc of tobacco juice toward the stove hearth. What a fool I'm making of myself, I thought. I couldn't remember the rest of the piece and retreated ingloriously.

Perhaps that incident left scar tissue on my mind and explains why, to this day, I can't appear before an audience without a spasm of uneasiness.

The old-fashioned farm home is itself an educational institution. A child with open eyes learns the ways of plants and animals, domesticated and wild. He learns to distinguish the characters of people in the family and in the neighborhood. The data of his experience are set up with large blank spaces around them, offering opportunity for thought and appraisal. The farm boy is drawn early into drudgery and learns how to take it off his mind through the development of rhythm. The talk of his elders, mostly tedious reminiscence or more tedious boasting of miraculous crops or marvelous fattened stock, does nevertheless float nuggets of wise old sayings, of unique situations, of legal maxims collected through jury service.

I was fortunate in living in a community of mixed origins. The difference in the status of the peasant or worker in Europe, as contrasted with the status of the American farmer, was vivid in the experience of the community. I was never to get over a sense of the wide difference between American liberty and the few acquired rights of the European working class, between the so-called classes of America, in which no ambitious youth expected to rest, and the rigid classes of Europe, which held their members secure, in default of a miracle. Above all I was fortunate in having natural educators for parents, and particularly the inspiration of my uncle, George Bille, who had a farm a mile away.

As a brilliant child in Denmark, George won the patronage of Provost Foens, who put him through the *Gymnasium,* or junior college, intending to push him on through the university and into the profession of law. But the pull of America was irresistible. George came on a ticket supplied by my father, and in six months had acquired an extraordinary mastery of English. He entered the examinations for teachers and won a first-grade certificate, which offered him immunity from further examinations for life. He taught school for a year successfully, but early marriage threw him back on the land.

Farming was not to his taste, but there was no escape from it. He managed, however, to find a little time for his unquenchable intellectual interests. He could afford few books, but they were good ones, like Grote's *History of Greece,* Green's *Short History,* Darwin's *Origin of Species.* He was deeply interested in the law and cut into the earnings of the local lawyers by giving good legal advice gratis to the neighbors. He subscribed to a New York architectural journal and took a lively interest in the rising Beaux Arts and classical tendencies, both of which he regarded as mistaken, inserts of European past cultures on the fresh soil of America.

As a student in Copenhagen he had participated in the struggle between the time-honored classical disciplines and the evolutionary science penetrating from England. He was passionate for science, and this had been one of the reasons he had rejected the opportunity of preparing himself for the profession of law.

In the farm community there were only two fields offering scientific stimulus, geology and botany. On my father's farm the creek had cut a deep gully, and the erosion that preceded the plow that broke the plains had made many dry confluent gullies. There before your eyes was the record of some millions of years, if you could read it.

High on the hillsides there was a limestone outcrop which reappeared at the same level for a dozen miles. It was overlaid by a yellow earth the neighbors called clay, but which my uncle ascribed to the dust blown in from the southwest for thousands and tens of thousands of years. When my father opened his quarry my uncle taught me to read the geologic record. In the surfaces uncovered by my father's gunpowder were all kinds of shells, some like oyster shells, some rather like crabs—trilobites, I think—some of totally unknown character. We puzzled over a hollowed surface the size of a plate with knobs a half-inch high forming a circle around it.

"You can see, Alvin," my uncle said, "this land was once ocean, shallow ocean, for there can't be many shellfish in deep water. These shells are millions of years old. There are none like them today."

Later we followed the brook and its tributory gullies.

"You see, Alvin, there must have been land here before that ocean we saw up on the hill. Look at that sand."

About twenty feet above the creek level there was a stratum of sand, an inch layer of nearly white, an inch layer of nearly black, an inch layer of red, two inches of white again, a thin trace of red, a wide layer of black, just trimmed with white, and above it true clay.

"This sand has been deposited by water, not sea water. There must have been five or six streams coming together here, from valleys among hills of different kinds of stone, gone millions of years ago. But there must have been an earlier ocean, to break the stone into sand."

I learned to look upon my father's farm as the product of millions, hundreds of millions of years.

Botany was more a matter of the here and now. There were no primordial plants to be discovered in our lime quarry. But the prairie was covered with plants for which there were no local names. My uncle asked me how many flowering plants I had seen. At least thirty, I thought.

Then he brought me Gray's *Manual.* With Gray's *Key* I discovered the names of more than two hundred flowering plants, most of which I had never noticed.

Veblen, who a decade earlier had been swept with the passion of botanizing, set down the impulse to find the names and relations of plants as mere "taxonomy," product of the obsolete genius of Linnaeus. Well, the insight into the variety of organic existence offered by Linnaeus was very important, for Veblen and me.

Suppose our primary object was just to find the names. What was the first intellectual feat in history? Eve's naming of the animals.

Without names you do not see things, or their differences. You call things gadgets, and let it go at that. By the end of our botanizing phase, Veblen and I knew a hundred times more about plant life than we had known before. And we knew more about human life, for all flesh is grass.

My uncle and I were not content with the mere finding of names or classifications. The descriptions in our Gray's *Manual,* based on the region east of the Mississippi, did not fit completely for our native plants. Our native vetches had leaves that were more hard-finished. Our native lupins were more prone or had more capacity for drooping and folding their leaves in the middle of the day. In every plant we had to allow for the effect of a more merciless sun than the East knew, for more damaging droughts. We did not know the word, but we became ecologists, students of the adaptation of plant life to locality.

My uncle had set me on the way of inquiring into the causes of things. Why were the misshapen hazelnuts always bitter? I collected hazelnuts in all stages, from the full-fleshed bland nut down to the miserable bitter dwarf. In some of them there was a dwarfed and perishing worm. In most of them you could see traces of a worm that had disappeared.

It was easy to see why the misshapen nuts were bitter. There had been a worm, and the plant had rushed all its capital of bitterness—tannin—to the spot to poison and gradually kill the worm. Then the plant had finished the nut, still a viable seed for the next spring, but not fit to eat.

I pursued with deep interest the devices of plants for sending their seed abroad in the world—the imperialism of the cottonwood, which could sow with its seed in the wind any sandbar within a hundred miles, the competence of the willow to float wherever the river might invite, the modest reliance of elm and maple and box elder upon the spreading winds.

Then I stumbled upon a problem. Trees producing acorns and nuts—how did they spread? Not by wind: an acorn won't blow fifty feet. Nor by the fur of wild animals, like burrs. Not by water, for oaks and nut trees can't live on sandbars or flood plains. Then how the deuce had they managed to spread from the Atlantic seaboard to the Pacific, from England to China?

My father's oak grove was expanding. All around it, up to one hundred feet of the edge, little oaks were appearing in the sod. How did they get there? Why, egoistic squirrels, having eaten all they could, buried the surplus, meaning to come back after it. They forgot, or something happened to them, and the oak advanced upon the prairie.

In that way, and only in that way, could the nut-bearing trees, the oaks, the walnuts, beeches, hickories, pecans, have spread. This rodent arboriculture had conquered both worlds. Could it be that our American world had evolved independently oaks, walnuts, beeches so like those of the Old World that they could cross and make fertile hybrids?

Impossible. There must have been a wide bridge between America and the Old World land mass. The oceanographers said there was no evidence of such a bridge. So much the worse for the oceanographers. For not less than a hundred milion years ago nor more than two hundred million, the rodents set out to plant east and west with nut-bearing trees.

A theory has since challenged the reluctant world of scholarship that the Old World and the New were once a single land mass. America seceded and moved west, Asia, Europe, and Africa moved east. That would account still better for the squirrel and the oak than the land bridge I assumed in my childish philosophy.

My uncle had made for himself a set of pedagogical principles suited to his own temperament and mine. I'm not sure they may not merit wider application.

"Never drive yourself to learn what does not interest you. If you follow your interest you will learn with pleasure, and your interest will expand into adjacent fields, ever widening, until you find that almost everything you are expected to learn is in the range of your vivid interest.

"Never be content with putting isolated facts into your memory. The chances are, such facts won't stay, or if they do, that you won't be able to find them. Every fact can be placed in a group of similar facts, hard to lose in memory. Best of all, fit it into a scheme of causes and effects, origin and development."

Following these principles, I have been able to make a show of good memory, although my memory for isolated facts, such as the names of persons to whom I am introduced, is abominable.

It was a part of my uncle's pedagogy that there is no difference between the child mind and the adult mind, except that the child mind lacks experience. My mother tacitly assumed the same thing. Her interest lay in human character rather than in scientific theories of evolution. The most fruitful field for the study of character she found in literature.

She would have me read aloud to her while she knitted or carded or spun. In the busy periods of farming I might have only an hour or less after supper; most of the year I had two hours or three. It was possible to cover a lot of literature in one to three hours, through half a dozen years. I read aloud to my mother most of the novels of Dickens, half of Thackeray, a third of George Eliot, Hugo's *Les Miserables,* Tolstoi's *Anna Karenina* and *The Kreutzer Sonata.* We discussed each character and situation as we encountered it, with no concession to the alleged limitations of the child mind.

My mother had an additional pedagogical reason for encouraging me in reading to her. It excluded what she called "skimming"—racing through a book for the high spots—what is now approved as "rapid reading." My mother felt that no book is worth holding in one's hand unless each chapter, each paragraph, each sentence, means enough to make you stop and think. One book thoughtfully read meant more to her than a hundred books skimmed. The habit of slow and thoughtful reading fixed itself upon me. In a long life I have not devoured the substance of more than five thousand books, but I have found nourishment in them.

The reading of fiction was not enough for me, and I followed with eagerness, in Green, the development of British liberty, from the folk meetings in the German forests to the early nineteenth-century British Parliaments. In Grote I followed the rise and fall of Greek democracy. I borrowed from my Uncle George, along with Green and Grote, Blackstone and Kent's *Commentaries* and learned that law is not just a struggle between paid lawyers before an ignorant jury and trembling clients, but in its true nature a practical philosophy of justice.

My sister Edith brought back from high school a copy of Caesar's *Commentaries*. In my hunger for literature I undertook to read it. Some sentences one could read straightway; some would yield if one referred to the vocabulary for a word or two. More sentences would succumb to a second reading. I bothered not at all with Latin grammar but puzzled out the language until the meaning and the situations came clear. In time Latin became to me a living language and Caesar a brilliant contemporary. I have never been able since to consider Latin a dead language or the great Romans mere antiquities.

When the time was approaching for my attempt to get into the University of Nebraska I wrote to the chancellor, James H. Canfield, for advice as to preparation.

This is what he replied. "My boy, in whatever walk of life you are destined to go, your most helpful tool will be a command of the English language. Take two books, one of history, one of fiction. Read a page of each very carefully, early in the morning. In the evening, after your farm work, reproduce those two pages from memory. Then compare your versions with those of the authors."

So I did, religiously, for a year. For history I took Grote, for fiction Harriet Beecher Stowe, for I wanted an American author. My versions could never compare well with Grote, but sometimes, I thought, were more effective than the author's in *Uncle Tom's Cabin*.

"Short horse soon curried," said the Indian as he walked away with the scalp. Short tale of my early education, soon told.

SEVEN

Vocational Dreams

M Y EARLIEST daydreams of a vocation were patterned upon my father's career. I dreamed of going far out into the West, taking up a homestead, clearing fields, building house and barn, finding a wife and bringing up a family. But the farm was to be bigger, with bigger trees, a bigger brook, bigger flash floods, bigger snowdrifts and hailstorms. House and barn were to be much bigger, and there were to be many more children. Like everyone else born in America, I had the instinct for bigness.

When I reached the manly age of seven I put away such childish fancies and dreamed of continuing my father's work on the home farm, or teaching school, or practicing medicine. The doctor's career seemed to me very enviable. Under the cloud of depression which settled on the family with a case of serious illness the doctor appeared like a bright light.

Suddenly the promise of a different career rose before me, soon to sink forever: the church.

One of my sisters had brought home an illustrated *History of the Bible,* a thick volume, with the difficult words syllabicated—Re-ho-bo-am. My sister Edith announced that she would read it through. Of course I determined to read it through, first. We entered upon a race. Whichever got the book first could hang on to it until weariness overtook him. Each of us had a bookmark, and Edith's bookmark advanced faster than mine. What could I do but scamp—practice "rapid reading"—so that every day my bookmark advanced ahead of Edith's. Edith has always been absolutely honest. She assumed that I was, and she worked faithfully to overcome the lead my bookmark was gaining. But I beat her to the end.

My triumph turned to ashes, for my conscience got hold of me and lacerated me severely. I had won by fraud. I imposed a penance on myself, to read the whole book through, pronouncing every word faithfully. What I had not noticed in the heat of competition was that the book was fascinatingly interesting.

From the first settlement of America until a half century ago the Bible was, for most families, not merely the Book par excellence, but the only book. As a library it was perfect. To the truly religious it offered light and comfort. It also offered precedent and justification for the genocidal attitude toward the Indians. Kill every male and every female who had known man: that was what the Lord's hero Joshua did; failure to do it was Saul's unforgivable sin, cause of the downfall of his family. For the dealer in wooden nutmegs Jacob's monkeying with the chromosomes of Laban's sheep was precedent; for the lecher or would-be lecher, David's affair with Uriah's wife and Solomon's immense harem were condonations.

For a boy, age-class conscious, what was most fascinating in the Bible was the recurrence of the boy hero: little Joseph, little Samuel, little David, little Daniel, the boy Jesus confounding the learned rabbis with his wisdom. There was also the little Isaac, bravely consenting to his father's intent to turn him into a burnt offering; little Moses, predestined to power from his cradle floating among the bulrushes. The annals of no other people exhibit such a galaxy of precocity. The nearest example I know is little Hannibal, sworn to destroy Rome. But the Carthaginians were Canaanites and spoke Hebrew.

There happened to come into our neighborhood an aging bishop from an Eastern city, who had set out with his good wife to explore the religious life of the prairie and bring light to those who sat in windswept darkness. He held services in our schoolhouse. After the sermon he was informed by a neighbor that he could take dinner at the Johnson house—the nearest to the schoolhouse. And so he drove his buggy up to our door and blandly informed my father that he had been advised to come to our house for dinner. My father led the bishop and his wife into the living room and brought the news to the kitchen.

What a crisis! No preparations had been made for a company dinner. My sisters had to scurry around and catch spring chickens, my mother had to prepare potatoes and throw together the materials for a shortcake.

Meanwhile the bishop and his wife sat in isolation in the living room. My father had unhitched their horse and had led it away to be watered and fed. I knew well that he would find other chores to do, in order to escape the bishop. This seemed inhospitable to me, and I slipped into the living room to do what I could to entertain the bishop.

Besides, there were a great many questions on which I wanted light.

The bishop beamed and questioned me about Sunday School. And could I read the little booklets distributed to the Sunday Schools by his people? Oh, yes. Why, I had read the *History of the Bible* through twice. The bishop applauded. I felt at home with him and could put my questions.

How could Abraham be called a good man when he was ready to butcher his only son as my father butchered a pig? And if the Lord hadn't sent a goat, Abraham would have butchered Isaac. The bishop gave me a long defense of Abraham, trying to find words enough of one syllable. I wasn't satisfied, but it wasn't polite to argue.

Why was Joseph so cruel to his brothers when they came to buy wheat? Here again I got a long explanation, soothing but not convincing.

When Shad-rach, Me-shach, and A-bed-ne-go were cast into the fiery furnace Neb-u-chad-nez-zar looked in through the isinglass and saw them walking around—which was all right with me, a miracle, but there was a fourth, who appeared to be the Son of God. How could that be? Jesus had not been born.

The bishop wrung his fat hands. "My child, you are too young to understand. The Son of God has always been, and He let himself be born a child, to die for our sins."

I was mystified.

The bishop put his hand on my head. "How would you like to be a preacher? You would go to fine schools, with fine teachers, and you would learn the answers to all questions about the Holy Book. You would preach sermons and make people better. You would visit the sick and you would take food to the starving."

All that sounded good to me. I had never thought of any such career, but I was prepared to try anything once—in my imagination. I probably appeared more receptive than I felt, for the bishop's wife picked me up and pressed me to her ample bosom.

The dinner, to my way of thinking, was magnificent, and the bishop and his wife did great havoc to the platter of chicken and the mashed potatoes. After dinner the bishop asked my father to come into the living room with him. Soon my father came out, his eyes blazing, and bright red showing on the cheekbones above his beard. He was awfully angry, I judged.

He got the bishop's horse from the barn, put it to the buggy, and bowed the bishop and his wife away. Then he went to the barn and kept away from us all afternoon. At supper he was cooled off, but very laconic. When I started to say something about the bishop my mother wirelessed me silence with her eyes. I hushed. We never again mentioned the bishop in my father's presence.

What had happened in the living room I learned later. The bishop had proposed to adopt me and take me back with him to Pennsylvania, give me a fine education and make of me a great ornament of the church. He would make me sole heir to his fortune, which he placed at half a million in government bonds, besides a mansion.

My father had replied, calmly, that he was not giving up his eldest son, who would somehow get all the education he needed.

My next enthusiasm was for Greek scholarship. I was reading *Tom Brown's Schooldays*. The boys had formed a gentlemen's agreement to balk on carrying the "construing"—whatever that meant—beyond a certain line. Tom forgot the agreement, carried away by the beauty of the lines describing the parting of Hector and Andromache. The lines were on the page before me, without translation. The Greek lettering seemed to me infinitely more beautiful than the ordinary English type. Some day, I promised myself, I would learn to read Greek. Perhaps I would teach it, in a school like Rugby.

For a time, when I read Blackstone and Kent, I flirted with dreams of the law. If you were a lawyer you would have a chance of becoming a judge. I'd like that, I thought. There was a young judge who sometimes appeared on circuit in our vicinity. My father, who hated lawyers, was full of enthusiasm for Judge Norris—the same man who later graced the Senate with his magnificent intelligence and statesmanship, the father of the Tennessee Valley project.

But after imaginary commitments to other vocations I always returned to my really serious interest, medicine.

At that time the prairies were served by doctors whose education was homemade. Our family doctor had come West as salesman for a hardware concern. He had settled down in a nearby town and opened a small hardware store, with patent medicines as a sideline. Persons afflicted with coughs, neuralgia, toothache, and innumerable other ills would come in and talk with the incipient doctor about medicines. His advice always helped. If one medicine didn't do the job he advised trying another. As they were all fifty per cent alcohol, they made one feel better, at least for the time.

Toothache, however, did not respond satisfactorily to Hostetter's Bitters or Ayer's Cherry Pectoral. The doctor acquired a forceps, and when you went into his store to buy nails or staples you might be greeted with an anguished "Oh!" from the chair by the hoes and rakes —the parting with a stubborn molar.

The doctor had to learn to set bones. Maybe they came out a bit crooked, but a crooked bone is as serviceable as a straight one. He had to acquire the art of obstetrics, but in a pioneer community a neighbor woman acts as midwife, and the doctor is useful mainly as comfort for an anxious husband.

Since cures are mainly psychological, and this doctor was a good instinctive psychologist, his cures were many. Wherever he went confidence and easing minds walked with him.

Another doctor came into the community, a man who had gained his medical training by apprenticeship to a successful self-taught physician. Patients left the old doctor and flocked to the new one, who had an entirely different set of patent medicines—still mostly alcohol—and even wrote out prescriptions, to be filled at the drugstore, probably with the ingredients of a familiar patent medicine.

Someone had told him that I meant to be a doctor, and he sent word to my father to bring me to see him.

The doctor occupied an unpleasantly new frame house at the edge of a small town. A woman, manifestly pregnant, ushered us into the office where the doctor sat, jotting down notes from a huge book. He rose and turned on us the full-blooded charm and noisy silence that constituted his extremely successful bedside manner. You could see that he was a man who cured.

He began with an account of his own apprenticeship, how he worked around the office of a great doctor, reading his books, eventually accompanying the doctor on his rounds, seeing how one lanced felons, bandaged injuries, learned to take the pulse, guessed at fever temperatures, judged the proper remedies—mostly patent medicines. After some years as observer he was permitted to handle minor cases, graded up to more important ones, until finally he could do everything his chief could do and was ready to start out for himself.

"How old are you, my boy?" he asked suddenly.

"Twelve," I said.

"That's when I began. I finished by twenty-one."

He launched out into a humorous, sometimes ghastly, account of the stupidities and mistakes of the college-trained doctors. What could they learn, handled as they were in bunches? As his apprentice

I'd see hundreds of cases, participate in handling hundreds, handle hundreds of my own.

My father had sat silent, all his reactions safely covered by his beard. "Doctor," he said at last, "just what would Alvin do, the first year or two?"

"Of course he'd want to earn his keep and instruction. He'd take care of my horses, milk the two cows, tend the garden, and help my wife with the housework. She's six months gone, and I can't get a girl who's any good."

"All right," my father said. "That's for his keep. What would he be learning?"

"For the first couple of years he'd be reading my library in his spare time. I've heard he is a reader."

"May we see your library?"

The doctor seemed embarrassed. He picked up the big book on the table. "That book has got everything we know about medicine. It's got everything known about medicine for thousands of years. Now there's Galen"—he made the name rhyme with gallon—"he's got more sense about what climate does to health than anybody nowadays. Take Hippocrates"—pronounced by the doctor in three syllables,—"Hippocrates knew more about the causes of dyspepsia than any of these college doctors."

"May I see the book?" my father asked. He turned some pages in a desultory way and lingered some moments over the title page.

"Thank you," he said, rising. "Alvin and I will think about it for a few days."

As we drove homeward my father said, after a mile of silence, "It seems to me what the doctor wants is a chores boy. You'd get a chance to read that book, but you can do that at home. I looked for the price. We can get the book for ten dollars."

Another half mile of silence. "The doctor told us what fools college doctors are. Some of them may be. But it seems to me you can't get too much education."

Another silence. "A doctor has to have a license to practice. I've heard that the college doctors are getting ready to run these self-made doctors out of the country."

Another silence. "If I were you I'd write to the state university and find out how you can get in—if you want to be a doctor."

That was all. We never again discussed the question of apprenticeship to a doctor. All my dreams turned toward the university.

EIGHT

Politics

M Y FAMILY were staunch Democrats. All Civil War veterans except my father were Republicans. My father had ardently supported Lincoln and had voted for him in 1860. He never lost his admiration for Lincoln. But he voted for McClellan in 1864, although he shared with the Western armies a thorough contempt for McClellan as a fop, a ladies' man more fit to lead a cotillion than an army.

In his company there was a man of grousing character, who declared that he meant to vote for McClellan. The company crowded round him and prepared to ride him out of camp on a rail. This outraged my father. He had come to America to live in a free country, where a man could think and speak and vote as he pleased. He had fought through the desperate war to save American liberty. He would not stand by and see a comrade bullied out of his rights.

My father slipped into his tent, got his gun, and wedged through the mob to the side of the frightened Democrat, who was backed up against the wall of a burned-out mansion. Deliberately fixing his bayonet, my father declared that he too meant to vote for McClellan and was ready to fight for his rights. The mob lost its enthusiasm and began to fall away.

It is hard, often impossible, to cow a mob with a pistol. The pistol may miss, or the bullets may hit the other fellow. A bayonet in the hands of a man skilled in handling it is a quite different matter. It threatens each man's very gizzard. These soldiers had experience of bayonet charges. My father was known to have had much more experience in European warfare, where the bayonet was brought into play in almost every battle. My father and the Democrat were permitted to vote for McClellan in peace.

That was the beginning of my family's adherence to the Democratic party. The end of it has not arrived.

The vindictive policy of the radical Republicans after the war

54

confirmed my father's democracy. As he saw it, although slavery had been at the bottom of the sectional antagonism that brought on the war, most of the Confederate soldiers had never been slaveholders. They had fought to keep the inevitable atrocities of war away from their homes, their wives and children. They had conducted themselves as valiantly and as decently as any army in history. Forgive and forget was my father's maxim. He bore no malice against the German settlers he had fought in the Schleswig-Holstein war. He bore no malice against the "rebels."

But the Republican party was keeping up the hatred of the South, a hatred that had always been far stronger in the civil population than in the army. Its principal political instrument was the Bloody Shirt. By what my father considered a wasteful and corrupt pension system, it was binding the great majority of the veterans to the party and using the power thus acquired to saddle upon the country a system of high protective duties, to the enrichment of the manufacturers and the impoverishment of the farmers.

In the weeks preceding a presidential election the veterans got out their old uniforms and paraded, breathing fire against copperheads and rebels. The shouting, the bugle calls, the firing of blank cartridges filled me with foreboding. Perhaps another Civil War was just over the hill, with burning houses and slaughtered men. It was a dreadful feeling, but no feeling of fear lasts long in the mind of a healthy child with an omnipotent father to protect him.

During the Cleveland-Blaine contest of 1883 I knew, or thought I knew, all about politics. I read eagerly the political news and editorial comment in the weekly issue of the *New York Tribune* and in a Democratic Omaha newspaper, as well as our extremely elementary local paper, the *Argus*. My spirits went up with the optimistic prognostications of the Democratic press and sank to the depths with the *Tribune* predictions of a Blaine victory. My father said that the Republicans had the money and were buying enough votes to win; moreover, if they lost, they would steal the election again. To my great rejoicing Cleveland won, and the Republicans hadn't the nerve to steal the election.

I deeply regretted that my Uncle George had voted for Blaine. Cleveland, he said, was a good solid New York provincial; Blaine was a statesman and realized that sooner or later America would have to take her place in international affairs. What if his reciprocity program was narrowly limited in its aims? It was a beginning. All this sounded too abstract for me. What was real was that the Democratic party was coming back into power after many years in the doghouse. Anyway, my uncle pointed out, both candidates were Easterners who knew nothing about the West and cared less. Life would go on with us exactly as it had before, whichever candidate won.

More important to us were our county elections, and the county conventions always left us the choice between two equally incompetent and corrupt cliques, each bound by gentlemen's agreement not to uncover, in case of victory, the stealings of its predecessor.

Local politics must come close to home to draw the interest of a half-grown boy away from the great affairs of the nation. It did come close to home.

In the early days of settlement roads had wandered at will over the prairie, following the courses of streams, aiming at low places on the long hills, seeking narrow points in the enormous gullies produced by ages of erosion. Ten miles west of my father's farm the prairie was gently rolling. There was nothing to prevent the roads from following straight lines for hundreds of miles. In that vast region the principle was accepted that section lines—the lines bounding a square mile—were or should be roads. Conversely, no road running diagonally across a section could be lawful unless it had been officially laid out and recorded.

This principle had no standing in common law, nor was there any federal statute fixing it. For level or gently rolling prairie it made sense, and so acquired something of the force of law, through general consent.

The region of my father's farm was a deeply dissected upland shelving toward the Missouri River. Section-line roads were unthinkable. One of the east-west section lines bounding my father's farm ran half a mile in swamp and scrub, climbed a steep two hundred feet, crossed a deep gulch cut by the brook, climbed a five-hundred-foot hill, descended the hill in a slope so steep cattle refused to graze on it, crossed another gulch to climb another hill. A road on this line might have been passable for horseback riders, but not for vehicles.

The actual road left the section-line pattern two miles above my father's farm, followed the easy contours of a branch-creek valley, crossed the main creek on the farm and rose in a curving course to a low point of a hill, and passed on through the Wigle farm to another easy contour leading to the Missouri bottom, where the section-line pattern could be resumed. This course of the road had been surveyed and presumably recorded.

But the Wigle farm was purchased by an Englishman of the type that regarded the Declaration of Independence as an unfortunate but transient aberration. Stirring around in the chaotic county records, he found that the county had failed to record the course of the road over his property. He cut a ditch across the road, put up a stout barbed-wire fence, and defied the community to disturb the obstruction. The lawful road, he claimed, had to follow the section line I have described.

There were some thirty settlers above my father's farm who had to use this road. They went by roundabout ways to the courthouse and demanded the opening of the road. The county authorities agreed that their case was good; the road had been there for a generation and had established itself by prescriptive right. But it might take two or three years to settle the matter in the courts, and in the meantime the settlers would have no access to the market for their grain and hogs. The county commissioners could indeed condemn the right of way and open the road immediately, but the county would have to pay down for the right of way, a matter of two hundred dollars. Unfortunately there was no money in the county treasury, and there would be none not committed to prior claims until the next summer at the earliest. Now, if the settlers would lend the county the money, the whole matter could be settled within a week.

A few days later the settlers met in the schoolhouse and discussed assessing themselves to make up the fund. But one after the other declared that he had no money available at all. And that was true. Farmers seldom saw any cash that was not immediately needed to cover purchases on credit. In the end they voted to ask my father to find the money. He would get it back the following summer. My father didn't like the proposition but consented.

He had brought with him from Denmark a number of ancient peasant traditions, of which the most important was always to have reserves on hand. He kept a three-year supply of bread grain in his bin, a two-year supply of corn for his stock, a reserve of hay good for half a winter. Neither drought nor grasshopper plague could affect his economy seriously. He practiced the "ever normal granary" principle before Henry Wallace was born.

Along with the reserves of food and feed he kept in the clock a reserve of gold—two stacks of gold coins, eagles and double eagles.

If expenses sometimes reduced the reserve he would sell a horse or some fat cattle to replenish it. Everybody knew it was there.

And so he went to the county commissioners and handed over two hundred dollars in gold. The Englishman was paid, his ditch filled and his fence removed, and commerce was restored.

At the proper time the next summer my father went to the courthouse to see about getting his money back. The chairman of the Board of Commissioners seemed much embarrassed. Counsel had advised him that the commissioners had exceeded their lawful powers in taking money from an individual, except as a gift, and therefore could not lawfully pay him back. He suggested that my father talk to a lawyer whom I shall call Jones. Lawyer Jones was extremely clever and might find a way to help my father.

At the time the courthouse was regarded by the farmers as a wasps' nest of crooks and scoundrels, of whom Lawyer Jones was the worst. The suggestion that he see Lawyer Jones did not sit well with my father; my Uncle George learned that he had advised the commissioner to go to hell, taking Lawyer Jones along with him. As for the two hundred dollars, the money was his, and the county would pay him sooner or later.

My Uncle George knew enough of law and politics to see that the assertion of *ultra vires* was a hocus-pocus. What it all amounted to was that the courthouse, finding a little money in a farmer's hands, felt entitled to some of it. If my father had gone to Lawyer Jones, that suave individual would have been so deeply sympathetic he would have taken the case without a fee. A week later he would have found a way for the county to pay my father his money in county warrants— worth fifty cents on the dollar. Lawyer Jones would have offered to cash the warrants at sixty cents on the dollar—to turn them in himself at face value when the first tax money came into the county treasury. Thus my father would get a hundred and twenty dollars and Lawyer Jones eighty dollars, no doubt to be shared with the commissioner.

For the first time in his life my father turned politician. A county convention was soon to be held, and the commissioner was counting on renomination. Delegates to the convention were chosen in precinct caucuses. My father got himself elected delegate and managed to get his friends in as the other delegates. Thus he had power enough to control the nomination.

The day after the caucus Lawyer Jones drove up to our house in a spick-and-span buggy. With bland smiles he informed my father that the commissioner had found a way for the county to pay him—whether lawfully or not. He would count on my father's being discreet about it.

"When?" my father asked.

"In about three weeks."

"A week after the convention," my father commented.

The lawyer laughed. "You get the point."

"Well," my father said, "you can tell the commissioner I had his word once, when I loaned the money to the county. I don't trust his word, even through you."

"Would you trust it in writing?"

"Maybe."

The next day the lawyer appeared again with a letter signed by the commissioner, promising to pay my father his money the Monday after the convention and expecting my father's support in the convention. My father put the letter in his pocket.

"Say!" the lawyer cried, aghast. "I was to show you this letter and give it to you if you promised support."

"I'm not going to support him. I'm going to put that scoundrel out of office. The convention will see this letter."

"But they will call it a case of bribery. And the recipient of a bribe is as much a criminal as the giver."

"Funny thing, to bribe me with my own money. But I'm not accepting the bribe."

The lawyer stormed and threatened to have my father arrested if he did not return the letter. My father laughed in his face.

Next day the commissioner himself appeared and begged for the return of the letter. There was nothing to be done about it. The letter was out in circulation—best for the commissioner to withdraw his name.

The commissioner stayed in the race and was roundly beaten.

Later he remarked bitterly to a talkative friend that his political career had been ruined by "that Dane." We should never have let the Danes into the country, to mess up the lives of true Americans.

This was the beginning of my political education. For years I had known that the county paid for jury service with warrants worth fifty or sixty cents on the dollar. It also paid ditching and bridge-building contractors in warrants, but these allowed for depreciation in their bids. I had learned to ask the why of geologic strata and plant forms. I began to ask the why of our local governmental setup and our county finances.

Years before some glib promoters had come along and sold—the proper word—the county commissioners on a railway to begin at the Missouri and traverse the county for twenty miles on its way west. They required the county to bond itself for twenty thousand dollars a mile. The county—or the commissioners—bit and signed the bond, without looking into the specifications of the construction project. What the promoters gave us was a narrow-gauge road, on which it would never be worth while to put rolling stock, and cheap light rails on cottonwood ties laid flat on the prairie sod. As the life of a cottonwood tie is not more than twelve months, the railway had entirely disappeared a few years after I began to take notice of economics and politics. There were a few rails hidden in grass and weeds. Some of them were carried off by farmers to brace corner fence posts.

This kind of construction could not have cost more than fifteen hundred dollars a mile, even in the greenback era. But the county was bonded for twenty thousand dollars a mile—four hundred thousand dollars! Naturally the county wanted to repudiate the bond.

The lower court was for the county, but the promoters appealed. The next higher court upheld them. The county appealed, and finally the Supreme Court of the state upheld the promoters and ordered the county to pay the principal and accrued interest on the bonds.

The county refused to pay. The promoters called on the courts to compel payment. The lower court refused. The tedious process of working up to the Supreme Court was gone through again, interest at six per cent accruing remorselessly.

For years every candidate for county office had to distinguish himself by the fervency with which he repudiated this unjust claim on the county. But with the Supreme Court twice committed against the county there was but one recourse left open to the county: to have no money in the treasury.

Money for taxes did come in. The farmers in my neighborhood had to pay. If they had no money they had to borrow from a usurer at two per cent a month. A few of them wisely came to my father and declaimed against the usurer, and went away with the necessary double eagles in their pockets. They always paid the money back, and offered interest, which my father refused to take. Whatever he thought of preachers, he took seriously the Biblical injunction to give, expecting nothing in return. He was always pleasantly surprised when the principal came back.

And so there was money, momentarily, in the treasury, but before ever it had a chance to sit down some insider, particularly the usurer who bought up warrants, got it. But however corrupt the county administration was, it never let the crooked railway promoters get access to a red cent. This virtuous illegality was for years the stock-in-trade of both party machines.

I have mentioned before the tongue-tied Dibble, the man who first imported and developed the shorthorn breed of cattle, capable of producing a thousand-pound steer in nine months as against the usual three-year minimum—baby beef, aliment of chambers of commerce and great bankers, until the Roosevelt revolution and its high wages enabled the workingman to snatch the choice steaks off the banker's platter. You admire a herd in Montana or Arizona and you are likely to be informed that they are purebred, from Dibble's herd in Nebraska.

At the time Dibble was not producing baby beef. He was producing gorgeous young bulls and heifers, to conquer the western uplands. The local prognostication was that he would go bankrupt with his ideas. But he was holding his own, and winning.

Dibble turned aside from breeding fine cattle to mend the politics of the county. He called a meeting. My father didn't want to go; he had had his bellyful of politics, he said. "But you go, Alvin, with George Bille. You'll learn something."

It was an exciting meeting, particularly to me, for at thirteen years, with no protection against blushing but the sunbrown on my face, I found myself accepted as a man among men.

Dibble made a speech, the most painful I've ever heard in my life. He stuttered, he got out a word, bit off its tail, and spewed it out again. Finally his ideas would burst through the barrier of his teeth, to use the Homeric phrase. The very difficulty of their a-bornin' made them totally convincing.

We were eight hundred farmers in the county, he reckoned. There were four hundred other families, including the officials, the pettifoggers, the usurers, the dealers, the craftsmen, among whom might be a lot of honest men. We had the numbers; but we were idiots. We let the natives hate the foreign-born, the Methodists hate the Lutherans and both of them the Catholics. For God's sake, let every man go to Heaven in his own way, or we'd all go to Hell together.

Imagine how that impressed me, at thirteen! Something real was

under way. Dibble took his time and at last presented his People's
party, to contend against the Republican and the Democratic party
alike. He nominated an engaging and brilliant Irishman for sheriff, a
domineering German for treasurer, an astonished unknown to serve
as attorney for the Board of Commissioners. For county clerk he
selected my Uncle George.

"Oh no!" cried my modest uncle. "I couldn't possibly be a political
candidate. I'd die if I had to make a speech."

"D-d-d-don't be a f-f-f-fool, George B-b-b-b-bille. Th-th-the
county clerk is in on everything. He sits with the com-com-commis-
sioners. Not a ra-ra-rake off passes him. He has the b-b-books on the
t-t-tax dodgers. We've got to have you. And you-you-you, shut up!"

My uncle shut up. The campaign went ahead. Republicans and
Democrats united against the farmer front and were beaten, three to
one. My uncle settled into office with misgivings, proceeded to uncover back taxes enough to pay off the infernal bonds, got re-elected
and re-elected until he was bored to death with his office and the
county was the most solvent in the state. After twelve years of service
my uncle refused to continue in office and went to California, where
he acquired a lovely piece of ground in the foothills of the Sierras,
fruit trees rising sweetly out of the red volcanic earth.

I reflected that the corruption of my own county could no doubt
be matched by corruption in other counties, and in state and federal
government. The organization of trade seemed equally corrupt. You
sold your wheat to a local dealer; he was likely to give you short
weight or pronounce it of lower than standard grade, therefore commanding less than the standard price. If you tried to ship your grain
or cattle to the large markets you paid twice as much for a car as the
local dealer would have paid; your car would be switched off somewhere on the road, and if you were shipping cattle they had to be
unloaded and fed on hay too coarse for them to eat but for which
you were charged fancy prices. One item of supply after another was
going up in price; the explanation given by the dealer, true or not,
was that a trust had taken over the industry and was fixing prices to
please itself. At the same time the New York papers gave rich and
spicy accounts of the doings of the Four Hundred and of the increasing number of millionaires.

It was natural that I should form the conclusion that the country
was blanketed by a "System" designed to shear the farmer to his very
hide, and the workingman too, if he didn't find some protection in his

union. I looked back yearningly to the good old times. But as I came to know more about those good old times, with their religious tyranny, their oppression of slave and indentured servant, imprisonment for debt, laws of settlement, I concluded that the conditions I detested went far into the past. The American and French Revolutions had fallen far short of raising the common man to a truly democratic level.

Bellamy's *Looking Backward* held me enthralled for some time. The picture of a rational socialist state with all persons equally enjoying the fruits of a super-efficient economic system stirred my longings. But then I reflected on the stubborn fact of personal inequalities. In a pioneer community, with all men having equal access to equally rich land, the differences in energy and intelligence strike one in the face. Who would operate that wonderful socialist state? How could the lazy and the stupid be kept off the necks of their personal betters?

No, I wanted a system which would leave each man free to work or not as he pleased, to build prosperity for himself and his family or reconcile himself to poverty. All my ideal required was the throwing off of the oppression of the "System." What I hoped for was a reawakening of the revolutionary spirit, to complete the work of liberating the masses. And the signs of the times, as I read them, promised some such movement.

Down in the South, up in Minnesota, a farmers' movement was gathering strength, the Farmers' Alliance. Labor was building a grandiose organization, the Knights of Labor, bringing under one roof all the organizations which had formerly gone each its individualist way. Was not this the promise of revolution? I dreamed that it was.

A lodge of the Farmers' Alliance was being formed in my own community. The organization meeting was held on my sixteenth birthday, a happy coincidence for me, since all persons sixteen years and over were eligible for membership, "except bankers, professional gamblers, and convicted criminals."

Some sixty farmers, mostly formidably bearded, attended the meeting. They proceeded to elect officers, president, secretary, treasurer, and sergeant-at-arms. But there was a fifth office, lecturer. Lecturer— what the hell was that? The organizer explained that at meetings the lecturer would make a speech about the organization and what it ought to do. He would give the members something to think about.

It was an office nobody wanted. An old bearded fellow rose and nominated Alvin Johnson for lecturer. There was a roar of laughter followed by a unanimous vote for me, hidden under my blushes.

But I did produce a lecture, of a sort, at the next meeting. It was on the coming revolution against the "System" and the absolute need for farmers and labor to join hands. It was not a popular idea, for the farmers regarded organized labor as part of the system of oppression, striking to get more wages for less work and pushing up the prices the farmers had to pay.

During the next two years, by assiduously reading the propaganda of the Farmers' Alliance and the adverse comments in the newspapers, I put together for myself the elements of a peaceful revolution:

1. Government regulation of railway rates.
2. Abolition of trusts.
3. Abolition of the sweat shop.
4. A graduated income tax.
5. Pensions to support the aged and disabled.
6. Government warehouses to store for the producer imperishable products like grain, cotton, and tobacco, with warrants for ninety per cent of the current price, circulating as legal tender.
7. Issue of paper money by government to finance public works in time of depression.
8. Guarantee of bank deposits.

With these reforms, I thought, the revolution would be complete and the common man could stand erect, with no oppression burdening his shoulders. Dreams of youth! I never imagined I would live to see those reforms realized, with yet much more to be done before our country could enjoy unmixed democracy.

In the neighborhood I passed for an extreme radical. My father never discussed my political views with me, but I felt that he'd have preferred more moderation.

Many years later, when I visited my parents in California, my father proposed a long walk—fifteen miles, not too long for his eighty-six years.

"There was something I wanted to tell you, Alvin," he said. "I have turned Socialist. When you were a boy I was afraid you were getting too radical. I thought you might go in for socialism. I didn't like the idea. The best life, I thought, was one in which every man stands on his own ground and looks after himself. I couldn't bear to think of being bossed around by a Socialist official, probably a crook.

"I feel that way still. But now we have this terrible war"—World War I. "The common people didn't want war. They never want war, but they have to suffer for it. It is the leaders who make the wars. In old times it was the kings. In these days it is the big bankers, big industrial magnates, big newspapers, that get into quarrels across national lines. Before they know, they have started a war.

"We have got to take the power out of their hands, or we will have a bigger war and a worse one in twenty-five years. That is why I have become a Socialist."

NINE

Emancipation

I T WAS a bright, cold morning in December. I had just succeeded in felling a huge old white elm tree and was trimming off its smaller branches when my father came up through the wood. He surveyed the fallen tree.

"That's a big tree, Alvin. Two foot and a half thick. But what are you going to do with it? You can't split old white elm chunks."

"John and I will saw it into stove lengths and let it stay here till it's frozen solid. Then it will split like blocks of ice."

"Where did you get that idea?"

"From you. That's what you did with white elm in Wisconsin."

"That's so." My father sat down on the log. "Alvin," he said, "in two weeks you will be thirteen years old."

"That's so."

"When a boy gets to be thirteen he thinks he knows more than his father."

"Oh no!" I cried.

"But it's so. It's so with all boys, and it makes a lot of trouble between son and father. Now, you wouldn't run the farm just the way I have run it."

I had no reply. That was true.

"You know, Alvin, in Bible days the Jews counted a boy a man when he was thirteen and made him independent. Saved a lot of rows. The Jews are a smart people. That's why ordinary dumb people hate them."

I had no comment. I was trying to catch the drift of my father's mind. Was he reproaching me for some unconscious insubordination?

"For the last three years you have been working the farm. You've worked it about as well as I did, before my health broke down. There's nothing on the farm you can't do. You are big as a man and stronger than most men. There are just two things I might criticize. You will

never admit when you are tired and keep on working when you ought
to rest. And you bite off more than you can chew. You always have
and always will. You can't help it.

"Now, Alvin, I'm going to follow the example of the Jews. You
are a man and ought to be independent. So I'm going to rent the
farm to you on shares. You will take two-thirds of what the farm makes
and you will give me one-third. You will run the farm to suit yourself.
You can come to me for advice if you want to, but I won't give
any advice you don't ask for."

I was speechless. To be sure, I felt I had the strength of a man in
me, and was rather arrogant about it. But to be officially recognized
as a man, and in my own home—what on earth could I say?

My father rose, gave me an understanding glance, and looked up
at the sun. "About ten o'clock. Don't work too long on that tree.
There's another day tomorrow. We'll talk to Mama about this after
dinner." He went away through the wood, humming an old Jutland air.

The truth was, I had been feeling shoots of discontent budding in
me. The farm was making a living but little money—and I needed
money if I was ever to go off to college. There was a twenty-acre lot
of pasture land where the grass grew too rank to interest the cows,
which had a great excess of pasture to roam over. I had thought of
asking my father to let me break up that lot and work it on shares, and
my mother had approved the plan but thought I should wait until I
was fifteen before broaching the subject. I wondered whether she had
talked with my father about my desire. Not likely. It was her principle
to let her children take their own initiatives.

Anyway, my father had the gift, granted to men of few words and
no books, of reading a person's mind.

My mother accepted the plan with enthusiasm. But was it quite fair
to my younger brothers? Wouldn't it be better to rent the farm to the
three of us together? Then, after five years, when I went off to college,
John could take over, and after him Harry.

My father stroked his beard. I was too surprised to find anything
to say. How could my mother raise the question of fairness to my
brothers? Was it not understood between us that I was only the representative of my mother's children, spearhead of their interests?

"Are you sure, Alvin," my father asked, "you three boys won't
quarrel about the division of your shares?"

"Heavens, no. If we ever disagree on anything, it will be because
each wants to give the others more than is coming to them."

"All right," my father said. "If you want to put the agreement in writing I'll sign it."

"Oh no. We don't need a written agreement."

It took me an hour's reflection to understand my mother's motives. My father saw them at once. She was afraid I'd be committed to staying on the farm. By providing for the succession of my brothers she would insure my liberation at the end of five years.

My father was right in surmising that we would not work the farm the way he had worked it. To him farming was a way of life. To us it had to be a way of making money—not for money's sake but for the sake of education.

In farming as a way of life you try to be as nearly independent of the market as possible. My father had his own bread grain, ground at a watermill for a toll of a quarter of the flour and the by-products. He killed his own meat, which was kept frozen for winter consumption or smoked or salted down for the warm months. The cellar always had a store of potatoes, roots, and cabbage sufficient to last until the spring gardening season. We were not successful in developing an orchard, but we had an infinity of wild fruit, gooseberries, plums, and grapes, which, preserved or turned into jellies and jams, satisfied our fruit hunger. In the attic we had a huge store of wool from our own sheep, to supply us with stockings and mittens, scarves and vests.

One does not need to keep a strict accounting of one's time, in farming as a way of life. So when we needed firewood or fenceposts we did not take the straight and accessible trees, which would have been easily worked up, but addressed ourselves to old gnarled trees, often growing on difficult slopes, from which the logs had to be snaked down to the wood roads, at great cost of time. In making hay we did not follow the local plan of mowing in September, when the weather is settled but when much of the nutriment of the grass has gone out. Instead, when the grass was in flower, in August, we'd be out at dawn with the mowing machine and cut a few acres. The grass dried quickly in the morning sun, and in the early afternoon, before the usual thunderstorm, we had it all set up in workmanlike cocks that would shed any deluge. After some weeks we would haul it to the hay-yard and stack it. In the winter, when we opened a stack, we would find the hay the color of light green tea, sprinkled with pressed field flowers that had kept their natural color. The cows liked that hay and kept as fat on it as on grass.

A way-of-life farmer makes friends of his animals and spares no pains to take care of them if they are ailing. So my father kept on pension the old mare that had drawn his family from Wisconsin. Her teeth were bad, and every day my father would boil a kettle of corn and oats until they were soft enough for her poor gums. He no more reckoned the time he spent taking care of the old mare than a city dweller reckons the time he spends on an ailing dog.

Why should the way-of-life farmer keep a reckoning of his time? Almost everything he does is essentially pastime. It is a pastime to thresh out with a flail a stack of beans or peas and winnow them by pouring them from the granary attic window onto a canvas on the ground, with the September wind carrying the chaff far down the field. The hour cost of the peas or beans may be heavy. What of it? They are to become a long succession of delectable soups. So we boys collected bushels of hazelnuts. They were worth fifty cents a bushel at the store, but they were worth many delightful hours at home.

Of course the way-of-life farmer had to buy a few things—clothing, kitchen ware and dishes, fence wire, sugar, tea and coffee. To pay for these he had to sell something—mostly butter and eggs, occasionally a fat cow, a wagonload of hogs, a horse. In this small sector of his economy the farmer had to submit to the play of market forces, usually juggled. Sometimes he was outraged, but he was not depressed or worried.

My brothers and I addressed ourselves through the winter months to plans for turning our way-of-life farm into a cash farm. And in the few years of our operations we did more worrying than my father did in all his life.

Our father had forty acres under cultivation out of his two hundred and forty acres. It had been his practice to let fifteen acres lie fallow every year. My brothers and I decided to break an additional twenty acres and work the whole sixty, with the hope of producing in the first year a great reserve of grain, to be followed the next year by a bigger crop. We would raise as many pigs and calves as we could. We judged that the place would carry at least three times the stock it had carried before our regime.

Man proposes, some other power disposes. As we meant to work our horses hard we wanted to produce plenty of oats. We sowed ten acres of very good land, hoping to harvest five hundred bushels. The crop was standing breast high, in its beautiful oat green, when one morning my father noticed that great patches appeared to be ripe though only in flower. We hurried over to find out what was the matter. Billions of chinch bugs—a pestilential little insect—blackened every oat stem, sucking out all the sap and life.

"Alvin," my father said, "you'd better run to the house and get some matches. The oats will burn; tomorrow all those chinch bugs will move into the corn."

In half an hour the whole field was a roaring flame. Some chinch bugs had already got into the corn, but not enough to ruin it. The great mass of them went up in the flames.

I could have wept for our beautiful oat crop, but I was a man, bound to exhibit my father's resolution. We put the horses on corn, and when their hair got brittle and their skin pricked with red points for lack of the right vitamins—not yet so christened then—we took wheat to the mill and brought back "shorts," the coarse meal that holds most of the wheat germ.

The year brought a mountain of corn. Anyway, it looks like a mountain after you have picked it ear by ear, a hundred ears to the bushel, fifteen hundred bushels. You begin picking corn after the first frosts have killed the stalks and the October winds have dried out the husks, so that they will rip off with two clawings of the husking pin. The team walks slowly down one row, drawing a wagon with double box and high "throw board" on the side opposite you. You follow along the next row, ripping the husks and throwing in the ears. If you can reduce yourself to a perfect rhythm, shutting out of your consciousness everything but corn and the will to pick it, you may attain the old American performance of fifty bushels a day. A Swede from the island of Gothland, well crossed with Esths and Finns, can pick seventy-five bushels; a pure Finn, one hundred and twenty bushels; a born Briton, fifteen bushels; a German, twenty bushels.

My brothers and I were first-generation Americans with no inherited capacity to shut off our consciousness and resolve ourselves into a husking rhythm. None of us rose above forty bushels. Without thinking, we'd think a thought—a bushel of performance lost. Still, we got the corn husked before the snow descended upon us.

We had the corn and were prepared to pass over to the other pole of the "corn-hog" cycle. We had bred every sow on the place, mature, too old, too young, and made preparations for a huge harvest of pigs in the spring. Some came too early, before the sow had a chance to supplement her diet with grass and wild Jerusalem artichokes, in which the field margins abounded. For want of vitamins a sow would exhibit a murderous neurosis, killing each of her pigs as soon as it was born. It was my job to be on hand with a stout club to beat the sow over the snout as she turned for murder. The pigs I gathered in a basket, to be kept warm, eight or ten of them. After two days I returned them to the mother. I kept the club handy, for the sow's mother love had returned, and she would have liked to kill me for kidnaping her pigs.

The summer months marched along at the head of our eighty swine, each eating enormously and growing extravagantly. In late October we would send seventy of them to the market, not one weighing less than two hundred and fifty pounds. We began to calculate their value; low as hog prices would be, we had in pen nine hundred squealing dollars. We quarreled a bit over the distribution of our collective share, my brothers ganging up to make me take more than my fair share. But there was very little substance to our quarrel, for the business of our higher education we recognized as a collective enterprise to be financed out of a common purse.

One September morning, as I went to feed the pigs, I found a four-hundred-pound hog dead by the water trough. I looked over the pen anxiously: two more were lying sick, indifferent to feeding. I asked my father to come and look at the hogs. He shook his head. Cholera: they would all die.

It was the custom of the commercial farmer, when his pen was smitten by hog cholera, to hurry every hog that could be got into a wagon off to the packing house. Some might die on the road, but by means of ten dollars rightly placed the load of hogs would get priority to the pig sticker; first priority for a hog that had to be pulled forward with ropes. This practice filled us with horror and disgust. We assumed that all the hogs had the malady in them and were unfit for food. They died and died, one day five, another ten. In the end all died but one, a sow that went around for months as a living skeleton, but then started to grow, and grew and grew until she was as heavy as a small cow.

At first we dug graves in the field and buried the hogs. It was a huge job. The Indians, who had no tabu on cholera meat, carted off about twenty of them. For the rest we selected a deep-cut gully, dug a ditch to divert storm waters from it, and made it into a huge collective grave. We planted cottonwoods on it.

Nine hundred dollars buried! Being my father's son, I had to put on a cheerful face.

Next we invested our hopes in the cattle, from which we had a record stock of calves. But that was a longer-time venture. They were ready for market two years after the hog disaster. We got them to the Omaha market, where we suffered all the discriminations then in vogue in city dealings with the farmer. Nevertheless we got some hard cash in our pockets.

But my eighteenth birthday was on the way, and I felt I was already terribly old for getting a start in education. The cornhusking was nearly over. I announced that when it was finished I would pack my trunk and set out for the university.

I had studied the catalogue of the University of Nebraska and found to my joy that students registering for the premedical course were not subject to entrance examinations. I had no doubt that I was advanced enough to do the work, but my homemade primary education might not pass a formal examination.

My father made no comment on my announcement of departure and for two days was unusually silent. But one bright Indian summer Sunday morning he said he would like a talk with me. We went to a bench under a spreading group of box elder trees, their still scattered yellow leaves golden in the sun. My father gazed in silence at the cornfield across the brook, a tangle of light buff, and the brown hill above, which threw a sheltering fold around the farm. He turned his face to the wood, now mostly leafless and showing a fine growth of straight young tree trunks.

"This is a pretty farm," my father said. "A good farm. You boys have made it produce twice as much as before, and you have just begun. You had bad luck with the hogs, but you are getting a new start, and the young cattle are coming on. The farm can sell a carload of fat cattle every year and at least three carloads of hogs on its own feed."

I had nothing to say. My father was going to persuade me to stay on the farm. I braced my resolution.

"Land is going up," my father resumed. "This farm might sell for twenty dollars an acre today, but by the time you are forty it will be worth fifty dollars an acre. Then there is Wigle's two hundred acres; the owner gets nothing out of it but taxes. He'd sell it in a minute for two thousand dollars. We could put our money together and buy it tomorrow, with a very light mortgage. Then there is the Lange quarter section north of us. They call it poor land, but ground that makes such a growth of weeds would make crops. We could get it for a thousand dollars or less. Then Okander's six hundred and forty. Okander is getting old and deeper all the time in law suits. The lawyers are eating him up; in a few years his land will be for sale, cheap.

"In ten years you boys could have twelve hundred acres, all paid for, and in twenty more years all this land will be worth fifty dollars an acre. You boys will be worth sixty thousand dollars." (The land was actually selling for a hundred dollars an acre and more before the end of thirty years.)

"If you leave," my father said after a long pause, "I'll have to sell the place. The boys will follow you soon, and I can't handle the farm." He waited for my answer.

"Papa," I said, "it hurts me awfully to leave you and the family and the farm. It is a fine farm, and I love it. I know we boys could get rich if we stayed, and we'll never get another chance. But I have to go. My heart has been set on education too long. I'd never be contented. I have to go."

"All right," my father said. He rose and looked at the sky. "Looks to me as if a storm is gathering. Glad you've got most of the corn husked. You'll finish tomorrow?"

Before the next week was over I had my trunk packed. My father was going to drive me to Dakota City, our railway station, fourteen miles away. Since I had to take my train in the morning we drove up in the afternoon and took rooms in the town hotel for the night. We had our supper and sat for a while in the cheerless lobby, where my father entered upon a desultory conversation with a traveling salesman. My father kept watching the clock.

"Well, Alvin, we'd better go to bed. We'll wake early tomorrow."

So we did. After three interminable hours the train puffed up from the east. We shook hands. I got on board and waved to my father as the train started up. He was a moving figure, so erect, his gray beard blowing out from his breast in the morning wind.

I had some terrible twinges of pain. I had had none of any consequence in parting with my mother, to whom I stood much closer, or my brothers, my constant companions since their birth. But I did not feel that I was parting with them. I was setting out to pioneer in education for the family, to break a road for my brothers to follow, to realize my mother's dream of professional careers for her children. My father had not participated in the dreams and plans, and parting left us with no solace.

Many years later my father reminded me of that parting. "Do you remember, Alvin," he said, "the time you went away, and the night we spent in the hotel? I didn't sleep that night. I cried most of the time."

What! My resolute father had actually cried? My mind went back to the conversation on the bench, and the cold cruelty of my response. "Papa, would you have been happier if I had taken your advice and stayed on the farm?"

"No. I didn't want you to stay. I felt it was right to try to show you, you could be rich if you stayed. But I never cared to be rich, and I knew you never would. From the time you were a little boy I knew you would leave me as soon as you grew up."

He was silent for some minutes. "If you had said you'd take my advice and stay, I'd have been awfully disappointed in you. I'd have felt like kicking you out."

After I left the farm my relations with my mother remained very close. We wrote weekly letters to each other down to the time of her death. She was aware of every problem I encountered, appraised every solution I found. My father never wrote letters and persisted in the view that the world I had entered was alien to him. So long as I remained in Nebraska, I spent part of my vacations at home, one year on the farm and after that in the village of Dakota City, where my father had bought a house after selling the farm. We conversed very little, mostly about local incidents.

And yet my father's personality was deep in my consciousness, perhaps deepest of all. But as he had no real relation to my educational life he will not appear again in these pages. I cannot forbear, however, from setting down here an incident that exhibits the deeper relations between us.

When I was in my middle childhood it was my duty to arise with the first streak of dawn and water and feed the horses so that they would be ready for the field when the day laborer appeared shortly after sunrise. I was a sleepyhead and for a time depended on being awakened by my father.

"Alvin!" he would call from his room. Immediately I'd be out of bed, still half asleep, and dressing myself with thick fingers.

Soon I had become conditioned to awakening at early dawn, and my father never again needed to call me.

One night, many years later, when I was a professor at Cornell, I was startled half awake by my father's voice, calling, "Alvin!" I was up and beginning to dress before I realized that it was just a dream.

Next morning I received a telegram from my mother in Palo Alto,

California. My father had died in the night. The letter that followed three days later told me that my father had been ill but not seriously enough to require my being informed. But about midnight he had sat up in his bed and called, "Alvin," and dropped back dead.

Just a coincidence, of course, but such coincidences may operate on one's unconscious mind with magical force. Since that time, as I have mentioned before, my father's simulacrum appears to me in a dream when I am deep in perplexity. He appears much larger and more majestic than in life, silent, but potent to thrust the pain of perplexity out of my mind.

TEN

A Prep Medic

IT WAS a late afternoon in early November when my train arrived at Lincoln. I got out, a little stiff from the novel experience of sitting still a whole day. There was a trolley waiting, marked for a destination unknown to me, but it would no doubt go through the town. I asked the conductor how one got to the university. Get out at Eleventh Street and walk north two or three blocks.

There before me, as I got out of the streetcar, was University Hall, as it was pictured in the university catalogue. I walked up to the gate, where I was almost trodden down by students scurrying from the classrooms. The building before me seemed huge and majestic. It had four strata of windows, some of them lighted, under a mansard roof. The building was topped with a square tower. To the right were three other buildings of varying architecture, all handsome to my country eyes.

But night was approaching, and I needed shelter. I picked up my bag and walked about in the streets near the campus until I came upon a sign, "Boarders." I knocked and was admitted by an emaciated land-lady, aproned and smelling of cooking. She led me to a room, about eight feet by twelve, with narrow bed, washstand, and table. Three dollars a week, room and board. I was content.

The next morning, having risen at five, I took a long walk to see the city and to kill the time until breakfast, served at the late city hour of half-past seven. I took another long walk to kill time until nine o'clock, when I surmised the offices would be open. What office? I did not know, but went to the campus and accosted a hurrying student. Where was the Secretary's office?

He shook his head. He didn't know.

I said I wanted to enter the preparatory department.

"Oh, then you go to the registrar, Ma Smith. But say, you're awful late. She'll kill you. She nearly broke my neck because I was two weeks late. But you can try her. First floor, offices to the left." The student raced on.

In those days youths expected to be rebuffed. It was part of the game of life you braced up to. I proceeded to Ma Smith's office without undue trepidation.

Ma Smith was an elderly woman with thin gray hair done in a hair-pinned bun at the base of her head. She was hauling an unlucky student over the coals, and the longer she talked the angrier she got. When I presented my modest request she almost frothed at the mouth.

"Enter now, with the term half over? No sirree!" She turned her back on me.

I retreated, not pleased but not crushed. I would try the chancellor. If he threw me out, I'd just hang around the rest of the semester and work up the courses by myself. After all, the chief function of the teacher was to make the student work, and I was quite competent to make myself work.

Chancellor James H. Canfield was a robust figure, not tall but, in a friendly way, very imposing. His mobile face was well bronzed, his dark eyes were bright and understanding. I was able to put my case without embarrassment.

"My boy," he said, "you are too late. You can't make it. My advice is, go home to the farm and come back September fifteenth."

"That wouldn't work," I objected. "I can't go back to the farm to do nothing. I'd have to plant another crop of corn and I'd have to husk it. You know, you can't husk corn before the end of October. I'd be just as late next year."

The chancellor smiled. "As I said, you can't make it. At least I think you can't make it. But if you want to try it, the chancellor has no right to forbid you."

"Then I can register?"

He nodded.

"Will you give me a note to Ma Smith?"

"*Miss* Smith," he corrected. "Yes." He wrote a note in his delicately perfect script, signed it with a flourish, and gave it to me. He offered his warm, cordial hand. "My boy, you'll make it."

In my senior year, when I counted Ma Smith among my best friends, she told me how near she had come to a "cat fit" when I presented the note from the chancellor. She said that in fixing up my program she tried to give me the toughest teachers on the faculty, of whom the very toughest was the "Lieut"—Lieutenant John J. Pershing, Commandant of Cadets, who taught elementary mathematics and studied law on the side.

Most of my teachers were very considerate and gave me more time than I needed to catch up. Not so Lieutenant John J. Pershing. I had been in his class one week when he ordered me to the board to work out a complicated problem in algebra. I asked to be excused on the ground that I had not had time to catch up with the class.

"You have been here a week," he said grimly. "Next Monday, be caught up."

I was.

Of all my teachers Lieutenant Pershing interested me most. I devoted myself more to studying him than to the progress of the class. He was my first experience of a professional soldier.

Lieutenant Pershing was tall, perfectly built, handsome. All his movements, all play of expression, were rigidly controlled to a military pattern. His pedagogy was military. His questions were short, sharp orders, and he expected quick, succinct answers. Woe to the student who put a problem on the board in loose or slovenly fashion! Pershing's soul appeared to have been formed on the pattern of "Present—arms! Right shoulder—arms! Fours right! Forward march!"

The ladies of the city were crazy about him—so it was gossiped among us students. But their adoration was vain—so the gossip ran— for the Lieut was ambitious and could not use a wife who did not bring a fortune. There were no adequate fortunes in Lincoln.

I admired Lieutenant Pershing, as a soldier. But never in the whole year did he give us a single glimpse of the Pythagorean enthusiasm for mathematics as an incomparable weapon for subjugating even the unknowable.

Where Pershing's abilities shone brilliantly was in his handling of the cadet battalion. He could take a body of cornfed yokels and with only three hours of drill a week turn them into fancy cadets, almost indistinguishable from West Pointers. The year before I came to Lincoln, Pershing had taken a body of his Nebraska cadets to a national cadet corps meet at St. Louis, and all but beat West Point.

The university population appeared to be made up of about equal numbers of preparatory students and collegians proper. Naturally my early associations were with the preps, but one encountered collegians in the boarding houses, where they tended to sit apart and patronize us poor preps. We were a body doomed to extinction but kept going for the time because of the inadequacy of the high schools in the state.

Most of us were from small towns or farms, and our preparation was woefully defective. I do not include myself among the unfortunate. I was comparatively well read and had an adequate command of language. Most of my fellow preps had read hardly anything. One, for example, told me that the only book he had ever read was *Robinson Crusoe,* and he was convinced most of it consisted of lies.

With command of language limited to the daily speech of the farm or the small town, one was terribly handicapped in one's studies. You had nothing to translate Latin or German into, and even the mathematical demonstrations were painfully myopic. A lot of my friends who had perfectly good brains nevertheless were dismal failures as students. In later years, as a professor of economics, I collected much evidence that success or failure in my classes was mainly a matter of English. The best students came, as a rule, from bookish families.

The next year I was confronted with the problem of military drill. I was a proto-pacifist and would have been glad to see the cadet corps abolished. But there it was, a condition of certain grants from the federal government which the university needed. One could substitute gymnasium work if one had good reasons for doing so, such as having to work in the late afternoon for board and room. I had begun, in desultory fashion, to do odd jobs to replenish my purse, but I had no time schedule that would serve as an excuse. My friends urged me to go in for drill while still a prep. Thus I could get five years of it and be fairly sure of an officer's commission. But that was distinctly what I did not want. My pacifism took the peculiar turn of willingness to accept the training of a private but not of an officer. I couldn't explain the distinction; it seemed to me like a mathematical axiom.

If you were out for a commission you served one year as a private, one as corporal, and a third as sergeant. If you were any good at all you got a lieutenancy, or even a captaincy, the fourth year, and on graduation you got a commission in the National Guard—mostly a paper organization.

Most cadets were dying to go up the promotion ladder and sycophanted the Lieutenant as intimately as they could sycophant that disintimate soldier. I looked on the whole process with equalitarian contempt.

At the end of the year I heard my name read out before the corps as one of the corporals for the next year. I wouldn't have it and went to Lieutenant Pershing to have my name taken off the list.

"Why?" he demanded in the first surprised tone I ever heard from him.

I tried to explain, but my explanation didn't get through to him. He frowned and said, "If you don't want it, there is another cadet who does."

About half a century later I met General Pershing at a party given by Bernard M. Baruch for the War Industries Board.

"I think I have met you before, Doctor Johnson," said the great general.

"Certainly," I said. "You have met hundreds of thousands, who all remember you, but you can't remember the hundreds of thousands."

"Was it in Nebraska, when I was Commandant of Cadets?"

"It was."

"And you were the cadet who refused to be a corporal. I never did understand your reasoning."

Imagine such a memory! Caesar was said to have known the names of all the soldiers in his legions. Commanding an army of ten regiments, to correspond with Caesar's army, Pershing might have learned the names of his men. He had had more to command his attention in his brilliant military career, first as Black Jack in the Philippines and finally in command of the huge American armies in World War I.

But to return to my education. As a prep medic I was privileged to carry more courses than could a prep student aiming at college. Also, the authorities were lenient in crediting me for work done in the vacation period. At the end of two years my preparation for medicine was complete. But my ambition had changed. I hungered for a life of scholarship, and registered as a freshman in the classical course.

ELEVEN

College

THE college proper of the University of Nebraska would have ranked as a small college today. It counted on graduating about a hundred and fifty students. As mortality in the lower classes was heavy, we may have numbered all told between seven and eight hundred.

As a prep student I had become familiar with the setup of the college. At the top was the chancellor. A mighty man was he, drawing a salary of five thousand dollars, said to be the largest salary in the state, whether in public or in private employment. We adored Chancellor Canfield. We regarded him not only as a shining representative of the world of culture, but as a true democrat, who used all his influence to abate the snobbishness of the students from the families that composed the rising middle class. He was constantly urging the more prosperous fathers to hold allowances to their sons and daughters to a minimum, that the university might not be cursed with caste formation.

We idolized still more his daughter Dorothy, a little girl still short of her teens, with lustrous brown eyes and abundant brown curls and the winning ways of a little fairy out of the storybooks. At college celebrations in the chapel she played for us on a mammoth violoncello, while a very tall Miss Mansfield played a diminutive violin. Dorothy Canfield was a bright star in our pioneer cultural dawn. She has remained a bright star ever since to the hundreds of thousands who have read her charming and wholesome books. No one works long in any good cause without finding himself associated with Dorothy Canfield Fisher, modest in prosperity, brave in disaster, never wavering in her faith in the essential goodness of human nature and in the high destiny of man.

Our beloved Jimmy, as we called the chancellor among ourselves, was soon to leave us for the University of Ohio. I never knew why. Many years later, when he served as Librarian of Columbia, endeavoring to make that great library into an intellectual power like the ancient library of Alexandria, I asked him why he had deserted us.

He smiled. "You know, Nebraska boasted of the fact that no chancellor could last with them for more than five years. Perhaps I simply left when the going was good."

In his place we got a handsome man who pronounced culture "cultcha" and informed us in his inaugural that hitherto the university had laid stress on quantity, but now it meant to stress quality.

That did not sit well with us. For the university, in the eyes of the faculty—except for late recruits from the East—and also in the eyes of the more awakened students, had a mission: to bring the light of education and culture to the prairie. We who knew Nebraska knew the need. I have described the kind of primary schooling that had been accessible to me. Many of my friends in the preparatory department had had nothing better. In my county there were two high schools, both poorly staffed. Their graduates were very inadequately prepared for college. But mine was one of the older and richer counties in the state. In the droughty western half of the state population was sparse and schools of any character were sprinkled very thinly over the monotonous landscape.

It was the chief mission of the university, as we saw it, to train young men and women and send them out to man the grade schools and eventually the high schools. A large percentage of the boys in the college, and a much larger percentage of the girls, expected to devote themselves, at least for some years, to this work of teaching.

The state was also short of educated lawyers, doctors, engineers. For want of resources the university had to give up its medical college, but it was handling competently the problems of legal and engineering education.

The older members of the faculty conceived of teaching Nebraskans as their essential function in life. Many of them had been students at the university in its early years and had risen through instructorships to the professorial ranks. Others had been drawn from neighboring institutions of the prairie states. Their teaching load was heavy, for the legislature, which voted the funds, considered it a rare privilege for a man to teach four hours a day and have all the rest of his time to himself. This seemed reasonable to the Nebraska contingent on the faculty but shocking to faculty recruits from the East, where ten hours of teaching a week was regarded as a heavy program.

The teaching, as a rule, was good, because the teachers believed in their mission. Like all good teachers, they rejoiced in the student of promise. But they did not give up the mediocre, nor even the poor student. A boy or girl who could never rise above a C+ or B might still bring the light of education into his home town up in the sandhills. A student aiming for the ministry might never be able to puzzle his way through Cicero's periods, or make anything out of the orations of Lysias or the dialogues of Plato. Still, his mediocre Latin and Greek might enable him to read the simple narratives of Genesis in the Vulgate, or the parables of the New Testament in Greek. Thus equipped, he might impress his congregation with the Word of God in more authentic language than the democracy's, or even the King's, English. A good part of the students would never find use for trigonometry in their daily lives, but the struggle to master the subject would bring home to them that real education is a desperately hard business. We all committed to memory what we understood to be the mottoes of Phi Beta Kappa: *Per Aspera ad Astra* and *Philosophia Biou Kybernetes*.

This new and perhaps crude university of ours was live; and life means strife. The faculty was torn by the conflict between the Arts, including the languages, literature, philosophy, and ethics, and the physical sciences, including, since the recent invasion of the techniques of Wundt, psychology. The political sciences were represented mainly by political economy, which both sides scorned as being neither flesh, fowl, nor good red herring. I detested the department and all its works, unfairly, for I could never be induced to attend a single political economy lecture. The "pol-econ" students who infested the boarding-house tables would fill the air with noisome abstractions like the Law of Diminishing Returns, and the principle that a demand for commodities is not a demand for labor. These "pol-econ" students assumed that with their abstractions they had the answer to the vital political issues that had been raised by the farmers and the labor movement. Bah!

Imagine how horrified I would have been if a true prophet had informed me that the time would come when I'd set up as an economist myself and develop great expertise in playing with abstractions in lieu of reality.

It was plain that the Arts faction was fighting a losing battle. You couldn't dramatize and publicize the virtues of patient classical study or the minute analysis of a piece of literature. The science departments could overwhelm you by demonstrating the invention of liquid air, then expected to be an important source of power. They could exhibit a world of microscopic life, whose control might banish disease; they could set up a table of elements including a number that had never been discovered but infallibly would be found.

The Arts faction asked what good these facts and speculations would be for the graduate struggling to raise the sunburned lads and lasses of Broken Bow or Weeping Water up out of the conglomerate matrix of farm and village preconceptions. The Science faction retorted: The backbone of your Arts system is a museum backbone—dead and petrified languages; your philosophy is a blizzard of dusty abstractions; your literature, women's club entertainment. Young people are live; science is live.

And already a rift was appearing in the victorious ranks of science, between pure and applied. The pure science of nitrogen was beginning to pipe small in the presence of the science of nitrogen as source of nitrate fertilizer. Contemplation of the stars in their courses had to yield to greasy overalls and the power and rumble of the dynamo.

I was happy at the university but not entirely at home in it. I was older than the average freshman. I was twenty as against an average of eighteen. And in that period of life one is extremely conscious of differences in age that later in life become negligible.

Being older, I was under constant inner pressure to make as rapid progress as I could toward my degree. As I was registered for the classical course I found a simple method for making up time: read, read copiously. Instead of mulling indefinitely with the class over a single play of Plautus or Terence, read all the plays. Soon you forget that you are reading a foreign language. Repeated contexts give you the precise meaning of words, and the grammatical forms that a class struggles with come to seem natural and inevitable.

I used one vacation to devour so much German literature that the professor pushed me ahead to his graduate seminar. The next vacation I did the same with Greek. In my second college year I was half sophomore, half graduate student, with the sophomore half in process of liquidation. In my third year I was a senior, with more than half my time to spare for work toward a Master's degree.

It goes without saying that with so much irregularity in my college course I could take no real interest in college politics, which for many students served as a valuable introduction to the real politics of village and city. There was wire-pulling, trading votes, distributing plums where they would do the most good. With one foot in the class of '98 and the other in the class of '97, I could not be interested in the contests in either.

Neither could I develop serious interest in general politics, as organized within the university in Republican and Democratic clubs. My enthusiasm for Cleveland of 1884 had wholly evaporated by 1892. I had been steeped in the ideas of the Farmers' Alliance and the Knights of Labor. I saw little choice between the Democratic party, bastioned by Tammany and the Southern aristocrats, and the Republican party, supported and controlled by big industry and big business. The time seemed ripe for the launching of a new party, and I was deeply interested in the formation of the People's party, dubbed the Populist party by its opponents.

The early nineties was a period of great social and political tension. The depression, which had afflicted the country since the early seventies, advancing or receding like a glacier, but as a rule advancing, was perhaps no more severe in the early nineties than it had been in the eighties or seventies, but it was felt as more severe, through the cumulation of stresses. Hundreds of thousands of men had given up all hope of regular employment and had developed tramping into a way of life. In the intermountain region tens of thousands of them followed the harvest in a more or less haphazard way, from Texas to the Canada line, never working in one place any longer than was necessary to earn a few dollars for cheap whisky or commercial love, sustaining themselves on handouts or on roasting ears or potatoes collected from the fields. Their mode of travel ordinarily was to establish themselves on top of freight cars, with clubs to beat off the advances of the brakemen. The more expert members of the tramping trade traveled much faster, lying on the rods under passenger or mail cars.

On rare occasions the masses of tramps exceeded these means of travel and had to resort to more energetic measures. Once the traffic on one of the North-South lines was thrown into confusion by the seizure of a train of empty freight cars by a thousand tramps, among whom were many experienced railwaymen. They started south with a wild hurrah, and all the railway authorities could do was telegraph ahead: "Keep the tracks open, for God's sake, unless you have jail room for a thousand desperadoes, mostly carrying pistols."

I wanted to know more about the tramps and their ideas of life. During one of my vacations I went up to Ames, Nebraska, where there was an enormous sugar-beet farm, relying on casual labor. Anybody could get a job there at twenty cents an hour—two dollars for a ten-hour day, with a charge of ninety cents for food and bunk room. The two dollars fell out if it rained—as it usually did—but the ninety cents went on remorselessly. In two weeks I netted a dollar and seventy-five cents, but I had to lay out a dollar and a half on Johnson's Horse Liniment, to abate the stiffness of my back and limbs.

We were thinning beets. The sugar beet then, and I believe still today, was an inhuman plant that sent up two, three, or four plantlets from just one seed. All but one had to be eliminated, if you were to have a real beet, and only the human thumb and forefinger could separate out the plantlets to be sacrificed.

We were two gangs of five hundred men each. In the morning we started out, each man with a row, which extended in a straight line over the flat Platte Valley landscape from the rising to the setting sun. At first I depended on the elasticity of my back to thin beets by stooping, but soon I saw I had to accept the tramp technique of getting down on my marrow bones in the soft, black soil.

Behind us three overseers strode back and forth, giving thunder to the laggards. Soft from college life, I would have caught it as a laggard, but a wooden-legged tramp next to me would push ahead with his own row and give a lift to mine. He was a rosy-faced, pleasant fellow, who had much good advice for me.

"You're new to this life, but I tell *you,* it is *the* life. You work when you want to, and when you don't want to, you needn't. You can always eat on handouts, and the best bedroom in the world is a haystack under the open sky.

"But the first thing you want to do is get a leg cut off. Mine was cut off when I was riding the rods on the Canadian Pacific. Those damned British roads are slow, and I fell asleep. Well, you know, after that I've had my wooden leg cut off four times, when I fell asleep on the rods. Besides, you get better handouts with a wooden leg."

He had a shack in Texas, where he had collected all the works of Emerson, to be read over and over in the winter months. Another tramp I was on good terms with carried a badly worn Bible—"damn good book, by God."

Returning to the university, how could I get heated up over Cleveland's free-trade notions, or even over his very laudable passion for Civil Service reform? Something more important was going on in the world.

A revolutionary impulse was abroad, a resumption of the democratic movement launched by Sam Adams, Tom Paine, and Jefferson, and extended by Jackson and Lincoln. The lines were being drawn. Cleveland found it necessary to suppress the Pullman strike in 1894 with military forces. In the Mountain and Pacific States "citizens' committees" were forming, to put down the "anarchistic" activities of labor. Bull pens were being set up, concentration camps for "agitators."

We had a literature, sometimes running to one-sided panaceas, like Harvey's *Coin's Financial School,* sometimes wild and disordered like Ignatius Donnelly's *Caesar's Column,* sometimes closely reasoned, authentically documented, like Henry Demarest Lloyd's *Arena* essays and his magnificent book *Wealth Against Commonwealth.* Against us was a literature of deliberate misunderstanding, bitter vituperation.

So it had been in the formative years of the Republican party. But the Republicans had found in Lincoln a great leader, master of political strategy. We had no great leader, only chiefs who thought they could play the political game. It came to be noised about that our party, the party of the people, saw a quick way to power through falling behind Bryan and the silver Democrats.

I had nothing against free silver. I had been convinced by the writings of men like Emile de Laveleye, and E. Benjamin Andrews' *An Honest Dollar* (for which he was fired from the presidency of Brown University) that the narrowness of the basis of credit—gold—had produced a continuous decline in prices since 1873 and had its share in the responsibility for the depression. But to my mind the currency problem was a minor issue among our many major issues, most of which, at the time, Bryan had apparently never heard of.

Our leaders were selling out, not only to Bryan but to the Democratic party, party of Croker of Tammany Hall, party of the rotten-borough politicians of the South.

Among the students I knew in my prep days there were many inclined like myself toward agrarian radicalism. Few of them survived through to the college classes. Politically I felt alien to the institution and rarely discussed politics at all.

In my urge forward in scholarship I had come very close to members of the faculty, particularly to the head of the Department of Greek, James T. Lees. He was a magnificent scholar. British born, with British conservatism dyed in his wool, educated at Johns Hopkins under the great classicist Basil L. Gildersleeve, passionate admirer of Paul Shorey, Platonist, despiser of his times and particularly of anything savoring of democracy.

"See here, Johnson," Lees would say, "you are in the wrong pew.

You know Greek culture, better than any other person born in Nebraska. You know Rome. You know the Renaissance. You know the Enlightenment. You know that every significant contribution ever made to culture was made by the few, the aristocrats. Every decay in culture has been due to the mob, the democracy."

"The case isn't so clear," I would argue. "Pericles was leader of the democratic faction not only of Athens but of all Greece; Socrates and Plato detested Pericles as you detest Bryan. Caesar may have been an aristocrat, but he rode into power on the shoulders of the Roman people. The Medici were wool merchants and bankers, probably detested and despised by the ancient aristocracy. Washington and Jefferson may have been aristocrats, but they threw in their lot with the common people of America instead of running with the fine-haired aristocrats of Philadelphia and New York in the Tory camp."

Professor Lees threw back his head, the Homeric way of expressing vigorous dissent. "Where are the aristocrats to lead your Populists today?"

"We haven't them yet, but sooner or later they will appear."

The aristocrat did indeed appear, but half a century late. Under Franklin D. Roosevelt virtually every aspiration of the Populists of the eighteen-nineties was realized. One may speculate on the problem of how our national life would have shaped itself if there had not been this half-century lag between democratic need and fulfillment.

I was also alien to the religious life of the university. A tattered flap of the Southern Bible Belt had covered much of Nebraska and was very much in evidence in the university. A very considerable proportion of the students I knew refused to register for any course under an instructor addicted to that horrible anti-religious doctrine Darwinism. They were sincere, frightfully sincere, these religionists. I will give one example. A good friend of mine, an able student of Greek, came to me so sunken in anguish that I feared he would commit suicide, and I stuck to him like a bur till his anguish abated a little.

He had gone skating on our salt lake on a cold January day. There was just one other man who had braved the bitter wind and was skating down the lake. As my friend followed him with the wind the idea cropped up in his head: Perhaps this man has not been saved. Perhaps if I accost him and plead, "Will you be saved?" his soul may be saved from Hell.

The stranger reached the end of the lake before my friend and started back. My friend could have intercepted him but his nerve failed.

He would do it at the starting end. He turned and skated valiantly against the wind, but the stranger turned and flew down the wind again. My friend started after him, but the stranger turned again and fought his way back against the wind, my friend following, out of breath.

At the end of the lake there was an interurban car waiting. The stranger got on—my friend was too late. The car moved swiftly away with the man who perhaps had not been saved. My friend took the next car and came home, to cudgel himself all night. If he had intercepted the stranger, who knows? he might have been saved. If the stranger was to burn in Hell, perhaps it would be the fault of my friend, who failed to skate into his path to challenge him to salvation.

This was a difficult atmosphere for my father's son.

Religionism in Nebraska produced its antidote in militant agnosticism, sometimes asserting itself to be atheism. When Robert Ingersoll came to town to lecture on the "Mistakes of Moses," you had to be up early in the morning, weeks ahead, to get standing room to hear this gross fat man, with a short-breathed wheeze that marvelously helped out his humor. I was among the standees and didn't tire of him. Yet I didn't like him or his crowd, for I knew life on the prairie and what religion meant to many poor souls dragging out their lives in grinding hardship.

Picture to yourself the prairie home of the eighties and nineties: the homestead, a grassy half-mile square, with not a tree or a bush except for a discouraged row of spindling cottonwood saplings, intended to grow into a windbreak in the course of years; the house, four-roomed frame, the clapboarding warped, the shingles curled by the sun, the plaster cracked and admitting drafts from the roaring winds, which kept the flame of the lamp perpetually flickering; no fuel, except soft coal too dear to buy, or corn in the ear, a very good fuel and cheaper than coal; excessive heat in summer, bitter cold in winter, and wind, wind, wind to drive one to distraction.

The state asylum for the insane was packed with farm wives, driven crazy, it was explained, by the isolation of farm life. I had a different explanation then, which seems to me even more reasonable now. I thought it was a matter of diet. These farm families lived almost exclusively on meat, potatoes, and soda biscuits. Some of them tried, in a halfhearted way, to plant vegetable gardens, but usually the weeds took over the ground while the farmer was occupied with his field crops.

When I visited the insane asylum I noticed that there were few insane women from the immigrant settlements, German, Scandinavian, Bohemian, Russian. All these immigrants cherished their gardens and ate enormously of the vegetables produced.

Whether it was from loneliness or a diet lacking vitamins, these farm women were a pathetic lot. When you passed by the prairie house you were likely to hear a woman singing, in thin, quavering tones:

> "We'll work till Jesus comes
>   When we'll be gathered home."

Or:

> "Nearer my Home
>   Nearer my Father's House
>   Where many mansions be
>   Nearer the Great White Throne
>   Nearer the crystal sea."

Or:

> "Come, come, angel band,
>   Come and around me stand,
>   Oh, bear me away on your snowy wings
>   To my immortal Home."

Would anyone rob these women of this shred of comfort in their lives?

On the other hand, I could not join the troop of the saved. One day a dozen of my good friends in the YMCA set themselves a job. They would pray for me continuously for twenty-four hours. Those boys woke one another up all night long to keep the praying going for the soul of Alvin Johnson.

It troubled me deeply. Why should those sweet friends of mine disturb themselves so much about my poor soul, hidden away somewhere in me and content with me if it could be sure that I accepted the brotherhood of man as a reality?

The Greek letter fraternities and sororities were already well established in the university; new ones were introduced from time to time. The majority of the students were anti-fraternity and were known as "Barbs"—barbarians. I saw nothing against the fraternities, nor anything for them. They were outside of my world. None of them would have invited me to membership, nor would I have accepted membership in any of them. A fraternity aimed at social and cultural uniformity. It dictated its members' associations with non-members—they had to be the "right kind"; it even decided what young ladies a member might properly call on and take out to parties. For my part I wanted to make my friends where I chose. As a rule I cultivated people who had a genuine taste for scholarship, but I also cultivated Jeremiah Rebmann, recently arrived from Germany, who was fighting desperately with our stubborn language and the more stubborn ideas of science and philosophy. From him I learned to pronounce German after the Württemberg fashion—very nearly good High German. I also cultivated a Negro student by the name of Johnson. I wanted to learn something about the Negro mind, commonly believed then to be essentially imitative, strong in its power to assimilate words, especially long ones of vague meaning, weak in the purely intellectual processes. This Negro Johnson was indeed a remarkable student of languages, both modern and ancient. But he was also prominent in mathematics, logic, and philosophy. An upstanding man, tall and handsome, bubbling with wit and good humor, he would have gone far but for the accident of his color, a beautiful and becoming blackbrown. I do not know what became of him: probably he found a privileged place among Pullman porters. I learned a lot from him. After associating with him I could never see the sense or justice in racial discrimination.

I was also on friendly terms with a number of young men who were Jews. At the time I never thought of them as Jews. Nobody did, although I believe the fraternities excluded them, on orders from the parent chapters in the East. There was nothing in their behavior or performance to set them apart from the general body of students. Some ranked with the brightest students, others with the stupidest. Of stupid students, Gentile and Jew, I had intimate knowledge, for after my freshman year I made my living and part of the living of my two brothers, who had joined me, by tutoring, especially in Latin and Greek but occasionally in English, mathematics, and elementary science. As a rule the students needing my services were dull, though too honest to crib. Sometimes I was fortunate enough to have a student of promise, as for example Wilfred I. King, destined later to be a distinguished economist. He astonished me by doing a translation of a whole book of Caesar in Alexandrine verse.

There were two literary societies among the "Barbs," the Palladian and the Union, made up of approximately equal numbers of boys and girls. I early became a Palladian and attended its Friday evening exercises with great regularity. Perhaps our literary performance was mediocre, but the association through years with eager young people of both sexes was worth while. We "Barbs" were mostly socially green, and the society of the girl students was a civilizing force. The Palladian girls were an admirable group, not, however, set apart from the girls of the general student body, who were in the vast majority earnest students, better disciplined intellectually than the boy students and gaining top rank in their classes so frequently that the male students, in self-defense, had to fall back on the antique dogma that the female mind is acquisitive, not original, and that the girls won honors by reflecting faithfully the professors' wisdom and foibles. Having been brought up with convictions of sex equality, I repudiated this dogma, and in argument with the champions of male monopoly of originality I would dwell on the fact that the two most original persons among our university students were Willa Cather and Louise Pound.

I was far from contented with my own social aptitude. I had a great many friends among the boy students, but few among the girl students. Each Friday evening the boy members of the Palladian society were expected to escort the girl members to the meeting. I met the requirement faithfully, but was always rather sorry for the girl whose evening was sacrificed to me. I had no small talk and felt hesitant about indulging in large talk—Plato's real place as the prince of the Sophists, Kleon as not at all the monster figured in upper-class Greek accounts but merely an ancient William Jennings Bryan, or the tragedy of the proposed Populist merger with the alien Democratic party. I was afraid of seeming a Winkhaus, with his unity of "time, space, matter, and the causal nexus." How I admired the young fellows who had only to face a girl in order to release a merry mutual chatter with nothing in it more responsible and exacting than in their exchange of smiles and pleased glances!

Almost all my friends were falling in love. That was inevitable: young men and women, meeting every day in classrooms and social groupings in an atmosphere of extraordinary emotional purity—how could they help it? Pessimistic spokesmen of the moribund aristocracy were even then charging that the coeducational college played the role of a matrimonial agency. Was there ever in the world so excellent a matrimonial agency? The boys and girls saw each other in classes, in laboratories, informal social groups. No bright girl fell for a four-flusher or dunderhead. No able boy fell for a girl who had looks and nothing else.

Through half a century I have kept in touch with those college mat-ings. They are as sweet and wholesome today as they promised to be then. If there have been any divorces I haven't heard of them.

My situation, however, troubled me deeply. My friends were falling in love and getting deep satisfaction, dreadful worries out of it. What was the matter with me that I was not falling in love? I knew many young ladies, very friendly, not bespoken. In some cases I tried to cook up a romantic feeling, but an evening at the Palladian, or occasionally at the theater, would leave me cold.

That was convenient, with my ambitions for a career in scholarship. I rationalized my coldness into realism and practicality. But yet all youth has flamed; you are young and remain cold. That is something uncomfortable to think of. But I suppressed such impertinent thoughts and congratulated myself unofficially on a disposition that fitted in precisely with my scholarly ambitions.

One day a fellow student, an editor of the college paper, showed me a sketch, just an English-class exercise, by a girl I had never heard of. I was at the time deep in the problem of literary style. I knew, or thought I knew, the secret of the overwhelming impression Demos-thenes made with the essentially trivial subject, *On the Crown.* I had analyzed Cicero's orations on Catiline before the Senate and his very different speeches to the Assembly. I knew the lovely prose of Seneca, and knew how Erasmus, following Seneca, made up a Latin prose fit to serve as a basis for French prose. I condemned the Ciceronian prose of Milton and rejoiced in the restoration of good sense in Hobbes and Locke and Hume.

Here in a sketch by an unknown girl was good prose, a rarity in the productions of university students. I inquired about the writer. She was a girl of seventeen, already a junior in college. Edith Henry was her name.

At the time I was custodian of the classical library. There was a young girl, blue-eyed, sweet-faced, who came to the library sometimes, treading as softly as May among the flowers. She wanted to take out a book. She signed a slip—Edith Henry. The girl of the perfect prose.

I couldn't get that girl out of my mind. I can't to this day: she is my beloved wife.

I can't remember the evolutions by which I got acquainted with Edith Henry. You can't remember what happens when you walk in a dream. But I do remember a day when I persuaded her to go with me out into the woods to hunt for violets. We found the violets, but what

I recall most distinctly is her sweet voice recounting a visit in the mountain region to the grave of Helen Hunt Jackson.

I was in love, irremediably. But I knew well, from Edith Henry's point of view and that of her family, I was totally ineligible. Her family were of the elect. Her father, after juvenile exploits in the Civil War, had come to Nebraska and made a fortune as trader, banker, dealer in land. He was a grand man, handsome, brave as a lion, successful. His wife was a descendant of John Alden, not remotely related to Longfellow. Edith had a brother, dynamic, certain of himself, and a sister who was a stunning beauty, with great ambitions.

Where could I, son of immigrant Danes, fit into this family constellation? Nowhere. But the Japanese used to have a saying: There were three men, suitors for the hand of a lady. One was handsome, one was rich, and one was persistent. Who got her?

I did.

TWELVE

Professional Scholarship:
First Approximation

To our sophisticated world, scholarship is just a profession like any other. The University of Nebraska, in the nineties, was not sophisticated. It bowed in awe before the great scholars who sometimes honored our rostrum, men like Edward Everett Hale, Jacob Gould Schurman. We experienced more than a trace of awe when we encountered men who had sat at the feet of Wundt, William James, Andrew D. White. They shone, if dimly, with induced radioactivity.

A declaration that you meant to devote your life to scholarship would have been regarded by most of our students as arrogance. You could announce your intention of devoting yourself to teaching, for teachers were made, not born, often out of coarse-grained, resistant material, and, in current folklore, all the better teachers for that. But for scholarship, as for sainthood, you needed a "call."

I did not share this reverential attitude toward scholarship. To my mind the ordinary man, if patient enough and bold enough, could achieve original scholarship, at least in minor degree. I knew no field in which everything had been done that needed to be done.

Take the simple problem of translation from one modern language to another. In the Germanic seminar it had been my task to compare the Ibsen characters as they appeared in the original Dano-Norwegian, the German, and the English. The German translations were faithful, as all German translations of the time were. The English translations, mostly the work of William Archer, were talented. But Hedda Gabler of Ibsen's conception, a high-grade Norwegian *Kjaelling,* was a strange personality in the German, for eternal wars had eliminated the man who lacked spirit to take a switch to the woman who needed it to complete her life. And Hedda in English was someone who could never have been on land or sea.

Or take Schiller. No commentator I consulted gave an inkling of the fact that what thrust a man of the poetic gifts of Schiller into a role that would have been that of minor writer in France or England was his miserable hankering after the security of approval by the powers that be. Though the creative movement of his time was revolutionary, and Schiller had to deal with revolutionary themes, his ignoble quest for security made him bend the knee to legitimacy, whatever and wherever it was, even to Gessler's cap. His hero Wilhelm Tell held himself and his sure arrows aloof from the movement for liberty, and only upon the threat to his son, a boy with a steady head and no other qualifications for history, did Tell play a hero's part.

One noble piece of literature Schiller produced, *Wallenstein's Lager.* That is a marvelous picture of mercenaries raked together from all the corners of central Europe, robbers, rapists, with not an ideal per thousand stomachs, but reciting the remarkable formula of Wallenstein:

> *"Die Tat ist stumm*
> *Der Gehorsam blind*
> *Das Wort ist frei."*

You commit murder, and shut up about it. You are ordered to murder: you do it, averting your eyes. But what you think of the whole process you can say, for speech is free.

Alas, after one noble essay on man as a reality, in the *Lager,* Schiller went on into his iniquitous sink of legitimacy. And throughout this country German professors set Schiller up alongside of the totally honest Lessing and the towering Epicurean Goethe.

Wherever one looked one could see work for the scholar. One of my fellow students, Nienhuis, uncertain whether it was worth while to make any scholarly effort, consulted Louise Pound, modest and extremely talented sister of the great Roscoe—Louise, who doesn't know to this day that at least one person considers her greater still.

"Scholarship," she said to Nienhuis, "is a mission. It needs many workers. If you can add just one cubic centimeter to the mass achievement of scholarship, you have not lived in vain."

I do not know what these words did for Nienhuis. But Louise Pound's principle sank deep into my heart. I would add a cubic centimeter to the treasure of verified knowledge.

I knew Latin and Greek. I read them like modern languages. In a long cold winter evening, before my potbellied soft coal stove, I might ready fifty pages of Tacitus or Thucydides. These were two friends of mine. They were honest as the day is long, but they were Optimates, Elite, judging all events from the elite standpoint. But because they were honest you could look through them to the common humanity, my kind of people, whom they hated and distrusted yet permitted to exist in their thought.

Plautus knew my people and presented them irresponsibly on the humorous stage. Terence yearned toward them and incorporated them in his tender philosophy. Pliny the Younger took humanity for his province, though himself of the ruling elite. Epictetus rose out of the muck to dominate the uneasy conscience of the elite, just as Paul Robeson, before the Russian propaganda got hold of him, made the racially oppressive world of America conscious of its mortal human sins.

In an earlier age Montaigne had woven the classical world into the life of his time. But Montaigne was of the early Enlightenment, pre-modern thinking. In our own time scholars are again bringing classical antiquity back into modern reality. As a student I was deeply interested in Jowett, with his faithfully sophisticated Plato, in Jebb, with his meticulous and extravagant *Homeric Question,* in Gilbert Murray, with his classics nobly confronted with British liberalism; in our own Paul Shorey, legitimate heir to the highbred snobbery of Plato, and Tenney Frank of Johns Hopkins, who knew Roman history better than Livy or Tacitus knew it.

I thought I could contribute my mite to the understanding of the majestic historical episodes of Greece and Rome.

But I had another string to my bow, philology. In my junior year I met a scholar of wide international reputation, Hjorth Hjalmar Edgren. He had held posts in many universities, for a time at Yale, where he had collaborated with the great William Dwight Whitney in bringing out a grammar of Sanskrit. I joined his Sanskrit class and, after a frightful struggle with an unconscionable alphabet, found that Sanskrit in its substance was closely akin to my own native tongue. Command the alphabet, use your knowledge of European languages, and it's no feat to read Sanskrit. It is worth doing, for there is an enormous literature, particularly dramatic literature of the sixth to the ninth centuries of our era, that nobody in our time, Indian or Western, has ever yet read.

In my student days philology was in an imperialistic ascendant. Max Müller had published his *Chips from a German Workshop.* It served as a textbook of Aryanism. This talented people, the North European blonds, originating somewhere in the Pamirs, had spread over the world in successive waves. The first wave, the Sanskrit-speaking peoples, thrust fragments off into Lithuania and Albania. The next wave overflowed Greece and Rome and the Celtic lands; a later wave, the Teutons and Slavs. And wherever the Aryans went they were conquerors, builders of states.

I accepted the Aryans for all they were worth, and more. I was also deeply interested in the Semites. I had studied enough Hebrew to realize that here was a totally different formulation of the rhetoric of human expression. The Semitic was a wonderful group of languages, hardly inferior imperially to the Aryan. Someday, I hoped, I might know enough about Semitic philology to penetrate into the prehistory of this brilliant group of peoples.

A vast philologic area was open to me. I meant to pioneer in it. But for the time all I could do was to assert that I meant to be a teacher of classics.

For any honest purpose one gets advice enough to sink a ship. My good friend Professor Lees, a noble classical scholar and a valiant Nimrod, who was member of a group holding power over a little lake where mallard ducks stopped to their woe on their way south, invited me to a duck feast full of birdshot.

"I've invited you, Johnson, not just to eat my ducks, though they are good. I want to give you some words of advice.

"You are a good Greek scholar. Do you remember that day we were reading the *Medea?* I had given my interpretation of a passage, and you said, 'But, Professor, how about this tense?' And my interpretation had all gone to the Devil, and I blushed and said, 'Yes, that is something; suppose we go on.' But, by God, Johnson, you humiliated me. I was wrong, and you, a cub off the farm, were right.

"You are a better Greek than I am, Johnson, but Greek is gone. They are cutting it out at Harvard and Yale. Soon there will be no colleges requiring Greek. Latin is going the same way. You are dreaming of a life of classics teaching. The classics are gone."

I listened politely, ate the mallard duck, and tried to keep from swallowing the birdshot. I was no more disturbed about the decay of classics in the required curriculum than I was about the mallard ducks with birdshot in their breasts and drumsticks, for I had sat through classes of Latin and Greek. I had heard *ad nauseam* the desperate attempts of students to reproduce, in terrible English, the smooth variety of Horace or Euripides. I agreed that there was no virtue in this ghastly business.

To me, all the college exercises in Latin or Greek were nothing but a vexation to the flesh and to the soul itself, unless the outcome was a competence to go on into the splendor of Latin and Greek literature. And of the hundreds, and thousands, who had struggled and fought with Latin and Greek in the University of Nebraska, I knew only one who had penetrated into the real secrets of the literature, and that was Roscoe Pound, who would use his wonderful command of Greek and Latin literature to *épater les bourgeois.*

Latin and Greek as pedagogical birch rods were dying. All right; I never did believe in them. But there was room enough still for an exponent of Latin and Greek civilization.

My excellent professor of Latin, Grove E. Barber, after sleeping serenely in the Latin chair for twelve years, went off to Chicago to have his eyes opened on the intricacies of Latin grammar by Professor William Gardner Hale. Returning, he made us all work our heads off on qui-quom clauses of purpose or "interest by the way." But he also tied up with a publishing company that wanted a textbook on the *Lives* of Cornelius Nepos.

My good professor had never read the *Lives,* and the truth was he couldn't read them. But I had read them and had a fair idea of what Livy also had written on some of the characters, and what might be learned from Plutarch. Professor Barber invited me to do all the work on the *Lives.* A text was to appear with Barber and Johnson on the title page. It was expected to be the making of me.

I accepted with alacrity, and somewhere in my archives, if I haven't thrown them away, are some very illuminating notes on Cornelius Nepos. But another publisher—damned be he!—brought out a students' text on Cornelius Nepos. Our enterprise was dropped.

I was young and took disappointments in my stride. Anyway, I had bigger game within range of my gun. With my chief Hjorth Hjalmar Edgren, I had a contract (Edgren and Johnson) to bring out a *Comparative Grammar* of Greek, Latin, Sanskrit, and Gothic. I knew Greek and Latin well. All there is in Gothic is Ulfilas, with a few inscriptions. I knew a good deal of Sanskrit. We could have produced a respectable book.

But a big dynamite manufacturer, fearing that war would become a matter of terrible explosions, undertook to set the world at peace. He offered a generous scheme of peace prizes and invited my beloved Hjorth Hjalmar Edgren to set up in Sweden as administrator of the Nobel prizes.

Our publishers informed me curtly that in the absence of Edgren the project was *kaput*. So much for me as philologist.

My graduation was approaching. I was invited to a teaching fellowship in Greek, Latin, or Germanics. I chose Greek, and the next year I strove manfully with a first semester class in Homer and a second semester class in Xenophon. It is a terrible thing to make a punishment for slackers out of the splendor of the *Iliad*. It is not much less terrible to carry an inert group of students one parasang or two or three with Xenophon.

I tried hard to make my class join with me in following this modest little secretary, Xenophon, deep into the center of the empire of the Persians. I tried to make clear his essential Yankee quality, when he harangued his men, asserting that there was nothing to fear from the Great King's armies, since the Greeks could go through them as a knife through a piece of cheese, but everything to fear from the long-limbed daughters of Mesopotamia, who could so easily transform Greek soldiers into lotus-eaters, forgetful of their dear fatherland.

I tried to inspire, wheedle, persuade, threaten my group of cornfed Nebraska boys and girls to a realization of the splendors of the deep insights Xenophon offered into the realities of Levantine life.

In vain. All my class wanted to know was, "How do our grades stand?" Who was I to introduce them to the majesty of the *Iliad* or the surge and splendor of the *Odyssey*?

THIRTEEN

War Fever

As a normal male child I was, of course, a militarist. What material for daydreams does a boy of six find comparable to dreams of military exploit? I took my first patterns from the Bible, David against Goliath, boy against giant; from Gideon and his small selected band, smashing the lantern pots and crying, "The sword of the Lord and of Gideon." I gloried in the eight years of military experience of my taciturn father, and in the family tradition of admirals and generals on my mother's side, Admiral Juhl and Admiral Just on my father's side. I read and idealized the accounts of fighting in American history, the French and Indian Wars, the Revolution and the Battle of New Orleans, the Mexican War. When I was seven or eight the press promoted a "Mexican War Cloud." It was anguish to me, for I was too young to be even a drummer boy.

The years brought wisdom. By the time I was ten I had accepted my father's philosophy that war is always a rich man's quarrel and a poor man's fight. I groped through a sanguinary illustrated book on the Franco-Prussian war. Why were those farmers and workingmen killed or mutilated just to decide who should sit on the worm-eaten throne of Spain? The writer of the book stated sardonically that the fields around Sedan, fertilized with blood, produced extraordinary yields of wheat, blood-stained wheat, that made uncommonly glutinous and tough bread for widows to chew at under their tears.

That choking thought did more to make a pacifist of me than the most eloquent arguments circulated by the American Peace Society, then a little band of brave men and women, mostly Quakers, gallantly attacking the god of war.

In my "prep" years at the University of Nebraska whatever time I had for political thinking was engrossed by the Populist movement. As for war, I regarded it as an upper-class enterprise which would emerge less often when the peoples achieved real democracy. My

101

first serious speculations on the structure and meaning of war were awakened by reading Thucydides. There, in a nutshell, was the anatomy of war: stupid antagonisms between two kindred peoples— and all peoples are kindred—two peoples closely enough akin in speech to detest each other's dialect; party interests crossing national lines, with the inevitable result that any war would become a civil war, with treason lurking everywhere; good patriots so blinded by party passion as to play into the hands of the enemy, as the Athenians did in neutralizing the efficiency of Alcibiades by loading him with poor old nephritic Nicias in the vital Sicilian campaign; fundamental breakdown on both sides, socially and morally, and the ultimate collapse of everything that had made Greece a shining beacon of civilization.

From Livy through Tacitus and Gibbon I followed the development of Roman wars, long triumphant but sapping the blood of the sound Roman people until the great empire was an empty nutshell with dried-up worms in the dust of the kernel.

As a naïve evolutionist, impressed by the role of selection in animal life, I was struck forcibly by a passage in Gibbon's *Decline and Fall.* At the time of Constantine, he asserts, there was not one single known descendant of the Fabii, the Curii, the Messalae, the Sallusti, the Ahenobarbi, or any other of the families that had made Rome great. All had been devoured, man, maid, and child, by war and imperial adventure. My reading of the history of Spain proved that the same consequence followed Spanish imperial enterprise: rise to the first place in Europe, great glory and overweening pride, declining swiftly to a status so mean that no one could be found to do honor to Spain. Notes from a lecture by David Starr Jordan, on a theme he later worked out in *The Blood of the Nation,* asserted that the Napoleonic Wars had resulted in a marked lowering of the stature of the French people. And, I asked myself, what effect had the deaths of three-quarters of a million young men, North and South, exerted upon the real constitution of the United States? Had those boys lived, could we have fallen under the control of the tariff hogs, the railway barons, the trust builders, and the venal politicians who served as obsequious door porters to the elite of insatiate greed?

I was pacifist not merely on the moral ground that war is murder, a truth I accepted, but also on the ground that war is folly, ruinous folly, ruinous to victor and vanquished alike. And noting the advance in all the leading nations of education and intelligence, I felt that we were on the eve of a new order of the world, an order of peace and cooperation. Were not our friends the English tired of colonial adventure? Had they not left the Christian filibuster Chinese Gordon and his gallant small army to be massacred by the fanatic followers of the Mahdi? Had they not repudiated the filibuster Jameson, with his raid upon the Afrikander republics? Had not the Blood and Iron Chancellor Bismarck declared that all the Balkans were not worth the sound bones of a single Pomeranian grenadier? Was it not rumored that the Tsar of all the Russias had become a confirmed champion of peace and international understanding?

The future of the world looked bright to me, in the early nineties.

But a cloud was forming over America. Cuba, restive under Spanish rule for more than a generation, was in open revolt. Division after division of Spanish soldiers had been sent to the island, but the insurrectionists were too mobile, too clever, to let themselves be brought face to face with Spanish regulars. Here and there a small squad might be cut to pieces, but the real force of the revolution was untouched.

The Spanish commander, General Weyler, known through the Cuban propaganda in the United States as Beast Weyler, invented a device destined later to enjoy a hideous history, the concentration camp. All the population of the rebellious districts were to assemble in camps under Spanish guard; all persons failing to assemble, men, women, or children, might be shot on sight.

Mostly the old, the women, and the children obeyed the order; the men who could fight remained in the bush. The Spanish soldiers dared to go nowhere except in large bodies, and large bodies sloshing around in swamp and jungle got nothing but weariness for their pains. In the concentration camps malaria and yellow fever carried off the women and children like flies. The epidemics passed on to the Spanish soldiers, on the sick list by the ten thousand, and the epidemics threatened to jump over the narrow seas to the United States.

It was inevitable that sentiment for a free Cuba should rise up everywhere in the United States. All people in the English tradition had detested Spain since the time of the Spanish Inquisition and the Armada. Spaniard: by nature a cold-blooded torturer.

There had been another Cuban insurrection a generation before. It had been put down with remorseless cruelty. Most young men I knew had read with horror the stories of the revolt published in the *Youth's Companion* by Juan Romero. To this day I shrink from the memory of the story of the Negro patriot tortured by the Spaniards to disclose the hiding places of the revolutionists.

We had assumed that civilization had advanced beyond the stage in which men were put to torture. But civilization had not reached Spain. It appeared to be our moral duty to force Spain to observe the laws of humanity, by war, if necessary.

Spain did not want war. Her replies to protests from the American government were conciliatory. She was willing to give Cuba autonomy, and in the end her definition of autonomy became more and more liberal, until it was hard to see any difference between autonomy and independence.

But the war party, led by William Randolph Hearst, became all the more violent as Spain became more conciliatory. After the sinking of the *Maine* the war party became irresistible.

I had assumed that the liberation of Cuba was the sole object of the proposed war. Professor Fred Morrow Fling, European historian, advised me to read the English papers, to get a better perspective than one could get from our own press.

At first I was somewhat bewildered, and even repelled, by the British attitude on the threatened war. Those omniscient British journalists calmly asserted that we were not actually motivated by the desire to liberate Cuba. What we were really after was the Philippine archipelago. We were? Why, hardly any Americans had ever heard of the Philippines, except perhaps in a romantic biography of Magellan. I looked up the Philippines in the Britannica. They were indeed a considerable territory, with a population mostly barbarous, among whom headhunting was a flourishing institution. What did we want with them?

The British journalists knew, although I felt sure President McKinley and Congress did not. What the British knew was that we wanted the Philippines as an outpost for our forces when the time should come for the partition of China. Already Russia and Japan were sharpening their carving knives. With America in the Philippines cooperating with the British, at least South China would fall into the right hands.

The French press had no such far-reaching notions as to the consequences of our war with Spain. They were sure that we were destined to be badly beaten. What was our army? Fifty thousand men, practically none of whom had ever been under fire. There were two hundred thousand seasoned Spanish soldiers in Cuba. On the sea we were very vulnerable. Our navy was new, with a few modern ships we had never handled in battle. If the Spaniards had less available tonnage, they were supposed to have better guns and better gunners. If they met our fleet in battle and sent it to the bottom, all our seaports would lie open to bombardment.

I had been against the war. We could win peace and freedom for Cuba, I argued, by diplomatic pressure. I became immensely unpopular with my fire-eating fellow-students. But when war was actually upon us and the President called for volunteers, I knew in my heart I should have to enlist.

I should like to be able to claim that it was entirely a patriotic compulsion that drove me to the recruiting office. At twenty-three one is a creature of mixed motives. Since childhood I had had a passionate sense of devotion to America. Later I tried to rationalize my feeling for America on the ground that it offered boys in every class opportunities no other country offered. There was something in that; I was proud of America's generosity. I was proud of America's resolute faith in individual liberty. But assemble all the reasons for loving your country, your home, your family: you haven't anything like an adequate explanation. You love because you love, and that's the short of it.

I was also actuated by personal pride. I had been opposed to the war. I was not opposed to it because I was unwilling to share the hardships and dangers involved in war. Being a pacifist, it seemed to me more incumbent on me than on a sentimental militarist to take my share in whatever came along.

Besides that I was restless, hungry for experience. The army was a way of life most of my ancestors, for a thousand years, had experienced. There was something extremely seductive in the idea of merging one's personality with one's fellows, shaping one's life by military orders, having one's self carried wherever the national policy required. I wanted particularly to get to the Philippines, to experience the wide ocean and sultry Oriental lands. I had come to accept the English view that the Philippine enterprise was America's bid for a share in determining the fate of China; and this might mean war with powers far stronger than Spain. If a great war had to come I wanted to be in it.

My friends in the faculty could see no sense in my wanting to enlist. Here was I, a promising teacher of Greek and student of philology with my Master's work practically finished. Had I a right to throw away my training on a remote battlefield, when the most ignorant unskilled laborer, or even a tramp, could stop a bullet as well as I—

perhaps better? The argument appeared to me undemocratic, decadent. If America left its defense to men it counted of no value, we were on the road toward the fate of the Byzantine Empire, where men of birth and breeding were too good to take the risk of fighting.

The State of Nebraska had two regiments of the National Guard. These were assembled in Lincoln, to be mustered into the national service and to fill out their ranks with new volunteers.

I waited to enlist until word came from Washington that the First Nebraska was to go south, to train for a Cuban campaign, while the Second Nebraska would go to San Francisco, to take ship for the Philippines.

I enlisted in the Second Nebraska, Company K, donned a uniform, and was assigned a blanket and a pile of hay in a tent. Much of each day we spent in drilling, green soldiers under greener officers. The First Nebraska was commanded by Colonel Stotsenburg, a regular Army officer who was then our Commandant of Cadets. Day by day one could note the progress he made in whipping his regiment into shape, while our homegrown Colonel Bills made small progress with his homegrown commissioned officers and noncoms. The time soon came when the orders from Washington were revised and the First Nebraska entrained for the Philippines. My regiment was to be prepared for the invasion of Cuba.

FOURTEEN

Chickamauga

EDUCATION had been to me from childhood a consuming passion. I wanted to know as much as I could about as many things as possible, but above all about the life of man. My interest in the classics drew its force from the numberless glimpses of human life under conditions very dissimilar to those of present-day America. I liked to sit with Horace in his cheerful evenings in Tibur, listening to the salty tales of his rural neighbors, over the musty old wine from the cellar depths. The study of language sometimes gave one glimpses into the life of the prehistoric past. The word "bran" appears not to be Celtic or Saxon but goes back to the earlier neolithic society, which must have milled wheat and sifted flour. Vergil in the *Georgics* takes the queen bee for male—a "king"—and the drones for pure parasites. But the Latin word for drone recognizes the drone's reproductive function. The peasants who formed the word knew better what the drone really was than the cultured and educated man. To look through words to the strata of preliterate life—that was one of the fascinations of philology.

I loved books, but I considered that books contained only fragments of men's ways and work. To hew a log square alongside of an experienced craftsman, to calcine limestone properly, slake it, and make a good mortar through immixture of the proper kind of sand—that too was educational, as was also the more or less irrelevant conversation of men working together. I learned a lot from men I worked with on the farm, and something, but not so much, from my fellow-students. They had had little experience they were able to formulate in speech.

I expected much more from my comrades in the volunteer regiment. Living together, drilling together, fretting together under military regulations—some truth about life was bound to slip out. They were a miscellaneous lot, ranging from eighteen years of age to forty.

Mostly they were born Nebraskans, but a minority were from the East and there was a scattering of foreign-born. Perhaps I might find somewhere in the regiment a group like Kipling's Soldiers Three.

My company had come from the Platte Valley, where they had joined the National Guard under a large landholder, who produced immense quantities of baled hay for the market. His son-in-law, another hay baron, was first lieutenant. Most of the men had worked for him in haymaking. Like the other companies of the National Guard, my company had refused to enlist unless they could keep their National Guard officers. They wouldn't hear of the West Pointers the government was supposed to be trying to foist upon us. Next in the order of their detestation were officers who had been trained in the university cadet corps and commissioned in the National Guard. The men felt that every university student was something of a menace to the legitimate hopes of the old Guardsmen for promotion. I did not want promotion, but I was suspect and was thrust into a group of tentmates that included two college students and two YMCA secretaries. Ours was known as the "preachers' tent."

My tent companions were agreeable lads but quite devoid of ideas or experience worth hearing about. As for the rest of the company, when they had exchanged their meager stock of obscene stories they had little to talk about. One exception was a German-American, Schroeder, who had gone through two years of military training in Germany. I learned a lot about the life of the German private soldier from him. Also, he undertook to train me in the use of the bayonet. My ribs took many bruises from him before I learned to tell where he would next thrust by watching his eyes.

For the kind of training we were getting in the company Schroeder had only contempt. Our officers were not only untrained but scatterbrained. Often in a company drill the captain would give an order, and a half-dozen privates would sing out, "That ain't right, Cap." Often a succession of orders would get us into a hopeless tangle from which the captain could not extricate us. He would exclaim peevishly, "What's the matter with you fellows? Fall out and fall in right."

To adjust us by an easy stage for campaigning in Cuba the government in its wisdom shipped us to Camp Thomas, Georgia. Thus we would become used to the heat and to water with mineral content different from that pumped from our prairie wells—an item then considered important by the army. The government took no account of the fact that typhoid, malaria, and hookworm were endemic in the region, nor that the assembling of forty thousand men, many of them from fever regions in other Southern states, would offer grave risks to a Northern regiment, especially since the government's ideas of sanitation were centuries behind those of Moses.

It was my first experience of life outside Nebraska. At first I found the change in the character of the landscape very exciting: instead of the boundless prairie, hills rising toward Lookout Mountain, all wooded except for clearings here and there for small farms; instead of the meadowlark, the mocking bird. Georgia was very hot, in June, too hot for much drilling except in the early morning. For most of the day we could wander around the huge Chickamauga battlefield, recently set up as a National Park. Besides, one could get out into the region of small farms without military permission. Our camp was bounded on one side by Chickamauga Creek, cut deep in the limestone, with precipitous banks. The Army never thought to post guards along the creek. A big tree had fallen across the creek, supplying a two-foot log for a bridge, and I made many an excursion deep into the back country and found out a lot about the conditions under which the Southern small farmer lived.

After a few weeks illness began to develop in the camp; dysentery and fevers the military doctors from Nebraska did not clearly distinguish but which later turned out to be malaria and typhoid. The theory of the doctors was that we were all being poisoned by the beef supplied by the Chicago packing companies. They were using newfangled preservatives, it was alleged, formaldehyde and benzoate of soda. Some able phrasemaker in Washington described the food as "embalmed beef," and a terrific popular rage developed against Secretary of War Alger. He was driven out of the Cabinet and out of political life, for good and all.

The fact is, the beef was good, and those of us who ate the beef and rejected the flyspecked bread remained well the longest. A regiment of regulars appeared to be entirely free of fevers, although they too fed heartily on the "embalmed beef." But they had traditions of cleanliness about their camp and covered their latrines. The volunteers left the latrines uncovered, providing breeding ground for billions of flies, which swarmed into the cook tent and dashed upon your beans or stew as you ate. That disgusted me; but I did not know how dangerous it was. Neither did the doctors.

The sickness increased and dysentery gave way to hemorrhage, mistakenly diagnosed by the doctors as "bloody flux," the local name for what later was recognized as a result of hookworm infestation. We were marched to the medical tent and required to swallow large doses of diluted camphor. This did not seem to help.

Day by day those of us who remained well were detailed to carry the seriously ill on stretchers to the hospital tent. I had more than my share of stretcher-bearing, for I remained well longer than most, and when I fell sick I wouldn't admit it. The sick in the hospital cots, fighting off flies from morning to night, were a terribly depressing spectacle. And too often I'd be sent down with a detail to carry a pine box to the truck, for shipment home for burial. It was a ghastly thing thus to carry off what had been a young and lusty fellow not ten days before. For some of them I sorrowed deeply. But too many were dying for much individual mourning.

I was troubled about myself. I did not fear death. It is a merciful dispensation of nature that when you are burning with a fever you look upon death with dim, stoical eyes. But I couldn't afford to die. I had set out to accomplish something in the way of scholarship; and, more important, I felt my responsibility to my two brothers and sister. I did not want to go home in a pine box. And I felt I'd somehow pull through if I could keep away from the hospital tent.

We did practically no drilling; too many of us were sick. For the few who were well there was a lot of walking guard to do, but the guard lines were mostly in deep woods and instead of marching back and forth you could lean against a tree when you were too dizzy to stand. When not on duty you lay in your tent and talked a little to your surviving tentmates or you just dozed.

A yearning came upon me to get away from the camp and out into the pleasant open country. I made my way to the log across Chickamauga Creek and soon found myself in a barren pasture all grown over with wild blackberries. I hungered for them but feared them. They might finish me if I ate them. But I would taste one. It was late in the season and the berries were very bitter. After a taste I could not resist the craving. I ate, I suppose, a pint of them, and slowly strolled back to my tent to await the consequences.

Next morning I was much better. The hemorrhage had perceptibly abated. I began to crave blackberries again and went across the creek and took my fill. And so I did every day for a week.

I was losing no more blood and my fever was abating. I no longer had to fix my eyes on the horizon in dizzy spells, to keep from falling down. I began to be ravenously hungry. I was afraid, however, to eat the Army rations and provided myself with hard crackers at the sutler's tent. I had learned from the Indians that you can satisfy your hunger with very little food, if it is hard enough to make you chew a long time. An Indian who wants to reduce doesn't fool with a count of calories. He eats parched corn and jerked beef as hard as leather. The stomach has no real sense of quantity. It gauges its requirements by the length of time given to mastication. Two hardtacks, containing less flour than one slice of bread, satisfied my stomach better than five slices of soft bread. And there were no flyspecks on the hardtack.

I was on the well list now, in fact and not by resolution to keep out of the hospital tent. In August the well list had dwindled to eight in my company of one hundred and twenty. One of our sergeants had been sent home in a pine box. My captain called me to his tent.

"Alvin," he said, "I'm going to make you sergeant."

"Captain," I said, "I appreciate that, but I think it would be a mistake. Your Platte Valley boys would get sore. Anyway, this war of ours has broken down. The Spaniards are quitting. In two or three months we'll be mustered out. Then a Platte Valley boy could go home as Sergeant Blank. The title would help him when he came to run for office. As for me, I'm going on in education. The name of sergeant would be of no use to me."

"Maybe there's something in that," the captain said with an expression of relief. "I'll tell the Platte Valley boys. They'll appreciate it."

They did, and from that time on I was forgiven my sin of being a university man.

One does a lot of hard thinking when death has been leering from behind a tree.

Why had this government of ours rushed gaily into a war that might have involved other powers besides Spain, if we had not had the unacknowledged protection of the British Navy? Why were the volunteer regiments from the North thrust into the fever camp of Chickamauga and held there with insufficient medical care long after their military effectiveness had been destroyed by disease? Why was no attention ever given to the problems of sanitation? Why were we left with obsolete rifles, old Springfields, with a fairly flat trajectory of a hundred yards and little penetrating capacity beyond four hundred yards, while the Spaniards had Mausers, as effective at six hundred yards as our rifles at two hundred? Why were we given no opportunity to fire our rifles at a target in the first three months after our enlistment, and then given only five cartridges, the total spent on us in our entire service? Not ten in my company ever hit the bull's eye, a black circle as big as a man's chest—and at a hundred yards. And any day we were expected to be ready to entrain for Florida, to be hurried to Cuba and engage the Spaniards.

Why had we no newspapers with the wide and deep knowledge of world affairs exhibited by the London *Times* and *Manchester Guardian?* Why were our national political ideas so childish? I reflected on the presidential campaigns from the end of the Civil War through a generation, won by sugar plums wrapped in the bloody shirt. Such childishness, while the trusts were devouring the independent businessman and the railways and moneylenders were decimating the independent farmers, bulwark of our democratic state!

Perhaps our political childishness had been harmless through the century in which we were sufficiently protected against foreign attack by the wide oceans. But now we had thrust our interests out beyond the Pacific. We could no longer rock along at ease in our impregnable isolation.

What were our colleges doing to open the eyes of their students to the political realities, domestic and foreign? Next to nothing. In my own university only Professor Fred Fling knew anything about the developing forces in world affairs; but this knowledge was his private luxury. His business was to teach loose-thinking young Nebraskans to use historical source material objectively. The economics department stood with all four feet solidly planted against the popular movements seething in the industrial cities and among the farming population. To the best of my knowledge, the same condition obtained in nearly all the colleges of the country, with only a handful of scholars, like E. Benjamin Andrews, Richard T. Ely, and John R. Commons, admitting that the popular reformers had a case; and these scholars were the objects of furious attack by the orthodox economists and had been ousted from their positions by orthodox trustees.

What was all that to me, a budding classical scholar? I could sink myself in classical texts, following the disastrous development of Greek politics or the mushrooming of business and political corruption in Rome. No board of trustees would throw me out even if I defended Kleon against Thucydides, Catiline against Cicero and Sallust. I might sometime be learned enough to write liberal essays on the classics, to counter the reactionary essays of Paul Shorey and Harry Thurston Peck. Only a corporal's guard of classical professors read

Shorey's and Peck's diatribes on ancient Populism. I could not hope for a more numerous circle of readers. I cared little about that. The joy would be in the writing, not in being read.

As I thought it over, it seemed to me that the most enviable life I knew of was that of my friend and teacher Professor Lees. Every year he would lead a select group of students through the classical historians, the dramatists, Theocritus, and Plato. Successive terms had made him expert at catching the unwary student and reducing him to abject submission. He also had a seminar in philology, but this was the charming discipline that antedated the terrible German scourge of thoroughness.

His teaching load rested easily on him; he had time to read widely, to make himself a mighty hunter of wild ducks and a formidable opponent at poker and at the kind of whist that Talleyrand regarded as a sheet to windward against the disabilities of old age. In a succession of summer vacations he piloted groups of eager Nebraskans through the palaces and museums of Europe, carrying his tourists as far as the Acropolis of Athens.

Could I ask for a better life?

And yet as I recovered my strength after typhoid I began to be harassed by doubts. Before I left the farm I had had space in my mind for ideas of militant democracy, of humanitarianism. I had thought of myself as prepared to take my place in the struggle for justice, for the restoration of the democratic ideal, badly battered by a generation of monopolistic greed and political chicanery.

Five years of intensive study of the classics seemed to have dulled the edge of my equalitarian zeal. It had made an Epicurean of me, bent on finding the pleasantest way of life, regardless of any obligations to my fellow men. I had of course justified myself with the argument that classics, and philology too, had a contribution to make to the general stream of culture. But this argument did not seem sufficiently cogent as I helped carry a stretcher with a desperately sick comrade, desperately sick because of the shocking incompetence of our society to care for its sons.

Finally I made up my mind that I would quit the classics and equip myself for teaching economics, political science, international relations. As soon as I should be discharged from the army I would set out for New York, to enter classes at Columbia. At the time Columbia was reputed to have the best organized Faculty of the Political Sciences in the country. Besides, it was in New York, home of Wall Street and Tammany Hall. I had cursed them often enough to feel the need of seeing what they actually were.

A mind made up is strong and determined in the morning, especially when you awaken from the deep sleep of convalescence. But by nightfall when one's spirits run low, doubts swarm up to assail one. Was it wise for me to scrap the considerable scholarly capital I had accumulated in the classics? Should I not find myself at a frightful disadvantage in competition with students who had specialized in the social sciences in their undergraduate years? Should I be able to stomach abstractions of the kind bandied about in the boarding houses by "pol-econ" students? I had always detested abstractions, except those of Aristotle, which bear so close a relation to the concrete that the mind takes them in without protest.

I wrote about my plan to a friend in the university, Hartley Burr Alexander, who discussed my case with Harry Wolfe, professor of psychology. Wolfe urged Alexander to dissuade me. I was good in languages; proficiency in language depended on memory. What the social sciences required was reasoning power—and memory and reasoning power didn't run together.

If I still had doubts they disappeared with the message from Wolfe. I had never thought much of him as a psychologist. He had worked with Wundt and was bent on fobbing off the student's natural curiosity about the workings of the mind with huge doses of the physiology of the brain and the nervous system. It was like him, I thought, to cling to the exploded notion of the incompatibility of reason and memory.

I was angry, and anger is a helpful factor in resolution.

The war was over. Rumors ran that one regiment and another was being ordered to its home state to be mustered out—but not our Second Nebraska, dwindling with hospitalization and deaths. Rumor asserted that the regiments from Cuba and Puerto Rico were to be shipped to Montauk, to wear off the tropical diseases that might otherwise be spread among the home population. It seemed to me that a similar reason was holding our regiment in the fever camp of Chickamauga. Washington, I surmised, feared to spread Georgia malaria and typhoid in Nebraska. Or did they fear the effect of our tottering lines marching down the Omaha streets to old Fort Omaha?

The thought of those inhuman Washington calculations enraged me, and rage demands action. I drew up a petition demanding that our regiment be shipped immediately back to our home state. I can't remember my wording, but I do remember that I applied more vigor than tact. In two hours I had a hundred signatures—not from my company alone, for we hadn't a hundred men alive and out of the hospital. I was sure that in two days I'd have the signatures of all the privates in the regiment. I'd have a specially pathetic edition for the poor devils in the hospital.

My captain sent his orderly to bring me to his tent, where he was lying sick. "Johnson," he said, "they say you are circulating a petition. That ain't right. Major Mapes says you'll get into a hell of a lot of trouble."

"All right," I said. "I'll go and see Major Mapes."

"Yes, I wish you would." The captain offered me his limp, hot hand.

The major was a Platte Valley beau, small-sized but always bearing in mind the stature of Napoleon. He puffed himself up in Napoleonic rage as I saluted.

"Do you know what you are doing?" he roared. "You are organizing mutiny in the face of the enemy. Do you know what the penalty is? Death! Death by hanging, by God!"

"Wait," I said. "There isn't any enemy. The Spaniards have surrendered unconditionally. No court-martial is going to hang anybody on account of the face of an enemy that is finished."

"But a court-martial would sentence you to fifteen years in Leavenworth."

"Perhaps I'd best go and see Colonel Olsen."

"Colonel Olsen! What does that Norsky know about American courts-martial?"

"After all, he is a West Pointer."

"Yes, a West Pointer, and you better not go near him. Those West Pointers will arrest you for a word, and then the jig is up."

I saluted and set off for Colonel Olsen's tent. He was only a lieutenant colonel, but the colonel had been sent North with a fever. Colonel Olsen was a slender, quick-eyed man, deliberate of speech, thoughtful of manner.

"Oh yes," he said, "I have a copy of your petition. I would suggest you address it to me instead of to the Secretary of War. Then I could take it to the general."

"Certainly, I'd gladly address it to you," I said.

"Perhaps you will sit down and make the change right now. Here

is a pen and a sheet of paper. You can attach the sheets of signatures.
You see, I'm reporting to the general in two hours."

I sat on a campstool with a board on my lap and reworded my pre-
amble, retaining the vigor but improving the tact. Colonel Olsen
glanced through it, folded it, and put it in his breast pocket.

The next morning he sent for me. "Well," he drawled, "the general
liked your petition. He wanted to know why the hell the boys didn't
get up a petition weeks ago."

Was I relieved!

Colonel Olsen continued, "The general dictated a message to
Washington: 'The whole Second Nebraska regiment has signed a
petition demanding their immediate return to Nebraska. The press is
trying to get hold of the petition.'

"Now," said Colonel Olsen, "you haven't got the signatures of the
whole regiment."

"No, but I'd have got them."

"The press never heard of you. But Washington heard of the press,
in the embalmed beef days." He laughed.

By coincidence, orders came in three days to entrain for Nebraska.
Colonel Olsen sent for me again and informed me with a twinkle in
his eye that the orders had come several days before my petition
reached the general. He had collected the petitions circulating, as of
no further use, and had destroyed them. If I had a copy would I hand it
to him?

I did. He laughed, and I laughed too. He offered me his hand.

"No hanging or Forth Leavenworth, this time," he said. "But you
don't belong in the Army."

I was young then, and possibly I felt a bit of oats as the train of
Jim Crow cars—we had gone down to Chickamauga in Pullmans—
proceeded from side track to side track on its way to Omaha.

Immediately on our arrival at old Fort Omaha I hunted up my
captain, who had recovered enough to keep shakily on his feet.

"Captain," I said, "we're going to be mustered out when Washington gets through the bookkeeping, which will take weeks. It's October,
and Columbia opens the first of October. I'm going to Columbia.
Can't I get an immediate discharge?"

"I don't know," he quavered. "You better go to Olsen."

Olsen lifted his brows as I saluted him. "Another mutiny?"

I told him what I wanted.

"Yes," he said, "it's another mutiny. I'll do my best to get you out of the army as soon as possible."

Five days later I had my honorable discharge.

I had envied the men caught by religion who felt that they had been born again. Now, with my honorable discharge, I felt born again, born into the gorgeous liberty of American civil life. In a week I'd be in New York, basking in the infinite possibilities of the great metropolis.

Two things I had to do first. I had to have a medical check-up to make sure I had no serious hangover from Chickamauga fever. I had to find two days to visit my parents. The check-up came first.

A friend had given me the name of a popular Omaha physician. I went to his office.

"Ah yes," he said, "you're in the Second Nebraska. Well, you'll be here a long time while they're unwinding the red tape."

"No," I said. "I'm a free man." I showed him my discharge. "I want to know—am I fit to go on to a university?"

"You mean to say they are letting you out without a physical examination? What proof will you have of disability if you ever apply for a pension?"

"I'm never going to apply for a pension. I just want to know—am I fairly fit?"

"Come in here then and strip. Kind of skeleton, ain't you? Step on the scales. One hundred and twenty-five pounds. What did you weigh when you went in?"

"One hundred and sixty."

"What did you have?"

"I don't know."

"What did the doctor call it?"

"I didn't go near the doctor. He buried too many of us."

"So you just walked around. Had fever?"

"Sure."

"What temperature?"

"I don't know."

"Hemorrhage?"

"Terrible."

"What did you think it was?"

"Typhoid."

"That's what it was. What did you do to get over it?"

"I ate blackberries. Bitter blackberries."

"My God! Blackberries!"

He put me through a lot of tests.

"For all I can see," he said, "what's left of you is sound. Black-berries! Blackberries." He went off into a roar of laughter. "I'll never be able to eat blackberries without thinking of typhoid."

I drew out my pocketbook.

"No charge," he said. "Patriotism. And besides, you've added to my education. Blackberries!"

FIFTEEN

Columbia

O CTOBER 1898 was well along when the ferryboat spilled me out into a countless throng hurrying along the cobblestones of Manhattan. I was still half intoxicated with the magnificence of the autumn foliage that clothed almost the whole landscape from Ohio to Jersey City. I had supposed that the Easterners had cleared their forests. Why, as far as the eye could see there were trees, golden, red, bright buff, at rare intervals giving way to fields and villages, themselves in the colored shade of ancient trees!

From the ferry I walked east until I came upon street railway tracks. A trolley came along, labeled Morningside. That, I had read, was the location of Columbia. I got on and took my station on the rear platform, to see as much of the city as I could.

I liked New York. It was not nearly as pushing and noisy as Chicago, or even downtown Omaha. Of course, I reflected, those cities made their living shoving around the freight thrust upon the railroads. It was natural for them to push and rush. From my post the cross streets looked sunny and quiet. People moved along the sidewalks at a normal pace, apparently not in a great hurry to get anywhere. Where did the money come from to support the infinite array of brick and brownstone fronts? Wall Street, to be sure, milked the country, but how did the milk reach these cross-street residents?

After an incredibly short hour I saw looming up on my left the unmistakable dome of the Columbia University Library. It was the first example of classical architecture I had ever seen. The dome was like that of the Pantheon, pictured in the classics textbooks. I walked around the building, viewing it from different angles, with deepening satisfaction.

I had never asked myself why so practical and stingy a statesman as the Emperor Augustus had undertaken to replace the brick and tile of republican Rome with marble and bronze. Now I saw the

119

motive. Every provincial walking in the shade of the great marble structures would be oriented toward Rome for the rest of his life. The temples and public buildings composed a bond of empire worth many legions. So here was I, a provincial, bound to Columbia for life by the calm magnificence of the Seth Low Library.

Entering, I met a janitor who directed me to the dean's office on the third floor. The dean, John W. Burgess, looked classic too, with the classicism of highbred British stock, or rather, of the cavalier stock that first settled in Virginia. Though he had enlisted in the Northern cavalry from Tennessee, he was Virginian in his melodiously fluent speech. He treated even the rawest student or a janitor's assistant with high courtesy and consideration. There were no bounds to my instant admiration of Dean Burgess. In later years I often found myself in utter disagreement with him, but his portrait remains in the gallery of my memory as one of ineffable charm.

I exhibited my Bachelor's and Master's degrees—the latter won without examination by the patriotic action of the state legislature, which voted the appropriate degrees for all volunteers who were approaching the conclusion of their requirements. He glanced at the diplomas and asked me what I wanted to study.

International relations, I said, political science, economics.

Then, he said, it would be best for me to major in economics, the strongest department. I'd need to make sociology one of my minors, according to the rules of the faculty. I could later decide what other minor I might like to take. He'd advise me to browse around freely the first year. Everybody ought to have some philosophy, and there was a famous course given by Professor Nicholas Murray Butler. Also, a course in literature might be useful.

He gave me some blanks to fill out, accepted them, and sent me to the bursar, who collected my semester's tuition and minor fees for privileges I didn't need.

So I was a registered graduate student in the School of Political Science. No question had been raised as to my antecedent scholarly preparation. Of course, I thought, the faculty would discover soon enough my ignorance of the field. They never did. I must have hidden it well.

I set out to look for a room and found one promptly on Amsterdam Avenue, near 122nd Street, the living room of an apartment looking out on Morningside Park. I found an expressman to go after my baggage and rushed over to the library to draw some books. I carried home with me Adam Smith, Ricardo, and Mill and read through suppertime and almost until morning.

I was very much excited. This science of economics, which I had despised as a farrago of barren abstractions, was plainly an extraordinarily effective implement of the mind. In that first twelve hours of reading a dozen problems that had puzzled me for years began to appear in a clearer light. They were not solved, but I thought I could safely assume that they would solve later, when I had studied enough.

In those days the financial position of almost every young man or woman who meant to pry the oyster out of the world was very precarious. We didn't mind it, for the words "security" and "insecurity" had not been given general currency by the psychologists. We weren't sorry for ourselves, and the older generation was not a bit sorry for us. Indeed, the older generation's injunction to us was, "Root, hog, or die."

I came to New York expecting somehow to support myself. But I found that it was extraordinarily hard to root morning glory stems, Jerusalem artichokes, and fat grubs from under the pavements of New York. Every day I spent some time looking for a part-time job, but nobody seemed to want me.

I had set out with money enough, I thought, to pay my railway fare, a semester's tuition, room rent for two months, and two months' rations. The university bursar threw out my calculations by imposing on me petty fees that ate up a month's rations. Well, one month should be time enough to find something. At the end of the month I found myself with a capital of sixty cents. I used ten cents for a trip to the wharves and return and invested the fifty cents in ship's biscuit. You can eat very little of that before your jaws, and your stomach too, cry, "Hold! Enough!"

On ship's biscuit, morning, noon, and night, I found my attention sharpened for reading and for hearing lectures. I had read that in India no philosopher will attempt to teach a boy who isn't held down to the starvation level of a handful of rice. I thought I had discovered the secret of intellectual proficiency. But the carnivorous barbarian is too near the surface of my skin. I went from saloon to saloon, offering to preside over the free lunch counter from six in the evening to twelve. At least some of the food would get by me to the patrons.

At last I found a saloonkeeper who would consider me. But when I said I was a student he shook his head. There were some pretty tough characters who came in late. I put on my most plug-ugly expression and said I was just out of the army. I passed.

When I got back to my room I found a long official envelope, forwarded from my home, containing a check for thirty-two dollars. Congress had got sentimental about the soldier boys and had passed an act giving each of us an extra month's pay. I rushed to the university to cash the check, and that evening I ate and ate, regardless of intellectual proficiency.

I never had to eat the rest of the ship's biscuit, kept in my drawer as a reserve, for I found a resource in the poor devils who feared examinations and placed their hopes in tutoring. I collected enough off them to feel fairly prosperous.

At the University of Nebraska it was said of one outstanding professor or another that he was distinguished enough to be called to Harvard or Columbia. The Columbia School of Political Science, under which I was to work for three years, was manned by professors too distinguished to be called anywhere, except to university presidencies or high administrative office. Naturally I could not work under all of them in my first year, but I could visit all their classes and judge for myself what men of top distinction were like.

Foremost stood the dean, John W. Burgess, gentleman and scholar, reputed first authority on American constitutional history and constitutional law. He was an imperialist. At the time the problems of war and peace occupied my mind, and I classified men's positions accordingly. Burgess had a grandiose idea of a permanent coalition among the three vital nations, America, England, and Germany, to rule the world. The decadent Latin nations were to be thrust into the role of charming museum pieces; the colored peoples and the half-Tartar Slavs were to be ruled with the firmness and justice of British rule in India.

Columbia men swore by Franklin H. Giddings as the greatest living sociologist. He was a large, genial man, with bluntly pointed red beard and a markedly dolichocephalic skull, of which he was very proud. In his view, all distinction in the world, all energy, all genius, were carried by the dolichocephalic blonds—Aryans, we called them then. Other peoples might acquire merit by imitation.

"Look at the Jews," he would say in the privacy of the Sunday evening meetings at his house. "They are middlemen in economic life and middlemen in the world of ideas."

Down the corridor from Giddings' office was the office of Franz

Boas, anthropologist. Logically he belonged in the School of Political Science, and in scholarly attainment, originality, and intellectual leadership he ranked with the best of them. Years later, when I was a member of the faculty, I urged the annexation of Franz Boas, then recognized throughout the world as the foremost anthropologist. Giddings vetoed the idea with the vigor of a Gromyko. Anthropology was either a natural science, having no proper place in a School of Political Science, or an amateurish sociology we could not afford to recognize.

Edwin R. A. Seligman was head of the Department of Economics. He was a strikingly handsome figure, with his thick dark beard, wavy in structure, with mahogany overtones. We called it an ambrosial beard; I doubt great Zeus had a handsomer.

No economist living had read so widely in the literature of the social sciences as Seligman. He had a catholic mind and found some good in every author, no matter how crackbrained. A man of large income, he was the foremost academic advocate of progressive income and inheritance taxes at a time when all regular economists abominated the idea of the income tax as a Populist attack on the wealthy and cultured classes. He was a staunch supporter of trade unionism and government regulation of railway rates. It was hard for me to distinguish between Seligman's populism and mine.

As a lecturer he was systematic and eloquent. He never appeared before a class without thorough preparation, and in the seminar meetings at his house he was always primed with all the facts and ideas that might supplement the students' papers. He was a great teacher, and most of the graduate students turned to him for direction.

The scholar who won my unreserved admiration and loyalty was John Bates Clark. In the nineties of the last century economic theory was undergoing transformation. Classical economics was giving way to neo-classical. A group of powerful thinkers, mostly Americans and Austrians, were working this transformation, and among them Clark ranked near the top. We Columbia students were convinced that he stood at the very top.

He was tall and slender, far from robust in health, of tender and humane religion, ethical in all his instincts. He was a convinced pacifist, rejecting utterly the doctrines of the superior racialists. All men were created equal, in his eyes, not only with equal rights but with equal claims upon the sympathy and help of their fellow men. He abhorred the idea of violent revolution but looked to gradual adjustments to solve the problems of dependent countries like India. He rejected Marxism and the idea of social revolution, believing that sound economic progress would in the end elevate labor to a condition so satisfactory as to leave no place for envy of the possessing classes.

He was a stimulating but not a systematic lecturer. He was always thinking when he was lecturing, and pure thought cannot be systematic. It flits from premise to conclusion and back again, often casting its searchlight on objects far to one side. To the mediocre and dull Clark's lectures were baffling; to the able students it was a priceless privilege to participate in the unfolding of his thought.

John Bassett Moore we regarded as a whale of an authority on international law and diplomacy. His capacious memory rejected no detail as too small; he could tell you what each statesman ate for breakfast at the Congress of Vienna, whether it agreed with him, and, if it didn't, how it affected his voice and vote. Frank J. Goodnow, later president of Johns Hopkins, was prime authority on administration and administrative law. He wrote huge, solid books with great gusto. He told me once he'd rather write a book than eat. They were solid books but singularly unappetizing.

Munroe Smith was professor of Roman and early European law. His passion was for clarity and precision. Roman law was a closed field, offering no new vistas to the explorer. It was difficult but necessary to a sound understanding of institutional history. Sometimes Munroe Smith hungered for the lush grass of less ordered scholarship. A newspaper had invited him to prepare a biography of Bismarck for its morgue. He took the assignment with deadly seriousness and must have put in half his time on it while Bismarck still refused to die. It is the best little book that has yet appeared on the Iron Chancellor.

Political theory was handled by William A. Dunning, a thorough scholar and a wit, often dazzling his class with a rocket burst of epigrams. Somewhat cynical, he insisted in season and out on the complete incapacity of political theory to exert any influence whatever upon political movements or institutions. It was purely a luxury discipline. In spite of his agnosticism he fathered a whole school of disciples, later to become professors of distinction throughout the country.

The last scholar on the roster of my Columbia teachers was Richmond Mayo-Smith, professor of statistics. Victim of chronic ill health, he presented a figure of profound sadness. With his students he was gentle and helpful, and no one ever tried more faithfully to give a semblance of life to the clattering dry bones of statistical science.

With a little money flowing into my pocket I abandoned my original plan of a room apart and breakfast and lunch on milk and crackers. I wanted to know how ordinary New Yorkers lived in their narrow brownstone or red brick houses. In the university secretary's office there was a long list of families that wanted to eke out their living by supplying room and board for a few "guests." I circulated rather widely among such families, promptly abandoning those that were uninteresting.

For months I lived in a small house on Convent Avenue, owned by a ward boss and his huge wife—I avoided skinny hostesses on principle: the food was likely to be skimpy. The "Boss's" food was good and abundant.

One of the boarders was an engineer, employed on what seemed then a colossal public work, the viaduct on Riverside Drive over 125th Street. One day he came from his work in great distress. The southern approach, a huge masonry abutment, had been finished, and the contractor was laying rails on it to carry the first of the great steel arches out to be let down by cranes on its prepared cement footing. The plan was to connect the abutment with the first steel arch, put on the essential girders, and extend the rails to carry another arch to be let down in place, and so on to the northern end of the viaduct.

An inspector had appeared and ordered a halt in the work. The foundation of the abutment, he declared, was not substantial enough to carry the vast weight of the steel arches. True, the foundation went down seventy-five feet, where the geological structure was a hardpan of clay and rubble, but it did not go down to bedrock, which was more than a hundred feet deeper.

To revise his plans in a way the inspector would approve meant a loss to the contractor of all his profit and money besides. He was talking of throwing up the job and dismissing his employees, to find positions as they could in a barren labor market.

As the engineer bewailed his fate over the supper table the Boss looked wise but remained silent. At the end of the meal he asked the engineer to go into the living room with him.

The next evening the engineer came to my room in high feather. "The foundation is all fixed up, and we can go ahead with the steel arches."

"How the devil—?"

"Well, I took the Boss to the contractor, and they went to the inspector's office. The Boss said to the inspector, 'A little money would fix that foundation. I think five hundred dollars would do it.' 'No,' said the inspector, 'it wouldn't.' 'Well,' said the Boss, 'I know, and you know, a thousand dollars would do it, and that's got to be enough.' 'Okay,' said the inspector. The contractor shelled out two five-hundred-dollar bills and the inspector got out his report and tore it up."

"Long live corruption," I said.

Next day I breakfasted alone with the Boss. He said, "I guess Mr. Brown told you that the viaduct business has been fixed. And how it was fixed. He's a fellow who can't keep his mouth shut. And I guess you and the other fellows up on the hill will be yelling corruption."

"No," I said, "we aren't going to do any yelling about confidential information. Just the same, it's corruption."

"Okay. But let me tell you, nothing can get done, in this city or any other, without what you call corruption. God help the city if you reformers ever get hold of it! There won't be a foot of pavement laid or a sewer extension where the houses are rotting in their own filth.

"Take your Riverside Park. In my father's day it was private property—belonged to some aristocrats. It was all spotted over with squatters' shacks, hangouts for the worst crooks in the city. The police didn't dare to go down there and arrest a man. Who got that land for the city? Your Tildens and reformers? No siree. They fought the plan, tooth and nail. Boss Tweed got it. Paid seventeen million for it. You couldn't touch it now for five hundred million.

"You'll say Tweed kept some of that seventeen million and handed out a lot of it to the boys—maybe two, three million. Sure he did. But where did the money come from? Taxes on real estate; and who owns the real estate? The Astors and that kind of aristocrat—not you and me.

"I'll tell you what you reformers are trying to do. You're trying to save money for the Astors, so they can pull swell parties for rotten European princes that show up. And you are trying to keep the common people down in the dirt."

After I left the Boss I fell to thinking about the immortal Pericles, Boss of Athens. Every year the allied cities on the Asia Minor coast sent to Athens a lot of gold and silver, to finance the building of ships against any possible attack by the Great King. Pericles grabbed this money and erected the Parthenon and set up a huge statue of Athena in ivory and gold. He made the Athenian Acropolis famous for the ages, and at the same time gave good jobs to the artisans, who made up more than half of the voting population of Athens.

In the view of Socrates and Plato, Pericles was the most dangerous figure in Greek political life. When you stand before the noble ruins of the Parthenon you do not deeply regret the ships that were never built.

We have today an answer to the puzzle, fertile corruption versus sterile reform. We have learned how to make reform fertile. Think of Robert Moses, David Lilienthal, Fiorello La Guardia and, looming high above them, Franklin Roosevelt.

At the university and in the various houses where I roomed I sought association particularly with unlike types, despite the doctrine of Giddings that the root of sociability is consciousness of kind. The graduate students were largely from the Middle West and had little that was new to contribute to my knowledge of life. I got much more out of Max Lazard, Frenchman; Edelstein, representative of a German export firm; and Gamargo Puga, Colombian politician in exile. But the man who interested me most was a Japanese, Zensaku Sano, who attended some of the same classes with me.

We took long walks together and formed a sort of exchange agreement, Sano to interpret Japanese life to me, I, American life to him. As our friendship grew warmer we decided to get rooms in the same boarding house. Landladies as a rule were shy of this unnatural coalition of Orient and Occident, but we found one who let us have the two rooms with a corridor, which made up her top floor. There we lectured each other alternately on our two civilizations.

When Sano first came to America on a two-year government fellowship he had it in his heart to bring back an American bride, for, he asserted, to my astonishment, Japanese regard American women as far more beautiful than Japanese. He had consulted the Japanese consul as to ways of approaching his heart's desire. The consul advised him to go to Poughkeepsie for his summer vacation, make known at the college his need of tutoring in English, offer good pay. There were quantities of charming Vassar girls who needed to earn a little money during vacation. He would be able to choose one from among a dozen, and with a daily lesson through three months he could let nature take its course.

Sano picked out a tutor he'd have been proud to present in Tokyo. She was tall and slender, dazzlingly beautiful in his eyes, vivacious and quick to fall into laughter melodious as temple bells. She quickly realized his object, and her demeanor did not say no, for he appeared to be wealthy, and the standing of his ancient family permitted the title of Count on his visiting card.

After a month he visited the consul to parade his improved English. But when he exclaimed over an astonishing incident related by the consul, "I'll be gum-swizzled," the consul raised his brows.

"Never use that vulgar expression," he admonished.

At another turn of the conversation Sano exclaimed, "Wouldn't that freeze your feet!"

Again the consul's brows vaulted up. "My friend," he said, "you must be associating with people of very low degree. You use such terribly vulgar expressions."

This cut Sano to the heart. His beautiful lady—no, she was no longer beautiful. Clearly she was of very low degree. And would any girl of high degree care to be exiled as wife of a Japanese, considered in America to be of a lower breed of men?

Sano went back to Poughkeepsie, packed his goods and his dreams, and returned to New York.

One evening we went downtown to a small exclusive restaurant operated for the personnel of the consulate and Japanese businessmen. We made a party of four; Sano introduced me to a visiting Japanese colonel and a civil official who had been interpreter at the negotiation of the Treaty of Shimonoseki which concluded the Sino-Japanese War. The official exhibited for my benefit the medal of the Order of the Double Dragon, conferred on him by the Chinese Emperor and entitling him to the privilege of having every Chinese fall flat in the dust before him, on sight of it.

The talk naturally was of war.

"In five years," said the colonel, "we will go after Russia."

"Russia produces terrible fighting men," I remarked. "It won't be a one-sided affair as it was with the Chinese. Besides, Russia has four times your population."

"We have gone over the situation, and we know we can win. Russia can keep two hundred thousand men supplied over the Trans-Siberia railroad—not more. We can keep half a million supplied, or a million. And the Japanese too are terrible fighting men."

"Then," said the official, "we will take Korea and Manchuria, with their vast supplies of raw materials and coal, and build up a great modern industry."

"We will build a mighty navy," said Sano, puffing himself up a bit. "And someday we will go after the United States."

"I hope not," I said. "We have no conflicting interests worth fighting about. But if we fight you will lose."

"Yes," said Sano sadly, "we will lose the war. But we will prove for all time we are not soft Orientals, to be treated as inferiors by the white races."

"And how soon is this war to come?" I asked skeptically.

"In fifty years."

That was in 1899.

By the end of the year I had become sufficiently Easterner to pity myself a bit for the precariousness of my living. It seemed best to get a job and save money enough in a year or two for the completion of my doctorate. A job as instructor in classics opened at Rutgers, and I visited the college to see whether I'd pass muster with the dean.

The sight of the campus was dampening to my spirits. Large trees, not noble; old buildings, not venerable. The offices of the dean and the department were murky and mousy, and the book collections emitted the characteristic musty smell. The dean was friendly and assured me that as the only eligible applicant I should no doubt be appointed at a meeting to be held in a week.

I came away realizing how far my mind had traveled away from its earlier classical ambitions. Already I was homesick for the light and life of Columbia.

Fortunately a belated applicant from Harvard turned up, and Rutgers, regarding Harvard classics as more authentic than Nebraskan, elected him. What a relief! I could return to Columbia.

The next year the sledding was not so hard. I had more tutoring to do and was better paid. Also, my beloved teacher John Bates Clark had me serve him occasionally as secretary, to take down in improvised speed-writing articles he was preparing. He asserted that I could follow his dictation better than a professional stenographer—which had more kindness than truth in it—and that in copying I'd be able to cut out repetitions and improve on the order of sentences and paragraphs, which I did very sparingly.

In the spring I was awarded a fellowship for the next year, which offered me adequate maintenance. I also wrote an essay on cutthroat competition for the Seligman Prize of five hundred dollars. As nobody else competed I won the five hundred dollars and was in a position to execute a plan of study I had laid out for the summer.

I was trying to write a thesis on the iron industry. The existing literature was spotty and mostly trivial. Many of the later developments were covered in the excellent journal *Iron Age;* but to study the iron industry effectively you needed to know iron and the unrecorded experience carried by the personnel of the industry.

Fortified by a letter from Professor Seligman to Senator George T. Oliver, I set out for Pittsburgh. I found Senator Oliver very obliging and carried away a letter placing me much higher on the levels of economic scholarship than I deserved. The letter was addressed to Charles Schwab, whom I called on next day.

Schwab glanced through the letter, instructed his secretary to give me a pass to the Homestead Works, and turned back to the report he was reading. When I visited the Homestead Works I was let in with the privilege of wandering around among the giant machinery which meant nothing to me. My pass was taken away as I came back through the gate, leaving me with no further access to the industrial plants.

I meant to get into the plants, nevertheless. One way to do it was to get acquainted with steel workers and go in with them. Where would I find them? I got a map of the city and studied the disposition of streets and institutions.

On a height overlooking the Monongahela, I noted, there was an institution, the College of the Holy Ghost. Catholic; and a lot of the steel workers were Irish Catholics. The height appeared to be a plateau, accesible from downtown by flights of steps. There was room for a lot of houses. Surely there would be boarding houses, and surely Irish workers would be drawn thither by the attraction of the Holy Ghost.

I set out and climbed what seemed to be a hundred steps to the plateau. It was set with comfortable houses, shoulder to shoulder, and almost every third house had a sign, "Boarders." I went from door to door, inquiring about room and board—and about the other boarders. If they were students, locally known as Holy Ghosters, I said I would call again. Soon I found a house that suited me. There were four boarders, all steel workers, one working at Braddock, another at Homestead, a third at Jones and Laughlin, a fourth in the old works down in the city.

The landlady was a plump person of fifty with a worried look. She surveyed my figure anxiously. "You look pretty husky, sir," she said.

"Thank you. I am."

"But you said you were a student."

"Yes. But a year ago I was in the army."

Her face cleared. "I charge four dollars a week. But if you think that's too much—"

"No," I said, "that's all right."

"The boys here are mighty fine boys, but they get drunk. And I'm scared of them. I want a boarder I can depend on when they get tough."

Boarder and bodyguard—well, I had handled enough drunks in the army. Their appearance of berserker strength I had found to be a fraud and a delusion. And if those boys got drunk and violent, they would be useful friends when sober. The "boys" were upstanding men, all muscle and strong bone, standoffish to me as a white-collar interloper.

The first Saturday evening the landlady burst into my room, sobbing, with a man after her—her husband, I soon learned.

"Ain't you 'shamed to break into the young gentleman's room? Ain't you 'shamed?" His air was very magisterial, but his steps uncertain.

"That's all right," I said. "She's a fine woman; you scared her. But now she's going back and I want you to sit down and have a talk with me. I need your help."

He looked dazed. I pushed him into the Morris chair. The landlady fled.

"Young gentleman," he mumbled, "I'm kinda under the weather."

"Take a nap," I said and fitted a pillow behind his head. In a moment he was asleep.

It was near morning when his fumbling about in the dark room awakened me. He was fully sober now and listened in a curiously eager way to my request for help in getting into the steel plants.

"Sure," he said. "I'll talk to the boys. They can get you in."

Through the help of the "boys" I got into almost every steel and iron plant in the vicinity. It was an exciting experience to watch the flood of molten iron burst from the blast furnace, flow down a main channel in a garden of blackened sand, spread into side channels and into minor channels off them until the whole area was a gridiron white hot, rapidly turning to yellow, orange, red, dull red, red brown, when workmen on soles eight inches thick walked out into the gridiron with crowbars, breaking the pig iron of the small channels loose from the sow iron of the large cross channels. Or to watch a white hot billet, in the wire-rod mill, pass swiftly through rollers, to be caught by agile workers and thrust back into the rollers, thinning down with each repetition and finally looping and coiling like a snake, seeking to enfold the workers in a red-hot caress. Sometimes, I was told, the rod succeeded in catching the worker. Then there was a funeral.

One night I spent with the open hearth process. A bright young foreman was in charge of several furnaces, each with a dazzling eye looking out into the dark space of the great shed. When an eye changed color in the direction of whiteness the foreman would rout up the crew, sleeping like tangled caterpillars in a dark corner, and they would bring up a handcar loaded with select scrap, to be caught by a mechanical arm and thrown into the boiling mess through a momentarily opened door.

Near morning the foreman, pointing to a particular eye of light—which to me looked like all the rest—declared that the furnace was ready for tapping. He roused the crew, and we went around behind the furnace, where a narrow ditch, twelve feet deep, held an array of molds. A lever brought a mold up to the mouth of the furnace; a workman with a crowbar broke in the fire-clay plug and the molten stream poured into the mold, hissing and shooting out a volley of great sparks, each with a minute nucleus of metal that struck your cheeks or hands like a quickly thrust pinpoint.

The platform on which we stood was too narrow for one to step forward or back. "Bad thing to get dizzy here," the foreman said. "Last week there was a Hunkie lost his balance and fell into the ingot mold as the metal poured in. Zip! He was gone. Not a tooth, not a button, could be traced.

"Those Hunkies are mighty religious, and when a man dies he's got to be buried with ceremony. First they insisted on burying the whole ingot—would have meant money, twelve feet of metal two feet thick. The boss got their preacher and explained that the poor devil would be mostly in the top six inches, with the slag and bubbles. We sawed off the six inches and they buried it solemnly. One corpse the worms don't get."

In six weeks I saw about all the processes of iron and steel working there were to see. I learned a lot about labor conditions—the long day, the night work of a continuous industry, the alternation between dawdling and extreme effort that makes a man most feel like a man, the knightlike arrogance of the man manipulating a machine that snipped the ends off railway steel like shears snipping thread. Unions were at that time regarded in the steel works as conspiracies, but I got into a number of secret meetings.

I could write up that industry, I felt certain. But I felt equally certain that it would take me four or five years to do it properly, and I had no such period of time at my disposal. Regretfully I decided to drop the iron industry and write my doctor's thesis on a theoretical subject I had opened in Clark's seminar, "Rent in Modern Economic Theory."

In my jaunts about Pittsburgh I had scraped acquaintance with a young civil engineer whose practical business was surveying coal-mine property. He had a small job in West Virginia, not far from the Ohio, and invited me to go out with him as his chain man. I grasped eagerly at this chance of new experiences.

In the rough country where the mine was located surface land titles have no geometrical character. The farm under which our company was taking out coal had boundaries running somewhat as follows: From the waterfall in Jones's branch along the branch upstream for 750 rods. From that point west by north to the white stone at the crest of Conko's hill, 335 rods. From the white stone, south by east 430 rods to Dead Indian Oak. From Dead Indian Oak to the waterfall, about 372 rods.

Imagine what that property shape looked like, underground at the coal seam, for by Anglo-American law those lines extended down and down till they shrank and coalesced to a point in the center of the earth. Or did they cut through the earth to the other side, neither extended nor diminished? That is a moot point, for Anglo-American law antedates Galileo.

In the utter dark of the coal mine you might run your shafts beyond your lawful boundary and grab some of your neighbor's coal. That was fine unless it was found out. If it was, a lawsuit followed, and the court was likely to make you pay over not only the profit you made on the stolen coal, but the whole value of the coal and money besides. It's hard for a proved thief, especially if he is rich, to get exact justice.

Our job was first to resurvey the surface lines, established about 1790, and then blueprint the areas underground from which the coal had been taken out. You'd think the surface survey would be simple, but it wasn't. In the first place, as we could establish by the uncertain lines of old stone fences, the waterfall in the title had walked back upstream nearly a hundred feet. Second, the white stone on the crest of Conko's hill—that hill had a double crest, and each crest had several white stones of equal magnitude. Third, the Dead Indian Oak had long since disappeared completely. Still, by count of rods, by noting directions, by sighting along old fences, we could retrace the old lines with fair accuracy.

Whatever possessed the early pioneers to build stones fences on such land was a question we could not answer. The land was good for nothing but to produce brambles and wild gooseberry bushes thickset with murderous thorns on every stem and branch, but also with green thorns on every berry, turning them into diminutive morningstars, the metal spheres set on clubs and adorned with sharp spikes, with which the early modern police tapped night marauders on the head, conclusively.

Besides, the hillside seemed to be a metropolis of rattlesnakes. I knew them in Nebraska, but seldom encountered more than two in a day, except in time of sexual orgy when one might see a whole mat of them intertwined and writhing. Here there seemed to be one under almost every bush. They did not much disturb me, for I knew a rattler could strike only from a coil, and then not more than two-thirds of its length. One had sufficient protection in a stout stick. My chief, being an Easterner, was uneasy about the snakes all the time.

I had always supposed that surface surveying was a simple matter of direction and measurement. But suppose, as happened with us, the line runs over a boulder big as a house. Are you going to count a hundred yards from end to end of the chain, or will you make allowance for the shortening produced by the big hump in the chain over the boulder? Or you carry your chain over a depression. Are you to pull it tight, raising it high above the bottom of the depression, or are you to follow the surface faithfully?

Tens of thousands of tons of coal are wrapped up in such questions. When they come to the courts for settlement, the courts can't come nearer certainty than you or I. They have to settle the problem by the rule of by guess and by gosh, a time-honored principle of Anglo-American law.

The underground survey was more exciting to me, as a wholly new experience. To work in the eternal darkness with only the miner's lamp on your cap to grope by—how can it be that miners find satisfaction in a life like that? They do. Our miners regarded work on the surface of the earth with pity and contempt.

We were working from a spacious enlargement of the shaft, a low-ceilinged underground hall more than four hundred feet square, without a single support left to hold up the overhead rock—probably a wholly unlawful treatment of the coal seam. Narrow shafts penetrated the wall at various points. It was my business to carry the chain to the end of a shaft. As I shouted the end my chief set down some notations to be worked into his blueprint. At one side half a dozen miners were on their knees, undercutting the seam.

Returning from a shaft, I noted that the miners had quit work and were looking around. Two of them ran toward the timbered entrance shaft. The other four began to run, but one paused to shout to us, "Hey, you damn fools! Get to hell out of there! Ceiling's coming in."

My chief grabbed up his instruments, and we ran. Just as we got into the timbered shaft thousands of tons of rock fell in. The gust of air threw us flat on our faces.

We picked ourselves up. My chief leaned against a post, shaking all over. An uncontrollable fit of laughter came upon me.

My chief was enraged. "Funny, ain't it, Johnny? Two seconds, and we'd have been dead and buried. Buried for good. The company would never have dug our mashed bones out. Laugh away, by God!"

"Sorry," I said. "I grew up among pioneers. When things went bad for them they laughed. I caught the habit."

I have since done much reflecting on the pioneer impulse to laugh in the face of danger, disaster, and even death. Is it hysterical? I hardly think so. It is probably a defense against the obsessions that might pry into one's deeper consciousness and ride one, waking or dreaming. I can't recall the resurgence in my consciousness of a single fear I have laughed away.

The pioneer culture, often regarded by city folk as mere absence of culture, was an organic development through a long period of time. Generation by generation, settlement moved westward by fifty-mile stages. Always the movement was piloted by hope, nearly always the hope led its victims into hardship, danger, disaster. That is why men had to learn to laugh.

I present a common example. Not far from my father's farm lived a man of pioneer stock, Lem Bates. Annoyed by the accumulation of tall dead weeds in his unused calf pasture, he set fire to it on a calm November day. Suddenly a gust of wind picked up a burning tuft of weeds and threw it on a haystack, which promptly began to blaze. Lem tried to keep the fire away from his other haystacks nearby, but the wind blew great firebrands into them. Soon his whole winter's hay supply was going up in towering flames.

A neighbor rushed up to offer help. Too late. He heard Lem muttering, "You always was a damn fool, Lem Bates." And then Lem moved back away from the heat and began to roar with laughter. The neighbor thought he was "tetched in the head."

By the time the pioneering waves reached Nebraska, a formidable, almost tangible mythical figure had developed, the Fool Killer.

"Wal," a man thrown from his horse and nursing a broken shoulder would say, "the Fool Killer tried hard to git me, but I fooled him." And then he would laugh uproariously.

SIXTEEN

The Committee of Fifteen

As the doctoral examinations approached in the spring of 1901, three of our group of students—Jesse Eliphalet Pope, Allan Willett, and I—spent much time together cramming. We were to be examined on the entire literature of our major—economics—and on the courses in the minors for which we had registered, in my case sociology under Giddings. It goes without saying that we hadn't a chance to load ourselves up for the particular questions we might be asked in a three-hour oral examination. Still we boned manfully.

Our Columbia professors were as a rule very humane. If a student seemed to be floored by a question the examiner made haste to substitute another and easier question. I felt I was getting on very satisfactorily under the questioning of Seligman and Clark. But then Giddings pounced on me with blood in his eye. He was having a feud with Seligman at the time and meant to take it out of my hide. He did, and I resented it, for he was my friend.

After the examination I waited in the corridor to hear the results of the examiners' deliberations. Soon Seligman came out and announced that I had passed with flying colors. Giddings followed, jovially slapped me on the back, and said, "Well, Johnson, I made you sweat. I knew it wouldn't hurt you. Seligman would have bulled you through if you had flunked every question. But say, you knew more of the answers than I'd have known if I hadn't loaded up for you."

So it was just good, clean fun, like pushing an absent-minded companion off an embankment.

We were all three candidates for teaching positions, and Seligman had a powerful reach out into the colleges of the country. Three openings came to his jurisdiction: an associate professorship at New York University, which he awarded to Pope, the faculty favorite; an instructorship at Brown University, which went to Willett; and a position as Reader at Bryn Mawr College, which he reserved for me. I was so very young, he said—all through my undergraduate life I had felt reprehensibly old. At Bryn Mawr I would give only one three-hour course and have nearly all my time for finishing my doctor's thesis.

Other faculty members warned me about M. Carey Thomas, president of Bryn Mawr. It might have been of her that Catullus wrote, "A woman's word is writ in wind and running water." I cared nothing about promises. I'd have a year to cut my teeth as an economics teacher. After that I'd easily get a position in some other college on the prestige of Bryn Mawr, which was nationwide.

When I called at the office of President Thomas for an interview I found her a majestic woman whose speech and manner had a dignity and classic style that reminded me of a passage in Sophocles. I was charmed. In the weeks following my acceptance the job evolved. The title of Reader stood, with its salary of five hundred dollars; but instead of one course of three hours I was to have three courses, a full-time professorial schedule. One was to be a graduate seminar in theory, the second a course for seniors on practical problems, and the third a general course on administration and administrative law, the dullest subject, as taught then, in even the widest curriculum.

President Thomas advised me to make my arrangements betimes for board and room. There was a room vacant in the Kaiserhof, an old house owned by the college, and an excellent table was set in the next house, also belonging to the college. I engaged the accommodations and came away reflecting: forty-one dollars and sixty-six cents a month salary, nine dollars a week board and room. In February I'd have a surplus of five dollars and sixty-six cents to squander. But in a disastrously long month like January I'd have only a surplus of a dollar and six cents.

But September 25 was far away, and I was confident the ravens would turn up to feed me. The ultimate authority does not report how kosher the meat was that the ravens brought Elijah. There is no record that he took damage from it. My ravens brought meat, of which I was a bit shy at first; but it was sufficiently nutritious.

At the turn of the century prostitution in New York City had grown rampant, or at least more rampant than usual. It infested the lower East Side and the theater district and was bold enough to throw its coils far out over the city. A bearded Columbia professor reported at a faculty lunch the horrible shock he had had when he had helped a young woman across the ice at the corner of Columbia; she had smiled at him and said, "Dear, would you like a nice time tonight?" Tammany and the police were in clover.

A group of fifteen highminded gentlemen made up their minds to curb if not extirpate this frightful abuse. They organized themselves into a committee known only as the Committee of Fifteen, for to specify more closely would have involved the use of unpleasant terms. The head of the committee was William Baldwin, Jr., president of the Long Island Railway, a magnificent example of American energy, who was putting through the Board of Alderman the project by which the Long Island and the Pennsylvania were authorized to tunnel their way into the heart of the city at Thirty-fourth Street. The spiritual head was Felix Adler, then at the height of his power as an apostle of Ethical Culture. The secretary was Professor E. R. A. Seligman.

The committee met and discussed the problem as thoroughly as it could be discussed without employing words that were tabu. In those days American culture was very word shy. The thing might be bad but the word was worse. The religious homilies of the time stressed always the dangers of temptation, and the straight avenue of temptation was through the ear—words. Close your ears against words if you would be saved.

The committee heard many high officials of the city government and many eminent medical men, and the collective judgment of these experts was that vice was much better handled in European cities than in America. Especially the Berlin authorities had known how to bring law into lawlessness, order into essential disorder. There all vice was congregated in a district out of sight of the general public, with compulsory clinical inspection to eliminate the menace of disease. The greater part of the committee was convinced, but Felix Alder held out stubbornly against the official recognition of prostitution as a permitted vocation. And Professor Seligman pointed out that there was a vast literature on the subject, which should be consulted before conclusions could be reached.

The justice of Professor Seligman's observation was recognized; but what could these highminded gentlemen do about it? Read the books? Where? In the bosom of the family? Certainly not. In their offices, where the secretaries would giggle over the stuff the boss was reading? Never.

Professor Seligman offered a way out. He would employ an assistant secretary, trained in research and capable of writing succinctly and with delicacy, to go through the literature and supply the committee with a confidential report.

He singled me out for the job. At first I didn't want it, for my mind too was crippled by the word-tabu culture of America. But after all, here was an important social problem scholars had no business to shy away from; and whatever results I might attain were for the committee alone.

The literature was indeed vast, unsavory, generally of dubious scientific quality. The authors were mostly doctors or police officials. The doctors were the worse. In those days when a doctor got an idea into his head he assumed that it was authentic and would fight for it tooth and nail. He particularly loved to throw statistics at the reader, statistics of uncertain origin and often nothing but a sum of guesses. The police officials were more conscientious but seldom well trained. One could, however, conclude safely that European regulation did not work with such perfection as most American medical men supposed.

The authorities were mostly old, with their scientific ideas dating from the eighties or seventies of the last century. A huge international conference had been held in Belgium in the late nineties, but its report, which ran into a dozen thick volumes, had not reached our libraries. I consulted Felix Adler, who said he was going to Europe and would have it sent to me.

Two months later he called me by phone from the pier. I was to come to his house in two hours. I did.

There on the table was a towering structure of paperbound books. It was the report of the conference. Felix Adler, after a few pleasant words, got a stout string and tied the books together.

"There," he said. "Take them away! You can't imagine how relieved I am to see them go. All the way over on the boat I worried. What if something happened to me and those awful books were found in my baggage?"

As I carried away the fifteen pounds of morally shocking literature I asked myself, "If the possession of these books would be compromising to the great Dr. Adler, acknowledged apostle of humane ethics, how about me, a young scholar just at the outset of a career?"

But I had already read widely enough in the literature to have delivered myself from the word-tabu and to view the problem in its sinister light as a shadow that had attended civilization from its first recorded beginnings. Moralists had inveighed against prostitution; legislators had penalized it; police had tried to regulate it; but the shadow faith-fully followed civilization. In the ancient world, while moralists, legis-lators, and police strove to cope with the evil, society tolerated the *leno,* the procurer and entrepreneur, who often bred slaves or kidnaped babies for his future trade.

What was our own society doing with the tens of thousands of girl children from broken homes, running wild, ground down in hopeless poverty? What was society doing to protect, to educate, to train them for a useful and satisfactory life? Nothing of any consequence. In effect, society was raising young girls for prostitution as definitely as was the Roman *leno.* Many, to be sure, escaped, as some escaped from the *leno.* But social stigmas stamped on adolescent sex offenders operated like the *leno's* branding iron to hold the girl to the function cut out for her.

The new body of literature placed in my hands by Dr. Adler was coldly scientific, competent, rational. Here were inquiries by trained scholars, statistics by expert statisticians. I was confirmed in my earlier conclusion that there was no validity in the accepted American view that Berlin and Paris had developed a scheme of regulation that held prostitution to the lowest limits and checked the spread of venereal disease. In neither city had the police been able to subject to regula-tion more than one-tenth of the women engaged in prostitution. In neither city had they been able to impose frequent enough, or thor-ough enough, inspection to affect the disease rate materially; nor did competent statistics of disease credit either city with an incidence of disease lower than that of many European cities with no such regula-tions. No comparison with American cities was possible, since we had no statistics worth a fig.

There was only one solution: for society to take care of its children, the girl children who were growing up to meet the supply, the boy children to present the demand. A slow procedure, and hard to follow for a society based on egoistic principles.

I wrote my confidential report, as brief and straightforward as I could make it, and sent it to Dr. Adler for submission to the committee, if he liked it. The next I heard of it was in a rather peremptory note from George H. Putnam, the publisher, which fixed a very inconvenient hour for me to come to see him.

I found him a little bald gray man with a face set to severity with authors. He was fingering my manuscript. "The Committee of Fifteen want to publish this report as a book. It is their unanimous view."

I was pleased. One always likes to see his sentences in print, even anonymously, as this had to be. Besides, the committee had at the outset held to the doctrine of the efficacy of the Berlin model of regulation. The only opponent of the doctrine had been Felix Adler.

Mr. Putnam turned the pages of the manuscript, scowling, trying to find occasion for scolding me. "Your manuscript is in longhand," he said severely.

"Yes. I prepared it as a confidential report, not for publication."

"And you have a copy of it in longhand?"

"No."

"That's what I thought. And what would you have done if it had been lost in the mails?"

"I'd have written it over."

Mr. Putnam snorted angrily. "A very young and inexperienced writer thinks he can reproduce something he has written. He can't. All his original zest is gone. He omits the most important ideas as old stuff."

I had nothing to say.

"I suspect," he grumbled on, "you had no conception of the importance of this document. Signed by fifteen of the most prominent men in New York, written, I have to say, with delicacy and good sense, it will go far to break the infamous conspiracy of silence. People will buy this book, thousands of them. It's the first book ever published in English a man will be willing to have on his desk at home."

As I walked away I noted that my appreciation of my own work stood considerably higher. This contravened a principle I had adopted for myself, never to permit the judgment of anyone else to affect my judgment of my own work. The work was published by Putnam under the title, *The Social Evil*.

I called on Dr. Adler. He received me with literally open arms. For two wonderful hours he unfolded for me his philosophy of life, his ethics. His ideas reached to the very confines of human life. They were compelling and true. If I could ever have been a disciple of anyone I would have enrolled on the spot as Dr. Adler's disciple.

I meant to keep him as a lifelong friend, and my admiration for him never abated. But he drew away from me when, some years later, I joined the staff of the *New Republic,* which, while devoted to the same ends as Dr. Adler's, the promotion of human justice and understanding, looked to political action. To Dr. Adler no good could develop out of politics. Every movement for political reform was bound to issue in half-baked radicalism. Only in the advance of ethics could there be any hope of a humane and healthy society.

It was no better when, later still, I took over the direction of the New School. Its object of assembling intelligent adults to study the dominant issues of the day, in politics and economics, philosophy and psychology, literature and the arts, could, in Dr. Adler's opinion, lead only to logomachies and callow radicalism.

Dr. Adler had a formula of his own for adult education. Address yourself to the laborer; teach him the relation of his job, however small and mechanical, to the organic whole of his industry, to the national and world economy. Thus he would come to realize the dignity of his job and his own personal dignity. He would no longer be victim to the delusive hopes floated by conscienceless labor leaders but would strive for cooperation and harmony.

I had no quarrel with Dr. Adler's views, but he had a grave quarrel with mine. The nearer I came to agreeing with his objectives, the more menacing my ideas seemed to him.

He was an apostle, and no apostle can endure deviation. Bunyan's Pilgrim found the greatest menace of all in the pleasant path that seemed to parallel the true road to salvation. Better a regiment of Apollyons than one innocent-seeming bypath.

The Kremlin today holds to the same uncompromising view of the menace of bypath deviation.

SEVENTEEN

Bryn Mawr

FROM the time of my appointment to Bryn Mawr I had looked forward to my classes there with eager anticipation and rigorously repressed dread. Bryn Mawr had a national reputation for the extraordinary ability and promise of its faculty and for its carefully selected, well-trained student body. My dread rooted in my recognition of an incorrigible shyness that had afflicted me since childhood. Would I be able to proceed boldly to the exposition of economic abstractions before classes of highly select young ladies?

Many years later I asked a friend, the great Hungarian psychoanalyst Sandor Ferenczi, to tell me why shyness should persist in dogging me through life.

"Was there ever anything in life you wanted very much and failed to get?"

I reflected. I couldn't think of anything.

"There is the answer," said Dr. Ferenczi. "Your shyness is a technique by which you get things, and your unconscious knows it. If your unconscious had let you appear as bold as you'd like to appear, you'd have failed often to get what you wanted."

It was a comforting explanation, but I still think I might have gone farther if I had been equipped with the nerve of one of the young fellows who can take a severe banker by the beard and shake an unsecured loan out of him. True, I can't cite instances of the actual working of that technique. And anyway, only a dark-eyed, dark-haired youth could possibly work it. One with so little pigment as I have blushes too readily.

At that time educational discussion was in the doldrums. The great educators like Andrew D. White, William James, and John Dewey were preoccupied with other issues, and the rostrum was occupied by little educators who were sure all college education was wrong, for the men's colleges did not turn out leaders and the women's colleges did not turn out mothers. Statisticians were at work on the more vital problem of motherhood. Too few of the graduates of the women's colleges married, and too few of those who married had children. The duty of propagating the race was coming to be concentrated on the uneducated and the unfit.

All that lore I dismissed as bunk. My own thesis was that the tuition-supported colleges, for both men and women, drew most of their students from the middle class, and the middle class was between the millstones of big business and the rising working class. Therefore it was becoming harder and harder for middle-class youth to found families.

President Thomas of Bryn Mawr had only contempt for the proposal to substitute, in the curriculum of a girls' college, courses on cooking, motherhood, and dressmaking for science, mathematics, and philosophy. Girls had exactly the same right to a thorough education as boys, and they would profit as much by it, or more. Bryn Mawr would make not the slightest concession to educational adulteration.

According to the prevailing myth, President Thomas had a unique rule for insuring the high quality of her faculty. She had in her private mind a fixed tenure of seven years. If a man wasn't good enough to be called to a post in a great university within seven years, she fired him. Like all myths, this one did not bear close inspection. I found two colleagues whose tenure antedated President Thomas's: George A. Barton, theologian, and Joseph W. Warren, physiologist. Hardly any of the other faculty members had been at the college for seven years, and most of them had been tapped for university appointments. They were young, mostly in their early thirties, working hard and joyously. The general atmosphere was, however, one of fluttering wings. President Thomas liked that. She never lost a man, she used to say, without replacing him with a better one.

The conversation of long-established scholars is apt to be thin. The great authority knows so much and you know so little, there can be a meeting of minds only on golf scores, college politics, or other trivialities. Young scholars in the first flush of their successful creative activity draw no line between shop talk and small talk. In all my life I never encountered such a wealth of interesting conversation as flowed freely at Bryn Mawr.

There I learned from Thomas Hunt Morgan how crucial the influence of mutation is in the formation of species. From Elmer P. Kohler I learned of the discovery of the molecular structure of a coal-tar fraction and the dazzling developments in industry that were growing out of this discovery. From Arthur S. MacKenzie I learned of non-Euclidean geometry and its bearing on the structure of the universe. From Barton I learned of the progress in Assyriology that was pushing our historical knowledge far back into the antiquity that had been shrouded in primordial night. From James H. Leuba I caught my first glimpse of Freud, a half-mythical figure who could clutch the unconscious by the neck and force it to tell all sorts of tales out of school.

Philadelphia was near at hand, and if I wanted an additional range of conversation I'd go down and spend an evening with old Simon N. Patten, who all his life had practiced the art of disputing axioms. But the best center of good conversation was the table of President Thomas. She entertained a constant succession of notables at her table, and knew how to make them and her faculty talk illuminatingly.

My first dinner at President Thomas's was the most painful social experience I ever had in my life. The guest of honor was a great journalist, packed to the gunwales with every sort of interesting information. I had my place next but one to the foot of the table, and the great journalist's wife was seated beyond me, dependent entirely on my conversation for her entertainment. I had always put a low valuation on my power of entertaining conversation, but I did my best to keep from being boring.

The moment she had finished her dessert the editor's wife leaned her head on my shoulder and went to sleep. I was paralyzed. So that was what my conversation could do! The general conversation went on, and nobody seemed to notice my frightful predicament. But I could forecast the jokes that would run through the faculty at my expense.

I walked back to my quarters with Dr. Hermann Collitz, the philologist.

"He is a very brilliant man," Collitz commented.

"Yes," I agreed, though I had been too preoccupied with the open-mouthed head on my shoulder to hear a single sentence of the great journalist's conversation.

"Wouldn't you think," Collitz reflected, "if a man has a wife with that weakness he'd leave her at home?"

"What weakness?" I asked, a gleam of relief breaking upon me.

"Why, she always goes to sleep immediately after the dessert. Didn't you notice it?"

"Oh yes," I replied. So it really wasn't the quality of my conversation that did it. I drank in the sense of relief with full throat.

I found my classes as satisfactory as I could have hoped. The girls were very intelligent; they paid gratifyingly close attention and they took part in discussion with courtesy and independence. My ingrown shyness had disappeared, I thought. But one afternoon the girls requested me to hold the session in the evening, so that they could attend a hockey game.

They appeared in the evening in charming party dress. There was no resemblance between this group of social beauties and the class I had been teaching. As I began to unfold the tangles of marginal productivity, my abstractions began to seem utterly stupid in the presence of those brilliant white young shoulders. I lost the thread of my argument, beat about forlornly, and dismissed the class, acknowledging that I was unable to proceed.

One recovers from anything. I had recovered from my defeat next day. And for the rest of the year I took much pleasure out of my teaching—though I found presently that there was a certain amount of mischief behind those fair masks of serious interest.

In those days I abominated Karl Marx. I regarded his monstrous work, *Das Kapital,* as the biggest hoax that had ever been perpetrated upon the reading public. Value was congealed labor, he dogmatized. It is not, and he knew it. Goods do not exchange in proportion to the labor that has gone into them. Marx asserted that they do, but he knew better. He knew that some things are almost wholly the product of labor; other things the product of little labor and a huge investment of capital. They could not exchange in proportion to the "congealed" labor, "socially necessary" or otherwise. Marx saw this difficulty, but instead of admitting it like a scholar and an honest man he postponed the explanation to his third volume, knowing that nobody would have the patience to plow through his work to that remote end.

Sometimes a Marxian idea would crop up in the comment of one of the students. I'd step on the idea, but another would crop up next time. Was it possible that these young ladies had taken the time to go through the formless volumes of Marx? I asked them. No, not one of them had read Marx. Where then had they gotten those ideas? They got them from Professor Keasbey.

Keasbey was my chief and my good friend. If I had known that the ideas had come from him I'd have demolished them just the same. But I would have done so with grave seriousness, not, as I had sometimes done, with facile ridicule.

Lindley Miller Keasbey was a scion of one of the old ruling families of New York and was related by four lines to the Four Hundred, still a potent social organization, our American hereditary aristocracy. He was a handsome figure, a delightful conversationalist, and an inimitable raconteur. He had married Cornelia Simrall, out of the Kentucky aristocracy, a charming and entertaining lady. For many of the faculty the Keasbeys set the social tone of Bryn Mawr. Keasbey was our Petronius, and if any faculty member wanted to select a suit of clothes that should be just right for him and for the occasions he needed it for, Keasbey's great expertness was at his service.

He had studied economic geography with Friedrich Ratzel at Leipzig and was the first American scholar to bring over the ideas of *Geopolitik*. Naturally his courses were heavily geographic. He was a most successful lecturer, although his lecturing vocabulary was as full of pedantries as that of any German professor of 1890. A scholar from the ranks like me would have put the class to sleep with the same pedantries. But Keasbey's aristocratic aura vitalized any expression he might choose.

He proclaimed himself a socialist. No one objected to that, for America was still a free country. And his conception of socialism was peculiarly seductive. It was to be brought about, not by a grubby and riotous rising of the proletariat, but by a coalition of the two anticapitalistic elements in society, the aristocrats and labor, the aristocrats supplying ideas and leadership and direction. He offered himself as a forerunner of this salutary coalition and dreamed of the time when he could appear before the masses with the fire of eloquence of a Ferdinand Lassalle.

All that was amusing to me. I had my own ideas of economic forces working onward to a world of abundance in which desperate poverty, as we knew it in city slums, would be abolished. Progress in that direction was dishearteningly slow, and I could not blame anyone for regaling himself with utopian dreams. Keasbey and I had many arguments, but they were conducted with mutual respect. And I had no desire to get into conflict with my chief before the bland faces of the students.

As spring came on President Thomas sent for me and told me how well satisfied she was with my teaching record. She had talked, she said, several times with every one of my students. I was surprised. How could so busy an executive find time for so thorough an inquiry into five hundred dollars' worth of instructor?

She was offering me reappointment, with improved salary and the position of associate, and she would like me to accept on the spot. I said I had to run up to New York and consult my friend Professor Clark. I had been informed confidentially by Professor Clark that I was being considered for an appointment as Tutor, the lowest regular position on the Columbia faculty.

I was on the fence. I wanted to go back to my good friends at Columbia, but I liked Bryn Mawr. One of my maturer students helped me to decide.

She came to my desk in the seminar room and asked me if I'd like to have her tell me something about the conditions in the college which she might understand better than I, having been in the college several years. There was grave friction, she said, between President Thomas and Professor Keasbey. President Thomas did not consider Keasbey's economics sound and had expressed great satisfaction over the reports of students as to my criticism of ideas originating with Keasbey. What President Thomas was counting on was my gradually taking economics away from Keasbey, leaving him his special sphere of economic geography. I had a very straight road to promotion, the young lady said, and ended the interview.

My mind was made up on the spot. I could not remain at Bryn Mawr, to carry on a war of attrition against my good friend Keasbey, and I accepted the Columbia post.

Three years later I received a telegram from President Thomas asking me to meet her at her hotel in New York. I did so with great pleasure. There was the same Sophoclean aura of classic dignity that had impressed me so much when first I saw her.

She went straight to the point. Bryn Mawr, alas, was losing Professor Keasbey. He had an utterly irresistible offer from the University of Texas, and of course Bryn Mawr could not meet the bid of so powerful a university. Therefore her board had instructed her to offer me the headship of the department with the title of associate professor.

The associate professorship at Bryn Mawr was a two-year appointment and carried only presumptions of tenure. With so imperial a head as President Thomas, the presumptions a college granted might be canceled or prorogued. I had tenure at Columbia and was unwilling to commit myself to a tenureless raft, however seaworthy and attractive. I regretfully refused to consider anything but a full professorship. President Thomas said the board would never stand for that, and I accepted her judgment as conclusive. For she was the board.

A week later she telegraphed me that the board had consented to make me a full professor and head of department. She requested a reply by wire.

In the meantime, however, I had a call from one of my Bryn Mawr colleagues, who gave me new light on the situation. Keasbey had indeed received an offer from Texas, which he had not the remotest intention of accepting. The Texas position carried a higher salary than he was receiving at Bryn Mawr. He had therefore demanded an advance in salary. President Thomas had refused the advance and had strongly urged him to accept the Texas offer. Keasbey said he would remain at Bryn Mawr at his old salary. No, she said; she had informed the board that he was leaving, and the board had instructed her to fill the vacant post.

I made further inquiries and found that this account was true. Professor Keasbey was being forced out.

Of course I could not accept the professorship.

EIGHTEEN

Four Years at Columbia

AT BRYN MAWR I had cut my teeth as an instructor in economics. I had not cut them very well, for the task of teaching small Bryn Mawr classes had been too simple. My students, without exception, had been intelligent and responsive.

At Columbia and Barnard, in the fall of 1902, instruction presented problems quite new to me. Sometimes the problems were perplexing, often annoying, but usually capable of some sort of solution. By the end of my four years at Columbia I had been whipped into the shape of a fairly good teacher, although I was quite incapable of rising to the quizmaster heights many heads of departments at that time regarded as ideal.

My principal function was to drill classes of juniors, at Columbia and Barnard, in Bullock's *Introduction to Economics*. At Columbia, Professor Seligman would lecture one hour to the assembled classes. At Barnard, Professor Henry L. Moore would likewise assemble all the students for a general lecture. Then I would take over the students in smaller, though still large, groups and try to polish them off by quizzing them. It was on the whole a bad method. Mark Hopkins at one end of a log and an inquiring student at the other end was an ideal educational institution. Mark Hopkins on the chopping block and fifty restless students on the woodpile could never have been the ideal of even the most fatuous alumnus.

At nine in the morning I would confront forty Columbia juniors, some earnest, some shattered by an evening out, some somnolent from their athletic exercises of the day before. The tradition of young instructors driven off by the class or pushed to the verge of suicide still hung over from the old Columbia College downtown. Rhythmic stamping, collective groans, and horse laughter were the chief devices for putting the instructor in his place—or pushing him out of it—and

151

in a room with a nine-foot cabinet it was possible to throw a captured dog up on top, to compete with the teacher in lecturing.

After an hour with the rambunctious Columbia class I would scurry over to Barnard, to confront fifty young ladies, quiet as field mice, apparently uniformly attentive. Later I discovered that a good third of those charming young ladies had learned the art of fixing a look of attention on their faces while their wits went abroad woolgathering. Then back to Columbia I went for a tussle with another Columbia section, and again to Barnard for peace and relief.

As the term progressed the Columbia classes quieted down and the Barnard classes came more generally alive. I found my classes increasingly enjoyable as the successive terms moved on. There were many good students among them. Two I particularly singled out as promising scholarly careers, Carlton Hayes, now professor emeritus of Columbia, and Meyer Jacobstein, now a great journalist of Rochester.

My teaching load was considered very light, for the four classes at Columbia and Barnard were scheduled to cover the same ground. But no two classes are alike. After a first meeting an instructor who likes to teach tries to adapt his method to each particular class. The four classes soon drifted far apart.

All were based on the same textbook, Bullock's *Introduction to Economics*. It was a good sound book, but often dull and frequently opaque to the student mind. Like any other college instructor, I felt that I could do a better textbook. An opportunity came with an invitation from a correspondence school to write a textbook that should be intelligible to the adult layman.

This was my first introduction to adult education. The book had to be written so simply that no instructor would be needed to interpret it. It would have to exclude interesting controversies of only historical importance. It could have no place for fugitive material like statistical tables. And, to avoid the wordiness that afflicts academic exposition, the author had to formulate briefly, for himself and for the reader, the gist of what each successive paragraph was supposed to show.

The correspondence school—I've forgotten its name—soon blew up and, as one of its assets, sold my *Introductory Economics* to D. C. Heath and Company. The publisher had me revise the book under the title *Introduction to Economics*, which made a modest career for itself. The chief criticism of it was rather flattering to me: it was too simple; it gave the student a delusive impression of the lucidity and inevitability of economic principles. They are in fact simple; how inevitable, that is another matter.

On the advice of Professor Seligman I offered a graduate course on the history of commerce. A graduate course entitled me to a seat on the Faculty of Political Science, a privilege I cherished. I was passionately interested in economic theory and would have preferred to work up a course in that field, but theory was a drug on the Columbia market. The greatest of American theorists, John Bates Clark, was still going strong. Professor Seligman ranged widely over the field of theory; the two new members of the department, Henry R. Seager and Henry L. Moore, were both accomplished theorists. There was no room for a neophyte.

I knew nothing about the history of commerce when I announced my course, but I knew that generalizations had to follow history stepwise; that foreign commerce is one thing when it is the main pecuniary interest in the economy, as with the medieval Italian cities and the Hanse cities, and quite another thing when it assumes a subordinate place in the economy as in most modern states. It is one thing when the gains of commerce come out of plunder of accumulated resources, as early Spanish trade with America, seventeenth-century Dutch trade with Japan, and British trade with India, and quite another thing when it carries an exchange of products between fairly equal economies.

The historical differentiation of commercial phases appeared to me to have a definite bearing on the problem of war. When commerce was loot, competition was intolerable. The English and Spaniards and Dutch had to fight for the loot of the Indies; the French and British had to fight for the furs of North America. Though the parent nations might be at peace, the commercial companies were at war, and sooner or later dragged in the parent nations.

Commerce as an instigator of war, I became convinced, had played out its role, except in the heart of obsolete policy-makers, the statesmen. America and England would never dream of fighting for the all-important trade of Europe. To be sure, trusts and cartels might seek monopoly positions and draw in the statesmen to back their claims. But America would hardly go to war for the Standard Oil Company nor Germany for Krupp.

There was indeed a flaw in my argument. I did not make sufficient allowance for the international commerce in arms. In the main, however, my thesis that commerce has lost its warmaking potency still stands.

I published my ideas on this in a *Political Science Quarterly* article, "Commerce and War," later republished by Frederick Keppel as an International Conciliation pamphlet.

It had been my intention to devote myself primarily to economic theory, even though the economics department did not need my services in that field. Economic theory was at the time a subject of ardent controversy. The marginal-utility analysis had gained a firm hold on the minds of all American economists except J. Laurence Laughlin, who maintained that all beauty and all truth were enclosed in Mill's formula: value for the moment is determined by supply and demand; in the long run, by cost of production. The center of controversy lay in the theory of interest. According to Clark, the rate of interest was determined by the marginal product of capital; according to Böhm-Bawerk and his American disciples, Irving Fisher and Frank A. Fetter, by the rate of discount of the future. To Clark the issue was a moral one. If the capitalist receives only what his lawful property produces, the existing system is fundamentally just. If he merely receives a premium for postponing consumption the issue of justice falls away.

I was convinced that Clark's logic was sound, although I could not accept his conclusions as to the justice of the existing system. I felt that Clark had not proved his case because he had not gone beneath the surface to the forces governing capital supply. I tried to indicate one direction in an essay I published in the *Political Science Quarterly* on "Influences Determining the Development of Thrift." Clark liked the essay but did not admit its relevance. He did not like at all an essay I published in the *Quarterly Journal of Economics,* purporting to show that technological improvements, far from operating automatically to raise the level of wages, might equally depress wages and raise interest—depending on the concrete situation. Clark did not quarrel with my logic but felt that I was giving aid and comfort to the socialist critics of the existing system.

Clark's system, as indeed practically the whole body of economic theory, was essentially static. Economics was reaching toward a theory of dynamics. I was convinced that pure economics could offer no realistic theory of economic dynamics. For that, I believed, one had to go back to the underlying motives of men, through psychology and sociology and to the social-economic-historical forces underlying technical progress. I proposed to enter this unknown field through a study of consumption and got permission from the faculty to offer a course on the subject. But I left Columbia before my study of consumption had attained to valuable results.

In sum, my literary performance during the four years I spent on the Columbia faculty was distressingly modest. A textbook, half a dozen articles, a dozen book reviews—that was all. My excuse was the usual academic one: too many things to do. And I was indeed rather fully occupied.

A part of my job was to serve as assistant editor of the *Political Science Quarterly*. This was a much more exacting job than I had anticipated. The style of the *Quarterly* had been set by a stylistic perfectionist, Munroe Smith. Every line of every manuscript had to be scrutinized painfully. Munroe Smith used to say that while there might be men in philosophy, literature, and the classics who wrote impeccable copy, there were no writers in the political and social sciences whose copy did not demand emendation. Every scholar should indeed be assumed to have a fundamental style expressive of his personality. It was the editor's job to find out what that style was and make his emendations within it so skillfully that the author would not be able to discover in proof that his lines had been tampered with. For a first task Munroe Smith gave me the manuscript of our dean, John W. Burgess, of whom I stood in awe. Everything I did with it proved wrong.

"You see," said Munroe Smith, "Burgess's fundamental style is turgid. Your emendations are in a simple style, Middle Western crossed with classics. Every word you wrote stands out like a sore thumb. Now look here—" And he proceeded to turgify my sentences, and the article came out all authentic Burgess.

For four years I did my best, every quarter, to master everybody's style. I should have been able to find a splendid style and make it my own. But always I dropped back to my own cross of Grote and Caesar, accelerated by Middle-Western impatience to arrive at the point. I have often regarded with envy the manuscripts of Frank Colby and Philip Littell, the original fair copy cobwebbed with marginal and interlined emendations aimed at perfection. I never could emulate them.

Another part of my job was to prepare, with Charles A. Beard, a "Record of Political Events," published every six months in the *Quarterly*. We split the job, Beard to take care of foreign events, I to handle the domestic. I read the newspapers every day and cluttered my office with stupendous sheaves of clippings. I spent untold hours watching the press refute today what it had maintained yesterday. But I saw that even so some truth would slip out. I began to yearn for journalistic employment; one could so easily do better than the editorial writers of the time.

One more job I had was to edit the doctoral theses to be published in the *Columbia Series in History, Economics, and Public Law.* Here I did not need to look for the author's fundamental style, for with one exception none of the authors had matured a style of his own. The one exception was Charles Beard's *History of the Justice of the Peace in England,* an essay with all the verve and power Beard displayed later in his rich series of mighty books. The essay was my first introduction to him, the most provocative and stimulating scholar I have ever known. Beard was making it his mission to compel his chief, James Harvey Robinson, to read Jaurès's vast *Histoire Socialiste,* a work that awakened Robinson out of his academic slumber and gave us the Robinson all liberals love. Beard and I were classed together as the radical wing of the faculty, but between us the differences in temperament and point of view were so marked that we never could meet without violent though friendly controversy.

One might say I had excuses enough for small productivity. I haven't set down the half of them.

Soon after the opening of my first classes Professor Seligman asked me to come to his office. He had a letter from Frank Moore Colby, then editor in chief of the *New International Encyclopaedia,* the first volumes of which were appearing. Colby was in a jam. The topic "Debt, Public," had been dropped by the professor to whom it had been assigned three years before, and the printing press was already devouring the "DA's." Colby entreated Seligman to write the article, but Seligman hadn't the time. I'd have to do it.

Of course I hadn't the time either, but it has always been my pose that I have plenty of time. It was Friday. I spent Saturday looking up the literature and sent in the article to arrive in the office Monday morning.

In a few days I got a letter from Colby with a check I had hardly counted on at all and the request that I go over half a dozen other articles that were badly needed at once. For revising an article the *Encyclopaedia* would pay a cent a word; for writing an article, two cents. As I was a rapid worker, never trying to write unless I knew well what I wanted to say and therefore having to waste little time on revision, I found myself suddenly earning more money as an editor than

I was getting from Columbia. I liked that. And I liked encyclopedia work. It justified me in reading widely in my subject. One takes in information in great gulps when one has to use it immediately.

I was breasting the flood of articles for revision and new topics fairly creditably, I thought, sometimes working down to the early morning. But I got an irritated letter from Colby. There was a topic that had come to his attention for which no provision had been made. I hadn't even mentioned it. Like the other professors he was so unlucky as to have to do business with, I had been sleeping at the switch.

Enraged, I went straight down to settle matters with Colby. "What do you mean," I demanded, "my sleeping at the switch? What do I know about your list of topics or about your contributors? You've been sending me a lot of articles to be written or revised, and I've tried to dispose of them promptly. If you aren't satisfied with my work, say it, in God's name, and don't try to haul me over the coals for something I haven't had anything to do with!"

"But you are our office editor for economics," Colby demurred.

"Since when?"

Colby called in his secretary. "Didn't I write a letter to Johnson three weeks ago, asking him to come in as office editor for economics?"

"You didn't finish it," the girl said. "You were going to add something."

Colby looked crestfallen. "It looks as if it was I who was sleeping at the switch. But I used to be a professor too. Suppose you stick around an hour or two and bother the staff. Nothing they like so much as to be interrupted in their work. Then we'll go out to dinner."

There were eight or nine office editors, each in a little room with opaque glass walls extending upward seven feet toward the twelve-foot ceiling, permitting a community of air and noise of gossip and typewriters. They were mostly young men and women with literary ambitions, holding their jobs discontentedly for bread and butter until their literary ships should come in. I never came to know them well, as I seldom went down to the office. The one I came nearest knowing was Simeon Strunsky, later editorial writer on the *Times,* who worked furiously and was worth more than any three of the rest.

In a long evening Colby unfolded to me the problems of the *Encyclopaedia.* The work had been planned four years earlier, with himself, Daniel Coit Gilman, and Harry Thurston Peck as editors, the last two being mainly of prestige value. Although Gilman answered letters and sometimes read proof, Peck withheld himself unless he wanted to make trouble. The real job rested on Colby's shoulders.

The publishers, Dodd, Mead and Company, had acquired the old *Johnson's Encyclopaedia* and had planned to revise it without radical departure from the old text. It was to be brought up to date, and new articles were to be added sparingly. But a competing encyclopedia project, the *Americana,* appeared over the horizon. After working for three years on the original plan the publishers decided to go in for a much more serious venture. They planned to double the size of the work, discard a much larger proportion of the old text, develop a great array of new articles. This was Colby's perpetual headache, for all the copy that had been prepared over the three years had to be revised, amplified; new topics had to be found, and new contributors. Most of the old editors felt terribly abused when the copy they had assembled was returned to them for revision. The economics editor had thrown up the job; hence the drafting of myself. Some months later the sociology editor flew the coop, leaving his department on my hands; and still later the political science editor also withdrew.

All this meant a lot of work for me, but I was content. I had already been forced to the conclusion that the social sciences needed to be integrated if they were to deal with practical problems realistically. To cultivate my wide domain I had to make myself at home in the whole range of the social sciences.

Colby, like most of his editorial staff, had literary ambitions. He was master of the style of the short essay of manners. While he was slaving away at the *Encyclopaedia,* writing letters to stir up phlegmatic contributors—who eased the strain of their failure to deliver promised articles by leaving their letters unopened—stoking copy into the angry maw of the printing press, checking slowdowns among the discontented office staff, Colby managed nevertheless to put together a delightful book of essays, *Imaginary Obligations.* In those days America had three men who could write essays with the charm of Charles Lamb: Clarence Day, Philip Littell, and Frank Moore Colby. Unfortunately that kind of writing, laborious as cameo sculpture, is not well paid. Clarence Day alone, by superhuman perseverance, could make a living by the art.

In a later year, when Colby visited me in Ithaca, he seemed a changed man. The slightly sardonic depression that had been habitual with him had lifted. He had a contract with *Harper's Weekly* to write a page essay a week, for a yearly salary of fifty-two hundred dollars. All his life, he said, he had dreamed of making a living by his pen, and at last the dream was being realized. Shortly thereafter Norman Hapgood took over *Harper's Weekly* and gave it an entirely new format. Hapgood regarded himself as an essayist of manners and dropped Colby back into the morass of encyclopedia and year-book editing.

Sometimes a picture, a phrase, an anecdote catches hold of a child's mind and becomes a part of his life pattern. So Charles Reade's soldier braced himself to every situation by, *"Courage, camarade, le diable est mort."* In my childhood I looked eagerly through the press for Alkali Ike, of the "Arkansas Traveller."

Alkali Ike was singing from notes in the church choir. Suddenly he emitted a many-directioned shattering roar. The preacher-conductor rushed up to him in consternation.

"What is the matter?"

Alkali Ike brought the sheet of music close to his eyes. "Oh, a mashed spider. But I sung him."

I have encountered many a mashed spider, and it has been my pride to say, "I sung him." Aware of this weakness of mine, friends have often unloaded on me difficult tasks. When Professor Clark found that a touchy, gun-toting Mississippian was immobilizing the seminar room by his billing and cooing, I was commissioned to tell the amorous bravo that it wouldn't do. When Professor Seligman made up his mind that an eager student hadn't the native ability to make the Ph.D., I was commissioned to advise the student to quit Columbia. I hated such commissions, but I sung 'em.

On the *Encyclopaedia,* Colby soon began to unload disagreeable jobs on me. A subscriber was coming in to raise thunder because his favorite poet had been omitted from the biographies. An enraged contributor, revised to the quick, was coming in to demand satisfaction. A neurotic discharged typist was coming in to tell the chief what a brute he was and what immoral doings were going on under his roof.

"Johnson," Colby would say, "I have to attend a publishers' meeting. Will you hold my office and take care of the author's grievance when he comes in?"

One day he presented, for me to sing, not a mashed spider but a mashed tarantula. Harry Thurston Peck (HTP, we called him) had come down in a wild mood, had sent the office boy for a bottle of champagne, and had proceeded to enjoy it noisily with the office boy and the stenographer, a demure and skinny lady in her forties. HTP *would* drink the champagne from the lady's slipper, and a shrieking commotion echoed through the whole office as HTP raped the slipper from the lady's recalcitrant foot. The champagne disposed of, the three stood on chairs and waved above the low partition—HTP the slipper, the office boy the empty bottle, the stenographer her notebook—and all shouted at the top of their voices, "To hell with Dodd, Mead and Company!"

It happened that Mr. Dodd was visiting the office and heard the whole proceeding, with horror. He was a courtly old gentleman with gray burnsides and stiff, correct clothes, a man of great piety who had built up the company largely by the publication of religious books. He requested Colby to admonish HTP on the enormity of his behavior and to exact a promise that nothing like that would ever happen again.

"That," said Colby to me, "is your job. He would take it from a professor."

"I'm not a professor but an instructor. He wouldn't take it from me. Anyway, nobody ever heard of HTP doing the same thing twice."

"But what will I say to Mr. Dodd?"

"Say you have assurances nothing of the kind will happen again."

Prophecy, not promise, held good.

Year by year my Columbia salary increased, for the first year, as tutor, by the regulation hundred dollars, then more materially by my promotion to the rank of instructor and a year later to that of assistant professor. My earnings from the *New International* amounted to twice my Columbia salary, and while that enterprise would come to an end in a few years, Colby had another job in sight, an American revision of *Nelson's Encyclopaedia,* on which he needed my help. I was thus in a position to bring to New York my two brothers, who wished to study law at Columbia, and my sister, who wished to study medicine. My sister had taught in the Sioux City, Iowa, grade schools for a number of years. She had been a successful teacher, but life runs thin and gray in too long a succession of fourth-grade classes. She resigned her teaching position and joined my brothers and me in New York. She wanted to take a year to brush up for the examinations comprising the entrance requirements at Cornell Medical School.

That was in 1903. The following year John and Harry, intending to practice law in California, transferred to Stanford Law School; Edith went to Ithaca for her first two years of medical instruction.

I am not writing a history of my family group, but, I may note, my brother John perished in the great flu epidemic following the first World War. Edith has practiced medicine these many years in Palo Alto, California, trusted and loved by her innumerable patients. Harry, after some years of law practice, was elected to the Superior Court of Northern California, where he still serves as judge, loving law much, justice more, and humanity most of all.

My mother lived to realize her dream of established professional position for her three surviving children. In my last hour with her the day before she died she said she was entirely happy, happy with the professional success of her children but happiest of all because whatever success we enjoyed, our childhood passion for the rights of the disinherited had never abated.

She rests in peace beside my father, among the flowers she loved so much.

By 1904 I had served my seven years of devotion to Edith Henry. We decided to marry. Edith intended to continue her study of philosophy under Frederick Woodbridge and John Dewey. Woodbridge, offering a seminar in Greek philosophy, set Edith the task of untangling the central issues of Aristotle's *Metaphysics,* a task for which she was peculiarly fitted by her proficiency in Greek as well as her philosophic training at Harvard under William James, Josiah Royce, and Hugo Münsterberg. The text of the *Metaphysics,* as it has come down to us, is often rather blind, and the English and French translations are harder to comprehend than the Greek. Through long and patient study Edith was able to piece together the argument that runs through Aristotle's text. Her essay, *The Argument of Aristotle's Metaphysics,* won her the doctoral degree. We published the essay ourselves. It sold out in a few years. Recently a university has asked permission to photostat it for the use of students.

In rereading it I note that it surpasses in distinction anything I have ever written. I speculate on the place in philosophy Edith would have achieved if she had not turned aside to rear and educate our seven children, all of whom she brought up to college entrance without a single day in school. Edith might well have written seven books of philosophy, to lay claim to a role in advancing our culture. But we agree: seven children bravely and eagerly marching forward in life carry more cultural potentialities than the seven books.

Teaching and encyclopedia work left me little time for cultivating friends outside of the faculty. I did for a time have entrée to Ida Tarbell's circle of militantly progressive journalists. Ray Stannard Baker was always there, grave, receptive, of few words. Lincoln Steffens, his round cheeks glowing red under a promised beard, was always bursting with delight over some new nest of municipal rottenness he had discovered. Ida Tarbell presided with the dignity of a queen and kept the conversation within the calm limits of liberal principles.

Another circle I frequented rather assiduously was that of Dr. Byron Caples and his brilliant wife. It consisted mainly of young people who had come from Fostoria, Ohio, to find their fortunes in New York. One of the most interesting was Clif Paden, who was working his way into the theatrical world through teaching in a dramatic school. Gradually he found a place as manager in a somewhat mediocre show, then in a much better one, and finally in a very good one, with Clara Bloodgood. But just as Clif had his hand on success Clara Bloodgood committed suicide, throwing Clif back many stages. The movies were coming in, and Clif decided to throw in his lot with this new art, under his stage name John Emerson. After a fair period of bafflement he found success, married Anita Loos of *Gentlemen Prefer Blondes,* and with her floated out of my ken to his proper place among the higher constellations.

The non-academic friend who had most to do in shaping my later ideas was Theodore Clark, a young architect whom I had met while we were both students at Columbia. Teddy was a devoted disciple of McKim, Mead and White. He was severely classical and therefore had reservations on Stanford White, classical without severity. Teddy had great difficulty in reconciling himself to the skyscraper but found a point of sympathy in the fact that the best architects proposed to give the skyscraper the proportions of a Greek column.

For years we went on frequent excursions together to study new buildings that were being constructed, skyscrapers, hotels, apartments in the city, villas and cottages in the suburbs. Even a layman could see that new influences were playing on architecture, radiating from certain strange figures I encountered first in Teddy's literature: Frank Lloyd Wright, revolutionizing architectural design in the West and bankrupting his patrons; Gropius, somewhere in Germany, developing an encyclopedia of new ideas; Mendelssohn, who was imposing on staid and stuffy old Berlin modernity and elegance; Joseph Urban, a brilliant creator of architectural design, an overwhelming genius in color and decorative form. Teddy did not like the innovators. I liked them. My taste in ancient art inclined to the Hellenistic, with its revolt against the severe canons of Hellenic art, its exuberance in experiment, its passion for color, its humanism. I decided that if ever I should have anything to do with building—something that seemed very improbable—I'd go modern.

Most of my social life lay within the School of Political Science. As assistant editor of the *Quarterly* I came to know well all the members of the faculty. They were all my good friends; of them all, John Bates Clark most commanded my devotion. He was not only a great scholar but a man of singular humanity and purity of spirit. I have never known his like.

Equality on the faculty was a principle rigorously observed. When I was elected to the faculty Dean Burgess gave me a little lecture on my rights. I was now endowed with voice and vote exactly equal to that of any department head or Dean Burgess himself. All decisions were by unanimous vote. If I did not feel that I could approve of any proposed action I should vote against it, and the proposal would be dropped. Burgess warned me not to be influenced by any of the older men. I was always to feel myself an equal among equals.

Nor were his words mere words. While I was on the faculty I never encountered one instance of departure from the principle of equality. On two occasions I held out against what otherwise was a unanimous vote. My vote was accepted immediately without question as an absolute veto.

An organization operating by democratic unanimity might be thought to fall short of working effectiveness. That was not true of our faculty. Every one of us came to the meetings with a grave sense of responsibility. One did not lightly pit his will against his colleagues.

There was, to be sure, a certain amount of personal friction, particularly between Giddings and Seligman. It was aired in the offices, not at faculty meetings. Giddings would encounter Seligman in the *Political Science Quarterly* office, where I was working, and would roar out his discontent with some plan of Seligman's. Seligman always remained imperturbably courteous.

Once I asked Giddings what he really had against Seligman.

"What I've got against him? I can't get under the skin of that infernal Christian. You know, Johnson, I sometimes think only Jews can really behave like Christians. The Jews created that religion, and it suits their temperament. It doesn't suit the temperament of us Aryans."

Munroe Smith gave me detail after detail of the history of the faculty. Dean Burgess, as a cavalry officer in the Civil War, had had much time for reflection on the stupendous folly of a war in which citizens laid waste other citizens' country and slaughtered each other without ill will. All the issues, Burgess believed, could have been compromised if the lawyers who controlled Congress and the state legislatures had been trained in history, political science, and public law. As soon as he was discharged from the army, after Appomattox, he set out for Germany to study the political sciences. He spent several years at different universities, forming friendships with the most famous professors and imbuing himself thoroughly with the spirit of German scholarship. On his return he accepted an appointment in history at Columbia College, then a pleasant young gentlemen's finishing school. He was permitted to offer courses in public law. Although these could not be counted for credit toward the A.B., many of the ablest students were drawn to his lectures.

From among his students he picked out four and enlisted them in a project for transforming Columbia College into a university. The four were Nicholas Murray Butler, E. R. A. Seligman, Frank Goodnow, and Munroe Smith. They were to proceed to Germany to get their doctorates. Butler was to study philosophy and education; Seligman, economics; Goodnow, administration; Munroe Smith, Roman law. The young men executed Burgess's command like good soldiers and in due time returned to offer non-credit courses at Columbia College.

Burgess's next move was to turn his group into a graduate faculty. Such a faculty had been set up at Johns Hopkins, the first in America, and commanded nationwide interest among educators. Burgess argued with President Frederick Barnard on the need of a graduate school in the greatest city of the country. After some years the Board of Trustees authorized in 1886 the setting up of a graduate School of Political Science, manned by Burgess and his disciples, now advanced to professorial rank.

Butler early stepped aside to develop courses he later organized into Teachers College. Burgess and his three younger colleagues watched for opportunities to enlist additional abilities: William A. Dunning in political theory, Herbert L. Osgood in American history, John Bassett Moore in international law, John Bates Clark in economics, Franklin Giddings in sociology. This process of expansion was going on energetically while I was on the faculty; Henry R. Seager and Henry L. Moore were enlisted for the economics department, Edward T. Devine and Samuel McCune Lindsay for sociology, James Harvey Robinson and later Charles A. Beard for history. In the meantime other graduate courses were springing up throughout the institution. The towering structure of Columbia University had risen up out of Burgess's small bottle.

Still in my time the controlling nucleus of our faculty consisted of Burgess, Seligman, Goodnow, and Munroe Smith. They all knew American colonial history well and had followed the step-by-step evolution of Massachusetts Bay from a settlement governed by a chartered company in England to a free self-governing community, germ of American liberty. Step by step Burgess and his lieutenants built up the liberties of the School of Political Science. They got the Board of Trustees to accept the principle of the absolute freedom of the scholar to pursue the truth as he sees it, whatever the consequences; the principle of absolute equality of the faculty members; the principle that no scholar might be added to the faculty without the unanimous consent of the faculty. The principle was established that the president and trustees could intervene in the affairs of the faculty only through the power of the purse.

President Seth Low, regarding himself justly as a recognized authority on administration, sought admission to the meetings of the faculty. He was turned down. A university president could not conduct himself as an equal among equals. When Nicholas Murray Butler became president he thought it would be a good idea for him to sit in with the faculty. After all, he had been one of Burgess's first panel. We voted the proposition down, unanimously.

Since my time the faculty has grown in numbers and its relations with other departments of the university have become closer. But the spirit of liberty and equality, established by Burgess and his lieutenants, still lives on at Columbia and has overflowed into the universities of America. From time to time a board of trustees steps outside its moral sphere and undertakes to purge and discipline the faculty. But established liberties stricken down are bound to rise again.

Many reasons I had for being contented with my position at Columbia, yet as the years went by I became more and more discontented. I was the youngest member of the department; my seniors were still in their prime. Naturally they occupied the fields nearest the heart of the science, leaving to me free choice of subjects on the periphery. I likened myself to a sapling growing up in the irregular air space among mighty trees. A sapling becomes spindling and crooked. If a hurricane levels the great trees, the sapling still must remain spindling and outward bent.

I coquetted for a time with an invitation to join the faculty of the University of Wisconsin and visited Madison to look over the ground. But here too the mighty trees monopolized the light, Richard T. Ely, John R. Commons, Thomas S. Adams, and E. A. Ross. The space offered me was more narrow and shady than the space I had at Columbia.

An offer of a professorship came from my Alma Mater, the University of Nebraska. The department was underdeveloped; my old friend W. G. Langworthy Taylor, with an assistant, held the entire field. I should have practically free range among the subjects that interested me.

Everyone experiences occasionally homesickness for his Alma Mater. With the years, the memory of the campus, the professors, the students grows cloudy but warm. So too the memory of the land of one's birth. Vivid pictures of the sunlit prairies, the friendly little whirlwinds marching in single file, teasing the straw and cornhusks up from the dry earth, the vast white sheets of snow covering level fields and the long hill slopes; the exuberant fertility of the brown wheat and the fields of corn, with the yellow ears flying rhythmically into the wagon box in the time of husking; the sudden burst of spring, with flowers and meadowlarks where last week the snow lay deep—that is Nebraska, the Nebraska of one's homesick dreams.

I tendered my resignation at Columbia in the spring of 1906.

President Butler sent word to me to call at his office.

"You are making a great mistake, Johnson," he declared magisterially. "You think you can go to a Western university, establish yourself in your science, and be called back to Columbia. You won't be called back."

"I'm not counting on that," I said.

"But you will want to come back. You will miss the association with America's foremost scholars. You will miss the libraries of New York. You will miss New York painfully. You will never have a chance to come back to Columbia. You have the reputation of a radical. No one would hold that against you if you stayed with us. You would be as secure, you'd be promoted as fast, if not faster.

But this is a conservative institution. It's not going to Nebraska to get a radical to join the faculty."

"I understand," I said, "but I doubt that I am more radical than you, President Butler."

"Well, do you think if I quit Columbia now they'd ever call me back?"

His eyes twinkled. I strove to suppress a smile. At the time Butler was deep in hot water over his action in forcing George E. Woodberry out and the consequent fiery resignation of Edward A. MacDowell.

"Well, my boy," he said. "I see you are bent on going. Good luck. I'll keep an eye on your progress."

Later, when I joined with James Harvey Robinson, Charles A. Beard, Thorstein Veblen, Herbert Croly, Mrs. Willard Straight, Mrs. George Bacon, and other liberals to launch the New School for Social Research I found in Butler our most savage critic. According to Butler, we were simply a little bunch of disgruntled liberals, setting up a tiny fly-by-night radical counterfeit of education. I wrote savagely about Butler too.

But years later, after I had set up the University in Exile, I once found myself sitting on the same platform with Butler. He was splendid, in appearance and speech, and I felt a glow of pride in my heart that I had sat under him as a student and served under him on the faculty. With all his faults he was a great educator and a great man.

After the program Butler offered me his hand and turned on me the super-power charm that had brought millions of dollars to Columbia.

"My boy," he said—I was already getting gray—"we are proud of what you are doing at the New School. I have a rather wild plan to propose, but I'll leave it to Fred Keppel to talk it out with you."

I allege to myself that I am beyond flattery, but the truth is, I felt stupendously flattered. I wasted no time in getting to Fred Keppel, at the Carnegie Corporation.

"You know, Alvin," Keppel said, "Nicholas Murray Butler is great on consolidations. If he had been in business he would have consolidated all the corporations in America. He proposes to take the New School under the wing of Columbia. I'm commissioned to persuade you.

"He sees a fruitful combination between your University in Exile and the Columbia faculty, your faculty to take care of the European point of view, ours to take care of the American. He sees a fruitful combination between your general courses and Columbia Extension and would make you head of the whole show.

"If Butler were twenty years younger I'd say, join up with him. But he may retire any day. And he is the only protection you would have against the Columbia trustees, who would see no reason why Columbia should harbor two faculties of Political Science, when the Columbia faculty, enlarged by two or three of your best men, would suffice. And they would expect you to shape your general courses to bring in large classes, and money for the Columbia treasury.

"I know a merger would solve your personal problem. You'd be set for life, yourself. But the New School would fade into history. And education would wait another generation or more for an institution that would take up the real adult educational job, of educating the educated."

I thanked Keppel for his good advice and came away in a sort of anguish. Personal security dangled before my eyes, but never in all my life have I given a hoot for personal security. There is no security for man except under a slab of marble or granite or concrete, and I have no preferences as among the three—or even a fourth, green sward with weeds to vex a curator. But in the here and now it was my job to raise money to support the New School, which meant mainly the University in Exile. If we merged with Columbia I'd never have to hear: "What can the New School do that Columbia isn't doing?" I heard that so often. I'd never have to go to reluctant contributors: "You gave me a hundred dollars last year; in the name of God, give me another hundred today."

The choice of Hercules was upon me, and I was not a Hercules. But I was a free man, resolved to be free.

Did I tell my board? No, I didn't dare.

NINETEEN

Nebraska

H OME again, in my native Nebraska.

The westbound tourist, seeing Nebraska from the Pullman window, thinks, "Good Lord, how monotonous!" He acquired his sense of landscape from the romanticists, who needed mountain scenery as background to their cloud-topped heroes. The rational classic writers detested the mountains. In Latin literature the only comments on the Alps are, "horrid, miserable, detestable." The classics loved the sweet plains, fertile, homelike, and homemaking, the rich lands along the sluggish streams exuberant with harvests, and the gentle slopes above, Bacchus hand in hand with the olive.

The Romans never laid eyes on such magnificent plains as those of Nebraska, and neither has modern man really seen them, his eyes blinkered by the literature of romance. For the Nebraska-born the gently winding streams with their flower-bedecked margins, the fertile bottom levels, the long swales of grassy hills, are quintessentially home, free and sunlit home.

Soon after arriving in Nebraska I visited the farm where I was born. There, on a grassy slope, was a small oak tree, perhaps six inches in diameter; it had been six inches in my earliest memory. It chose to live, not to grow. It was the tree to which my father tied up his horse when he came from Wisconsin, years before I was born. I looked out upon the landscape, with my father's pioneer eyes. Before me a descent to a stream; beyond, level ground covered with a plum thicket, rising to a green slope embraced by two hill spurs reaching forward from a long green range closing the horizon, with a saucy knoll coming forward between the embracing main hill arms. As I looked and contemplated, dusk came on, and over the range of hills the evening star appeared, dim at first and then a brilliant gem. I was back in my father's spirit. This is home. Home.

I returned with joy and reverence to the bosom of my Alma Mater.

169

But my Alma Mater had dolled herself up. According to the fashions of the time, she hadn't any bosom, but cold and stiff whalebone.

The old University Hall of my early dreams and awe still stood, but there were plans to pull it down. Nebraska Hall, built by the painful labor of farmboy students and convicts from the penitentiary, was condemned and in process of liquidation. New buildings had gone up, of varying styles, not answering to either my earlier classical architectural instincts or my later modernist ideas. The city of Lincoln, which in my day had claimed, falsely, a population of twenty-five thousand, in 1906 flaunted its fifty thousand and looked forward to the inevitable hundred thousand. The two great mansions of my student time, built by lucky paving contractors, were thrown in the shade by elegant mansion upon mansion along streets that had been cow walks.

The student body had changed with the swelling prosperity of the state. There was no longer in evidence the kind of student I had known, particularly one who had walked in from Loup City, a hundred and fifty miles, with a broken ankle, to save a few dollars on railway fare. All the students had money and bicycles, and here and there one had a "buzz wagon," a primordial automobile that would carry a crowd of laughing boys and girls to the near woods where crickets and frogs squeaked and croaked welcome. The dean of women was growing haggard and gray, breaking up parties on campus benches where the young men's wooing was getting too *handgreiflich,* as the Germans say—too "handgrabbish."

Wo bist du, du gute alte Zeit?

But life is one thing and education is another. I was there to serve as educator. I had submitted discreetly worded descriptions of three courses I proposed to give, covering the very center of interest in my science of economics: a seminar in economic theory, a course on labor problems, and a course on public finance. That made nine hours of instruction, and the statutes of the university still required twenty hours from every instructor. But what are statutes among friends? And I was among very good and true friends, on the faculty and on the board; and the chancellor, E. Benjamin Andrews, a man huge physically, mentally, morally, though not knowing me, knew my wife and all her family and loved them.

Surely I could find, among the thousands of chattering, flirting, footballing young cornfed Nebraskans, the fifteen or twenty serious students per course I needed to function well as a teacher. Had I not

come back with the aura of a great Eastern university shining round
my head?

My grandmother, as a child in Odense, knew the boy Hans Christian Andersen, son of a sad drunkard and of a handwringing worn-
faced mother. My grandmother saw Hans Christian set off for Copenhagen, amid the catcalls of his schoolmates, bravely asserting that he
would come back in triumph. He did win triumph, but not enough to
astonish Odense. On his return he expected the city council, with
vehicles decked with the gorgeous flowers for which Odense was
famous, to come a stage or two to meet his coach. Instead, he was
met, toward the end of the last stage, by a crowd of his former schoolmates, running along the coach and shouting, *"Orangoutang! Orangoutang!"*

My homecoming was not so dramatic as that. The thousands of
students had no time to notice it.

My new chief, W. G. Langworthy Taylor, head of the Department
of Economics, was a man of a type which has since been discontinued.
He was altogether a creature of will power. In his last year at Harvard
he had had a devastating nervous breakdown, which he overrode by
sheer force of will—acquired from his teacher William James. He
forced his way through to his degree and proceeded by inhumanly
exacting exercises to keep himself upright. When he came to Nebraska
as professor of economics his nerves were still so rebellious that often
as he lectured everything went black before his eyes and he had to
cling to his desk to keep from toppling over; but he made his lecture
go on. It was not always intelligible to his students; but they ascribed
his unintelligibility to his depth of thought and originality. He did
think deeply, and originally, but one had to be a well-trained economist
to follow the leaps of his thought over the neurological abysses.

He was much better in health when I joined his department, but he
was still training himself. He had bought in Kentucky two beautiful
horses, similar in character to the man-eating horses of Diomede.
I wouldn't go in front of one of them for fear of having a shoulder
bitten off; nor behind, for fear of getting the daylights kicked out of
me. Taylor rode one of those dynamic horses every afternoon and
made his wife, a good economist and a particularly timid person, ride
the other, to build up her will power.

Taylor loved to teach, but the object of his teaching was to develop
the students' will power. To that end he used as a text Mill's *Prin-*

ciples, expurgated by J. Laurence Laughlin of all Mill's lapses into humanity. If a student could not get the sense of a passage—and there are stubbornly resistant passages in Mill—Taylor would have the student commit the passage to memory, so that later in life, in the midst of his riper experience, it might flash upon him. "Ah, this is what Mill meant!"

In the nineties of the last century, when all Nebraska was sunk in the poverty of the depression and the whole population was fighting despair with will power, classes of fifty or sixty, mostly mature and argumentative men, would struggle their way through Mill with Taylor. But in 1906 the state was prosperous and will power an antique. Taylor's class had dwindled to less than a baker's dozen, for the most part immature and non-argumentative.

Only students who passed in the Mill course were eligible for registration in the elective courses, of which there were ten. Our ten electives had to compete for the survivors of the course in Principles, supplemented by rare students of earlier vintages.

Two students registered for my course in labor problems, five for my course in public finance, four for my seminar in economic theory. It did not greatly hearten me that I had about the maximum possible registration in the circumstances. You can never expect more than one really promising economics student out of five. I had one in my course in public finance, Fred Garver, later to serve with distinction as professor of political science at the University of Minnesota, a dyed-in-the-wool pessimist whose dark colors remained true and fast throughout his career. There were two promising students out of four in my seminar. As for the course on labor problems, one of the two students was called home by the death of his father and the necessity of taking over his father's shop. The other simply disappeared, and I had a third of my time on my hands.

I was far from contented. My actual function was virtually that of a private tutor on a professor's salary. I was clearly not needed in the department, and I made up my mind to seek another position. This I reported to the chairman of the Board of Regents, Charles Allen.

"I never expected you to have more than a handful of students the first year," he said soothingly. "I had suggested to Taylor that he give you the course on Principles; you'd have had plenty of students, and there would be a lot going on into the advanced courses. But it would break Taylor's heart to give up drilling and training the beginning students. And Taylor is a royal good fellow: neither you nor

I would push him out of his heart's desire. If you will stick around for a few years the problem will solve itself. The board appreciates you and are going to raise your salary."

"For private tutoring," I said pessimistically. But they did raise my salary at the next meeting.

Still I was not happy in my work and could not foresee a future condition that would satisfy me. Underneath the froth of social life and athleticism there were great treasures of talent in the student body. But the best students were not inclined in the direction of economics.

The physical sciences appeal powerfully to the innate instinct of curiosity; literature and philosophy appeal strongly to the emotions. Interest in economics rises out of practical economic problems, the restlessness of labor in poverty, the crushing down of the small farmer, excessive burdens of taxation, the threat of monopoly. Nebraska had been intensely interested in economics during the eighties and nineties, when each year brought lower prices and deeper poverty than the last. But by 1906 each year showed higher prices and better incomes than the last. And economics came to seem a shattered sheaf of boring abstractions.

Besides, the idyllic faculty society I had assumed when I was a student looked altogether different from the inside. The Greek professor could not endure the sight of the Latin professor; the American historian was continually at war with the European historian; literature and English were on perennially hostile terms; my own department found sociology and political science hard to bear. These warring professors were men I had worked under in my student days. I knew them to be sincere scholars and devoted teachers. It distressed me deeply to find them mutually embittering their lives, apparently without cause.

Roscoe Pound, who was then dean of the Law School, was equally distressed by the internecine academic warfare. As dean, as a scholar of universal interest, as a man of abounding energy and drive, he commanded immense prestige in the university. Some of us peace-loving professors urged Pound to get the whole faculty together, from time to time, in academic sociability. We engaged the assembly room of one of the hotels; Pound issued a compelling invitation, and all the faculty assembled. Professors who had avoided each other for years found themselves seated side by side, and they meant honestly to like it.

The program was song and "reaming swats that drink divinely." Pound led off with the ballad of the bold Dick Turpin, borrowed from his sister Louise, top authority on the ballad. One after another professors who for years had used their voices only in lecturing and in academic politics drew old college and university songs out of their dusty memories. We roared *"Gaudeamus igitur"* in virtual unison:

> *"Vita nostra brevis est.*
> *Brevi finietur,*
> *Venit mors velociter,*
> *Rapit nos atrociter,*
> *Nemini parcetur."*

The German university students had borrowed from the Romans and Greeks the custom of inviting Death to their feasts. Not death as a step to immortality, but death for good and all. *"Nox est perpetua una dormienda"*—Death, the leveler of ambitions and strife.

Our party was a great success. But a group of ladies were having a party of social reform on the next floor. All the serenity of their thought was destroyed by our professorial roaring. They reported us to Chancellor Andrews, who told us, gently but firmly, nothing of the kind was to happen again.

I had assumed that I could never be drawn into the factional strife, but I stumbled into it unawares.

There was an opening in the department of philosophy, and I thought I knew exactly the right man, Hartley Burr Alexander. We had been students together at Nebraska and had graduated in the same year. By universal acclaim he had been set up as the intellectual giant of the student body. Indeed, many students feared him, with his swift generalizations flaming through the all but opaque walls between the disciplines. Later we both held fellowships in Columbia, Alex, as we all called him, in philosophy, I in economics. We received our doctorates at about the same time.

His road had been much more difficult than mine. Economics was an expanding field, with many approaches all fairly tolerant mutually; philosophy a static if not a shrinking field, and, moreover, a highly contentious one. Philosophy is forever compromised with theology, and every syllogism points toward heaven or toward annihilation. Inevitably philosophers must be fighters. They must fall into factions striving each to ban all heretics from the profession.

The prevailing philosophy, at the time Alex and I became doctors, was Neo-Hegelianism, living on fairly easy terms with Neo-Platonism and Platonism itself. Alex's philosophy was fundamentally Aristotelian, with overtones from science and the arts. All his applications for positions were emphatically turned down, although one gentle professor tempered his negative with a word of advice.

"Young man, if you go on in the way you are going, you will number among those who are seeking to destroy all the values the true philosophers have painfully established."

Frank Moore Colby found a place for Alex on the staff of the *New International,* as official copy cutter, and later Alex joined the staff of *Webster's Dictionary,* then being revised. Alex went on blithely writing philosophical articles, mostly rejected by the journals though decidedly possessed of merit.

My wife and I saw in the depleted department in Nebraska an opportunity to launch Alex as a professor. We felt certain that once a professor, he would get the hearing he deserved. I went to Chancellor Andrews to present the case.

He listened gravely to my encomiums on Alex. "What does Edith think about Alexander?" he asked.

"My judgments on his philosophy are hers."

"Mine will be too." He smiled. He had read Edith's book on Aristotle's *Metaphysics* and knew her for an exceptionally well-trained philosopher.

Then I went to the acting head of the department—and pulled down an unanticipated storm that raged in the faculty long after Alex's appointment.

As a professor Alex proved a brilliant success. With his extremely intelligent passion for art he became an important figure in the cultural life of the city. The remarkable scheme of decoration of the new State Capitol building grew out of the collaboration of Alexander and Goodhue the architect.

In sharp contrast to the tense academic gatherings were the meetings of a businessmen's club, a branch of the chamber of commerce. Professor Taylor and I attended occasionally as guests. I was attracted strongly by the fact that William Jennings Bryan, who had set the prairies aflame in 1896 with his Cross of Gold speech, and who still could command the Democratic nomination for the presidency whenever he chose, was in fairly regular attendance.

Time had altered his appearance very little. He had mellowed, and his silver voice had taken on golden overtones. He was very impressive, especially when seated; for, like all the great orators from Odysseus down, his body was long in relation to the length of his legs. His manner was genial and engaging but uncompromising.

The discussions rarely brought up the subject of free silver, but Bryan had occasional opportunity to assert that his position in 1896 had been fortified by subsequent events. He maintained that the long depression from 1873 to 1896 was due to the fact that there was not gold enough in the world to serve as a satisfactory medium of exchange for the world's expanding business, except at a steadily declining price level, ruinous to the debtor classes, enriching the creditor classes unjustly. By 1896 South Africa and Australia had begun to pour new gold into the world system. This, Bryan argued, arrested the downward progress of prices, cause of chronic depression, and was even pushing prices upward, generating prosperity. Therefore the need for remonetizing silver was temporarily not urgent. But the world's business would again outrun the capacity of gold, and the silver question would again be the dominant political issue.

Most of the members of the club were hard-shell Republicans. They had other explanations for rising prices: McKinley and higher protective duties; the Spanish war and the expansion of American dominion overseas. But they could listen tolerantly to Bryan's theoretical exposition of the quantity theory of money, since there appeared to be no danger that he or anyone else would ever be in a position to tamper with the currency. Indeed, they found his arguments stimulating. Bryan had read and digested every authority on money, from the Romans down. The Nebraska layman had a passion for education, and Bryan's exposition was highly educational.

The members of the club were not so tolerant of other points in Bryan's system. A graduated income tax—that would kill the spirit of enterprise; inheritance taxes—robbery of widows and orphans; regulation of railway rates—socialism; guaranty of bank deposits— ruin of the credit system. The two banker members argued that under a bank-deposit guaranty deposits would flow as freely into the unsound banks as into the sound ones; and on the inevitable failure of the unsound banks, the sound ones would be ruined by the taxes levied to make good the guaranty.

On Bryan's most passionate interest, prohibition, the club was openminded. Most members had fortified themselves a bit before Bryan arrived, but they were agreed, alcohol never did anybody any good.

Bryan carried himself magnificently in the debates. No member of the club could wrestle him in argument and come off unbruised. But the club liked him. When he was absent the other members were warm in their admiration of his ability to make the worse seem the better reason. I was reminded of the classical anecdote of the orator Aeschines, driven off the rostrum and into the professorial chair by the overwhelming oratorical power of Demosthenes.

As an exercise in oratory Aeschines recited for his students an oration of Demosthenes. To the students, who went wild with enthusiasm, he shouted angrily, "But you should have heard the beast deliver it himself!"

At first I marveled to find these businessmen, selfish materialists, so much more tolerant of opposing opinion than the professors in the university. On reflection I saw that business materialists, for whom every issue resolves itself into money, can well be tolerant, for all money issues can be compromised. To the idealist, men's souls are at stake in every issue. The idealist can't compromise.

In reviewing the history of conflicts, domestic and international, I saw that naked pecuniary interests seldom if ever produce effective action. They must dress themselves up in shimmering garments of idealism. We didn't fight the presidential campaign of 1896 merely to raise prices or keep them down. We fought for justice on one side, and honor on the other. We did not fight Spain for the sugar and tobacco of Cuba, the coffee of Puerto Rico, the approach to Asiatic trade afforded by the Philippines. We fought to liberate the islands from the inhuman Spanish yoke.

It is one of the tragedies of history that after the underlying materialistic interests have reached a position where compromise and peace are possible, the idealistic front still cries for war and more war.

By moving, a body greatly increases its visibility. In the four years in which I sat in the shade of the big trees of Columbia, I had one invitation to return to Bryn Mawr, another to come to Wisconsin, and a third to return to Nebraska. Within three months of my long move to Nebraska I had two tentative invitations, one from the University of Missouri, the other from the University of Texas.

I had friends in both institutions. Isidor Loeb, professor of political science at Missouri, was an old friend of Seligman's and so a friend of Seligman's protégé. My old chief from Bryn Mawr, Lindley Miller Keasbey, was professor of political science at the University of Texas.

David Houston, president of the University of Texas, dropped into Lincoln to look over Professor Heald, in botany, and myself. Houston was a powerful figure who carried himself modestly, was quick and sharp in his judgments, and of rather sardonic humor. I had the privilege of showing him around the campus while we talked economics. I wanted to take him out to our show place, the agricultural college, but he refused. He had been president of Texas Agricultural and Mechanical College for six years, and he had learned that when men give their lives to the problems of fat steers and hogs their spirit takes its quality from fat steers and hogs. By the irony of fate, Houston was later to become Secretary of Agriculture.

We parted friends. I agreed to visit the University of Texas during the Christmas recess.

I arrived in Austin the morning before Christmas of 1906, to be greeted by the most brilliant, the most godlike sun I had ever beheld. I am by nature a sun worshiper; I attribute that to my Scandinavian blood. We blue-eyed blonds were never meant to be thrust into the cold and fog of Northern Europe. We are not equipped with the black eyes of Eskimos and Samoyeds who can face the gleaming sleet surfaces without snow blindness. We do not have their short, round bodies with fat insulation under the skin. We can support winter cold only by eating enormously, meat, fish, blubber. Through the ages we have been distinguished for our tremendous eating power.

I think our native home, after we left the Pamirs—where, like the local goats, we developed blue eyes—was the land bridge between Europe and Africa. When the bridge broke down, part of us were left on the European side in Italy, part in Algiers and Tunisia. An infinite number of the small, dark Mediterranean race crowded in and pushed our European half into the forests of the North, to become Nordics; our African half into the highlands of Algiers and Morocco, to become Berbers and Kabyles.

We have never been contented, and as our manpower grew we have pressed back toward the Mediterranean, Cimbri and Teutones, Alemanni, Ostrogoths and Visigoths, Vandals, Longobards, Vikings, Hapsburgs, Wilhelm II and his dream of a place in the sun.

A big reason for the small fact that I love the sun.

A few minutes after I left the train my friend Keasbey drove up in a victoria, drawn by two blooded Kentucky trotting horses, and took me out to the edge of town where he was living in a temporary cottage while building a mansion. Inshallah was being built according to designs conceived by his wife, genial designs whose realization involved building an arched doorway and pulling it down, moving a wall forward and then still farther back. The end result, as anyone could foresee, would be unique and beautiful—and building labor was cheap.

There was a tract of ten acres alongside Keasbey's "ranch," with a three-room cottage fronted by a noble grove of oak trees, a promising grape arbor, a fig tree, and a Japanese persimmon with most of its Christmas decoration fruit still on its branches. I made up my mind to buy it, if the appointment came off.

The next day we were to have Christmas dinner with Sidney E. Mezes, dean and second in command to Houston. At breakfast Keasbey urged me to make a good impression on Mezes. We set out early to make Christmas morning calls, a charming institution I had never before encountered. At each cordial house—half a dozen of them—we had to partake of eggnog, a beverage of which I had no experience but whose smooth and bland innocence I highly suspected. Arriving at the house of Mezes, I made a resolve. If speech is silver, silence is golden: I'd go in heavily for silence.

I did. Yet somehow I came away with a reputation for learning and a keen sense of humor.

The appointment was in the bag, but the regents could not act before the coming June meeting, and at the University of Nebraska you could not resign later than June 1. I was not prepared to resign on the strength of a prospect. Texas would have to be postponed for a year.

Anyway, I had something on my mind far more important than any university position. My wife and I expected our first child toward the end of the summer. To escape the blistering hot winds of the Nebraska summer, we secured a little cottage in Palo Alto, California, where on September 16, 1907, my daughter Dorothy was born.

In her first half-hour of life Dorothy lay still, crying softly to herself, for she could not know that there was anyone else to cry to. "Dorothy," I would say, for we had already named this great gift of God. She would stop crying with a shadowy look of puzzlement in her eyes. Then she would resume her crying, and again I'd say, "Dorothy," and she would hush, looking more puzzled.

I realized that the notions of fatherhood I had held hitherto were all wrong. She was not just a treasured possession of her parents. She was not a plastic bit of humanity to be shaped by parental love and wisdom. She was an independent member of the family group, possessed of her full share in its counsels, its rights and privileges. She would be shaped, but fundamentally only by the inherent laws of her own being. Far more priceless than the most priceless possession, she granted us the great privilege of having her one of us.

TWENTY

Texas

A s A practical economist I had often inveighed against home ownership for labor. In the sweeping migrations of industry labor
would have to follow or languish in steadily worsening unemployment. I disapproved especially of home ownership for college teachers,
essentially migratory workers, in an era of irregularly expanding college and university development. I could cite instance after instance
of professors chained by the leg to house and lot, when their best
scholarly interests would have drawn them half a continent away.

In accepting a professorship at the University of Texas I assumed
that I was passing out of the class of migratory scholars. Some institutions at the time were extremely subject to the lightning strokes of
"calls" from more powerful institutions; lightning struck repeatedly
at a college like Bryn Mawr. Texas was virtually secure against such
lightning. Once there, you assimilated rapidly into the independent
State of Texas, with its Lone Star floating from the capitol tower.
You adapted your teaching, your research, your very manner of exposition and your style of speaking and writing to Texas requirements.
You became a mere memory to the belt of Northern educational institutions.

In my brief visit to Texas I had met Dr. Milton B. Porter, a superb
mathematician who would have lent distinction to any university department; Dr. Edwin W. Fay, the choicest Latinist I ever knew; Dr.
William J. Battle, almost a naturalized ancient Greek; Dr. George
P. Garrison, one of the half-dozen best-known American historians;
and Keasbey, with Bryn Mawr behind him and a reputation as the
best-trained economic geographer in the country. None of these men
expected to be called to the great universities, and, so far as I know,
none ever received a call. But none wanted it.

So I conceived that I was taking Texas for better or for worse and
could wisely yield to the primordial urge to home ownership. My heart

turned to the little cottage and the ten-acre lot I had examined on my first visit, mine own vine and fig tree, my grove of gnarled and knotty century-old oaks, my gently sloping, well-drained field, lying just right against the north for a peach orchard. I wrote to a real-estate operator I had met to buy the place for me. It cost me twenty-five hundred dollars, about all the money I had, but of course I could borrow enough money on such security to enlarge the cottage into a livable house.

As soon as my classes were over at the University of Nebraska in June 1908, I prepared to set out for Austin. As Texas had a well-earned reputation for summer heat my wife decided to remain with Dorothy at the home of her mother in a pleasant village in southern Nebraska.

The Austin summer begins in the middle of May. The temperature rises to 94 degrees at ten in the morning and stays there until four in the afternoon, when a grateful breeze sweeps up from the Gulf, to cut the heat to about 80, a level maintained through the night and early morning. That, I feel sure, was the temperature of the Garden of Eden, and I can appreciate the nostalgia of Adam and Eve.

The evening and night temperature held steadily through the summer. But the midday temperature rose about half a degree a week to a maximum of 98 or 100. Then a slow decline set in, reaching 94 by the middle of October. After that the weather was unreliable. It was headed for the heavenly sunlit days of winter; but at any time a norther might descend from the Colorado mountains, cutting the temperature down as low as 20, or even 15 or 10, under a savage wind. At such times the Negro population hovered over fire-clay buckets of blazing charcoal, or, if the charcoal ran out, went to bed, pulling the quilts up over their heads.

The heat in June did not greatly depress me. Humidity was low, indeed, almost at a vanishing point. I possessed myself of clothes made of something like "handkerchief linen" and promptly found that I was sunburning through them. My whole body exhibited the textile pattern. But sunburned skin regulates perspiration far better than the cellar-white of the heavily clad body. I soon accepted the Texas formula, "Finest climate in the world." But it was clear that I would have to consider the climate among the premises of my plans for building.

This the local architects did not do. They built cottages after the patterns of New England. Out in the country and in the more remote suburbs cottages were set two feet off the ground on cedar posts—

"so that the hogs could go in and eat up the snakes." So my own cottage stood, purposelessly, for while snakes were much in evidence I'd never have any hogs. Floors were single, and the boards inevitably shrunken, leaving cracks between them for the 20-degree norther, at forty miles an hour, to make long, slender cold drafts for one's feet.

I decided to be my own architect. The cottage I had bought consisted of three rooms in a row, each sixteen feet square, making a length of forty-eight feet. I would parallel it with a member of the same length and width, with a connecting member twenty-four feet long and eighteen feet wide. I'd throw a single roof over the whole structure, thus creating a vast garret in which half a dozen rooms could be finished off, and allowing wide verandas at front and back of the middle member, designed to be the living room. At the front, which faced north, I'd tilt up the roof to make a wide, deep sleeping balcony. I'd put a stone foundation under the whole house and build five stone fireplaces for the small rooms and a magnificently tiled fireplace in the living room. Stone was cheap. There is a local limestone that lies in convenient level strata nine inches thick, so soft when it comes from the quarry you cut it with a crosscut saw, like soft wood. It hardens on exposure to the air and exhibits lovely little shell surfaces of amber color and rose.

I laid my plans before a builder, who estimated that he could do the whole job for twenty-five hundred dollars, including all material costs. I was impatient to go right ahead. I went to the Capital National Bank to negotiate a loan. One could surely borrow twenty-five hundred dollars for improvements on a twenty-five-hundred-dollar property, unencumbered.

Then came my first realization of the uniqueness of Texas institutions. I could not borrow a cent on my property, for it was legally my homestead.

The early Texas legislators had regarded moneylenders as birds of prey and meant to keep their claws off the home of the innocent though perhaps imprudent citizen. Therefore they had enacted a law making the home of a man with wife, or of a widow, or of minor children, exempt from seizure for debt. Were not wife and children a man's preferred creditors? A single man had no homestead, but any man might marry, defeating the claims of the moneylender, however well established prior to the marriage. Furthermore, a supremely humane Supreme Court justice had held that although the state had made it a penitentiary offense for a white person to marry a Negro, still the institution of illegitimate unions persisted; and who so helpless, so deserving of the protection of the law, as a man's illegitimate mulatto child? The judge's decision conferred homestead rights upon such children, and all other illegitimate children as well.

There was another decision of the Court that made a homesteader's place of business also exempt. The banker told me of a man who had a house worth forty thousand and two hundred thousand in a business plant. He could bid his creditors go whistle, and in fact they were whistling and would continue to do so until they scaled down their claims.

Some weeks later I had dinner with an Englishman whose business was to place English money in Texas eight per cent loans. He inveighed savagely against this peculiar Texas institution. None of the vast volume of Texas real estate could be used for security. I asked him how much money he had out on loan. Eight million pounds sterling. About what were his annual losses, through homestead repudiation? Never a shilling. I reminded him of the doctrine of Jeremy Bentham, great English philosopher, that there should be no legal enforcement of contracts. An honorable man would fulfill the terms of his contract, and no intelligent person would care to do business with a dishonorable man. Was that not about the condition in Texas real estate?

"Yes, but they could borrow ten times the money if it weren't for this crazy law."

Fortunately there is always a way to get around the law, even a crazy law. The good legislators of Texas felt that labor too had to be protected and made the mechanic's lien ultra sacred, even taking precedence over the homestead law. The banker showed me how I could make a contract with a working builder, giving him a lien covering not only all labor but all material. The bank would endorse such a lien and sell it to an investor.

"For how long a term would it run?" I asked.

"No term at all. It is collectible any day the holder may choose. No Texas investor would bother you about the principal so long as you pay the interest. But if it falls into the hands of a damn Yankee, pay it off if you have to beg, borrow, or steal."

"And how great is the risk of a damn Yankee?"

"There's not much risk. You see, in Texas a man may get shot for less than that, and the damn Yankees are gun-shy."

I was reassured, and soon my building operations were going blithely ahead.

I was sleeping in my cottage, picking up my meals where I could. To enjoy to the full the Gulf breeze at night, I placed my cot under an open window and left my doors wide open. As there were no mosquitoes and no more flies than enough to feed the little scorpions that kept house with me, I did not put in screens. For protection I kept a monkey wrench on the window sill beside my cot.

One night I awoke to see an animal in the lozenge of moonlight before my window. He was ghost pale, about two feet high; his nose approached the floor, as did his stiff, hairless tail. What the deuce was that? I reached for the monkey wrench. In a wink the animal disappeared.

It was just a 'possum.

But I got to thinking how defenseless I was, a thousand feet away from my next neighbor. My lot was long, and on the far end of it was a well-beaten path trodden out by the Negroes from the densely populated Del Valle region, on their way to the city. Men and women and children; enormous plantation hands; grizzled Uncle Toms; sooty black, dark and light brown; occasional blue-eyed redheads—all flowed along the path in long streams, on Sundays and holidays. Being green to the country, I became rather nervous about them. It took me time to realize that these were the most harmless people in the world.

Anyway, everybody had a gun handy; I ought to have one. I went to a dealer in guns and hardware.

"No. I can't sell you a gun. It's against the law. But I can lease it to you, say, for ninety-nine years or, if you like, nine hundred and ninety-nine years. Same price."

I picked out what looked to me like a good type for a professor, small caliber, pleasantly chased surfaces.

"I wouldn't advise you to take that gun. Shoot a man with it, you only aggravate him. You want a gun that will stop a man. Now this forty-five Colt. You hit a man with that and he goes flat on his back."

I handled the gun and liked it. It had belonged to an Army officer at Fort Sill, evidently a man who liked nice things, for the stock was mother-of-pearl with a noble spread eagle in relief. A practical man too, for he had filed off the trigger guard, so that his finger might not fumble in a crucial moment.

I supplied myself with cartridges and returned to my "homestead," meaning to learn how to shoot. I set up a tin can on a post and tried my hand at fifty feet. My first shots went wild but my fifth shot punished the can. I set it up again and hit it with my third shot. Evidently the art could be learned—with patience.

The long lines of Negroes from Del Valle no longer came through my place. They had heard my artillery. Their ancient route had been displaced a half mile to the east.

The use of pistols was fairly common in those days—only in self-defense. A succession of judicial decisions had greatly expanded the concept of self-defense. Of course it was self-defense to shoot a man who was shooting at you. Any court would let you go free. But, "He reached for his gun," came to be a valid plea. Next it became sufficient to say, "I thought he was reaching for his gun." And if he hadn't a gun, "I thought he had a gun." Under these principles anyone could shoot any man, with impunity.

One day I went to call on a lawyer friend, Peter Dudley, at his office. A man was half stumbling down the stairs from the office. Peter's voice was roaring after him, "You get out of this town, Jim Bellows! If ever I see you on the streets of Austin I'll kill you. I'll sure kill you!"

Peter was fondling his pistol as I entered his office.

"Say, Peter," I said, "I saw a man coming down your stairs in a mighty big hurry, 'like he goin' to leave the place.'"

"That damn skunk! You know what he did? He said I throwed his case. He hadn't any case. I did the best I could for him, but he was bound to lose. And then he had the nerve to say I throwed his case. If I ever see him on the streets of Austin I'm sure going to kill him!"

"Is that so simple, Peter? How can you plead self-defense if you've announced you're going to kill him?"

"He'll have a gun, won't he, if he ain't a damn fool? He'll reach for it, won't he? But I'm quicker than most men."

Once I was lunching with a venerable judge who boasted of the law-abiding character of Austin. "I've been on the bench for seventeen years. Not one case of serious crime has come up in all those years."

"But, Judge, how can you say that? I've been here only five months, and six men I've met have been shot down."

"I wasn't speaking of homicides," the Judge said calmly. "As I see it, every man is going to have so many good days and about as many bad days; so much pleasure and so much pain; so much happiness and so much sorrow. You kill him, and that just about balances his account. But if you steal his horse, that leaves him worse off. That's a crime."

Neither did the matter of homicide seem so grave to me as it had seemed before or as it seemed later. If a man would be a bravo about town it might easily happen that he would have to shoot or be shot. Ordinary peace-loving citizens lived in an atmosphere of mutual courtesy, in greater safety than in most cities, for holdups and burglaries were absolutely nonexistent. One could leave his house with doors unlocked for months, certain that no one would enter and disturb his possessions.

I felt I had wasted my money in "leasing" a gun. But one day when I was sweltering in the room that temporarily housed my books, trying to get through a tough German work, Stammler's *Wirtschaft und Recht,* Uncle Ned, a charming old Negro employed as mortar mixer at Keasbey's place, came bowing in, declaring he had come to dust my books. I told him I didn't want them dusted; they would soon be dusty again.

"Lor', Doctah, ain't good foh books to be dusty. You got a gun, Doctah? I lika see it."

I showed him the pistol.

"Fine pistol. But it ain't loaded. Now what's the use of a gun that ain't loaded? Got any cartridges?"

I showed him my box of cartridges. He took them and lovingly pushed cartridges home in the six chambers.

Uncle Ned bustled around dusting my books, sweeping my floors, straightening out my kitchenware, until I became uneasy about his absence from his job.

"Uncle Ned," I said, "how can Doctor Keasbey get along without you to mix mortar?"

"They don't have to plaster this evenin' " (evening was all the day after one). "They's two bad boys hangin' round an' I don't want to see 'em."

I learned later, Uncle Ned had been in a drunken row and had killed a man. His white patron went to the police authorities, who were looking for Uncle Ned, and said, "Look here. If three niggers—or three white men—get drunk and get into an argument, one of 'em is like to get shot. Which one? The unlucky one. You going to arrest the lucky one? What's the use? I've known Uncle Ned all my life, and he's a mighty good nigger."

Uncle Ned wasn't arrested. But he had "two bad boys" looking for him—brothers of the man he had killed. Hence his insistence on dusting my books and his care to load my pistol, in case the "bad boys" came over to my house.

Professor Keasbey had to go to Nova Scotia to look after a summer inn he was operating and asked me to take charge of his place and settle any difficulties that might come up. It was a light duty, for the place was well organized, manned by two white boys and two Negroes. Of the Negroes, Wesley was a sad-faced man downtrodden by Lily, his wife—"a mighty mean woman," he said, "but not so mean as she was before she got religion"; Louis was about the handsomest man I had ever seen. He was six feet two with shoulders near a yard wide, narrow hips, long narrow feet on which he carried himself with the silent grace of a fine dancer. His color was a beautiful mahogany with copper overtones, his eyes great agates, his nose strong and slightly aquiline, his lips just thick enough to premise generosity. And he was as true and faithful and intelligent as he was handsome.

The two white boys, Henry and Goetz, had been printers in Milwaukee. They were Socialists, and since they could find no places in the Austin press, they came to Keasbey, who was generally known to be a Socialist, asking for jobs on his "ranch." Keasbey took them on although he didn't need them.

One day Keasbey's little daughter Cornelia came running to my house, all out of breath.

"Doctor Johnson, come right over. There's trouble between the white boys and the Negroes. They're threatening each other with knives and axes. Get your pistol."

They were indeed threatening each other. The white boys were displaying their new acquisitions, murderous bowie knives. Louis had an ax, and Wesley, behind him, a pitchfork.

"What's the matter here?" I demanded, making show of inspecting the pistol in my hand.

"Doctor Johnson," said Louis, "we ain't done nothin'. We been doin' our wohk de way Professoh Keasbey tole us to do it. Dese white boys keep pickin' on us, an' now dey want to knife us. If dey don' let us alone I sure will kill dem. I know I'll buhn, but I sure will kill dem."

"Goetz!" I said. "What have you got to say?"

"We won't work with no damn niggers."

"Fine Socialists you are! You don't have to. You're fired."

"But Professor Keasbey hired us."

"And left full authority to me. You're fired. March yourselves down to the shanty and pack your suitcases. And make it snappy."

"Don't be pointing that thing at me. It might go off."

"It's likely to go off. March!"

They marched. I ordered the Negroes back to the barn and followed the white boys. I wasn't at all happy. This melodramatic business of threatening men with a pistol didn't comport with my picture of myself.

What if I had had to shoot? I'd have shot at the boys' feet. That would have been sufficient to make Milwaukee Socialists dance. But if I had had to threaten Louis my gun wasn't big enough.

The boys were in the shanty, packing their suitcases. Goetz came to the door. "Say, Doctor, if we promise to behave and quit ragging the niggers, can we stay?"

"No. I don't want to see Socialists that act like you anywhere around."

"We did act like damn fools, and we'll say that to the niggers. By God, we'll apologize."

"All right." I pocketed my pistol and we went down to the barn. Louis and Wesley watched us coming, from the door.

"Louis," I said, "Henry and Goetz have come down to apologize. If you say so, they can stay."

Louis drew himself up to more than his six feet two and looked down on us.

"Louis," said Goetz, "we've been acting like damn fools. We're sorry. We promise not to do it again."

Louis's fine eyes rolled about for a moment. He swallowed hard. "Okay," he said finally.

"And now you boys shake hands," I commanded.

Louis stepped back. "I don' haf to shake hands with no white man."

"But you'll shake hands with me."

Louis extended his mighty hand with a beautiful dark smile. The episode was closed. I returned to my cottage and thrust the pistol as far back in a drawer as it would go. Pistols didn't go with my temperament.

Louis did not remain long at the Keasbeys'. I've often wondered what became of him. He was ten times as impressive, personally, as Paul Robeson, and when his song burst forth, it was of the melodiousness and volume of a pipe organ. White, he could not have missed fame. But he was a Negro, and in Texas.

In the long summer I tried to get a clear view of the Texan attitude toward the Negro. It was, of course, intensely racialist, but it did not follow precisely the patterns Northerners have invented for the South.

I was having lunch with a cotton broker and prepared to leave a tip for the waiter.

"Don't do that," said the broker. "You'd hurt him. He looks after you well because he likes you. What you got to do is, show him you like him. And if he serves you often, remember him at Christmas. What you Northerners don't realize, a nigger is by nature a gentleman. He's got finer feelings than you or me. And a finer sense of people. If you want to know what a man is, ask his niggers. They can tell you, exactly."

Another friend lectured me a bit. "You Northerners have got the Negro problem all wrong. You think the Negro is an inferior race and it won't hurt to educate them. By God, the Negro ain't inferior. Educate him, and he'll take this damn country."

It was twenty years in the penitentiary for marrying a Negro woman, but the law had nothing at all to say about mating with a woman of Negro blood, loving her faithfully, bringing up children by her. Of course there was social ostracism, but the Texas he-man doesn't care much about that.

A curious case occupied much space in the newspapers at the time. A Texan had married a beautiful blond girl and lived happily with her until some busybody, browsing around in birth records, found that the girl, unknown to herself, had the eighth of Negro blood that makes one a Negro; beyond one-eighth, Negro blood doesn't count. The popular misconception holds that eighth-bloods are physiologically incapable of begetting or conceiving children.

Unwittingly the Texan had committed a crime and was due for twenty years in the penitentiary. But a group of good citizens, including the judge who would have had to condemn him, got up a generous purse to buy out his small business and give him a start in another state where he could live in safety with his beautiful wife and his true Cupid of a sixteenth-blood baby.

I decided that it was not for me to judge of the institutions of the great State of Texas or of its brave, courteous, generous, and humane people.

There were a few Socialists in Austin, who were disposed to forgive me my bourgeois ideas because I was a staunch advocate of freedom of thought and speech and defended trade unionism whenever I got a chance. I had many a friendly argument with the Socialist group.

One evening when I was sitting idly under one of my oaks in the moonlight a young Socialist I had met appeared at my gate with a little old woman, who came up with quick short steps through the long grass.

"Doctor," said the Socialist, "this is Mother Jones, on her way to the strike in the cypress lumbering field. She wanted to talk with you." He shook hands and left us.

"Young man," said Mother Jones, "you may have heard of me."

"Sure," I said. "You are the red flag of labor troubles. I read of a strike in Colorado or Montana or Washington that is going along peacefully, then Mother Jones appears, and violence breaks out."

"That ain't right," she said gently. "I'm always against violence. For why? The bosses have the clubs; the boys have only their thin skulls. I always say to the boys, 'No guns, boys; no explosives. For why? The bosses have all the explosives they can use and the Army. You use explosives once, they'll use them ten times and lay it to you, and the Army will knock you in the head.' "

She went on to tell incident after incident of labor troubles in the Western mining and lumber camps, of judicial murders, of bull pens, deportations. In a recent strike the bosses had seized her, put her on a train, and dumped her off in the desert, a hundred miles from a drop of water. She walked the tracks, determined not to get off for a train. A freight came along and tried to whistle her off the track. She wouldn't go, and the train stopped and picked her up and gave her the water for which she was near perishing.

"Speaking of water, comrade," she said, "you don't happen to have a drop of whisky in the house?"

I fetched a pint and a pitcher of cold water.

"Make it thin, comrade," she said. I did, for it had to last, as she gave no indication of leaving me. Her narratives ran on, while the great white moon raced westward. What a contribution to the romance of labor history, I thought, if it could be recorded!

She told me all about the lumbering camps she was about to visit, of virtual slave labor in the cypress swamps, men working in water and mud up to their knees, hard-shelled little alligators scraping against their rubber boots, the mud full of bloodsuckers that managed to get under a man's pants, the air thick with mosquitoes and stinging flies and wasps, the food in camp moldy bread and maggoty meat, and nothing for the men to live for, nothing except rotgut whisky to make sleep possible in spite of itching all over the body. The whisky was supplied compulsorily by the boss in quantity more than sufficient to eat up the margin of wages and put the worker in debt, subject to arrest if he tried to leave the job.

"Have you the time on you, comrade?"

"Sure. It's about four o'clock. It will soon be daylight."

"My train goes at five. I got to leave you. Say, comrade, have you a spare five dollars on you? I've got my ticket but nary a cent for grub and a drop to drink."

"Sure," I said. I produced the bill.

"God bless you, comrade. I got to go. It's most an hour's walk."

"I'll go with you," I said.

"No, comrade. It ain't safe. The bosses' spies know I'm here—I seemed to see something move behind that oak over there. They can't shoot an old woman, but they might shoot her accidentally, shooting at a man in the moonlight. Good-by—I'll pray to God for you, comrade."

The papers reported, two days later, that Mother Jones had appeared at the strike scene; violence had broken out; a striker had been killed and several wounded; but the strike was by way of being settled, with concessions to labor that would have been granted—so it was asserted—without a strike.

Near the end of the summer David Houston, who had accepted the presidency of Washington University in St. Louis, came down to wind up his Austin affairs. I had opportunity to tax him on his fickleness.

"I accepted the Texas appointment on the premise of your presidency, moved by your eloquent account of the glories and promise of the State of Texas."

"As I see it," Houston said, "there are two States of Texas; one is the North and West, where everybody is making money hand over fist and thinks of nothing else; the other, East Texas, land of malaria and hookworm, which saps everything out of a man but his ability to talk. The fruit of talk is politics; Texas politics is East Texas. In the last analysis Texas is governed by hookworm and malaria; and there's no hope for the university."

Dr. Houston's successor was Sidney E. Mezes, a native Californian of Spanish descent, a philosopher whose doctrines were Aristotelianism filtered through the subtlety of the Spanish mind, who met your every point or argument with, "We must distinguish." He had married one of two sisters endowed with super Texas charm; the other sister was married to Colonel Edward M. House, a man distinguished at that time as the only Texan who knew his way around in national politics. When I met this modest, soft-voiced gentleman I had no idea that he had in him the power of key figure in national and international affairs—of king maker.

I had three courses, a graduate seminar, a general course in economics for undergraduates, and a combined economics and political science course for a special group of law students known as the Longhorns.

My graduate seminar had only three students, but they were all well equipped; and one of them, a young instructor in history, was the best student I ever had, Walton Hamilton, later to win national acclaim as economist, political scientist, jurist, and expert in government departments. My general course had about fifty young men and a dozen young women. They were extremely respectful to the teacher, so respectful that my attempts to conduct the course by classroom discussion were a failure. No one would venture to dispute even the most glaring paradox. I went over to the lecture method, which worked perfectly well if I managed to make the lectures interesting. I worked very hard on that. I had to, for in the warm afternoons of the Texas autumn, if the professor dropped into droning of obvious ideas, the class dropped into slumber.

The Longhorns were reputed to be a serious problem for the instructor. They were from the cow country; many of them had been cowboys, and some still walked with the cowboy straddle. They were a humorous lot and liked to have a little fun with the instructor. From the first I liked them.

Believing that the cow business had seen its best days, these young men were casting about for a new career; and having seen lawyers collecting large fees for just a bit of paper work and talk, they meant to make lawyers of themselves. As they had no high-school records, the university had set up a special law course for them, with the law enriched by one course in English and another in so-called political science, my course. The English professor, a Harvard man, was having a bad time with them, but to me they were a lot of fun.

They were a belated remnant of the old American expansionist, filibustering type and looked forward confidently to seizure by the United States of Mexico down to Torreón, for Mexico was in the throes of revolution. A group of them invited me to join them in a filibustering expedition to seize a wonderful valley. It had a sparse population we could easily chase out, and only two narrow entrances, at either of which six men with a machine gun could hold off the whole Mexican army. I demurred: what would I be worth as military material? It made no difference; they said I could set up a tent and teach them philosophy while they were waiting for the Mexican Army to attack them.

Some of my academic friends, when they heard I was bent on going to Texas, had warned me that I was bidding adieu to academic liberty. I would have to think as the Texans think, or keep my thoughts altogether to myself. There had indeed been a time when the University of Texas was just a football of politics and every ignoramus was privileged to give it a sound kick. For example, the geologist had to reconcile the findings of his science with the chronology of Genesis. He had to get the trilobites and the dinosaurs and the eohippus within the six thousand years since Creation according to Moses. The geologist had only one loophole for escape. He could argue that since God was omnipotent He could develop and extinguish the dinosaurs, lay down stratified rock to the depth of six miles, in a split second of time.

By my time the university had come to be controlled by a Board of Regents consisting of true Texas gentlemen—political reactionaries, perhaps, from my point of view, but men who had the antique American spirit of liberty. The disastrous systems of thought control that have grown up as a result of two World Wars lay far in the future. The regents and the president of the university would rather have seen the institution closed down than endure the suppression of any opinion advanced by honest scholarship. As a political scientist I could argue for socialism if I chose, revolutionary socialism, for did not Thomas Jefferson argue that it might be well for us to have a revolution every twenty years?

I am not sure that the freedom of gun play was without bearing on the Texas spirit of liberty. Certainly the framers of the Constitution saw in arms-bearing a guaranty of the liberty of the citizen: the Constitution guarantees to the citizen, among other rights, the right to bear arms. We have quibbled that right away by excluding "concealed" weapons from the category of legitimate arms. No pistols; but you still have a right to walk down Broadway with a whole arsenal of rifles and shotguns on your shoulders.

Outside of the university, to be sure, Texas could be oppressive, especially in matters of religion.

One day an emaciated, neurotic-faced man in Civil War long coat appeared in my classroom. He was evidently somebody, for the class kept eying him all through my lecture. At its close he rose and asked in a sepulchral voice, "Doctor Johnson, do you believe in the doctrine of evolution?"

"What do you mean by the doctrine of evolution?"

"That we are descended from monkeys."

"No," I said, "I do not believe we are descended from monkeys. The monkey, especially the American monkey, is a highly organized animal. Except in point of brain, it is more highly organized than man. There is no precedent for the development of the less highly organized animal out of the more highly organized."

The questioner looked puzzled, shook his head, and departed. A dozen students came up to my desk.

"Do you know who that old fellow is? K. Lamity."

"And who is K. Lamity?"

"He's the editor of K. Lamity's *Harpoon*. Magazine with the biggest circulation in the South—four hundred thousand. He's always hammering at atheism and nigger-loving. He came to make trouble for you, and we were all ready to throw him out."

Toward the end of the year one of the Longhorns came to my office.

"I'm in a peck of trouble, Doctor Johnson. I planned, soon as I got my degree, I'd go out to Amarillo, where a friend of mine's got a law office and more work than he can do. He'd make me junior partner. And as soon as I got established I was going to marry the sweetest girl there ever was. Here's her picture, Doctor."

The photograph did indeed present a face of wonderful loveliness.

"But now they won't let me have my degree. You see, Doctor, I was out three weeks with flu. When I came back to the English class the professor was handing out some papers. I asked, 'Professor, what are those papers?' 'Those are the essays I assigned three weeks ago; I haven't found yours.' 'But, Professor, I been sick; this is the first I heard of those essays.' 'That's very well to say,' the professor said.

"That hurt me. 'Professor,' I said, 'are you sayin' I'm lyin'?' 'Draw your own conclusions,' said the professor. Well, what could I do? I drawed my gun and said, 'Professor, you take that back.' He took it back but reported me, and now they won't let me have my degree. Don't you think you might be able to help me?"

"I'll try," I said. "But if the case has gone to Dean Battle there isn't much hope."

I went to the English professor, who was at first very cold to my suggestion that he join me in a plea to Battle, but finally he yielded. But Battle was obdurate. It was time, he said, to put a stop to students' toting guns and pulling them on professors.

I've never heard what happened to the poor victim of this reform. But I don't think his friend in Amarillo or the sweetest girl there ever was could have turned him down on a mere technicality.

For the first term of my second year I was on leave to give courses in the fall quarter at the University of Chicago. I had to find a substitute to carry my courses, and I thought I had a very satisfactory one, Doeson, I'll call him, for he may still have relatives living. I had come to know him in New York. The University of Texas needed courses in commerce, and I thought a temporary appointment would enable Doeson, whose field was commerce, to edge in. I got together a lot of my best friends among the students and pledged them to do everything to help Doeson adjust to local conditions.

In Chicago I was glancing through the headlines of the *Tribune* and struck one that arrested my attention: "Texas Students Run a Professor off the Campus." My eyes flitted through the item. My man Doeson! Apparently he had not only been run off the campus but had left Austin as if the devil were after him.

When I got back to Austin a group of twenty-five or thirty of my students turned out to meet me. After shaking hands all around and exchanging terms of affection I asked, "But what did you do to my friend Doeson?"

"Hell of a friend! He never gave a lecture he didn't try to pull you to pieces. Ridiculed you for ideas he said you had but we never heard of. Said you were a Socialist in disguise. Finally we said, 'Professor, we've heard all the attacks on Doctor Johnson we're going to hear. You are going to get off this campus in a mighty big hurry and never come back.'"

I kept a solemn face, but laughter was bubbling within me. Doeson had set out in good faith to push me off the nest and had enjoyed an experience no Northern professor had ever had, of being chased off the campus by his students.

"But didn't Doeson appeal to President Mezes?"

"What appeal?" one of the boys asked in astonishment. "He had to git, skedaddle, vamoose, and he saw it."

"Oh yes, you boys all had guns."

"No, Professor, not half of us toted guns. But that skunk would never have given us a chance to use them."

Battle's reform hadn't gone very deep.

As a friend of Keasbey and President Mezes I was elected to the Town and Gown Club, an organization manned half by twelve professors, half by twelve lawyers and businessmen. We met every month, sometimes with additional meetings when distinguished guests were in town, like David Houston, Colonel House, Franklin K. Lane, who was a California friend of Mezes, Albert S. Burleson, our congressman. We discussed everything under the sun, from the origin of the Aztecs to non-Euclidean mathematics.

Years after I left Texas a profound change came over the Town and Gown Club. David Houston, Thomas W. Gregory, Franklin K. Lane, and Albert Burleson were all translated into Wilson's Cabinet. Mezes was offered the Commissionership of Education but preferred the presidency of City College in New York. Robert L. Batts was put in charge of the prosecution of the New Haven Railroad. And Colonel House, who had made Wilson president, served as a kind of top Cabinet member at home and abroad.

Washington had reached into the Town and Gown, skimming off practically all the layman cream, leaving the academic skim milk to sour.

I must bid farewell to Texas, although I could write on about the state indefinitely. During my two years there I wrote little but read much. I learned much from my colleagues. From Porter I became familiar with Poincaré and non-Euclidean mathematics, with its profound reach into the constitution of the universe. From Fay I learned to appreciate better the meaning of rhythm in Latin oratory. Through Battle I came nearer than I had ever been to the spirit of Sophocles. There was hardly a professor I knew who did not supply a bit of honey for the intellectual comb I was trying to fill.

But the colleague who meant most to me was Stark Young, then an instructor in poetry. At first we seemed to have little in common except a passionate love of Botticelli. Soon we found we had a world in common. Many of my happiest hours were spent in conversations with Stark; the happiest of all, in his delightful cottage, with his serene and beautiful sister, not destined, alas, to live long. Stark remains to this day a friend I deeply cherish, my colleague in the great, unorganized university of America and the world, where I claim a modest place as an accepted instructor.

TWENTY-ONE

The University of Chicago

FOR a Columbia man to receive even a temporary appointment in the Chicago economics department was an event without precedent. J. Laurence Laughlin, who had headed the department from its beginning, was at feud with Columbia and, indeed, with most of the Eastern institutions. Alone among important economists, he had refused to join the leaders of the profession in launching the American Economic Association in 1886 and held himself aloof from the organization throughout his career. The association was infected, he asserted, with *Kathedersozialismus*—socialism of the chair—and was supporting even more socialistic tendencies. Professor Seligman, with his coquetting with organized labor and his advocacy of an income tax; Richard T. Ely, with his sympathetic exposition of French and German socialism; Henry C. Adams, serving as statistician of the Interstate Commerce Commission (long an organization without power) and working tirelessly for real control of railway rates—they were in Laughlin's eyes men who were sapping away the foundations of the American republic. He condemned Frank W. Taussig too, for what is called nowadays "guilt by association," for Taussig lived on terms of friendship with the chief villains.

Thorstein Veblen, who was a naked revolutionary but whose style, to borrow a phrase of Colby's, "was his sufficient fig leaf," had long held a position under Laughlin, but two years before I came to Chicago he had been forced out. Herbert J. Davenport, a bold fellow of Scotch descent, with style formed on Carlyle, could not stand the atmosphere of the department and left shortly after. There were two members of the department who had served for years, John Cummins and William Hill, but oppression had driven them to twilight habits; one rarely caught a glimpse of them. The working department consisted of Laughlin and a group of young associate professors, Leon Marshall, Robert Hoxie, Chester Wright, and James Field, all ardent teachers and promising scholars. Except for Hoxie, I had not known these men personally, but the general university opinion was that now at last the Chicago department was coming to life. I welcomed the opportunity to join it for a term, somewhat puzzled that it came my way, in spite of Laughlin's hatred of Seligman's students. The explanation was simple. Laughlin was away on a long official and academic junket in Latin America. Leon Marshall was acting head and, being eupeptic and humorous, decided to surprise the old chief by presenting me, on his return, as a temporary member of the department.

Laughlin was a gentleman of the old school—the only school of real gentlemen—and though he must have swallowed hard when first he heard of my presence he greeted me with distinguished courtesy. His tolerance of me soon developed into friendship, and long before the term was over he invited me to become a permanent member of the department.

On my part I came to have a warm affection for Laughlin. Like my Nebraska chief, Langworthy Taylor, Laughlin had had neuroses gnawing at his vitals through all his adult life; but, unlike Taylor, who disciplined himself according to William James, Laughlin had only the discipline that makes the gentleman—a fine thing in maintaining consistency of demeanor but impotent to still internal anguish. Laughlin could not distinguish between his autonomous feelings of distress and his judgment of the hopeless confusion of the external world.

One day when he was feeling despair more keenly than usual he told me of the wife of his youth, beautiful, exquisite, who was carried off by death when still very young. He all but perished for sorrow. But now, when he thought of all the cruelties, injustices, treacheries that fall to one's lot if one lives in this horrible world, he saw that hers was the better lot, to die while the morning illusions of life were still dewy and sunlit.

I do not nowadays often encounter such hopeless neurotics as freely besprinkled the academic landscape fifty years ago. Perhaps it is because the modern scholar lives under the menace of the psychiatrist, prepared to take the neurosis out of the live soul by means of the painful psychological knife and forceps. A wise scholar takes himself in hand while the neuroses are still small. Or perhaps it is because scholarly diet has improved in vitamin content. Scholars ate abominably fifty years ago.

It was hard for me to make up my mind to leave Texas for Chicago. The house I had built had proved "functional," to use a term that came later into vogue. Of nights the wealth of windows filled the house with the cool air from the Gulf breeze; with the windows closed in the morning, the house could resist the midday heat for hours. I meant to set up a gate with tall posts of white stone and run a white stone wall along my five hundred feet of highway front. I had plans for starting an orchard and for planting edible grapes to supplement my arbor of mustang grapes, a native type that had evolved a skin tough enough to withstand the sharp bills of the pestilential mocking birds, which claimed prescriptive right over all fruits and threatened to put out my eyes when I intruded upon my own fig tree.

I liked my home and I liked Texas. But, as the saying runs, Texas is heaven for men and horses and hell for women and children. Men and horses, living mainly in the sun and developing proper perspiration control, suffer hardly at all from the heat. The same is true of the passionate horsewomen. But the health of the housekeeping woman languishes in the heat, and the health of little children gives the parents much concern. The most popular physician of the city advised mothers to keep breast-feeding going for three years if they wished their babies to remain in lusty health. Industry and advertising had not supplied the wealth of prepared baby foods now readily available.

As far as we could see, if we continued to live in Texas my family would have to go North every May to return in October. That was not a cheerful prospect. And so, after much hesitation and with many regrets, I accepted Laughlin's invitation to join the Chicago faculty the next academic year. We had to return to Texas for the winter and spring terms of 1909–1910. There were now four of us, for my wife had given birth to a boy, huge of head and chest, with strong long limbs and an air of determination he has never lost, our son Alden.

Chicago was shivering under a blizzard when we boarded the train for Austin. The next day we had passed out of the range of the blizzard and could look out on brown fields and pasture lands, touched here and there by resistant residues of snowdrifts. Then we penetrated the South, with pastures green and roses blooming around the railway stations. Finally we left the train at Austin, stepping out into the most delightful spring weather under a sky most heavenly blue. It was a painful thought that we should never again experience the joys of Texas winter.

In the Texas of those days it was nearly impossible to sell real estate. In any other state I could have sold my house, taking a little cash and the rest of the value in a mortgage. Under Texas homestead institutions a mortgage was worthless. You could sell a house only for cash, and there was very little cash in Texas. But you could exchange one piece of real estate for another. And as Texans were restless people there was an immense business of real-estate swapping going on. I had several opportunities to exchange my house for other property. One was for a plantation a dozen miles from Austin, with fields that were said to yield a bale of cotton to the acre. It had pasturage enough for a herd of forty or fifty cattle and immense areas of huge prickly pear cactuses. These were declared to be an asset, for in time of drought, when forage ran short, you chopped down the cactus with a machete and held it over a fire to singe off the prickles. Then the cows could eat it.

I didn't bite.

Then a man came down from Missouri to take over a lumber yard inherited from his brother. He liked my house and proposed to trade for it a farm he owned in central Missouri. The proposal looked worth considering. I made a trip to Missouri.

The farm lay on the first prairie level above the Missouri bottom and on the slope running down to the bottom land, of which the farm had a few acres in brambles flattened down by the rubbish left in the last Missouri flood. The slope was much dissected and covered with woods of every kind of tree I had ever seen, North or South, a fair proportion of it merchantable oak and cedar. About half the land, two hundred acres, was cultivated, or had been cultivated. A hundred years of slipshod tillage had pretty completely exhausted the fertility, but the soil was of good texture and would respond fruitfully to modern farm practices. There were two houses, one old and the other new, both very satisfactory as farmhouses go, and a huge broken-backed barn that could be set straight with beams from the wood.

I liked the place and swapped my house for it. The farm represented a sheet to windward if ever a storm of academic persecution should blow up. In the first decade of the century there was very little persecution of professors on grounds of opinion, and most scholars labored under the pleasant delusion that the evil phase of history in which a professor might be fired for teaching free trade or bimetallism was closed forever and that academic liberty was now a settled institution. I was skeptical. My reading of American social history had proved to me that persecution for opinion lies deep in the mores of America. It may slumber for a time, but on the first occasion it leaps into savage life.

Originally the habit of persecution grew out of the warring of religious sects. What was at stake in Colonial times was men's souls. To put out of the way or to imprison men who taught heresy, or even listened to the teaching of heresy, was a Christian duty. The mechanism of persecution, perfected for religious purposes, could as well serve social, economic, political purposes, as in the hunting down of Tories, of Abolitionists, of Copperheads, of pro-Germans, pro-Russians.

A small group of intelligent leaders, steeped in the humanism of the Enlightenment, gave us a Constitution with a Bill of Rights designed to insure the liberty of the citizen and protect him against persecution of opinion, religious, social, political. We have always had champions of liberty, and we have had courts, usually impartial, to defend our rights. But the veneer of liberalism is still very thin over the solid oak of persecuting orthodoxy. A live force like persecutionism can always find ways to go around the law to its oppressive ends.

Economics, in times of political stress, is on the firing line. It did not lie in my temperament to seek martyrdom; but I was born free and was determined to live out my life as a free man. I would use whatever mental power I had to arrive at opinions sound and reasonable and just. Once I had established such opinions, no force could make me retract them. Thus I might well find myself an object of persecution. If worst came to worst and my academic career became untenable, I could retire to my farm, where I might have to live laboriously, but as a free man.

I kept hold of the farm through most of my active career, although it never proved to be a financial asset. I was an absentee landlord, dependent on the local variety of tenants to work the farm, and the tenants were of the border-state variety, who eat up what they produce and leave it to the landlord to pay the taxes.

Rent, according to Ricardo, is the payment for the use of the original and indestructible properties of the soil. It isn't. It is the return a landowner gets out of the acquired and destructible properties of the tenant population.

In June of 1910 my wife and I found a pleasant little house in Chicago not far from the university and from Jackson Park, and we planned on long walks with our little children through the park and along Lake Michigan, usually smooth and blue but occasionally whipped up by the wind and liquidly far-sounding. But our summer plans were disrupted when I received a telegram from E. Dana Durand, the new Director of the Census, inviting me to join a group of economists he was assembling in Washington to overhaul the traditional Census schedules and prepare for a Census that would tell the truth about American economic conditions. I took the invitation for a command, and, besides, I welcomed the chance to see the inside of one section of the Washington bureaucracy.

I found an interesting group of economists, among them Thomas Nixon Carver, Professor Taussig's wonder child of theory; George F. Warren, agricultural economist of Cornell, chief academic advocate through the years of the hated McNary-Haugen heresy, germ of our present agricultural policy under which we live well and pay well for it. A very active member was Earl Dean Howard, who later worked with Joseph Schaffner of Hart, Schaffner and Marx to set up a plan of industrial relations under which subsequently Sidney Hillman and the Amalgamated Clothing Workers waxed great and powerful enough to destroy the sweatshop which had disgraced America.

We worked hard and drew up a set of schedules which really meant something. They were handled with scorn by the permanent Census staff, who regarded any proposed change as of the devil. Their scorn proved to be justified. When Durand took our schedules to a meeting of the National Association of Manufacturers they were denounced as subversive. Why, if business answered the questions on our proposed schedules, anyone could tell pretty certainly where business stood, knowledge that would prove a death knell to American free enterprise! The NAM committee helped Durand revise our revision of the schedules. What he brought back were practically the old schedules we started with.

Some of our group inveighed against the weakness of Durand, unjustly; for it wasn't Durand's weakness but the weakness of the legal position of the Census. There is warrant in the Constitution for a Census of Population, the necessary basis for apportioning represensation in Congress. The Constitution makers never contemplated inquiries as to how much Bessemer, how much open-hearth steel we make; how many calves see the light in a Census year, how many eggs our national hens lay. Such inquiries make up the staple employment for the thousands of worthy Census employees. And there was enough strict constructionism in those days to warn the Census officials against raising questions in a way to bring the courts down on their heads. They could ask any questions they pleased of a little man; if he refused to answer they could have him fined. But if a big man refused to answer, they bowed themselves out and made up his answers themselves, honestly entering them in red ink.

I came away from Washington somewhat disillusioned, but the experience had been highly educational. Every good citizen should come to know the ways of the capital of this country if he gets a chance.

Teaching in Chicago I found very stimulating. The students were as a rule much older than those I had taught in Columbia. They were also much more earnest, but abstractions were more puzzling to them. I did not encounter the elementary students, for these were divided up into small sections to be quizzed by the other younger men in the department. Under the chairmanship of Leon Marshall the instructors met every afternoon and often in the evenings, working out a syllabus to serve as a common text for all the classes. I was exempt from this kind of corvée service and greatly appreciated my liberty.

Of all the faculty I most enjoyed Robert Hoxie. He specialized in labor problems and had the enterprise to bring before his class all types of labor leaders, to state their aims and unfold their hopes. He had in unexampled degree the art to bring even the most stubborn-tongued labor leader to an adequate expression of his views.

Hoxie was square built and well poised, of ruddy complexion and bright eyes, well equipped with wit and humor, and, you'd have said, here, anyway, was a scholar well adjusted to life. But the fact was he was subject to terrible nervous crises. He imputed his condition to an attack of poliomyelitis in his childhood, which, while it did not cripple his limbs, impaired permanently his nervous structure. I questioned the validity of his explanation until I came to know him.

He was my good friend, and we saw a lot of each other. Whenever he could get free from his office he'd come to mine and insist that we go for a walk, even if the cold wind was blowing at forty miles an hour. However busy I was I would comply, for if I did not he would fall into a lamentable fit of depression, asserting that I no longer found him interesting.

When he was scheduled for a seminar paper I had a choice of unattractive alternatives. If I did not attend, he put this down as my judgment that he had nothing to say. If I attended, he felt sure that I detected all the points where the author of a seminar paper sidesteps difficulties.

Matters were simpler when we were alone together, on our walks or over the beer at the White City, where we could argue to the accompaniment of an orchestra playing with great éclat the scores of *Traviata* or *Aïda*. So far as I could, I kept away from contentious economic subjects.

One subject of contention would, however, inevitably intrude: Veblen. Hoxie loved Veblen with a love that passeth understanding. I admired Veblen's genius, but Veblen and I could never get nearer each other than arm's length. He regarded me as a plodding Dane; I regarded him as a romantic Norwegian. Whenever we found ourselves together in company we spoiled each other's style. On occasion friends would urge me to remain away from a Veblen party, for Veblen never made himself interesting when I was around.

I considered Veblen good reading for the scholar who knew how to discriminate, but a singularly dangerous guide for anyone who followed him blindly. I asserted that Veblen's *Theory of the Leisure Class* was really a satirical essay, with literary potency and scientific intent closely parallel to Carlyle's *Sartor Resartus*. Both authors counted on the pleasure a reader gets out of judiciously worded insults to himself. Both liked to make use of the principle that two half-truths make a whole truth.

Such observations filled Hoxie with indignation, but pleasant indignation, for they proved to him that I fell far short of him in the understanding of the man he considered the greatest economist of all time. Hoxie boasted that his whole system of thought came from Veblen. It was Veblen who had taught him that all ideas of reconciling the interests of labor and the employer were a fantastic delusion. For the minds of labor and of the employer were built out of completely different philosophic elements. The philosophy the worker had hammered into him by his job ran in terms of cause and effect—the efficient cause. The employer thought in terms of values, purposes, final causes. As well try to mate a sheep with a tunny fish as try to bring efficient cause and final cause to an agreement.

I argued that this contrast was just a hocus-pocus. The employer, in considering the properties of a machine he is tempted to buy, or in considering how to cut the waste of material, is thinking in terms of cause and effect. The worker in demanding an enlarged take-home is thinking in terms of values.

I refused to concede that there are impermeable septa between the thinking of any two classes, indeed, between any two individuals. Business conceptions, labor conceptions, wander afield. Does one not encounter the divine who calculates on the "unit cost of saving souls"?

Years later Hoxie visited New York and asked me to come to his hotel for the evening. He was frightening in his appearance.

"Johnson," he said, "I'm finished. I can see now, all my work has been bunk. All my writing, every lecture I have ever given, has been bunk."

"What in heaven's name has happened to you, Hoxie?"

"I've come to see through Veblen. You partly saw through him, but not the way I do."

In an evening that extended until four in the morning—for I did not dare to leave him—Hoxie unfolded the rather inconsequential course of his deconversion from Veblen. They had disagreed on a personal matter and Veblen had treated Hoxie rudely. But Hoxie had always known that Veblen could glory in rudeness.

Such an incident could have been effective only as a catalyst. Hoxie had been working for months with Frey, a distinguished labor leader, on a book, *Industrial Management and Labor*. Undoubtedly he had been unconsciously accumulating cases that exhibited the shortcomings of Veblen's theories.

"I got to thinking," Hoxie said, "how could a man be so great a scientist and such a damn fool? And the more I thought, the more the idea rode my mind: how great a scientist is he? Johnson thought his science was phony."

"No," I said, "I never thought that. I thought you had to watch him. His equations didn't solve, and he patched them up by rhetorical 'by and large,' 'for the most part.' Almost all economists do something of the kind sometimes."

"Veblen knew his equations didn't solve, but he used them just the same. And his class dope; he pretended it was psychology. It was pure abstractions; no, not pure, but with a purpose."

"We're all purposive, Hoxie."

"I wouldn't care if it was just the matter of my finding out a phony I had taken for okay. But Veblen has been the premise of all my work. My work is all rotten with Veblenism."

"Hoxie, I've read about everything you ever wrote. Your work stands on its own feet. Sometimes you're wrong—not often."

"Johnson, you know the basis of my labor theory. Two philosophies, the employer's and the laborer's. The first based on the final cause, the other on the efficient cause. You called that bunk the first time we met, when we were both on the American Economic Association program."

"It is bunk," I agreed. "But all that enormous amount of concrete investigation you have done is quite independent of any such premise. It stands."

"No, it doesn't. It's all diseased, from that premise."

I argued with Hoxie for eight hours at a stretch. Our positions were reversed, Hoxie was attacking Veblen, I was defending him. I marshaled as many telling and meaningful passages as I held in my memory, from Veblen's *Theory of Business Enterprise, Imperial Germany, The Engineers and the Price System,* even from Veblen's most sardonic and least sincere book, *The Higher Learning.* Finally Hoxie seemed to be calmed down enough, or wearied enough, for sleep. I left him, promising to visit him in Chicago and renew the discussion.

But before I could get around to a Chicago trip Hoxie killed himself.

The Chicago winter of 1910–11 was bleak, cold, and dark. Unusually disagreeable it was, according to older Chicagoans. It was hard on all my family. Down to our baby son, we all suffered cold after cold. But what most distressed Edith and me was the grim darkness. Nebraska born, we were creatures of the sun. Nebraska might have terrible blizzards, but once the wind dropped the sun shone gloriously upon the waste of glistening snowdrifts. In the morning the sun often rose accompanied by two "sun dogs," concentrations of light brilliant as the sun itself, at distances of 23½ degrees on the horizon.

In the early spring David Starr Jordan, president of Stanford University, telegraphed me that he would be at the Palmer House four days later and would like me to join him at lunch. I had never met him, but I was deeply interested in his writings on the folly and wastefulness of war. I was associated with groups of men and women who were trying to rouse public opinion to support a serious movement for world organization for peace. In 1906, when I had first attached myself to the peace movement, it was already clear that a great European war was in the making. In my judgment the disaster would break upon the world in 1913. I was wrong by one year.

I supposed David Starr Jordan meant to invite me to join some committee working for peace. But as soon as we had shaken hands he said, "I have come to invite you to accept the headship of the economics department at Stanford. As you may know, at Stanford a department head has full powers, under the president and board. He may fire, demote, or move around any other member of the department to suit himself. Only he can't promote anybody until we get more money than I can see ahead.

"Of course you'll want time to think it over. And now I've finished my business with you, I propose we go down to lunch and talk about world affairs."

There is no one born in Nebraska who does not sometimes dream of going to live in California. Land of gold and golden oranges, vast vineyards and apricot orchards, olive trees shading the red volcanic earth with their gray foliage, great trees that were already old when Troy fell and when Moses led the Hebrews out of Egypt, land of soft sunshine and roses blooming through the winter: how can a Nebraskan resist the lure of California? There were powerful family forces drawing Edith and me. Edith had her Uncle Jim in San José, a blithe and engaging man who had built himself a comfortable fortune, and Cousin Bess, the sweetest lady I have ever known except my wife. And my parents, my sister, and my two brothers were all living in California.

I called up Jordan the next morning and accepted.

It was hard to tell my colleagues, my very good friends, that I was leaving them. It was hardest to tell J. Laurence Laughlin.

"Johnson," he said, "Veblen had to leave me; the world doesn't know why. Davenport left me. Now if you go everybody will say, 'Nobody can get along with that old fellow J. Laurence Laughlin.' "

Few partings in my life ever pained me so much.

Years later Laughlin visited me at my home in Nyack. He had retired and aged, but he carried himself straight. He was on his way to a new home in New England where he said he would weather into the granite landscape.

"I won't need to do anything at all," he said with forced cheerfulness. "Fact is nobody wants me to do anything. The magazines used to solicit me for articles, paying me unreasonably high honoraria. Now there is no magazine that has space for an article by a time-expired old fellow like me."

He braced himself, smiled a wintry smile, and took his departure with consummate courtesy.

TWENTY-TWO

Stanford University

THE economics department at Stanford was manned by Albert C. Whitaker, who had been my colleague as Fellow at Columbia, Harry Millis, destined for a professorship at Chicago and an overwhelming repute in labor arbitration, and Ira Cross, a young man of force and enterprise, later to become a professor at Berkeley. The department also had a semi-independent associate, Professor Burt E. Howard, political scientist, who had been a preacher, but whose sermons had been too bewilderingly intellectual for his Los Angeles congregation.

Whitaker had a better claim to the headship of the department than I. He was a brilliant teacher, an expert in economic theory, and a first-rate authority on foreign exchange. He had a mind of surpassing keenness, and I found great delight in discussions with him. But his mental rapier was very sharp, and one who chose to fence with him needed thick-padded armor of humor. President Jordan, who liked him and admired him, was deterred from making him department head by the hostility of the other three members of the department. As Whitaker's friend, I too was at first regarded by the department as an enemy. At best I was a choice between evils. But this situation, when I learned of it, did not trouble me. Enmities are a demanding crop; you have to cultivate and water them well, or they wilt away. I have never been able to acquire expertness in this kind of gardening.

At a preliminary meeting of the department I asked the members what courses they felt I should offer. Millis told me solemnly that as department head I had a right to any course I pleased. I said I pleased to take courses nobody else wanted. In the outcome I was put in charge of the introductory course, to give three lectures a week, with the class then to be divided into sections for quizzing by Cross; a course on railway problems, nearly the most boring of all economics subjects; and a seminar in theory. Also, I had a bootleg course for engineering students. The engineering school was so jealous of its students' time that they were given not one hour free for economics, which many of them thought they needed. I made private arrangements to meet a group of them on Saturday evenings. We were agreed to say nothing about it; for if the engineering school learned that any of its students had time for economics, the school would clamp on an additional engineering course.

Economics was a required course in the college, and this meant an introductory class of about two hundred and fifty. California is a land that is kind to its children, feeds them well, and gives them plenty of sun. I never before had encountered so large a group of well-grown, good-looking, frank-faced young men and women as in this class. I glanced over the class list. To call the roll would eat up too much of the fifty minutes at my disposal. I announced that I would not call the roll; any student who thought he could make more progress in economics outside of the class could take cuts with impunity. Of course this put me at outs with the office of administration. For a time a secretary would come in to count my students, hoping to prove that cutting was becoming a scandal. But attendance kept up satisfactorily. Indeed, the secretary once found three hundred persons in the room. Fifty persons not registered; I had to put them out. "How?" I asked.

At that time the Eastern colleges were ridden by a garden variety of psychology, degenerated from William James, which distinguished between the "active" and the "passive" in experience, as a substitute for the old distinction between virtue and vice. Listening to a lecture was passive; sitting in a room with thirty persons being quizzed by an instructor was "active." Psychologists of this school inveighed constantly against the "lecture method," oblivious of the fact that listening to a lecturer like William James was about as "active" an experience as the nervous system will stand.

Unfortunately I was not a William James; but my lectures got all the response they were worth. Returns on examinations were entirely satisfactory. An extraordinary proportion of the papers contained active arguments against the position taken by the instructor. I liked that class and was very well satisfied with it.

The university had set up the institution of student advisers among the faculty. A student chose an adviser according to his own free will; after the choice his free will abdicated, for he could register only with his adviser's approval, and he could change from one course to another only with the adviser's consent. I soon found I had been chosen adviser so widely I could have given my whole time to the job.

Two students came to me and asked permission to drop Shakespeare and take up Forge.

I demurred. If they had wanted to exchange Shakespeare for Browning or Tennyson or even Mark Twain I'd have approved. But Shakespeare for iron work?

One of them said, "Professor, before you turn us down you ought to go with us to one session of Shakespeare and one of Forge."

It was a fair challenge. I agreed.

I found the Shakespeare session competently conducted but without enthusiasm, except where the instructor touched on points of scholarly differences—of no interest whatever to undergraduates. The session of Forge was another matter. An eager young scholar who knew iron from Tubal-cain down, in whose hands the metal was a responsive plastic, kept all his students on their toes with interest. As I had long been convinced that whatever excites vivid interest is educational and whatever bores is not, I was forced to agree to the exchange of Shakespeare for Forge.

Stanford appeared to be marking time. President Jordan was still in residence, offering drafts of scholarly spirit to all who came in contact with him; but he was scheduled for early retirement. So was the Old Guard of professors who had joined Jordan in the launching of Stanford. It was asserted, mischievously, that when Jordan accepted Senator Stanford's invitation to build a new university he was thirty-seven years old, and in making faculty appointments considered anyone over thirty-eight too old, anyone under thirty-six too young. There was indeed a remarkably unified age grouping in the Old Guard. This meant that they were dropping by platoons into the abyss of the Carnegie pension system. After its first years the university suffered severe financial embarrassments, and it had never been possible to bring in much new ability, with opportunity for full development. There were able men in Stanford of later enlistment, but under the shadow of the Old Guard they too often presented a spindling character of scholarly growth. Budget difficulties still harassed President Jordan so severely that faculty members who affected sardonic wit asserted that he regarded the sudden death of a professor as good news.

The social and political atmosphere of Stanford was quietist. Several years earlier the political life of San Francisco had been torn to painful shreds in the struggle between the good government faction, led by Hiram W. Johnson and Fremont Older, editor of the *Bulletin,* and the corrupt ring of political boss Abe Ruef, supported by the powerful United Railways and the Southern Pacific. Ruef had been convicted of bribery, along with a number of fellow-conspirators. But the cases were appealed, and the higher court ordered the cases to be heard before it. As the higher court belonged to the old order, it was a foregone conclusion that the convictions would be upset, as they indeed were in the case of all the accused except Ruef. His appeal had been acted on favorably by the court, but the five members had not all been within the borders of the state to sign the appeal order on the same day. On this technicality Older and Johnson seized Ruef and hurried him off to the penitentiary. Now, in 1911, Johnson was governor.

Soon after arriving at Stanford I gave a day to looking over San Francisco. While waiting at the gate for my suburban train, I caught sight of a huge man, certainly six feet four, with a strong, gloomy face and a pugnacious air. I thought how well a battle-ax would have become him, at the side of Richard Coeur de Lion. An idea occurred to me. Surely he was Fremont Older. I accosted him. He was.

Older was taking the train to San José, ten miles beyond my station. We shared a seat as far as Palo Alto, discussing many things but mostly politics, disagreeing on some points but agreeing on most. As the train approached my stop, Older invited me to dine with him the next Sunday at his house on the mountain. His car would pick me up at the San José station.

Older had made his paper, the *Bulletin,* a knotted cat-o'-nine-tails for evil-doers, little and big. Imagine my surprise when, seated at table in his dining room, looking out over the Santa Clara Valley, the shining bay and the rose-tinted hills beyond, I glanced up at the butler serving the soup to see a man with the revolting face of a hardened criminal.

Mrs. Older, who sat beside me, read my feelings. "Doctor Johnson," she said when the butler had left the room, "he is only the burglar. The murderer is in the kitchen."

After dinner Older expounded his views of crime and punishment. Criminals, that is, the professional ones, composed a minor nation at war with a greater nation, the law-abiding. As in all such wars, the minor nation put up a dirty fight, and the major nation, if it had any sense, used dirty means when it needed them. Convicted criminals, in Older's view, were prisoners of war. There was no just reason for mal-treating them in captivity, and there was no sense in trying to reform them. When at last released they went back to their nation. What else was there for them to do? Who wanted to employ them? At least Older himself could give a few of them a chance; hence the murderer in the kitchen and the burglar as butler, together with an assortment of criminals working around the place.

I wondered at Mrs. Older, a lovely, gentle person, spending her days alone in her mountain house, surrounded by men of crime and violence. But she seemed to take the conditions of her life very blithely.

On occasion, Older said, the arts of crime had proved useful. Once when Mrs. Older was visiting in the East and Older had given his men a vacation, retaining only the butler to look after his house, he had returned from San Francisco, picked up the butler at San José, and driven home. As he mounted the steps he realized that he had left his keys on the inside of the locked door.

"Don't worry, Mr. Older," said the butler. "You see, I'm a second-story man." In a minute he had shinned up a porch post, slipped through an open window, and unlocked the door.

Some months later, when I was again dining at the house on the mountain, I noted that there was a new butler—a suave, polished gentleman, he seemed. He was a forger; the murderer in the kitchen had been replaced by a rapist.

"Yes," Older said, "they left me. They hated to do it, but they were getting awfully bored. What could I offer that would compare in excitement with a hold-up or a burglary? Still, there is always a chance that some of them will reform. I want you to take a good look at the family that's coming in this afternoon. I'll tell you their story later."

The family that called consisted of a handsome, charming young man, whom Older introduced as Doctor, and an extremely pretty lady, his wife, and two children, a boy of eight and a girl of six, very bright and well behaved. The Doctor was a popular dentist in Southern California, and, having business in San Francisco, he brought his family along to present to his true friend Fremont Older.

Afterward I heard the story. The man had carried on two professions, salesman for a firm supplying dental equipment and burglary. He had broken into a mansion on Nob Hill, closed for the summer, and had assembled a suitcase full of silver and jewelry. But as bad luck would have it, a passing policeman saw him crawling out of the window and picked him up, suitcase and all. Naturally his first move was to call up Older, Protector of the Poor, who brought a lawyer along to interview him.

"There's no way out," said the lawyer. "You were caught redhanded. All you can do is plead guilty and throw yourself on the mercy of the court. We'll plead guilty to second degree burglary."

Under California law burglary by daylight was second degree and carried a penalty of ten years in the penitentiary. Burglary by night was first degree and worth twenty years.

The judge was one Older said needed to drink a little blood every day, to get out of his chronic depression and feel himself a man again.

"Burglary in the second degree?" he roared. "Fetch me a calendar. Let's see. He was picked up at six-one. Sunset on that date, five-fifty-nine. Burglary in the first degree."

"But, Judge," the lawyer expostulated, "the crime lay in breaking in and collecting the material. He did all that by daylight."

"No quibbling!" stormed the judge. Turning to the accused, he said, "I find you guilty of burglary in the first degree and sentence you to twenty years in the penitentiary at San Quentin."

"But, Judge, how can you sentence him? You haven't arraigned him."

"Mr. Blank, you are very near contempt of court."

"Then I call all spectators to witness, there is no arraignment in this record. And I remind all present that to tamper with the record as taken down by the court stenographer is a penitentiary offense."

There are many things in the law that have puzzled me, and one of the most puzzling was a principle of the California law that if the record of a man's conviction was defective, after serving a year and a day in prison he might sue out a writ of habeas corpus, and if the defect was proved, he went scot free, as if he had never committed a crime at all. At the end of the year his lawyer got a writ, and the burglar was a free man.

"Lightning never strikes me twice in the same place," he said. "I'm off burgling for life."

In the practice of his two professions he had often thought, in calling on dentists with his catalogue of supplies, how much more satisfactory the career of dentist was than that of burglar. He yearned to go through a dental school, but the dental schools required a high-school diploma. He had a fiancée, a girl of great beauty and ingenuity, who got herself a position as secretary to a member of the legislature. When she had succeeded in getting the member under her charm she had him put through an amendment to the educational law, by which a record of two years of traveling for a dental supply house could be counted as equivalent to a high-school diploma, for entrance to a dental school.

Our friend finished his dental course with honor, opened an office, and soon won great popularity for his skill and humaneness.

Older tried to work out a moral for the story but gave it up. "A true story never has a moral anyway."

I called frequently at Older's *Bulletin* office, where I was known to the staff as "Old Abstract Philosophy." There I met for the first time Clarence S. Darrow, at the zenith of his reputation as a redoubtable defender of persons accused of serious crime. No murderer defended by Darrow was ever executed.

Years before he had defeated William E. Borah, who was prosecuting Big Bill Haywood, Pettibone, and Moyer, top officials of the I.W.W. for the murder of ex-Governor Steunenberg of Idaho. Borah was a mighty lawyer but no match for Darrow, who won by his victory the universal execration of all solid-headed citizens. For the I.W.W. was as much detested and feared then as the Communists are today, and perhaps on good grounds, for does not Nicolai Lenin tell us, somewhere in his writings, that he developed Communist tactics after a thorough study of the I.W.W.?

I expected to find Darrow a nervous, fire-eating type. What he proved to be was the plainest of plain men, never dressing better than the least well-dressed man on a jury, never using language that the least-educated juror would fail to understand. He did his best not to be a "personality" but failed dismally, for his personality was in fact most compelling.

I once saw him in operation in court. His client was plainly innocent, but the prosecution meant to convict him, and when the jury found that the accused was to be defended by the terrible Clarence Darrow, they got their backs up and meant to convict, whatever the evidence.

Darrow slouched in a seat facing the jury, smiling into their indignant faces. A witness fumbled along with his made-up evidence; Darrow would ask him to repeat a statement—it didn't come out the same—and Darrow would smile at the jury. When it came to cross-examination Darrow didn't bullyrag the witness but asked gently questions that appeared irrelevant but were vital. With each admission of the witness Darrow would smile at the jury.

In an hour Darrow held the jury in the hollow of his hand. It took the jury less than half an hour to acquit.

Some years later, after I had returned to New York, Darrow did me the honor of asking me to his hotel when he came to the city. I had full opportunity to sound out his philosophy.

Everybody, he held, is guilty. Is there any man, he asked, who has never had murder in his heart? Is there any man who has looked in at a jeweler's window without feeling that if he could get away with it, how nice it would be to lift a ring or a bracelet? Is there any man who has got into a jam who doesn't wish he could forge a check, if he could float it successfully?

We are all criminals, said Darrow; but those of us who haven't had the opportunity or the nerve to carry out the crimes that are in our hearts sit in judgment on those who have carried out their crimes. Put them away, if we must, in self-defense. Execute them if necessary. But punish? Who is pure enough to arrogate to himself the right to punish?

A man of quite different type to whom Older introduced me was Andrew Furuseth, champion of the seamen. Before Furuseth, seamen were serfs. At sea the captain could flog a seaman, put him in irons, hang him. If a ship touched at an American port and a seaman, in revolt against the treatment the captain handed out, tried to jump ship, the local police were required, under international law, to hunt him down as a deserter and return him handcuffed to his master. And in all the world there was no man fighting for the liberation of the seaman except Andrew Furuseth.

Andy was a spare, Norwegian type, heroically ascetic on principle. He took me to his room: it was four feet wide by ten feet long, not a chair to sit on, no furnishings other than a cot, a stand with a washbowl, and an eight-inch square glass to shave by. He took me to his eating place, where we lunched for twenty cents each. Andy told me that he had never in his life paid more than four dollars a month for a room or more than twenty-five cents for a meal. He had never married and had never let any person become dependent on him. For salary he accepted only the pay of a seaman of the lowest class.

"I like the good things of life as much as anyone," he said. "But if I lived well I could be controlled, by the threat of taking away my pay. If I had a wife and children they would be hostages against me. When you fight what looks like a hopeless cause, you've got to be a monk or you are licked."

Andrew Furuseth worked patiently through many years, building an organization among the serfs of the sea. Finally he managed to get an interview with Senator La Follette, and he set forth the conditions of the seaman's life so vividly that La Follette caught fire. The result was the Seaman's bill, fought furiously by the shipping interests through several years but finally passed in 1915. Under this law a sailor, American or foreign, whose ship touches an American port, has a right to demand his wages down to the landing date and to leave the ship if he wishes to do so. If he is an alien seaman he has a right to remain in our port a reasonable time until he can pick up a job on an outgoing ship. And if instead of going out on a ship he slips away and takes a job in Skaneateles or Little Rock, who is there to find him and throw him out of the country? There are tens of thousands of such unlawful immigrants scattered through the country. They are the one completely law-abiding element we have in our population, for if they get into court the fact of their jumping ship comes out and they are sure to be deported.

The La Follette law also prescribed decent living quarters for sailors. Look at the freighters in the harbor, with their cumbrous superstructures above decks. Those are the handiwork of Andy Furuseth, living quarters to replace the suffocating holes in the hold where the seamen and cockroaches used to be accommodated; fit living quarters for the men Andy freed from serfdom.

One other interesting character that I met through Fremont Older was Abe Ruef. At first Older was happy over his success in putting this corrupt political boss into the penitentiary, even on a technicality. But his contentment oozed away. Like a hunter who is thrilled by bringing down a fawn, only to torture himself with remorse when he sees the poor wounded creature's anguished eyes, Older would have set Abe Ruef free. He appealed to Governor Johnson to pardon Ruef; he broke with Johnson over the case and carried on a constant propaganda in the *Bulletin,* under the caption, "Abe Ruef Is the Private Prisoner of Hiram Johnson." In vain. There was no mercy in Hiram Johnson.

Finally Abe's term, shortened by good behavior, came to an end. Older, who had made himself trustee of Ruef's property interests while Ruef was in the penitentiary, and had fought off the cormorants, Abe's associates, disputing for the plunder they could get out of the absent Boss, set out valiantly to rehabilitate Abe. He organized a big dinner party ostensibly to honor the "good" Spreckels who had financed the prosecution (there were other Spreckelses not so good), but really as a coming-out party for Abe.

Older seated Abe between Mrs. Older and me, and we were commissioned to entertain Abe so well that he would not notice the good citizens' eyes glaring at him from across the table.

Abe was a little man, not attractive, apparently not happy over the honor of dining with the men who had put him in jail. As was bound to happen, some of the speakers touched on the horrible corruption of earlier years and the present purity of San Francisco politics. At such times Mrs. Older stepped up her conversational energy to double speed.

"Poor Mr. Ruef," she said to me after dinner. "I tried hard to keep him from hearing what they said."

Some years after I left California Mrs. Older visited New York. Of course I inquired about our common friends, and finally asked about Abe Ruef.

"Mr. Older and I feel rather cool toward him. You see, there was a crook just out of the penitentiary who came to ask Mr. Older for money to take him to Phoenix, where he said he had an uncle who would give him a job. Mr. Older wasn't feeling very flush at the time, so he asked, 'Who sent you to me?' 'Abe Ruef.' 'Funny thing for Abe to send me a man I never saw.' 'Oh yes, you've seen me, Mr. Older. You remember the time at the Beach House, when the man behind you had a pistol at your back, meaning to kill you; but another crook who was for you sat behind him with a pistol at his back? Well, I was the man hired to kill you.' 'I see,' said Mr. Older. 'I ought to give you some money, you think, because you were hired to kill me. Who hired you?' 'Oh, don't you know? Abe Ruef.' 'And that's why he thinks I ought to give you some money!'

"After that," Mrs. Older continued, "Mr. Older has felt rather cool toward Abe Ruef."

California was wonderful. My associations at the university and outside of it were delightful. But I was going through a highly political phase. I was passionate about the Progressive movement, which appeared to be on its way toward capturing the presidency and inaugurating an era of honest and efficient government. Although California had Hiram Johnson and Fremont Older, the state was remote from the real centers of Progressive strength.

At all costs, I felt, I had to go East. An invitation to become professor at Cornell University came to me at the midyear. I accepted.

TWENTY-THREE

Three Years at Cornell

ITHACA and Cornell I saw first on a brilliant winter day in 1912. Some inches of soft snow had fallen in the night, and all the streets, all the trees, all the roofs, were clad in pure ermine. The taxi had to puff strenuously to take me up the steep and curving street to the plateau where Cornell sits in state, looking out over the pleasant city and the long greenish-blue ribbon of Lake Cayuga.

I had come from California on the invitation of the president, Jacob Gould Schurman, ostensibly to give four lectures. An economical institution like Cornell does not invest four hundred dollars on lectures by a man who has no reputation as a lecturer. What the invitation meant was a question: Shall you be open-minded to a call from Cornell if after a week's acquaintance the university is inclined to enlist you on its faculty? On both sides we understood what we were about.

My first call was of course on Schurman in his office. He was one of three great university presidents of the time, along with David Starr Jordan and Benjamin Ide Wheeler. They were all disciples of Andrew D. White, founder of the institution with Ezra Cornell, and had imbibed White's serene and serious outlook upon the world, his passion for truth and freedom from fear. Schurman's greeting was brief, cordial, and adequate. He had command of my admiration and friendship, for life.

Schurman turned me over to my host for the week, Jeremiah Jenks, who for years had been the pillar of the Department of Political Science but who was leaving Cornell to head the Alexander Hamilton Institute in New York, an ambitious venture in what we now call adult education. Jenks was a man of irresistible charm who had only to smile at a man to make a devoted friend of him. He held the friendship of Theodore Roosevelt in fee simple. Whenever Roosevelt wanted to set up a commission of inquiry he wanted to put Jenks at its head. So Jenks was put at the head of the Industrial Commission, which produced an enormous report on the whole state of American business and industry.

Jenks was a competent economist but had no use for the refinements of current economic theory. He had still less use for the developing refinements of statistics. He used statistics, but as sand on the road, to keep the smooth wheels of argument from spinning too fast.

Jenks's personal demeanor had frozen at the stage of development of a successful and popular college senior. He loved practical jokes that did not draw blood and was capable of engaging in hazing, as I soon found out.

Frank A. Fetter had held the chair in economic theory but had resigned to go to Princeton. The department had been run by the trio Jenks, Fetter, and Walter F. Willcox, of whom only Willcox remained. Willcox's mind impressed one like a bust of Parian marble, the most human of all marbles, which in aging develops overtones of gold and rose but holds its splendor forever. I found him a man of few words, but all of them pertinent and meaningful. He wrote little, but what he wrote was of supreme good sense. He still writes occasionally, in his nineties, and what he writes is still as meaningful as his writings of any time in the last sixty years. He still lives in Ithaca. When I have the rare good fortune to spend an hour with him I rejoice in his Parian mind, perfect in form, with the gold and rose gaining on the clear marble.

There were two younger men in the department, John Bauer, an excellent teacher, and A. P. Usher, a remarkable research worker in economic history. Jenks told me, in a friendly way, after he knew I was to be on the faculty, that he had meant to fire Usher and was sure I would want to. I thought he had another guess coming, for I knew Usher's work, modestly superb.

Andrew D. White was still living on the campus, Nestor of the American historians, once intimate with Darwin and Huxley, with American and British statesmen who had achieved greatness or were destined to achieve it. How old he was I never thought to inquire, for his mind was ageless; if affected in any way by the years, it was in the direction of copiousness. He was a king among Cornellians and could do no wrong, though he was likely to hijack your guests and take over any discussion you were staging. Once a distinguished French economist came to Cornell particularly to discuss some moot points with me. He was to be my guest. White heard of the economist's coming, waylaid him at the train, and carried him home. All I ever was permitted to see of the economist was a glimpse at a crowded tea.

I met also the historian, George Burr, disciple of Andrew D. White. Burr never consented to manumission. He was the most exquisite historian in America, capable of working years to establish once for all a point that would never command more than a brief paragraph in the biggest historical volume. To him, history was a fine art, and its fineness had transformed his personality into the finest example of living art. His colleague, Charles H. Hull, affected a gruff air but carried around over his diaphragm a heart big as the full moon.

Cornell had two distinguished philosophers, James E. Creighton and Frank Thilly, both Progressive in their political views; counting me a Progressive, they enrolled me among their friends. But no such happy relation could last, for they were philosophers. I had learned in my life how to get on pleasantly with farmers and merchants, engineers and philologists, writers and editors, lawyers and politicians, even political crooks, burglars, and murderers. But except for my beloved friend John Dewey and my colleagues Horace Kallen and Kurt Riezler, I am singularly unsuccessful in my relations with philosophers. That is not to their discredit nor to mine.

The philosopher is essentially the theologian *in partibus infidelium*. He is custodian of the immortal soul; he holds the gate of Heaven ajar for those who believe. Unbelief is the one mortal sin. The philosopher may make show of hospitality to relativity, skepticism, but his essential nature is absolutistic. An economist moves entirely in the world of relative values. He knows no absolute good, only the better than the worse. He knows no absolute truth, only the more probable above the less probable. How can he sit in a pew with a true philosopher?

I knew well enough, after meeting my future colleagues, that whatever the outcome of my lectures I was pretty sure to be invited to join the faculty. If I had had any doubt it would have been dispelled by inside information supplied by Johnny Bauer, who was destined to become a sharp thorn in the side of the Long Island Railway and other public service corporations trying to gain what they insisted were their rights.

But I still had those four lectures to give, and, Jeremiah Jenks informed me, I was to give one before the Law School, one before the faculty, one before the huge body of elementary students, and the fourth before the graduate students. I had prepared myself for a series of four consecutive lectures, and the new program was disturbing.

I was under no illusions as to my performance as a lecturer. To read a written lecture was to my mind the most effective way of putting an audience to sleep. To write a lecture and commit it to memory was impossible for me. I'd get so bored with it that I could not fail to bore the audience. My expedient was to devote an intense two hours to my subject beforehand, and then shape my exposition according to my judgment of what the audience would take. I might begin at the point where an idea ought to begin and work through to the end, or begin in the middle and excavate toward both ends. The results were never satisfactory to me, but audiences are forgiving.

At four in the afternoon, Jenks told me, I'd meet the elementary students. I went into a brown study to decide what to say to them and walked up not too reluctantly with Jenks to Goldwin Smith Hall.

As we came through the door Jenks said, "By the way, there has been a change in the program. You will speak to the faculty now."

And I was loaded for the elementary students! Well, you always have a few minutes to marshal your thoughts while you are being introduced, and fortunately Jenks was long-winded in his introduction, little of which was pertinent to me.

The next day I was prepared for the law students. As Jenks took me to the hall he announced a last-minute change: I was to have the graduate students. There seemed to be a method in his procedure. I'd be prepared for either the law students or the elementary class next day; but I was eager to see whether Jenks would make another substitution. He did.

I knew I was going to get the appointment anyway. Jenks was just hazing me. I couldn't resent it, for he was too charming. But, I said to myself, life is long, and Jenks doesn't realize what a good memory I have.

Years later I was invited to the Williamstown Institute to discuss the new dollar diplomacy adopted by the State Department. Latin-American countries, particularly insolvent ones, were naturally eager to borrow money in the United States. If the faction in power was pro-American in spirit the State Department would encourage our great banks—rather forcibly—to underwrite a loan. The security was worthless, and the great banks knew it, but they could make their country correspondents take the bonds and place them with private investors trapped by the approval of the loan by our State Department. At the next turn of the wheel of Latin-American politics the pro-American party would go out and an anti-American party would repudiate the loan. The private American investors could blow on their cold fingers.

Recognizing that a scholar must be cautious in attacking the State Department I had written an address which was a model of caution and, of course, rather boring. When I presented myself at Williamstown the first man I met was Jeremiah Jenks. Would I let him see my address? He might like to take part in the discussion. I handed him my copy, asking him to return it in two hours, as it was the only copy I had.

I went to the Secretary's office to register.

"May I have your address?" he asked.

"In two hours," I said. "I loaned it to Jeremiah Jenks."

"The deuce!" he said. "When the State Department learned you were to speak they telegraphed Jeremiah to come up and refute you."

Well, I thought to myself, it would have been nice of Jeremiah to have told me he was to be my official refuter. I'd have given him my manuscript anyway. And then I recalled that Jeremiah had once told me that, contrary to the general impression, he never spoke impromptu. He made very careful notes and committed the points to memory. He's in for a little hazing himself, I thought.

Before the audience I discarded my manuscript and my caution and described as vividly as I could the skin game the State Department was operating on the innocent investor. As I warmed up to my subject the audience warmed up too. I was enjoying myself, and all the more because, out of the corner of my eye, I could see Jenks stirring around in the copy of my address he had had made by his own permission and consulting a parcel of notes.

Jenks started his refutation with a compliment to a young man who knew the business of the State Department better than the department. For that he got booed. He stirred around in his notes and tried to draw damaging conclusions from something that was indeed in my manuscript but not in my speech. He made a polite, totally irrelevant remark and got a hostile response. He got a little angry and said something sarcastic about me and got booed again. Finally he sat down, with the applause of just one pair of hands.

The audience, three or four hundred, funneled toward the door. Driven at random through the crowd, I found myself half a dozen feet behind Jenks, who was walking with his one applauder, Archibald Coolidge. Jenks was saying, "Alvin Johnson is the trickiest man in the whole economics profession." "Utterly unreliable," said Archibald Coolidge. As for me, my conscience should have hurt me, but it didn't. As Clarence Darrow maintained, there is a germ of cruelty in every human breast.

In accepting appointment I intended to make Cornell my permanent home. True, I had meant to stay out my life at Columbia, Nebraska, Texas, Chicago, Stanford. Home: I have always had a deep and powerful yearning for a place I could call home. But I have an equally deep and powerful desire for what lies beyond the horizon. Perhaps it is because the horizons I knew as a boy in Nebraska never really closed the landscape but invited one to what lay beyond. Or perhaps the contradiction may be resolved on the principle that to a Middle Westerner home means the whole United States. When I'm away from America for a few weeks homesickness comes upon me, for the whole United States, East and West, North and South, my own magnificent country, my beloved home.

Solidly as I felt myself settled at Cornell, within a month I was ready to yield to the temptation to move. I visited New York, just to renew my old acquaintance at Columbia. I called first on Seligman.

"Alvin," he said, "now you've come so far East, why not come a little farther, and join us here at Columbia?"

"I'd like nothing better," I said. "But I doubt the faculty would want me. There are two other men who would supplement the department better, Wesley Mitchell and Allyn Young."

"They are fine scholars," Seligman assented. "We have considered them. But you are one of us."

For months I heard nothing from Seligman. I knew that his proposal had blown up. Still, he had been so positive about it, I wanted to find out what had happened. I went down to New York again and called at his office.

"Alvin, you are not going to get a call to Columbia. Columbia doesn't need you."

"All right," I said. "I don't need Columbia." Both statements were true, but I hadn't the real explanation yet. I couldn't get it, I knew, out of Seligman, for he was bound to keep to himself what went on inside the faculty. I went to see another friend.

"You see, Alvin, we have the rule of unanimity. We were all for you but one. He vetoed you."

"Who was he?" I was curious: was it my old friend Giddings?

"That I'm not permitted to say."

I went to another friend.

"Does it hurt you, Johnson, that we turned you down?"

"Not a damn bit. I'm perfectly happy where I am."

"Then if I tell you who it was, you won't bear a grudge?"

"No. I'm too superficial a soul to bear grudges."

"Well then I'll tell you: it was X. Y."

"Oh, X. Y." I laughed with relief. None of my true friends had gone back on me.

"You see, X. Y. has a new fine-haired theory for the faculty. He argues that we ought to take on only professors who have independent means enough to live in style. He wants the Columbia faculty to be in a position to cotton to the New York moneyed aristocracy. You haven't got the independent means; and besides, you don't give a damn for the New York moneyed aristocracy."

"That's true," I said. "I'm a dyed-in-the-wool Middle-Western democrat. I see I'll have to dress up when I call on you Columbia people in the future."

"But you won't."

As the train carried me toward Ithaca I did a lot of reflecting. I hadn't really wanted to go to Columbia; but there *was* something I wanted, vaguely, unconsciously, but persistently. It was something I hadn't been able to find in any of my teaching positions.

My scholarly forte was economic theory, but economic theory by 1912 had fought itself to a virtual standstill. Through the analysis of marginal utility, marginal productivity, discounting of future values, it had built up a competent and consistent picture of an economic world based on perfect competition. In the real world there is no such phenomenon as perfect competition, and the ablest of the younger economic theorists, like John Maurice Clark, were turning to analysis of monopoly and restricted competition. Other economists under the leadership of Wesley C. Mitchell were subjecting the phenomena of economic crises to a wide-reaching analysis, developing new statistical and mathematical techniques for the purpose.

But it seemed to me that economic science was drifting farther and farther away from the comprehension of the intelligent layman, for whom Adam Smith, Ricardo, Malthus, and John Stuart Mill wrote their powerful books. Here and there you might find a businessman who displayed an amateur interest in the work of the modern economic theorists, but only as you found occasional businessmen who stood as proficient amateurs of philology or Aztec civilization. The divorce between academic economics and the intelligent public was nearly complete.

It is true, we had the youth in colleges and universities and consoled ourselves with the notion that we were shaping the minds of the coming generation of leaders. But when you met an alumnus of several years' standing you found it hard to discover in the alumnus mind a chemical trace of the ideas he had accepted blithely in class.

I had often heard persons in the Indian Service mourning over what happened to the young Indians from the reservations, on their return from fancy Eastern Indian schools. Within a few months the young Indian "returned to the blanket." He had to do so if he was to be accepted by his reservation associates. So I would find that the young alumnus had returned to the blanket of popular economic ideas. And I was forced to the conclusion that economics would never be able to contribute seriously to public opinion and public policy until it learned how to reach the lay blanket of ideas.

What I felt was most needed was higher adult education, although at the time I did not use the term. How could the economist reach the intelligent public? By writing, I thought. I had written for the academic journals and had thought little of the efforts of economists like J. Laurence Laughlin and Jeremiah Jenks to make a place for themselves in popular magazines. I was wrong, I saw.

What could I write that a popular magazine would take? I thought of a theme that might interest Ellery Sedgwick of the *Atlantic Monthly*. Immediately I got a pad out of my suitcase and scribbled an article amidst the jerking of the train. A patient typist translated the article next day to clean copy. I sent it off, and in three days got a cordial letter from Sedgwick, with a check and an invitation to contribute more articles. It could be done, I saw.

Cornell was rich in good students. I greatly enjoyed teaching both in undergraduate electives and in graduate courses. The undergraduate students were very responsive and very patient with my peculiar methods of handling a subject. Sometimes they were a little too patient.

I was giving a course in taxation and public finance, inherently a dull subject besprinkled with uninspiring statistics. When half the term was over a student raised his hand to ask a question.

"Professor Sampson—" he began.

"Professor Johnson," I corrected.

The student stared. "Aren't you Professor Sampson? And isn't this course English Fourteen?"

"No, I am Professor Johnson, and this course is Economics Ten."

The poor boy was out of luck. He had registered for the English course and had half a term's cuts against him. He hadn't registered in time for my course and couldn't get credit for it. He couldn't get his degree that year as he was three hours short.

Among the graduate students who interested me most were Harold Reed, later to become a professor in the economics department; Hu Shih, destined to be a Chinese statesman and sometime Chinese Ambassador to Washington; and Frank Knight, who became a professor at the University of Chicago, one of the ablest of American economic theorists.

Knight came up from Tennessee, where border-state diet had endowed him with dyspepsia and a graven expression of pessimism. He was majoring in philosophy under Creighton and Thilly and doing a minor with me. I found him the keenest student of theory I had ever had. When I was elaborating some theoretical subtlety he would turn on me the gray light of his skeptical eyes, seeming to say, "I don't believe a word of that." Sometimes he would attack my position, very competently. I liked that. It was stimulating to wrestle over points of theory.

One day in the spring Knight came to me with an unusually sad face. "Doctor," he said, "I thought all along I was doing pretty well in my philosophy major. But Creighton called me in and gave me the most frightful hauling over the coals. Said I was totally unfit to study or teach philosophy; indeed, that I ought to drop the idea of teaching anything, for with my attitude I'd do more harm than good. I went to Thilly for comfort, and he gave it to me still worse."

I was astonished. Could two such clear-headed philosophers make such a mistake about so promising a student as Knight? I couldn't believe it. I went straight to Creighton.

"Knight?" he said bitterly. "It isn't that he is devoid of ability. But with his ingrained skepticism he repudiates all the values of philosophy. As a teacher or writer he will be not just the blind leading the blind into pitfalls. He will destroy the true philosophic spirit wherever he touches it."

"I see," I said. "Knight has been miscast. He should not have majored in philosophy, where his work and attitude are so unsatisfactory, but in economics, where he does excellent work. Suppose I take him over?"

"Do as you please," said Creighton acidly. "We in philosophy will have nothing to do with him."

I had a fellowship at my disposal and gave it to Knight. When this appeared in the *Bulletin* the break with Creighton and Thilly became complete. They would barely nod when we met. And they adopted a department rule that no philosophy major could take a minor in economics, nor could any economics major take a minor in philosophy.

I was grieved, for Creighton and Thilly had stood with me in the Progressive group of the faculty, a group which was in correspondence with other Progressive faculty groups, an informal organization under the leadership of Morris Raphael Cohen at City College.

The 1912 victory of Woodrow Wilson over the Republicans, split between Roosevelt and Taft, was not a heartening event to academic Progressives. Wilson was indeed a liberal, but of the old-style liberals of the nineteenth century, a man admiring the British Constitution more than the American, a believer in the dogma that the best government is the one that governs least. We Progressives no longer believed in spiritual laissez faire. Nor were we happy to see the rise in the influence of the South in our national government. Still, we regarded Wilson as a great improvement over Taft.

Some years earlier Andrew Carnegie had set up the Endowment for International Peace, and in the first organization Professor John Bates Clark became head of the division of economics and history. He was having studies made of the world-wide peace movement and of forces making for war, such as military organizations, armaments, and armament industries. The work had been parceled out to scholars throughout the world, and bulky volumes in English and approximate English were steadily coming in. This meant a monumental task of editing, and Professor Clark invited me to join his department as editorial secretary. The work, while heavy, did not interfere with my duties as a Cornell professor.

What I saw in these studies was profoundly disturbing. The European continent was moving swiftly and irresistibly toward war. There was indeed a peace party in every country, but it was a feeble force to pit against the war party. There was no European power without its statesmen and generals calmly calculating the profits of war. The

Germans meant to win their place in the sun; their eyes were fixed on Poland, the Ukraine and the Balkans, the Berlin-Baghdad railway line, nerve of a Baltic-Persian Gulf commercial and military empire. The Austrians were bent on stamping out Serbia and the ceaseless intrigues of the Serbs, Croats, and Slovenes within the empire borders. The Russians were concerned with breaking German military power, forcing the South Slavs under the Russian wing, and acquiring Constantinople and a good slice of Turkey. The French meant to recover Alsace-Lorraine and greatly extend their hold on Syria. The British meant to put an end to the menace of the German navy and the competition of the German merchant marine. The Italians wanted to wrest the Trentino and Trieste from Austria and seize the Dalmatian coast up to the mountain barriers fencing off the Greek lands. All these war parties were perfectly cynical in their intentions and plans, but it took a German philosopher to declare, "Universal peace is but a dream, and not a beautiful dream." And the great armament firms were persistently exploiting, sometimes even manufacturing, rumors of warlike moves, to stimulate the demand for ships and guns.

We had some volumes in page proof, more in galley and corrected manuscript, when the war actually broke out. At the Carnegie offices we had a hurried meeting and decided to put all the material into safe-deposit vaults. Published, it would supply propaganda to the unrighteous as well as the righteous, if indeed such a distinction could be drawn within the confused confraternity of warmakers.

At first most Americans regarded the European struggle as one between nations equally guilty and equally matched. President Wilson issued a proclamation on its outbreak, warning Americans to observe neutrality in thought and deed. Theodore Roosevelt issued a pronunciamento to the same effect. But gradually a party of intervention, with Roosevelt at its head, formed and became increasingly savage in its demand that America should enter the war on the side of the "democratic nations," England, France, and Imperial Russia. The war party was joined by a more moderate party demanding "preparedness." To the peace party, to which I adhered, "preparedness" meant only the removal of the strongest obstacle to our being dragged into the war— our military impotence.

I did not want to see either side wholly victorious. I recalled Caesar's message to Pompey after crossing the Rubicon: "You have a powerful army; I have a powerful army; if we fight, one of us will win; which, lies with Fate. Without fighting we can make a fair compromise; if

we fight it will be impossible for the victor to be just to the vanquished."
Later I printed the idea in the *New Republic* in an article extolling the
merits of an "Inconclusive Peace," to the great indignation of the bitter-
enders. President Wilson developed a similar idea, "Peace without
Victory," and drew all the bitter-end rage to himself.

I was continuing my efforts to limber up my style so that in time
I might really reach the nonacademic reader. To write easily and
simply you need to have written a lot, and it occurred to me to do a
sketch of my experiences in Texas, which would give me interesting
practice and would leave an amusing memoir for my children. But,
reflecting on my material, I saw that I'd not have a real place for
hearsay or for the development of the potentialities of incidents I had
seen in germ. Fiction would afford a much freer medium. So I invented an imaginary river and city and university, an imaginary college president, and a professor with a rather shadowy love affair. I
set myself a stint of a chapter a day, and in thirty days I had completed
the project. In the course of the composition I came to like the piece
fairly well, named it for the river, "On the San Juan Obispo," and
showed the draft to Frank Moore Colby, who put it into the hands
of Dodd, Mead and Company's readers. They liked it, except that no
book could sell with a place name; they invented *The Professor and
the Petticoat,* a name very uncharacteristic of the piece. I asked them
to return it to me for revision, but they demurred. Its virtue lay in its
negligent exuberance, they said; if I took hold of it with academic
fingers I'd spoil it.

The book sold badly; the publisher let it go with the first modest
printing. Soon it was sold out. I had only a few copies, intending to buy
more. The publisher hadn't any. I tried the secondhand bookstores
without success. For some reason I could not divine a bookseller in
Australia took a big section of the edition, and in Australia the pests
promptly eat a book up. One secondhand copy did come into my
hands in forty-five years, picked up by my friend Mary Lynn, who is
always equal to anything.

In 1914 Henry Holt, the publisher, launched a new quarterly, *The
Unpopular Review,* which he intended as a challenge to the super-
ficiality of his time. Inquiring for possible contributors, he got my name
from Ellery Sedgwick and invited me to have tea with him at three
o'clock in the morning. I was intrigued by what I had heard of his

habits and groped my way through the dim streets to his brilliantly lighted house.

Henry Holt in his eighties persisted in his habit of sleeping only in the daytime. The evening was his working time; his dinner, at twelve or one at night; his sociable hours, from three to six in the morning. The tea he served me at three was scotch and soda, the only really wholesome milk for an old man, he asserted, and not unnutritious for the mind of a young man.

His scheme of magazine construction was to print articles without signature and leave it to the readers to guess the authors, for three months, until the list of names appeared in the next issue. He thought guessing was a great game for the leisured reader, and such persons would read far more attentively in the hope of becoming able to guess right. To give an advantage to the writers, he assembled all the contributors to the forthcoming issue for a superb dinner, scheduled for twelve at night but actually as late as one-thirty or two.

The scheme sounded amusing to me, and I went back to Ithaca and wrote an article I called "The Soul of Capitalism," arguing that, for all its injustices, cruelties, vulgarities, capitalism is a spirit that works through the ages to defeat primordial poverty, the Egyptian darkness of primitive ignorance, the hatred of man for unlike man. Henry Holt made it the leading article and assembled the guesses. Not a single person guessed Alvin Johnson, but the article was imputed to almost every good writer in America. Thenceforth I was a "good writer" for Henry Holt and as such highly recommended to Herbert Croly, who was launching the *New Republic*.

My years at Ithaca are memorable to me for two great gifts of God, my son Thorold and my daughter Natalie. Thorold promptly assumed the humorous charm of a little figure then appearing on everyone's desk, a little Buddha, and Frank Knight refused to remember the name Thorold and called him Buddhie, a name by which Knight remembers him to this day. Natalie was born on Christmas Day, a shining Christmas light in the family life.

TWENTY-FOUR

The "New Republic"
and the Carnegie Libraries

THE progressive groups in the universities had long yearned for an adequate journalistic voice. The *Nation,* after its acquisition by Villard, was an excellent liberal organ, but stronger critically than "constructively." We rejoiced when "one of ours," Norman Hapgood, took over the old reactionary *Harper's Weekly* in 1913. We expected great things from the bold editorial initiative of Norman Hapgood. But except in devising a striking new format, Norman appeared uncreative.

Therefore we were greatly elated when we heard that a new weekly was to be launched under the editorship of Herbert Croly. We knew Herbert Croly from his *Promise of American Life* (1909). It was a powerful book, powerfully hard to read; but if one worked one's way through the involved sentences and the long-worded abstractions, one found a real philosophy of American progressivism. We were still more excited to learn that Croly was associating with himself Walter Lippmann, a very young man who wrote like a seasoned political scientist, and Walter E. Weyl, an accomplished high-class journalist and writer of books, deep in the Progressive movement.

Herbert Croly wrote me at Cornell that he would like to have me take lunch with him at the Players when next I came to New York. Naturally I came to New York very promptly.

I found him a spare, slight figure with heavy head and face of unrelieved gravity. It was hard at first for us to open lines of intercommunication, but after some minutes absorbed in martinis, Croly told me that he was one of the persons who had guessed wildly on the authorship of "The Soul of Capitalism" and had decided, whoever the author was, he should be asked for occasional contributions to the *New Republic,* soon to issue its first number in November 1914.

The *New Republic,* like most enterprises I've encountered in life, was in large measure the creature of accident, as I learned from Croly's account when he warmed up. He had sent a copy of his *Promise of American Life* to Theodore Roosevelt, who had written him enthusiastically about it, only querying passages on pages 117 and 235. The natural inference was that Roosevelt had read the book from cover to cover, something I doubted vehemently. Roosevelt had the habit of ennobling authors by reading just specimen pages of their works. Anyway, Roosevelt had recommended the book widely, and it had fallen into the hands of Willard and Dorothy Straight, who invited Croly for a weekend at their home in Long Island.

Naturally the new face of *Harper's Weekly* came up for discussion, and Croly produced a weighty and convincing statement of what *Harper's Weekly* should be but wasn't.

Finally Dorothy Straight said, "Why don't you get out a weekly yourself, Herbert?"

"Where would I find the money?" Herbert asked despondently.

"I will find it," Dorothy Straight said simply.

Croly was nearly stunned. But his doubts reasserted themselves. He had been editor of the *Architectural Review* and knew a lot about the costs of magazine publication. Probably Dorothy Straight had no idea how much money would be involved.

"It would take a lot of money," Herbert said. "About a hundred thousand for the first year. The next year should show a smaller deficit and the third year still less. It might take five years to make the paper self-supporting."

"Yes, I understand," said Dorothy Straight. "It may take longer, much longer. But let's go ahead."

This was the conversation as Herbert Croly related it to me. I doubt the accuracy of the reporting. Nobody has ever reported a miracle accurately.

Herbert returned to New York, his heart glowing, his head spinning. To think that he had found an angel for an enterprise he had only dreamed of!

And such an angel as Dorothy Straight! How could it have happened that Fate should have placed an immense fortune in the hands of a woman so brave, so true, so beautiful as Dorothy Straight? A real angel: in the years I was associated with the *New Republic* I heard hundreds of persons speak of her and I have heard hundreds more since. I have never heard one voice of criticism of Dorothy

Straight. Not one person ever detected the faintest blot on the white purity of her spirit.

Later in the day I met the other editors: Walter Lippmann, not far out of college but very far in the world of political wisdom; Walter E. Weyl, who looked like a saint and fundamentally was one; Philip Littell, who was very witty but silent in editorial company; Francis Hackett, born in Kilkenny on soil so provocative that even the cats have an eternal place in the folklore; Robert Hallowell, a fine water colorist, drafted for business manager; and Charlotte Rudyard, in charge of make-up and technical editing, an exquisite stylist, but with a fatal disposition to take favorite pedantic expressions out of an editor's living hide.

Croly was under the illusion that he had enough manpower on his staff to supply the twenty-five thousand words he needed weekly to fill the issue. All he would need was an occasional contribution from outside, and he invited me to contribute occasionally. I accepted, with reservations as to the "occasionally." For I knew that you can't get more than three thousand words out of anybody, week by week, through a year. His manpower was equal to only three-fifths of his requirements. I went back to Ithaca and thought up a scheme of articles, editorials, book reviews I'd try on Croly from time to time. Through the year there was hardly an issue in which I failed to appear—mostly anonymously.

The *New Republic* came into existence when liberalism, often called progressivism, was emerging in scattered nuclei through America: in Boston around Louis D. Brandeis and Felix Frankfurter, in New York in many interpenetrating circles, in Pennsylvania around Gifford Pinchot, in Cleveland around Newton D. Baker, in Wisconsin around Governor Robert M. La Follette, in Iowa around Senator Jonathan P. Dolliver, in Idaho around Senator William E. Borah, in California around Hiram Johnson. The *New Republic* was set up to draw these nuclei together into a coordinated liberal movement.

At the outset the *New Republic* was successful in this enterprise. Every progressive or liberal nucleus in the United States welcomed the *New Republic*. There had not been available any organ of up-to-date liberalism. We had the *Nation* under Villard, representing the intensely honest liberalism of John Stuart Mill and Carl Schurz. But the times had changed.

In its early years the *New Republic* operated like a Committee of

Correspondence of the time of the American Revolution. In every part of the country it could enumerate among its friends the leading liberals and progressives. It could count on like-minded groups abroad, the *Nation* group and *New Statesman* group in London, the Dreyfusards in France, Lajpat Rai and the Indian Independence movement, Hu Shih and a galaxy of enlightened Chinese and Japanese.

In the summer of 1914 Henry S. Pritchett, president of the boards of the Santa Fe and the Carnegie Corporation, asked me to come down to New York to see him. He was concerned about the activities of the corporation in planting libraries. Andrew Carnegie had been more passionate about libraries than about anything else in his whole passionate life, and in his will he had made colossal provision for the planting of libraries. Fifty millions had gone into the venture, and the corporation had never even inquired how the libraries were functioning. A community applied for a library: the corporation examined the figures for population and, according to the figures, made a grant of ten, fifteen, twenty-five, or fifty thousand, with the stipulation that the community should supply every year fifteen per cent of the grant for maintenance. The service was administered by James Bertram, employee and friend of Andrew Carnegie, who after Carnegie's death made a sort of religion out of planting libraries. The only control Bertram exercised was over the architectural plans, which he tried to keep uniform from Bangor, Maine, to Calexico, California.

Certain items of information as to the operation of the libraries had come, more or less accidentally, to the corporation. For example, the corporation learned of a library in Texas surrounded by a twelve-foot-high board fence, with no gate for entrance. The corporation had granted funds for the library, and it had been constructed properly according to Bertram's plans. But while it was building, a new town council was elected, which resolved that since no council could bind its successor, they were free to repudiate the pledge of fifteen per cent for maintenance; and this they did. The citizens gave the library any books they did not care to keep, and the aged daughter of a Confederate general volunteered to serve two hours a week as librarian, taking her reward in the form of sociability. After a few weeks people ceased to come. The librarian locked up the building and went home.

Soon the town was afflicted by an epidemic of depredations by tramps. The community could not imagine where the tramps were harbored; but the sheriff found that they had burrowed into the

basement of the library, warming themselves over a fire on the concrete basement floor, started with books and maintained with library
shelves. The sheriff chased them out, and the council decided to put
the building up at auction.

The only bidder was a barber, who thought that the basement would
do for barber chairs and a hairdressing shop, and the main floor, with
the book stacks removed, might do for Knights of Pythias and Odd Fellows meetings. The barber bid a thousand dollars and the building was
about to be knocked down to him when a political purist rose to declare that if the building were sold the thousand dollars would have
to be sent back to Mr. Carnegie. That was a shocking idea: send money
out of the State of Texas? The auction was closed, and the building
boarded around to keep out the tramps.

Another bit of information had come in from southern Ireland,
where there were nine Carnegie libraries with not a single book in
them. This condition came out of a natural compromise. The sheriffs
wanted the libraries, for a sheriff got a guinea for every public building
in his jurisdiction. The priests didn't want them, for they were supplying their parishioners with all the literature that was good for them.
Finally it was agreed that the libraries might be built on the condition
that there should never be any books in them. So the sheriffs got their
guineas, and no harm done.

What Pritchett wanted of me was ten weeks of my time, to go
through the country on a sort of sampling tour, to take a look at the
operations of as many libraries as I had time to visit. I thought a
professional librarian could do a better job, but Pritchett didn't agree.
What the corporation needed was not a comprehensive report but a
series of impressions of libraries and their place in the community. As
I always loved travel I accepted. I proceeded on a zigzag course
through the Middle West to the Coast, back through the South and
Middle Atlantic States, and finally through New England.

I saw many good libraries, well integrated into their communities,
and many bad ones, particularly in the South, where the chairman of
the library board might tell me, seriously, that the Carnegie Corporation owned the publishing houses and meant to make back, in
fifteen per cent maintenance, whatever it had invested in buildings.
Also, I would frequently find board members who thought reading a
futile and usually an injurious activity. I found relatively few towns in
which the library had been located where it would be most accessible,

and some towns where the library had been located on a practically inaccessible site, to oblige some powerful real-estate owner.

Some libraries, great and small, had made themselves into vital organs of the community life. The librarian would make it his business—more often her business—to know everybody in the community and his potential library needs. If a birth was announced the mother got a card with a list of books on child care. If the community was contemplating improved roads, the authorities received lists of books on different kinds of paving and the use of the split-log drag. And knowing the needs of the community, the librarian spent her modest book appropriations with a view to maximum community use.

Other libraries in towns of the same size, with population of the same character, were absolutely inert. The book collections were built up on abstract library principles and had no relation to local requirements. The librarian was mere custodian of books and eyed with suspicion anyone who wanted to draw out a book. Could he be counted on to return it or might he leave the community, taking the book along with him? Would he leave the book in the hammock under the tree, for the night dew and perhaps the morning rain? Such things happen, every librarian knows. Librarians differ in the importance they assign to losses, relatively to services.

Not buildings nor even book collections, but trained, intelligent, enterprising library service makes a real library. This I saw as clearly in my sampling experience as I could have seen if I had had time to visit all the libraries of the United States. And the libraries, by and large, were the Cinderellas of the educational world, with no prince upon the horizon. The librarians were all underpaid—most of them shockingly underpaid. The salaries even of the best librarians filled me with shame for my niggardly country. Few had any training other than an underpaid semi-apprentice job in a library afforded. But work with books is by nature so attractive to intelligent young women that they will accept almost any kind of salary, put up with any kind of difficulties in equipping themselves for the job.

I had gone out into the country to get up a report criticizing the libraries. I came back with a report criticizing the communities and the Carnegie Corporation, sowing libraries broadcast with not an effective thought on the vital factor of library service. My report was brief. Except for the necessary illustrations it could have been put in a nutshell.

First, I recommended the setting up, by the corporation, of a machinery for bringing in, every year, a detailed report of the operations of all existing Carnegie libraries.

Second, no more libraries to be planted except after a thorough survey of the community, its sentiments, its needs, its realization of the importance of trained library service, and its willingness to pay for service.

Third, divert as much as practicable of available library funds to the promotion and support of library training.

I was called to a meeting of the corporation board after submitting my report. Elihu Root presided. In a five-minute talk of crystal clarity he summarized my report for the board. Then Mr. Bertram swung his hatchet.

"Your proposals, Doctor Johnson, fly straight in the face of Mr. Carnegie's intentions. He wanted to give libraries to communities and leave the communities absolutely free to manage them any way they might see fit. He abominated centralized, bureaucratic control. That is exactly what you want to introduce.

"Mr. Carnegie never wanted an unnecessary cent to be spent in the administration of his charities. I have administered the whole huge enterprise of establishing libraries with just one secretary, with a desk in my room. To do what you propose would require twelve secretaries and at least six rooms—a big unnecesary expense."

"Not so huge an expense," I ventured to say, "for keeping track of an investment of fifty millions."

"A big expense, and unnecessary," Mr. Bertram reiterated. "And as for library training, Mr. Carnegie never believed in it. He believed in having books where anybody could get hold of them. What made him, he used to say, was a private library a philanthropic gentleman opened to him. A librarian's business is to hand out the books. That doesn't require a long, expensive training."

"What does the board propose to do with the report?" Mr. Root asked.

"I move," said Bertram, "the board thank Doctor Johnson and reject his report."

I rose to go. Mr. Root offered me his hand. "Come and have tea with me, Doctor Johnson, at half-past four, in my apartment. I'll have Pritchett too. He's sorry he couldn't be here for this meeting. We all prefer scotch, don't we?"

"Yes, thank you."

I had never met Elihu Root before that day. I was in awe of him, as the greatest American lawyer, and against him, as a reactionary. But I found him a delightful host.

"We were all for your report, Doctor Johnson, except Bertram. But, you see, Bertram was in Carnegie's service for years. He loved Carnegie, and Carnegie was devoted to him. And we can't do anything to hurt the old fellow, who retires before the year is out. However, you will see, your recommendations will presently be in force."

The next day I called at the corporation office to ask for one of the copies of my report. "I'm sorry," the secretary said. "Mr. Bertram had it destroyed."

The report out of the way, Mr. Bertram became my cordial friend. He often invited me to join him for so-called "tea," and if the tea was abundant enough, he admitted that there was much in my report worth taking into account. He was sorry it had been destroyed.

But apparently one copy survived, for about fifteen years later a librarian from Melbourne, Australia, called on me and mentioned my report, which he had read several years before. I went to Fred Keppel, then president of the corporation, and asked for a copy for myself.

Over the strenuous objection of his secretary Keppel gave me a printed copy. I think it had been edited somewhat. I did not see in this printed copy any serious criticism of the corporation's past policy, or any recommendation for a permanent office of Carnegie library reports. But there was enough still unchanged to make it recognizable to me—about all any author can expect of manuscripts I have edited myself.

TWENTY-FIVE

An Editor of the "New Republic"

CHARLIE BEARD used to say that so long as American political science was cultivated by lawyers and men of affairs it was creative and significant. One found real political thinking in the writings of Hamilton, Jefferson, John Adams, Madison, Calhoun, Alexander Stevens, Henry Clay, Stephen A. Douglas, Abraham Lincoln. But after the Civil War political science fell into the hands of the professors, who proceeded to systematize and sterilize it.

There was always a kernel of truth in Charlie's assertions, even the wildest. The man of affairs, if interested in political ideas, discusses them with mature men and women of varied experience. The professor discusses his ideas occasionally with his peers, in association meetings, but most commonly before his students, whom he has trained to take, not to give. The lay political scientist reads, but unsystematically, taking what runs in his own line of thought wherever he finds it. The professor has to know the literature of his subject. He has to distinguish between the more authoritative book and the less; he has to trace the origin and filiation of ideas. Too often the discipline he imposes on himself inhibits creative thought of his own.

Beard's doctrine of the sterility of the professorial mind was refuted by his own rich and varied contributions to political science. But the palm of leadership in the philosophy of the Progressive movement had been won by Herbert Croly, with his *Promise of American Life*.

Herbert Croly takes an honored place in the long line of lay political thinkers. I doubt that he had ever read a *Grundriss,* a *système,* or even a *trattato.* He had read widely in the works of the early American thinkers and knew the British thinkers well. He was adept in the philosophy of William James and John Dewey. The literary works he loved best were the writings of Henry Adams and Henry James. He had gathered into his list of friends, with quicksilver infallibility, men and women of free, adventuring mind.

What other influences went to make up the character of Herbert Croly I could not know, for Croly was utterly reticent as to his own spiritual 'career. In the seven years of our intimate association I cannot recall a single conversation revealing any part of Croly's early life. His oldest friends could tell of a profound spiritual crisis he went through in revolt against Auguste Comte, the god of his father, who had had the unique idea of baptizing the newborn Herbert in the philosophy of Comte. This crisis was alleged to lie at the basis of Croly's profound, often anguished seriousness.

In the second year of the *New Republic* Croly invited me to join the staff of editors for a year. I welcomed the opportunity. It was not difficult to get a year's leave from Cornell, as the department had been enriched by the accession of Allyn A. Young, one of the most brilliant of American economists, and the university budget could stand a momentary relief.

It was far from my intention to abandon academic life for journalism. I knew I could never compete with Walter Lippmann, then unfolding his wide wings, nor could I approach the brilliancy of style of Francis Hackett, who made of the book review a pungent essay in literary criticism. But I felt that I could, for a term, do fair yeoman service on a "Journal of Opinion," and, for myself, get nearer to the mature lay public that the economist would have to reach if his ideas were ever to mesh with political realities.

Life on the *New Republic* I found excitingly educational. The Great War, as we called it then, loomed over the horizon. Every week brought news from the battle fronts, in which Americans were involved only as sympathizers or as suppliers to the Allies. Still more important for America was news from the diplomatic front, and this front also involved the domestic political situation. Our editorial staff was in practically continuous consultation, but early in the week—Tuesdays if the paper was scheduled to go to press Wednesday nights— we had a prolonged meeting to lay out the editorial plan for the forthcoming issue. Often the discussion was acrimonious, for Croly and Walter Lippmann leaned heavily in their sympathies toward England, while Francis Hackett, as a militant Irish patriot, though detesting the Germans most of all, detested also the English handling of the Irish question. The movement for Irish independence was strong and growing steadily stronger. English policy was one of suppression, usually by means that were tolerable, but sometimes ruthless. Croly and Lippmann did not accept the view that England was denying independence to a people rightfully bent on freeing itself. There was Ulster, utterly opposed to Irish independence, and not a simple problem of a unified province that could go its own way, but a problem of a wide margin of mixed populations, mixed in religion and to a hypothetical extent in blood.

All our differences of opinion, however, ironed themselves out in the staff discussions, and the paper as it issued carried our unanimous views.

The staff conference allocated the tasks of composition to the several members. The leading editorial, usually dealing with the international situation, lay in the province of Croly; Lippmann might write an article seconding Croly in the international field or might devote himself to an exposition of national policy. Walter Weyl and I divided the field of economics, Weyl usually dealing with labor problems while I handled fiscal and trade problems. On rare occasions I broke into the leading place, through emergency. Croly might call me up from his apartment on the eve of our going to press.

"Alvin, have you seen the evening papers? The news cancels out my leader. Will you write an article to fill the space, about twenty-one hundred words?"

"Sure." It was Croly's innocent notion that whatever I had was always on tap. I'd rack my brains for a subject sufficiently pontifical and fall to. For the presses were to start at one, and I'd have to get the twenty-one hundred words, more or less, into the hands of our faithful copy editor, Charlotte Rudyard, then at the press reading the proof as it came, the ink still wet.

We all had a hand in the brief editorial paragraphs and were expected from time to time to contribute signed articles for the middle section of the paper—light middles, we called them. I liked to write light middles, as a relief from the responsibility of the editorial pages. Sometimes I printed them over my own name, sometimes I used one of several pseudonyms. Later I collected a number of the articles, supplemented by a longer sketch, and made a book of them, *John Stuyvesant, Ancestor.*

Quite as educational as the staff meetings were the informal discussions at the *New Republic* lunch table. Croly had a marvelous net out for notables and a genius for drawing out their opinions. So I met Gifford Pinchot and Albert J. Beveridge, the Thomas W. Lamonts,

Brandeis, Cardozo, Learned Hand, Newton D. Baker, Acheson and Berle, McAdoo, Chester Bowles, Ned Burling, George Rublee, Salmon Levinson, Amy Lowell, Dorothy Thompson, Edna Ferber, Sinclair Lewis, then a writer for the *Saturday Evening Post,* who gave us ten reasons why the life-size novel he was working on could never sell. The novel was *Main Street.* I also met the publishers Alfred Harcourt and Ben Huebsch. I first took Ben for a Don Quixote, because he let Francis Hackett persuade him to publish the complete works of Veblen, an enterprise that could never pay. But on closer acquaintance I found Ben something much rarer than a Don Quixote— a publisher with ideals and public spirit.

But our most instructive guests were Englishmen on brief visits to America. Gilbert Murray, Lord Robert Cecil, Sidney and Beatrice Webb, John Maynard Keynes, H. N. Brailsford, S. K. Ratcliffe, Norman Angell, John Masefield, H. G. Wells, Elizabeth Bibesco, daughter of Lord Asquith and wife of Prince Bibesco, Ambassador from Rumania. And a vistor so frequent as to be almost a member of the staff was Harold Laski, then an instructor in Harvard.

What impressed me most in our English guests was the openness and wide reach of their minds. They looked upon the Great War in the perspective of history. While Americans viewed the war as a wanton criminal enterprise of the Kaiser and the German General Staff, the Englishmen saw in it the culmination of forces over which no single nation had had actual control, in the existing state of international anarchy. We Americans were all deeply affected by the tales of German atrocities widely circulated by the press—the worst ones by word of mouth. The attitude of most of our English friends was that war itself was a ghastly atrocity, but that the Germans were not more atrocious than a nation in the German position, between formidable enemies on the East and the West, might be expected to be.

But in spite of this British fairness of mind, or perhaps because of it, our English friends were utterly resolute in defense of the British war policy, wholly prepared for any sacrifices to be borne on the way to victory.

Of all our English friends, the one I most admired was John Maynard Keynes. I held many reservations on his economics, yet I recognized him as far the most creative economic thinker of our time. He represented the most splendid achievement of civilization, British liberty, liberty to think and to act in spite of oppressors from above and below. There was a marvelous charm in his personality, upstanding, brave and free, human, as passionate about the art of his wife, a distinguished professional dancer, as about his own compelling economic doctrines.

I had a talk with him soon after his book on the *Economic Consequences of the Peace* appeared in America.

"Keynes," I said, "you weren't fair to Wilson. He is a Presbyterian, yes; he has a long body and short legs, like all the great orators of history; but was there ever a man more deeply devoted to humanity?"

"True," said Keynes. "I was unfair. I had to be unfair. For the prestige of Wilson was the support of the monstrous Treaty of Versailles. I had to destroy that support if I could."

Many years later, when Keynes had come over to discuss economic policy with President Roosevelt, he came to see me.

"Alvin," he said, "maybe what I say will offend you. I don't think your President Roosevelt knows anything about economics."

"You don't offend me," I said. "I wish he knew a bit more about it, but I'm for him anyway."

Some memoir of Roosevelt records his opinion of that time: John Maynard Keynes seemed to him, not an economist, but just a mathematician. I trust those two great and true men may be meeting in the Elysian Fields, and between them solving the problems that beset us on our stupid but fertile black soil.

Public opinion in America was rapidly deteriorating, to employ a term borrowed from diplomacy. Except for the small body of irreconcilable pacifists, the anti-British Irish, and a fraction of the German-Americans, the whole American population was drifting away from neutrality. President Wilson was composing one note of protest after another to the belligerents. Both sides were violating American rights under international law, the Germans by their submarine warfare, the British by their unwarranted extension of the categories of contraband and by their blockade on the high seas, which virtually dried up our trade not only with Germany but with the European neutrals. As between the two wrongs, the submarine warfare was infinitely the more outrageous. The successive messages of President Wilson slanted more and more away from neutrality. The *New Republic* was undergoing the same shift away from the sentiment of neutrality, and soon found itself a fairly consistent supporter of Wilson. Often its editorials looked like a preliminary rehearsal of a Wilson pronunciamento. In wide circles the *New Republic* came to be regarded as a Wilson organ, a reputation perhaps helpful to the circulation but not unembarrassing. For the *New Republic* saw greater crises approaching and meant to retain its freedom to criticize.

All the official information made available to the public exhibited confidence in Allied victory. We of the *New Republic* were not confident that without American intervention the Germans could be beaten. They were indeed held in stalemate on the French front, but the Russian front did not look good to us. The Russians had unlimited manpower but scant and unreliable fire power. The Russian publicity would gloat over the preference of Ivan for the bayonet, as against rifle and machine gun. To us this meant that the Russians were out of ammunition and were forcing their soldiers to charge with bayonets against withering German fire. How long could the bravest army hold out under such conditions? We feared that Russia would be knocked out and that all the forces on the Eastern front, at least one-third of Germany's military power, would be transferred to the French front. In such case the only barrier to German victory would lie in the intervention of the United States. This the *New Republic* saw; but we were by no means sure that Wilson saw it, or would act upon it. Nevertheless, we were in favor of the re-election of Wilson in 1916. We did not like the slogan "He kept us out of war," because we foresaw that he, or Charles Evans Hughes, if he won the election, might have to take us into war. But we conceived that much turned on what conditions we fixed to our belligerency, and we knew that Wilson had thought deeply on this.

The war party was growing stronger, day by day, and more violent. All who were not for an immediate declaration of war were denounced as pro-Germans, pacifists. As Theodore Roosevelt, in the period of his neutrality leanings, had been friendly to the *New Republic,* so after his conversion to war he became particularly bitter against us. He would let loose a swarm of winged words, of the wasp variety, such as that the *New Republic* was run by three anemic gentiles and three international Jews. To make up the number of anemic gentiles he must have counted Francis Hackett, whose hot Irish blood was diluted with cayenne pepper; to make up the number of international Jews he must have counted me.

My year's leave of absence was drawing to a close. Since I was not prepared to leave academic life, I had either to return to Cornell or accept a more attractive position at Stanford, offered me by the new and vigorous president, Ray Lyman Wilbur. I went to Stanford.

As in the East, the war party in California was becoming more and

more vociferous. Wilson was anathema to them. Anything to beat
Wilson; they had inaugurated a whispering campaign on Wilson's
private life. He was charged with having loved more ladies than one.
He had indeed carried on a long correspondence, through many years,
with a charming and distinguished lady, who had kept the letters in a
suitcase. This a sneaking Republican had stolen and delivered to
Roosevelt.

What the letters were like is known to a journalistic friend of mine,
who was commissioned to read them through. Exercises in literary
composition, mellifluously soporific. Nothing else. Roosevelt refused
to use them. Scandalmongering, he declared, had never proved politically effective.

But there were men in the party who thought Roosevelt was overlooking an important new factor. For the first time women were to
vote for president. Would they not apply the Caesar's wife criterion of
fitness for the presidency?

I was invited by organizations of women voters to discuss the issues
of the campaign. At my first meeting I inquired what issues they wanted
me to discuss. The chairman told me frankly they wanted to know
how much truth there was in the awful stories circulated about Wilson.

I addressed a question to the meeting. Would women, now voting
for the first time, be swayed by such stories, even supposing they were
true, at a time when war and peace were in the balance; and if war,
what should be the conditions of our belligerency? The whole audience
seemed to unite in an emphatic no. I was glad. I had been an ardent
advocate of women's suffrage all my adult life. Now I was assured
they would vote responsibly.

As the year went on the war situation became more and more grave.
I kept in touch with the *New Republic* by correspondence. We were
agreed that America would soon be forced to enter the war. Russia
was breaking down.

In the early spring of 1917 I got a telegram from the *New Republic*.
"War is inevitable. Come back and join us. We need you."

I had some difficulty in persuading President Wilbur to give me an
immediate leave of absence. What of my students? I said that in four
weeks practically all of them would be off to officers' training camps,
and he himself would be in Washington. That guess was a shot in the
dark, but it hit. Wilbur told me that he was already arranging for an
office in Washington, to help in securing a proper official position for
his friend Herbert Hoover, who would have to leave Belgium, where he

was serving as Commissioner of Food Relief. With that he granted my application for leave.

War had not actually been declared, and the pacifists were making one last desperate effort to keep America neutral. My old friend David Starr Jordan invited me to a meeting called by Emily Green Balch, to make plans for marshaling the lovers of peace. I called on Jordan and told him I loved peace as much as ever and hated war. But, I said, as of the moment Germany had won the war. If we did not come in the Allies would sue for peace, on Germany's own terms, and within a very few weeks Germany would take as much of Russia as she pleased, retain Belgium and French Lorraine, reduce Hungary, Bulgaria, and Turkey to vassalage, and stand forth, the overwhelming power of the Eurasian continent. Would she be a peaceful power? She could not be. She would have to maintain a mighty army to hold the vast non-German populations in order, and the German General Staff would become the most powerful body in the world.

"If I believed that your analysis is sound," Jordan said, "I too would urge America to enter the war. I do not believe it."

A year later he wrote me, recalling our talk. "You were right," he concluded his letter, "and I was wrong. But we will still work together for universal peace."

TWENTY-SIX

The War Years

For a brief time the *New Republic* enjoyed the privilege of standing with the majority. The majority—at least the articulate majority—were for war, and the *New Republic* had declared itself for war in advance of President Wilson. Naturally we alienated those of our friends who persisted in opposition to American participation in the Great War. Intervention, we called it. To the general public participation and intervention meant the same thing. To us the difference in meaning was vital. Participation meant throwing our forces in with those of the Allies, with our war objectives borrowed from them: intervention meant aid to the Allies to the extreme extent of our power, but on condition that we shared in shaping the objectives of the war. The Allies, we had been authoritatively informed by our English friends, were bound by secret treaties to pursue the war until each member of the alliance secured certain advantages. Even without our sources of information we would have known that the "sacred egoism" of the Italian statesmen would not have permitted Italy's joining the Allies without substantial promises, at least for the acquisition of the Trentino, Istria, and Dalmatia. The decrepit empire of Turkey was to be carved up; obviously Russia was to have Constantinople and the lands washed by the Black Sea. Who was to have the southern half of Asia Minor? Italy, of course. For was not France to extend her hold on Syria deep into Cilicia, far beyond the upper Euphrates and into the Armenian highlands? Was not England to have Arabia and Mesopotamia, thus consolidating her control of the Persian Gulf?

The *New Republic* was ardent for war against German imperialism, but not for war to promote Allied imperialism. Since American intervention offered the only force that could save the Allies from defeat, America was in a position to demand the cancellation of the secret treaties and the throwing upon the table of the peace conference all the problems of the international situation, to be settled with a free hand. We trusted Wilson to make some such conditions. If we as private citizens could know of the secret treaties, surely the President of the United States would have exact information about them. To our astonishment, Wilson at the beginning of the Peace Conference asserted that he had never heard of the secret treaties.

Our insistence on the defining of the objectives of the war alienated more and more of our warlike friends. The American mind is simple. Objectives of a war? Why, the only objective worth considering is victory, total victory, the crushing of the enemy.

"Lay on, MacDuff, And damn'd be he who first cries, 'Hold, enough!' " That's American, even though it's Shakespeare.

"Inter arma silent leges," wrote a Roman philosopher. The laws are mute amid the clangor of arms. No one was ever so unrealistic as to assert that private interests go into hiding when the flames of war sweep over the horizon. War has always been attended by an orgy of profiteering. How could it be otherwise? The demand of war for matériel is insatiable and instant. There is no time for bargaining with the suppliers of arms and munitions. The army purchasing agent asks not, How much? but, How soon? If a billion dollars' worth of smokeless powder and high explosives is to be shot away, what does it matter that the army paid two billion for it? Anyway, it was assumed that the victorious Allies would collect the whole of the cost of the war from the defeated enemy countries. Why try to bargain down our own purveyors, profiteering, in the last analysis, at the expense of the enemy?

When America entered the war in April 1917 we had already developed a powerful, if disorderly, war industry for supplying the Allies. Our industrialists had organized themselves under gentlemen's agreements not to compete and spoil one another's markets.

Some minor items remained uncornered. A brilliant and ardent student of philosophy announced to his friends that he was tired of starving as a philosopher: he would follow the example of Thales, who cornered the olive presses and by this practical coup immensely enhanced his repute as a philosopher. Our young philosopher made a scientific study of the requirements of the Allies and found one item that had not been cornered—machine-gun parts. These were procured at shamefully low prices from the little machine shops scattered up and down the Atlantic seaboard. Our friend borrowed a little money for traveling expenses and organized the machine shops into a combine that could exact real prices. The machine shops more than doubled their take, and our philosopher was soon a millionaire. But, unlike Thales, he never went back to philosophy.

Our industrialists had liberated themselves from the scourge of competition, but the Allied governments competed merrily. British, French, and Russian agents would race to the promising sources of supply and outbid one another scandalously. Eventually the situation became intolerable, and under the auspices of the House of Morgan a combined Anglo-French Purchasing Agency was set up. The agency did good work in curbing the exactions of American industry, particularly through the expert service of Leland L. Sommers, of all men I have ever known the most widely and precisely informed on American industry. But the agency had to be gentle with the industry of a country which through its loans was paying the bills. Some of the prices charged the Allies made me gasp.

The most crucial industrial issue of the time was shipping. Submarine sinkings, even before Germany decided on unlimited submarine warfare, far exceeded new construction. Every British and French shipyard was working desperately to finish off new bottoms and could not wait for their own steel industries to supply them. The key material was the ship plate, and our own steel industry was putting out plates in what for the time were huge quantities.

I was responsible for gathering material on production and prices for the *New Republic* and got inside information where I could, naturally never absolutely accurate but good for all practical purposes. I learned that our steel industry was collecting thirty-seven cents a pound for ship plates. Years earlier, in browsing among the steel plants in the Pittsburgh district, I had learned that ship plates could be supplied profitably at two cents a pound. Costs had of course risen, but I doubted that they could have risen more than four hundred per cent. My economic conscience would have settled for eight cents a pound. Later, when Bernard M. Baruch finally was given power to control prices, he fixed the price of ship plates at four cents a pound. I had been damned as a pernicious radical and busybody intellectual when I had urged a reduction to eight cents.

The first months after our entry into the war were very exciting for a journalist. New York and Washington were crowded with men with projects, who were eager to lay their plans before anyone who could get them into print. A project for supplementing our dwindling shipping was presented to me by an engineer with wide industrial connections, Fred Clark, son of my beloved teacher John Bates Clark. While sinkings were running ahead of ship construction, the yards building wooden ships were idle all along the coast from Maine to Texas. They had turned out small schooners and fishing craft mostly, but occasionally a windjammer to carry Australian wheat cheaply, though tediously, to the European markets. Why should they not turn out a swarm of small ships? They could build a thousand-ton ship good for several years at sea. A submarine could hardly afford one of its precious torpedoes for a thousand-ton ship; and if it did waste torpedoes, it was impossible to dispose of ten thousand tons of cargo carried in ten separate units with the same facility as ten thousand tons in a single steel ship.

I carried on a vigorous campaign for wooden ships, only to be set down as an ill-informed amateur. We did build some wooden ships, more to make employment in politically important localities than to contribute to the solution of the problems of bottomry. Instead of the thousand-ton ship with the partial invulnerability of insignificance, we built wooden ships of four or five thousand tons, too big to be held together by their timber structure in heavy seas, and even more vulnerable than the steel ship, since they could not safely be speeded up. The steel men offered a solution: a great new steel shipbuilding plant to be set up on the bottomless mud of Hog Island on the Delaware. When the war ended Hog Island had sunk several hundred millions in the mud and promised optimistically to begin production in two years, or in three at most. With peace, the whole project was abandoned.

On our entry into the war a great swarm of charming British gentlemen, civilians with titles we Americans had known only from the English novel, and army and navy officers in striking uniform, came swiftly over the sea. They were socially the most acceptable people America had seen since the Revolutionary occupation of New York and Philadelphia. Whatever they did was correct and worthy of imitation.

In the quarter-century before the war the cigar, the *ancien-régime* aristocrat of the tobacco world, had established an unchallenged dominion over all successful Americans. This had been accomplished partly by advertising, but mainly by the finesse of drawing the writing public into an unpaid propaganda. No politician could appear on the stage or in fiction without his big black cigar. No gentleman in letters or in life could be without his perfecto if he were a solid head of a household, or a panatela if he affected well-groomed hands and an esthetic air. There was indeed a Jacquerie, which included even some of the gilded youth, who took to the cigarette—coffin nails, in the parlance of the time. But the pipe—that was a proper adjunct to the Irish laborer digging up the street or excavating basements.

There were some of us for whom the pipe was a necessity. We had to manage it like a secret sin. At no social gathering could a man light up a pipe without evoking a smiling admonition. At no first-class restaurant could you take two puffs from a pipe without incurring the disciplinary action of the headwaiter. The clubs were out of bounds, except that the fine old liberal Century Club had a room up under the eaves where a man could furtively smoke his pipe.

Our English visitors were entirely unconscious of the established smokers' hierarchy. They were all pipesmokers, except Winston Churchill. They smoked their pipes everywhere, "downstairs and upstairs and in my lady's chamber." Timidly other pipesmokers came out of hiding. How many of them appeared! Soon by force of numbers they gathered confidence. The pipe was at last free.

The reader may think I've wasted a lot of space on a triviality. Triviality? The freeing of the pipe was the sole contribution of the Great War to American liberty. How could an honest historian fail to celebrate it?

Nothing can match the attracting power of confusion. Washington had become the world center of confusion; accordingly, everybody wanted to go to Washington and add his bit. Dollar-a-year men swarmed to Washington and flew around in circles. Of course I accepted eagerly an invitation from Wesley Mitchell to join his division in the Council of National Defense. He was working on the statistics of supply and requirements. Supply was not easy to determine, for the data were meager and often discordant. But requirement was an anarchy. There were forty divisions, each convinced that its particular requirements should be met in full, and for the sake of prudence each marked them up with a multiplier. It was my job to go around among the divisions and by accumulating and comparing figures for requirements work nearer to an estimate of what actually was required.

Mitchell and I were uncertain as to what we would do with our results, if we attained to useful results. We were at first under the Council of National Defense, a body of outstanding business and professional men under the chairmanship of Bernard M. Baruch. The council was a coordinating body, but it was clothed only with the power of discussion and advice. Soon a more select body was segregated out under the name of the War Industries Board, of which Baruch was chairman. Nor had the War Industries Board any tangible power to enforce coordination. President Wilson was a strict constructionist of the Constitution and was hesitant to extend the powers of the Executive, even in time of war. What was needed was the power to allocate men and materials and to hold prices in check. The board did not have those powers.

But we were confident Baruch would manage to get them. He was in almost daily contact with President Wilson, who loved him and trusted him. But there was much sentiment in favor of turning all the powers of coordination over to a new Cabinet officer, Secretary of Munitions. Many favored transferring the Secretary of War, Newton D. Baker, to this new post. The Army was said to be supporting the elder Stettinius.

I had known Baker before the war as an important leader of the liberal movement, and so I encroached occasionally on his precious time to urge the necessity of coordination of services. Baker was surprisingly friendly, for so high an official, and talked the situation over confidentially—but not frankly. I made bold also to ask Baker why Theodore Roosevelt should not have the command of a division in France he so ardently desired. On this point Baker was energetically frank. As Secretary of War he was under obligation to see that when our boys came to face the enemy they were as well equipped and as well led as possible. We could not risk a repetition of the San Juan Hill affair, with the commander rushing his men into a situation from which only luck extricated them.

For Secretary of Munitions, if there was to be one, Baruch was the choice of every dollar-a-year man I met. People who did not know much about finance and industry regarded him as simply a very successful speculator. And, indeed, Baruch described himself as a speculator. No doubt he was just a speculator in his early career. But later his activity consisted in investing his capital where he had good factual reasons for anticipating success. Properly, he was a venture capitalist in the speculative market.

To invest with reasonable safety in a new or an expanding industry one needed to know a lot about the market for its product and the competitive situation. Baruch's experience had taught him that quite as important was the character of the men running the industry, not the stuffed shirts holding the presidency of the company or the chairmanship of the board, but the key men actually operating the works, whom the public hardly ever heard of. He was busily building up an organization of key men in the War Industries Board. Given power, the machine would work.

Sometimes I would see Baruch pausing for a few moments as he issued from the White House, tall, slender, his handsome face wreathed in serenity, and I would ask myself, Has he got the authority yet? It came much later and in a way that seemed almost accidental.

The steel companies had patriotically offered to reduce the price of ship plates to fifteen cents a pound for our own government, expecting to get a better price from the Allied governments. President Wilson insisted that we had to give equal treatment to our Allies, and the steel men consented reluctantly. In the meantime Baruch had found out that ship plates could be produced with a good profit at four cents. But of course the steel men would refuse to come down, unless they were compelled to do so. President Wilson's indignation was stirred, I surmise. Anyway, he gave Baruch a letter authorizing him to commandeer the whole steel industry, if necessary, to secure fair prices. When the steel men saw the letter their adamantine resolution to resist "confiscatory" prices vaporized.

Baruch was Secretary of Munitions without the title. If he could commandeer steel he could commandeer anything. There was no longer any question about his power to allocate materials and control prices.

We were at last in condition to prepare for war.

It was profoundly heartening to me to see an effective organization of war industry rising out of the confusion under the wand of Bernard M. Baruch. I also derived great satisfaction from what I saw of the Food Control organization under Herbert Hoover. I had first met Hoover in the apartment of his friend Ray Lyman Wilbur, shortly after his arrival from Belgium. Hoover was walking the floor in disgust at the way he was being treated. The Department of Agriculture claimed that it had all the resources of personnel and organization needed to handle the food problem. It did not need his help, although it could use his name to head its propaganda work.

"If all they can use me for is to knit, why did they send for me?" Hoover demanded indignantly. Wilbur tried to ease Hoover's mood by dwelling on the universality of the jealous obstruction of the permanent departments to any outside help. President Wilson, he said, was quite alive to the situation and had promised him soon to issue an executive order establishing Hoover's independent position.

When I came to Washington in June of 1917 as a dollar-a-year man Hoover's organization was functioning powerfully. It had command not only of the sources of supply and the channels of trade, but also of the hearts and will of all the housewives of America. If reports came in that butter supplies were running short, an order went forth to all the American world: "Save butter and win the war." Immediately butter became an iridescent film on the gray surface of the war bread—especially thin in the hotels and restaurants. If the reports of shortage proved erroneous and protests came in that butter was oozing from the warehouse eaves, another order would go out: "Thanks to the patriotism of the American public the butter crisis is over. Butter may be eaten freely, with moderation."

At the Department of Agriculture I was told that many of the Hoover orders were unnecessary. There was plenty of food; we would have surpluses far beyond anything we could export. I doubted the validity of these assertions. But granted that there might be something in them, they were beside the point. Hoover was building up a national morale behind our war effort such as we had never had before.

I was continuing my discouraging efforts to get together figures for the real requirements of the several services. I had collected a lot of information, before I came to Washington, on the stocks and current production of the various key materials. I thought this information would prepare me to be useful. It did not. Wherever I went I was given an account of requirements and supplies, but everywhere I had to promise to regard the information as confidential—too confidential to go into a bulletin to be circulated among the forty divisions. Thus I found that along with any new information, about everything I knew in advance was being ticketed as "confidential." My official mind was being reduced to a *tabula rasa*.

The Navy wanted a certain amount of wool—three times our annual clip. The Army wanted four times our annual clip. Other departments you wouldn't have thought of as needing wool made up an imposing aggregate. And the only department that was making any effort to economize in its wool demand was civilian consumption, under the chairmanship of Professor Edwin Gay of Harvard. I found Professor Gay delightful, rich in information, which he gave freely but, of course, confidentially. In Washington, he declared, there is no such thing as a confidence that is kept. Distribute a circular marked "Absolutely Confidential" to forty responsible officials: you will find that five or ten have friends in the press who would like a discreet eyeful. Of course the editor or special writer promises absolutely confidential treatment;

he wants the information only to help his newspaper to steer away from pitfalls. All those promises are given in good faith; yet somehow the matter gets into the press, and the devil is to pay.

With this warning Professor Gay gave me an account of an incident the press might have liked to use, but to the serious injury of the national interest. I promised to keep it confidential for twenty years. When the twenty years were over I narrated it at a meeting organized in Professor Gay's honor. It gave him a slight shock to hear my public statement of confidential matter, but he was not seriously displeased.

The Army and Navy needed wool, but wool was also needed for women's skirts. Their coats could be part shoddy, but shoddy can't be used in sheer woolens. And sheer woolens were a necessity of life, essential to the national morale. Gay had calculated the minimum requirement of wool for women's wear.

A disturbing announcement came in from Paris. The couturiers had got together and decreed that women's skirts were to be lengthened by four inches. The amount of wool required for this additional length was equivalent to the uniforms of several Army divisions.

Someone suggested to Gay that the French Ambassador, Jean Jules Jusserand, might help. Gay put the problem before him.

"That is simple," said Jusserand. "I will cable my government. They will take it up with the couturiers."

A week later Jusserand reported that the couturiers, assembled in extraordinary session, had decreed that skirts, instead of being lengthened by four inches were to be shortened by four inches. And thus women's knees, after untold years of seclusion, came out into the open to help win the war.

It was a relief to turn to the division of wood industries. There I wasn't afflicted with the confidential inhibition. We had timber enough, if we could get it out, and that depended mainly on labor. Forest labor in the Northwest was seriously infected by the sabotage techniques of the I.W.W., but that was being taken care of by a special setup in the Labor Department, which handled the problem successfully by diplomacy.

But there was a minor problem of shortage which illustrates the procedures of the era of confusion.

We needed black walnut for gun stocks and airplane wings. It is a strong, compact wood; and Civil War experience had shown that while stocks made of other woods might shatter on the impact of a bullet, blinding a soldier with slivers, the bullet would bore a clean hole through black walnut.

There are no heavy stands of black walnut; only trees here and there in the forest or planted along village streets. The black walnut, like other nut-bearing trees, is in nature dependent entirely upon squirrel arboriculture for propagation. The nuts can't be borne by the wind, and if they are carried by water they are deposited in swamps or on sandbars where walnuts won't grow. Squirrels carry them a distance from the tree and bury them for later use, as with other nuts. But the black walnut is so dramatic in size and shape that the squirrel rarely forgets to go back after it. Hence walnut trees are rare in the forest.

We had commandeered the beautiful old walnut trees on the village streets, but they met only a tithe of the requirement. What was the next best wood? Mahogany. It too is rare. An isolated tree towers above the jungle of the highlands of Central America. It is cut and drawn by a forty-ox team to a dry run which will be a river when the torrential rains come. As mahogany is too heavy to float by itself, two equally large cedars are cut and the logs lashed to the mahogany log. With good luck the mahogany is carried down to the seacoast, with the cedar logs that make paper-light material for cigar boxes.

Unfortunately there was a revolution going on in Central America, and the guerrillas had eaten up all the oxen. There was no way of getting the logs to the dry run. So mahogany was out. But there was a fine wood in West Africa which passed with the furniture trade for mahogany. We detached a lot of our desperately needed shipping to bring over these African "mahogany" logs.

When we ripped them open we found a lot of them were affected by "wind shakes." In the violent winds of West Africa the trees are whipped about, with much internal breakage of fiber. The wind over, the tree proceeds to repair the lesions by a mixture of gum and wood fiber. This makes a beautiful wood for furniture, but it breaks easily at the shakes. It wouldn't do for military use.

The furniture trade was up in arms. If all this condemned mahogany were thrown on the market it would disrupt the mahogany trade, to the grave damage of the national morale. The government had to agree either to export the logs when peace returned or burn them up. I've never heard of those logs since, nor, though I am ardent for mahogany, have I ever seen in any shop the beautiful wind-shake mahogany I saw in sample at Washington.

Finally it occurred to our wise men to put the question to representatives of our Allies: "What do you use for gun stocks and airplane wings?" They used oak. Oh, well, but that was English oak and French oak. The foreign experts assured us that neither the French nor the British oaks were as strong or finished so well as the American white oak. But how about the blinding slivers? The experts assured us that this was a problem of the 1860s, when large caliber bullets fired at low velocity were in use. The modern small-caliber, high velocity bullet bored a clean hole through anything.

I would gladly have continued as a dollar-a-year man to the end of the war, but, as I saw it, the confusion in the War Industries Board was clearing up. On the other hand, the confusion in public opinion was growing steadily worse. I felt that I was more needed on the *New Republic* than on the War Industries Board.

It was already clear that the Central Powers were doomed to defeat. The unlimited submarine warfare was Germany's last throw. It had been her hope, through ship sinkings, to cut off the flow of American manpower and matériel across the Atlantic. Although sinkings were still a grave problem, the techniques of defense against submarines had so far advanced that immense American forces were getting across. The Central Powers had lost their superiority in manpower. They still held superiority in the air, but victory could not be won through air power.

It was true, Germany had won the war against Russia. Fighting with bayonets and clubbed rifles against machine guns had broken the spirit of the Russian soldier. He mutinied against his generals, Sukhomlinov, Minister of War, and the Tsar himself. A revolution was on, headed by the socialist liberal, Alexander Kerenski. America hoped that Kerenski might galvanize the Russian soldier into new efforts of resistance. The Tsar had been deposed; the soldier would be fighting for a republic. Wilson sent Elihu Root to Moscow by way of the perilous voyage to Archangel in the hope of persuading Kerenski, with unlimited promises of American aid, to organize an offensive against the Germans. Kerenski tried it but failed. American promises could not replace the cartridges the Russian soldiers lacked. Kerenski had to fall back in defeat: and Lenin and Trotsky rose up to take over. They had a scant following under the horrid-sounding but etymologically innocent name, Bolsheviks. But they proclaimed their intent to make peace, and all Russia wanted peace. Russia was in their hands. They signed the Treaty of Brest-Litovsk early in 1918, giving Germany everything she asked for.

Russia, we felt, or rather Lenin and Trotsky, had betrayed us. We forgot the Russians, without cartridges, mowed down by the Germans like standing grain. We forgot the Russian soldiers plodding in the Carpathian snows with nothing on their feet but bast shoes, worn through in twenty miles to leave a fleck of blood on every foot imprint in the snow. We had forgotten Sukhomlinov's irritated reply to Stanley King, who was offering to supply New England shoes. "Oh, shoes! I've had so much trouble with shoes, I've decided not to get any."

Lenin and Trotsky had betrayed us. After the war, perhaps we'd have something to say to them. The Allied capitals and Washington filled with Russian propagandists for war on Lenin and Trotsky. Wherever there was a chance of publicity these agents appeared. Of course they were for an American type of republic in Russia. But Lenin and Trotsky and the Bolsheviks!

One day, not long after the Armistice, Bob Hallowell, our *New Republic* treasurer, brought to our lunch table an extremely pretty and clever lady, whom I shall call Madame X. She was a Social Revolutionary, she said. She hated Tsarism. She had been passionate for Kerenski. But Lenin and Trotsky were the arch criminals of creation. Madame X intimated that the Jews were behind them but, feeling the atmosphere cooling off, admitted that Lenin, né Ulyanov, was no Jew, though animated by the Jew Karl Marx. Then she went off into descriptions of Russian liberal life, so eloquent and charming the editors felt very warm toward her.

After lunch Bob came to me in discontent. Madame X had said that all the editors were very nice to her except Dr. Johnson, who appeared to be suspicious.

"I am," I said. "She is some kind of spy. I'm going to warn the editors to watch their step when she's around."

"Listen," said Bob. "How did I come to meet her? Charlotte and I were airing our dog on the Atlantic City boardwalk. We met a lady with a dog. The dogs made up. That's how we came to meet Madame X. Is that the way you get in contact with a spy?"

"You were registered, as from the *New Republic*. You were set down as possessed of a dog. She hired a dog."

Bob left me in high dudgeon.

A few days later Madame X called me on the phone. A brilliant

Social Revolutionary, Mr. Y, had just arrived from England with a document of enormous importance for every person in journalism. Would I come to tea?

I was far from thrilled, unsure how I should deport myself in a nest of spies. But it has always been my rule: Try anything—once.

Mr. Y was a kind of Russian jumping jack, who'd say some cryptic words and hop up and down. They offered me some prewar vodka, but though that could have interested me I professed a passion for that safe and useless beverage, tea. I waited for the document.

It was a manuscript entitled "Protocols of the Elders of Zion." I browsed through the pages: a horrid conspiracy for the Jewish conquest of the world, involving wars the nations could be pushed into by the Jews, like the World War just over, proletarian revolutions like the Bolshevik revolution in Russia, to the end that the Star of David should be the morning star of a Jewish-ruled world.

"This," I declared pontifically, "is a forgery. The whole idea is lifted out of a crazy French novel I read years ago."

"I assure you," said Madame X, "it is not a forgery. We have the documents to prove this project of ruin was adopted at a meeting of the leaders of Jewry. There was an honest rabbi present, who was horrified by the inhumanity of the project. Mr. Y, show the doctor his deposition."

I looked at it. "That too is a forgery."

"It is not!" said Madame X energetically. "I will tell you why I asked you to come. You are suspicious of me, outrageously and, I may say, impolitely. But you know publishers. This document is to be published. You could find a publisher who would put it out with a warning, not to charge the millions of innocent Jews with the crimes of the leaders, the Elders of Zion. I give you my word, if it is published and not published right, millions of Jews will die for it."

"I'm sorry," I said. "It is a patent fraud. I don't think any publisher will touch it."

I rose to go. I offered my hand. She wouldn't take it; but Mr. Y took my hand and bowed deeply, with the sardonic smile only a Russian can produce.

A few weeks later Madame X called me again by telephone. "Doctor Johnson, you said I couldn't get a publisher. I have one. Don't you want to come and take tea with me?"

"Yes," I said.

She was in high feather. "One of the six richest men in America is standing back of the publication. It will reach a hundred million people. And, alas, millions of Jews will die for it."

"Madame X," I pleaded, "you are employed by some interest which I don't know. But you are a woman, a very beautiful and accomplished woman. You are cultured, you are human. You know very well the document is a forgery. You know it may bring distress, perhaps death, to multitudes of innocent persons. How is it possible for you to view your work without horror?"

Madame X rose. "What has been done has been done. I'm sorry for the men and women and little children who will die for it. Good-by, Dr. Johnson. We will never meet again."

We never met.

Though Germany could not win, she could make us pay a ghastly price for victory. We could root the Germans out of their trenches: we proved that later in breaking in the St. Mihiel salient. We could no doubt force the passage of the Rhine even under German air superiority. We could bull our way through to Berlin, plowing out defensive forces on every stream and height of land. But the defensive is always in a better position than the offensive, given equal determination to fight on both sides and equal equipment. In such a campaign, for every German killed, two of ours, if not three or four, would perish. The most conservative military estimate of the cost of "marching" to Berlin, given bitter-end resistance, was a million and a half killed on our side—mostly Americans—for half a million Germans.

But how strong was bitter-end sentiment in Germany? We had ample evidence that the German civil population was utterly weary of the war and that the morale of the German soldier was not at all what it had been when the German Army came roaring down through Belgium. What kept Germany fighting was fear, fear that the Allies and America meant to destroy Germany, literally. There had been many wild threats by Frenchmen and British in the days of their military strength. They would push the French boundary to the Rhine and the Polish border to the Oder; they would dismantle German industry and dry up German trade; they would exact as indemnity everything Germany could produce above the most meager subsistence of the population. These were not official threats but were uttered by persons of sufficient prominence to inspire the German morale propaganda.

Naturally America, being fresh to the war, had had no time to calculate costs. To Berlin! And fertilize the fields all the way with German blood. Kill Huns—kill them. A screaming hurricane of wild hate swept America. One who did not throw his own screams of hate into the venomous cacophony was pro-German, or at least "seditious," the term used in that old time where now we would say "subversive."

All this played marvelously into the hands of the German bitter-enders. If Germany was to be destroyed in any event, better to go down fighting to the end. If German blood would richly fertilize the fields, Allied blood was just as good fertilizer, and there would be more of it.

The editors of the *New Republic* knew that peace was to be had on infinitely less exorbitant terms. The Germans would willingly give up Alsace-Lorraine, that pestilential "hole in the Vosges," as Bismarck prophetically called it. They would willingly give up Posen— a headache through decades—to the newly created state of Poland. They would willingly abolish the monarchy and set up a republic according to Western models. They would pay such indemnities as they could, grudgingly, of course. And that was about all they would do.

And that was about all any intelligent person on the Allied side wanted the Germans to do. It was all the *New Republic* wanted, all President Wilson wanted. Even if we had been willing to pay the price of carrying the war through to Berlin we would not have stood for the total crushing and peonization of the German people. There was a warning in the East, where the total defeat of Russia was turning that great land over to the Bolsheviks. We did not then realize the full meaning of communism, but we did not want communism to make the Rhine its western boundary.

A solution was obvious: President Wilson should issue proclamations assuring the German people that we had no intention of destroying them. President Wilson didn't need the urgings of the *New Republic* to make up his mind that this was one thing he had to do, but perhaps his stride was accelerated by the frequent interviews he granted our Walter Lippmann. Walter was young, earnest, ardent, the most persuasive figure in the whole field of political journalism. Woodrow Wilson would have had to be adamant not to be affected in some measure by Walter's seductive good sense.

We attacked any project of annexations that would tear integrated members from the living body of Germany. Alsace-Lorraine, yes; but the Rhine frontier, no. Posen for Poland, yes; but Silesia, no. For

Italy, the Trentino and Trieste, yes; but Dalmatia, no. The Croats and Slovenes to Serbia, yes; the Slovaks to Bohemia, yes. The German colonies, and the members of a dissected Turkey, if Turkey were cut up, to the League of Nations.

As to indemnities and the postwar position of Germany in world trade, I was assigned to formulate the *New Republic* policy, as the economist of the staff. On indemnities I took my cue from Bismarck's handling of the indemnity problem after the victory over France in 1871. Bismarck wanted all the French money he could get; he didn't want money he couldn't get. After consulting his economic experts he decided that five milliards of francs—about a billion dollars—was all the French economy would stand. It was a rich economy, very little damaged by war, and in a very short time, through domestic and foreign loans, France was able to pay off the indemnity and rid herself of the German occupation. The French citizen, in paying taxes toward interest on the loans, was paying his own fellow-citizens and friendly foreigners, not German victors. In the circumstances a Frenchman would pay.

A defeated Germany should pay all she could; but how much could she pay and still maintain a stable government? Before the war the value of all German properties was at the outside one hundred billion dollars. With her productive energies canalized for war industries, with the loss of Alsace-Lorraine and the Polish territories, and with the loss of her shipping and foreign outlets, her capital value could not exceed eighty billions. Her income, which had been ten billions, could not exceed eight billions, postwar. Ten per cent on capital was to my mind the absolute maximum any country can pay by way of total indemnity. Ten per cent of income, I calculated, was the maximum annual installment that could be paid. On this basis I estimated that the maximum indemnity Germany could be expected really to pay was eight billion dollars. Bismarck would have set me down as an academic ignoramus for venturing so high a figure. Bismarck would have judged that three or four billion was the maximum that could be taken off the international security market in three years.

But I was not a responsible Iron Chancellor and could cheerfully stand by my figure of eight billion. Allied war costs, excluding American, exceeded fifty billion dollars. Obviously it was a case for priorities.

It had been a principle of German military theory to push the theater of war into enemy territory, so that all incidental damage should be borne by the enemy state. Pursuant to this pernicious theory, the Germans had pushed the theater of war down through Belgium to the Marne. They ruined the country, and incidentally ruined themselves.

I thought it was a good idea to step on this theory by making reparation for such damage a claim in any circumstances upon a defeated aggressor. And so I drew a distinction between reparations and indemnity. As I figured the just claims of France and Belgium for damages to civil property, they amounted to about six billion. But nobody fails to inflate his damages. The claims would certainly be inflated to the outside possible eight billion.

I would not be so conceited as to think that it was my editorial, on reparations but no indemnities, that found its way into the Fourteen Points. Unfortunately, at the Peace Conference, President Wilson didn't understand the practical bearings of the principle. Nor did he quite understand my other editorial, "No Economic Barriers," intended to exclude differential duties against German goods. It proved not to be clear to President Wilson whether this meant no protective duties. Protective duties are not an absolute barrier against the trade of any state unless they are differential. But for good or evil, the principle, "No Economic Barriers," found its way into the Fourteen Points.

At that time I was a member of the Authors' Club, by the generosity of Andrew Carnegie housed on the top floor of Carnegie Hall. Occasionally I'd drop in there in the hope of meeting a living author. The nearest I came to that was a pleasant hour over scotch and soda with Hamlin Garland. For the rest, the authors I met were not entirely dead.

One evening I dropped in, for a Diogenes search for a real author. A group of old gentlemen whose books had been forgotten since the administration of Grover Cleveland invited me to sit with them.

"I have been reading the last *New Republic*," said one of them suavely. "I read the *New Republic* as I read the enemy communiqués. I see that you want to let your dear Germans out of the indemnity they ought to pay."

"You should have noted," I said, "we are for reparations, and reparations would take all the money Germany could possibly pay."

"Could possibly pay! She could pay the whole cost of the war she made. A hundred billion would be too little. Let the Germans be slaves for a century, to pay it."

"You're dreaming," I said. "A slave economy produces nothing but a little margin for the slave-driver."

"That's what you pro-Germans argue. I wish we had a real man for president. You New Republicans would be shot at sunrise."

"Thank you for your kind wish," I said, rising. "If wishes were horses, what a wild ride you'd have. Good night."

Externally I could take refuge in humor, but I was boiling inside. What the devil am I doing here? I asked myself:

> "Here where men sit and hear each other groan,
> Where palsy shakes a few last sad grey hairs."

I was grateful to Keats. His lines, in my memory, quieted my indignation. My extrovert psychology is not hospitable to indignation. It is a thorn in the foot.

But my doddering author was not alone in his attitude toward the *New Republic*. The American public was drinking deep drafts of hate. To Americans, hate is an unfamiliar beverage, as seductive and disastrous to them as hard liquor to primitive Indians.

All through the country solid citizens drunk with hate were ramping gloriously. To hell with the Huns and everything Hunnish—German names, the German language, Goethe and Lessing—to hell with them! German was ripped out of the high-school curricula. My own sedate birth state penalized the teaching of German, even by a father to his little son within the four walls of his house.

I winced for shame of America, my own beloved America. I was seeing much of the English. They were rational, tolerant, determined, fixed in their objectives, fully conscious of costs. I asked myself, Why are we Americans so inferior to the English in common sense, in tolerance, in moral courage, in respect for the rights and dignity of man? I still ask myself this question.

Is it because our English stock has been diluted by hordes of immigrants from the Continent, like my father and my father's son? No. The worst offenders against Jeffersonian principles of liberty and tolerance are the authentic old Americans, the men whose ancestors are supposed to have fled from England to establish liberty in America.

I think history would afford an answer, if one ever sat patiently at history's feet. The Colonial settlers of America did not come here for liberty, but for *their* liberty. Did not Cotton Mather propose to send out an armed ship to intercept and capture William Penn and the Quaker miscreants headed for the Delaware, and sell those miscreants into slavery in the West Indies? Liberty, yes, to serve God in your own way, and to hell with anyone who has the infamous delusion that there might be another way of serving God.

Religious intolerance was in the blood of the early Americans. When religion faded, intolerance remained in the deep channels it had dug in the American soul. Political intolerance had these channels to flow in.

But the English who had remained at home fought it out. Sure, they were likely to be beheaded or hanged; accused, they accepted liberty on their own recognizances, and appeared blithely for a trial rigged against them, like Sir Thomas More, who could have gone over to France but stood a trial he knew would condemn him and asked only that he might put his honored beard to one side, in the beheading, for his beard had never offended the king.

As a true American I am Anglophobe. But as a historian I know there can't be so many generations of man that the last one will not hold in honor the record of the indomitable English, separated, as Vergil wrote, from all mankind.

The Fourteen Points were proclaimed before Congress on January 8, 1918, and an additional six points of clarification followed later. To the English and French, they were a masterly venture in statecraft, worth at least twenty divisions for breaking the German war spirit. To our own bitter-enders, they were a pro-German document, a dastardly surrender of our right to inflict condign punishment on Germany. The hurricane of hate received new impetus. Whoever stood for Wilson and his treasonable "points" needed to be hunted down and exposed. I had the great privilege of being attended, wherever I went, by some of the stupidest of mankind, then drawn into the secret police. If I went to call on a lady, I gave a real job to my guardians. Who else ever called on that lady; and was he a German agent? They composed a dossier on me, thin paper twelve inches deep. I'd give much to have that dossier, to reprint it here. The reader would find that Alvin Johnson is not the commonplace figure who appears occasionally through earlier chapters of this book, but a romantic, sinister figure, too clever to be caught.

The Germans accepted an armistice, based on the Fourteen Points and the supplementary Six Points, in October 1918. Our bitter-enders shrieked themselves to inarticulate hoarseness, but all the peoples of the world drew deep breaths of relief. The war was over. But peace, not yet.

President Wilson determined to go to the Peace Conference that was to be assembled at Versailles in the spring of 1919. We of the

New Republic did not want him to go. Our argument was that he needed to remain at home, to control the opposition of the isolationists in Congress. My own opinion had another base. I admired Wilson as the greatest moral leader of our time; but the essential items of the peace would be economic, and Wilson not only knew nothing of economics but despised every economic idea. I wanted Louis D. Brandeis to head our delegation. Brandeis was our greatest lawyer, our profoundest practical economist, a wise man who knew the past and could foresee the future. When I put it to him in a personal interview he said, "No. The men who are to meet at Versailles are in the position of gods. They can give the world universal peace or universal chaos. I am not a candidate for the position of a god."

Since Wilson insisted on going to the Peace Conference, we of the *New Republic* supported his going, but with misgivings. We rejoiced in the colossal welcome given him, as king of peace, arbiter of the destinies of all mankind. We rejoiced to find that England and France took the Fourteen Points seriously, as the basis of peace. No annexations: this point was taken seriously, though Wilson, who admitted knowing nothing of geography, permitted Italy, in recovering the Trentino, to cut deep into the Austrian Tyrol and seize the German area that had produced Arnold Winkelried, hero of a hundred thousand schoolboy declamations.

But what was a little territory in this wide world of ours? I waited impatiently for the decisions on the nub of the peace, reparations versus indemnities.

And here the sky-topping morality of Wilson and his total incapacity in economics destroyed all my hopes for a peace that could last. I had calculated closely: Germany could and would pay reparations of eight billion dollars, a large sum but conceivably payable. The other great moralist, Jan Smuts of South Africa, presented Wilson with the argument: If we require payment to a French peasant woman for the hut the Germans destroyed, why should we not give her reparation for her chief breadwinner, her husband, shot by the Germans? Why should we not give indemnity to all the peoples, including South Africans, whose sons were killed by the Germans in the war?

Morally there was no answer to this question. Wilson said yes. The rest of the commission, mostly legally trained, told him that no lawyer would accept this extension of the reparations idea. Wilson is reported to have said, "I don't give a damn for the lawyers. I mean to include pensions and separation allowances in reparations."

This increased the outside figure of reparations from the eight billion dollars that conceivably could have been paid to sixty billion that could not be paid. It was the total ruin of the hope for peace.

I wrote a leader for the *New Republic,* "A Punic Peace." Later John Maynard Keynes, a better journalist than I, put it, "A Carthaginian Peace," in his *Economic Consequences of the Peace.*

We of the *New Republic* realized perfectly and painfully that the two great moralists, Smuts and Wilson, had let a djinn out of the bottle that would loom to the skies and tread down into dust the hopes of mankind for peace. We knew that the new German republic could not function, as a child stricken in infancy by poliomyelitis cannot play an athletic role.

Our Wilson, the Wilson we loved, the Wilson for whom we had let ourselves be a hissing and a byword, had sold us out for the empty approval of a moralist more unrealistic than himself. What we foresaw was a long, embittered jangle between the victors and the vanquished over "reparations" that could never be paid. We foresaw the impossibility of any German government raising money enough to support itself, let alone paying anything on reparations. We foresaw the ascent of incipient German inflation into the realm of the Milky Way. We foresaw a new German autocracy and another world war, rising out of the djinn bottle of those excellent moralists, Wilson and Smuts.

We repudiated the Treaty of Versailles and all its works and found ourselves lined up with our old enemies the isolationists, who did not welcome us as heartily as our old friends, thick and thin for Wilson and the League, detested us. Very well; we still had our virtue and our sense that we were right to clothe us.

I could not be very hopeful about the position of the *New Republic.* President Ray Lyman Wilbur of Stanford, who had kept my position open through the years, was insisting that I come back to the university.

I loved Stanford and the sweet California environment. I realized how pleasant it was to stand on the lecture platform before hundreds of hopeful boys and charming girls and expound pleasantly the principles of economics. But that was no longer for me. I had formed my relations with an adult public. Half of them hated me, but even hatred is a vital relation. I made up my mind to stay in New York. If the time came when the *New Republic* didn't need me, I could find something else to do. Indeed, there was a newspaper editor who offered me a humorous column. Imagine: a solemn figure like me pounding out a humorous column!

Since I meant to stay in New York, whatever happened, I began to think of a home of my own. There was a grave and increasing disadvantage in rented quarters, because I had become addicted to antique mahogany.

I had thought nothing of the antique. Good solid Detroit oak looked right to me. But my wife, who through my life has opened my eyes to nearly everything worth while, had me get her a little antique sewing table. It was so beautiful that next I got some antique chairs. A friend introduced me to a dealer, who introduced me to a queer fellow named Liebowitz, who made it his business to go through Virginia and the Carolinas, buying up century-old pieces which some degenerate heirs wanted to replace with bird's-eye maple. He'd get the mahogany for a song and sell it to me for two songs. I still boast that an antique sideboard I got for very little was so attractive when I had it refinished that I was offered a profit of a thousand dollars if I would part with it. Of course I wouldn't.

I thought I was above ideas of authenticity, but I was put to the test when I was introduced to an old lady in Brooklyn who had a little card table, with a letter proving it was done by Heppelwhite's own hand. I wanted the table; but the lady asked four hundred dollars, far too much for me. Later she died, and her effects were auctioned off. I bid for the table and got it for thirty dollars. But the charming letter of Heppelwhite, presenting the table to a friend, was lost. Still, I have the table and love it.

Clearly I couldn't subject a quantity of priceless mahogany to successive movings. With my wife and children, now augmented by a fifth, Felicia, an incredibly lovely baby, I drove my car through every suburb of Westchester and deep into New Jersey looking for houses, my ten-year-old daughter Dorothy admonishing, "Parents, when you have found the place that suits you, buy it, so I can have a garden."

One day I saw as small an advertisement as will run in a newspaper: "Gentleman's estate on the Hudson." It had been my dream to live by a river. I called up the agent. The house was in Nyack, the town of all towns that most attracted me. I took the first train to my place in White Plains, packed my family into the car, and drove over to look at the house. It was big and in bad repair, of Norman architecture; there were three acres of grounds running down to the river with grass so tall that my children, running through it, were just progressive waves in the grass.

Back at White Plains, I took the first train to the city, hurried to the agent, and made the down payment. Somebody else put in a down payment with another agent, but two hours later. He could whistle.

There I have lived since 1919, there I will live until "the Master of all good workmen calls me to work anew." There my sixth and seventh children were born, Ingrith and Astrith, from their birth to this day, pure joy to me. There my wife set up her educational system, to train her seven children herself up to the point where they could enter college. There we have noble trees of our own planting, and gardens and gardens, violets and daffodils and hyacinths, tulips and peonies, roses and roses and roses, and lilies, chrysanthemums, and all the wealth of the westering year.

There we are at home.

TWENTY-SEVEN

The New School

IF YOU want to live at ease in the political world, be a practical reactionary. Say that you want the government to put a prohibitive duty on paprika, to promote your Carolina plantation; you can find someone who wants a prohibitive duty on South African lobster tails, in favor of the New England lobster pots. You two can get together a hundred similar interests, including those of office-seekers and contractors. You can all win together, following the politician's version of the Golden Rule: "Scratch my back and I'll scratch yours."

It is much harder to live at ease, or even in peace, as a liberal. For liberalism is by nature uncompromising, intransigent. I have my ideal of the public interest. You have yours. I can't get you to support my ideal in return for my support of yours. Ideals don't cooperate. They fight.

A liberal must make certain assumptions as to the character of what Veblen calls the "underlying population"—roughly, the farmers, the manual workers, the housewives, the routine white-collar workers. To promote the interests of the underlying population is the accepted objective of all liberals. But how? Is the underlying population a mob, to be held in check for its own good? Is it the People, whose voice is the voice of God? Shall we say that the underlying population is fundamentally sound but ignorant of its real interests and needing leadership from the "higher" classes, to discover and define those interests, and promote them, whether the underlying population wills or no? Or is "leadership" a misnomer for the activity of the liberal democrat? Is it not his proper business to understand and clarify the interests of the people while leaving it to the people's will to decide?

The Middle-Western liberal assumes that the underlying population is sound and endowed with good sense. They are the People. The Western attitude is well expressed in Bryan's acceptance of his defeat, "The People have given and the People have taken away: Blessed be the name of the People."

Nowadays instead of "the People" we say, "the grass roots," a metaphor that means nothing to Easterners, who use it nevertheless. To the Middle Westerner, all flesh is grass; grass goes down with the frost or withers in the drought; but the roots abide, ready to put forth again.

Croly's assumptions as to the underlying population were the friendly Eastern assumptions; mine were the Western. His theory of leadership implied finding out what was good for the people and doing it for them. Consent? They might consent after the event. Croly's ideal leaders were Alexander Hamilton, in history, and Theodore Roosevelt and Woodrow Wilson in our day. Mine were Thomas Jefferson, La Follette, Norris, Brandeis. Croly admired Brandeis; but when we had Brandeis at the luncheon table Croly's eloquence froze up. He could not talk with that equalitarian, states' rights liberal.

In all practical issues Croly and I were in complete agreement. Still, I felt a bit lonely in the nest of Eastern liberals and seized an opportunity, when we were enlisting assistant editors, to draw in a man of my kind of liberalism. He was a teacher in a California school, who sent us a poem of exultation over the fall of the age-old oppressive dynasties of Russia, Germany, and Austria. The poem breathed the spirit of the Peasant Revolts and the storming of the Bastille. I wanted that man and got him—Maxwell Anderson.

Anderson was exactly what I surmised he would be, an uncompromising Western liberal. I took great comfort from his presence on the staff. But the edges of his liberalism had not weathered off like mine and were often lacerating to Croly's fingers. Finally Croly picked a quarrel in which he was in the wrong and removed Anderson from the staff. That didn't hurt Anderson. After an interlude in daily journalism he entered upon his real career as dramatist, one of the most powerful of our time.

Croly and I had often discussed projects for a new educational institution. We envied England the London School of Economics, as we saw it through the eyes of Harold Laski. The London School was not handicapped by mobs of beef-devouring alumni, passionate about football and contemptuous of scholarship. The London School had enjoyed unchallenged liberty all through the war; in America professors departing by a hand's breadth from the prevailing war doctrine were fired. A frequent newspaper headline had been, "Another Professor Goes Pop."

Being free, the London School could address itself to real problems, even the most contentious of the time. It could train leaders for the Labour party and for the labor movement in general. Croly had glowing dreams of a school in New York where intelligent young men and women would be trained and go forth to supplement the planning work of the two-fisted union leaders. I had my doubts on this point. The militant union leaders I knew would accept our trained helpers humorously and set them at licking stamps. But I had no cold water to throw on the warm idea of a new school.

The need of a new institution which should be honestly free was actively discussed in other circles. Beard and Robinson had resigned from Columbia in disgust with the oppressive action of the trustees, not actually directed against them but, as they saw it, vitally affecting them. John Dewey was in revolt against academic timidity and futility; Wesley Mitchell, although invulnerable as a statistical economist, was deeply discontented. We had meetings at the *New Republic* with one after another of these men.

What we lacked was a catalyzer; and this lack came to be supplied by Caroline Bacon, wife of George W. Bacon, head of a great firm of consulting engineers. Caroline Bacon was a scholar in her own right, having been a professor at Smith. She drew us together in frequent meetings at her apartment, our number supplemented by Mrs. Willard Straight, Mrs. George Haven Putnam, Mrs. Learned Hand, Mrs. Victor Sorchan, and later Mrs. Thomas W. Lamont. Finally Thorstein Veblen came in from the University of Missouri to join us.

We were by no means agreed as to the kind of institution we wanted. Croly wanted a modest research and training center. Beard wanted a modest research center, without many concessions to the idea of supplying planning experts to the unions. Robinson wanted pleasant quarters where professors as cultivated gentlemen could present their ideas informally to cultivated gentlemen and ladies. He was agreeable to the plan of having a few research workers, preferably post-Ph.D.s, who would wander around freely, consulting the professors when they pleased.

My own view was that we ought to create a true school of advanced adult education. Under Albert Mansbridge a great movement for adult education was under way in England. But Mansbridge could premise great numbers of Englishmen, as able as any, who had never had access to high school. In America there were considerable groups of men and women who needed elementary and secondary instruction, but these were to be found mainly in the deep South or among groups of new immigrants. Their education, it seemed to me, was a job the public schools could undertake.

My own objective was an institution for the continued education of the educated. To my mind, the educated, particularly the college graduates, bore a heavy social responsibility. Nearly every one of them was in a position to influence the social and political action of a number of persons not privileged in education. It was therefore of the utmost importance that the educated mind remain clear and steady. But in America it was the educated who responded most promptly to the waves of dominant opinion. Through the war and postwar periods the educated mind had been subjected to torrents of emotion-bearing catchwords—pro-German, pacifist, sentimentalist, socialist, red, pink, fellow-traveler. These torrents had eroded the minds of the educated as violent summer storms erode the fields, carrying away the fertile topsoil, gashing deep gullies, leaving the field incapable of growing anything but witch grass and bull nettles.

I have always recognized that my own mind is just as subject to ruinous erosion as that of anyone else. Therefore I have put in cover crops from time to time to preserve the soil. Sometimes I discontinue my political reading for a time and devote myself to Montaigne's *Essays,* or Erasmus; or, better, I return to the Latin authors. The language itself and the thought take one's mind away from the current problems that only time can solve. So every three years I reread Plautus and Terence, Horace, Vergil, Tacitus, Seneca, and, with most delight, Pliny the Younger. For I seem to know Pliny personally. I think he was just like my beloved Professor Seligman. Like Seligman, Pliny was widely learned, possessed of ample fortune, and prominent in the highest political and social circles of the time. Pliny stood as close to the Emperor Trajan as Seligman to Theodore Roosevelt. Pliny had a modest pride in his achievements and his position, but he never forgot his obligation to the less fortunate. In his time what passed for the publication of a literary work was a public recitation under a portico in the Forum. Pliny was never too busy with his own affairs to go down to the Forum to hear and encourage even the youngest poet. Seligman would have done just that.

The English educated gentleman did not carry his classical textbooks to the old-book store but kept them through life and used them, as I do, to keep his mind from the deterioration that results from living wholly in the present crisis. I think that is one of the reasons the English are so much more level-headed than we are.

Whatever its character was to be, our new educational institution was forming. I did not consider it worth while to go deeply into the discussion of its functions. Once launched, an educational institution develops its own character and functions. But the prospective educational infant had to be named. At first I proposed to name it after some distinguished authority, Adam Smith, David Hume, James Madison. That idea met no response. It was too pedantic. After trying all sorts of names we accepted as a compromise The New School for Social Research.

Mitchell claimed that it was I who invented the name. If that is true, I deserve to be punished for it; and indeed, I have been punished, whether the sin was mine or not.

For this is New York, where people are too busy to distinguish between terms that look somewhat alike. The New School for Social Research looked somewhat like the Rand School of Social Science. Hundreds of thousands of New Yorkers, thirty years ago, assumed that the two institutions were the same. And as the Rand School was a socialist institution—and a very distinguished one—it was assumed that the New School was socialist. In time it has come to be realized, except in paleolithic circles, that the two institutions are different. But the delusion has persisted that they follow the same doctrine, a delusion that has cost us tens of thousands of students and hundreds of thousands in contributions.

The fact is that from the very beginning the New School has been what the Marxians call "bourgeois." We believed in free and untrammeled teaching. We wished to understand the other party's point of view as well as our own. But that, the Marxians said, was a typical bourgeois attitude. Where were our views different from the professed views of any ordinary university? At no point, except that we were trying to work out an educational plan under which professions of academic liberty could be taken seriously. But to the Marxians there is no truth but their truth, and the whole duty of a teacher is indoctrination.

We had our name, and under it a tentative educational plan not too inhumanly coordinated. A lecture program addressed to the intelligent adult was accepted, although lectures are not research. Thus Robinson and I were to have what we wanted. There was only one point of disagreement between us. I wanted the students to have a large share in determining the program. Robinson didn't object to my idea but was not interested in it.

To satisfy Beard we agreed to appoint three research fellows, and we counted on Mitchell to develop a research center in social and economic statistics. To satisfy Croly we leaned hospitably toward a project he was planning with Robert W. Bruère, a Labor Research Bureau which was to offer its services to labor unions in return for substantial fees. I didn't like this project. It was chaining one of our organs to a particular group. But I wasn't looking for trouble and presented my objections merely for the record.

We had three problems to dispose of: legal organization, location, and finances. Robinson had hoped that we might get on without a board of trustees. The function of an educational trustee, as Robinson saw it, was to thrust thick, blunt fingers into the delicate texture of intellectual policy. We convinced Robinson that we could not get a charter without a board. But we agreed that the board should concern itself only with finances and physical plant.

As for location, Beard argued strongly for renting space in some office building, as much as we needed and no more. If our following grew we could take additional square feet. Our venture was highly experimental. If it failed we would just cancel our lease, pack our papers into handbags, and go our way in peace. To own a building was to chain yourself down and force all sorts of compromises upon your free spirit.

All the rest of us revolted against Beard's idea. What following could we ever get in a flimsily partitioned space in a Forty-second Street skyscraper? Besides, the idea of remodeling a group of buildings for our use was very seductive to some of our members, particularly to Croly, former editor of the *Architectural Review,* and Mrs. Sorchan, an amateur architect of great talent. We voted for setting up the school in a group of buildings in the Chelsea district, not far from the offices of the *New Republic.*

As for finances, Beard insisted on a hand-to-mouth plan. No endowment; for every educational endowment tempts pirate educators to clamber over the gunwales, dirk in teeth. We should collect each year what we could in student fees and appeal to our friends, year by year, to cover any deficit. Just as a bank must be prepared at all times to meet lawful drafts upon it, so a school, to be solvent educationally, should be prepared to meet the current expectations of its followers and supporters. If it fails to meet those expectations, it has proven to be educationally bankrupt and should be foreclosed.

I did not agree with Beard. In my academic experience endowments had proved oppressive only through inadequacy. I believed that the adult educational program could in the end approach self-support. But research is another matter. Research earns nothing. It is never possible to determine in advance how much time a serious piece of research may require. Without resources that can be counted on, research is just an aspiration.

We could have procured a modest endowment fund at the time. We had generous friends. But after hearing Beard's passionate denunciation of endowments they were content to let us take our annual chances of solvency.

The New York educational authorities were cold to our petition for a charter, so we turned to the District of Columbia, which at that time would charter anything with any powers save letters of marque and reprisal. We acquired three old houses in London Terrace on West Twenty-third Street, well-built houses, once the homes of the minor aristocracy, but in our century degraded to cheap boarding houses. We acquired three houses on Twenty-fourth Street, backing our Twenty-third Street houses across a set of ashcan and alley-cat back yards. What we acquired was not the land, but the houses, with ground leases having still ten years to run.

In the fall term of 1918–19 Mrs. Sorchan and her assistant architect worked a true miracle. The second floors of two of the buildings and the party wall were removed to form a lofty, well-columned auditorium. The basement of another was transformed into refectory and kitchen. The back yards were transformed into a dignified court, with high walls at either end.

In an indifferent city like New York the plant of an institution appealing to the public must exhibit personality if people are to remember where it is. Mrs. Sorchan and her architect had given our plant a seductive if modest personality.

Professional scholars rarely have any appreciation of the subtleties of public appeal. Members of our faculty liked to criticize our plant as developed by an "interior decorator." Certainly the plant had shortcomings. The auditorium was the only room where we might lawfully assemble more than thirty persons. There was no chance under heaven of self-support from student fees if we observed the law. But those were the days of Prohibition, and the law counted for little among friends. Still, after I had assumed responsibility I was troubled about our top-floor lecture rooms, where Horace Kallen held sixty to eighty select liberals spellbound over Beauty and Use, or Dominant Ideals. If a fire should break out very few could squeeze through the narrow fire-escape stairway, to run over the roofs. The bulk of them and Kallen himself would have gone up in smoke, a burnt-offering to liberal philosophy.

Robinson's plan of academic administration was simple. As chairman he would be available for consultation for some hours each week; but most faculty business would be transacted informally over the lunch table. The functions of secretary, registrar, and treasurer were combined into a job for Emma Peters Smith, a determined young woman who had been adviser to graduate students at Barnard. The physical plant and the lunchroom were looked after by the superintendent, Fred Grote, who remained faithfully with the New School until well past normal retiring age.

The New School opened, with éclat, for the spring term of 1919. Every liberal in the city was excited by the novel venture of an institution headed by two such dynamic figures as Robinson and Beard, self-disfrocked from the conventional academic life.

I went over to the school the evening of the opening. The long, narrow reception room was jammed. I saw there about every liberal I knew, and a lot I had heard of. Miss Smith was writing down registrations in hectic haste, filing bills and checks under paperweights on her desk. From time to time she would jump up, wave a bill over her head, and cry, "Who gave me this twenty-dollar bill?"

A needle in a haystack. They had all been giving her twenty-dollar bills. But it was jolly.

The next year opened with what for the time was a true galaxy of liberal professors, drawn together as part-time lecturers by the prestige of Robinson and Beard. The year 1920–21 exhibited still further growth in prestige. As a concession to the practicalities, a business manager was added to the administrative staff, Lawrence K. Frank, whose principal function, I surmised, was to fight over prerogatives with Emma Smith's totalitarian attitudes. But Larry built up an impressive course on Mental Hygiene, given by a group of the most distinguished psychiatrists of the time. This may be set down as the germ of the psychoanalytic and psychological developments that came later.

But, alas, dissension soon penetrated our educational utopia. I think it began with the board, although I cannot say with certainty, for my attendance at board meetings was spotty. The meetings were devoted to money-raising. I had never raised a dollar in my life, and, I was confident, I'd never be able to raise a dollar. So my presence at board meetings seemed useless.

But the board saw two ways of raising money: by soliciting contributions and by increasing tuition receipts through an intensified campaign for students. Emma Smith had been in charge of publicity, but the board was dissatisfied with her announcements as too academic and added to the staff a trained publicity secretary, who proceeded to put out advertising abhorrent to Miss Smith, who ran to Beard with the newspaper clippings. "Good God," exclaimed Charlie. "They are selling us like a new brand of cheese."

And naturally, being vitally interested in attendance, members of the board would look over the catalogue and might suggest, to Robinson or Beard, that a certain lecturer was bad medicine. Robinson laid back his ears. Interference with academic liberty!

A more serious problem arose out of Croly's discontent with the performance of the institution. A school of social research: what research was it actually carrying on? Student attendance was growing: what of that? The school was becoming a mere lecture center, a one-horse Chautauqua.

The intellectuals of that time were very snooty about lectures. Chautauqua and all other lecturing institutions aroused their derision. As a rule they were abominable lecturers themselves. But even Charlie Beard, the most exciting lecturer in the whole academic world, was violent in his dispraise of the "lecture system." His ideal was the small, compact group of students in a give-and-take discussion with a professor. Strangely enough, Beard had never been good at that. He really welcomed the advancing deafness that made the discussion group unworkable for him.

Croly had come to detest Robinson and all his educational ideas. When Robinson offered him the manuscript of a book for the *New Republic* series, Croly wouldn't look at it. The book was *Mind in the Making*. It readily found a publisher, who sold more than a hundred thousand copies. None of us on the *New Republic* was very happy over our lost opportunity.

The only section of the New School that Croly considered worth while was the Labor Research Bureau, operated by Bruère, Ordway Tead, and Heber and Mary Blankenhorn. Croly started a campaign among the board to throw all the resources of the school to the Labor Research Bureau. The faction headed by Caroline Bacon resisted. The bureau was already absorbing the contributions raised by Croly and his friends. What justification was there for demanding more?

I had not taken part in the struggles going on inside the school and among the board, except to offer a few suggestions of compromise, which were of no effect. I had seen too much of academic rows to take this one very seriously. But Mrs. Sorchan, Mrs. Bacon, and Mrs. Putnam invited me to tea and laid the problem of the school before me. Nearly half the board were threatening to resign; Mitchell had returned to Columbia; Robinson and Beard were talking about resigning, and the rest of the faculty were at sixes and sevens and hardly spoke when they met. It was my duty, Caroline Bacon asserted, to go into the whole problem of the school and work out a plan by which it could be saved. Any plan I might propose they would back up.

I spent a week looking into matters. They were worse than had been represented to me. Most of the contributors had fallen away, and of the remaining contributors the most generous, Mrs. Straight, would leave us if the threatened secession from the board took place. I interviewed board members and faculty members; for the most part they were too angry to have useful opinions. Veblen, of course, was imperturbable. He invited me to give up the school as a lost cause and devote myself to raising thirty-five thousand dollars a year for three years, to enable him to go to England with his assistants on a research project to show that the British Kingdom and Empire were just the publicity façade of British business.

I drew up two possible plans and called a meeting of the board. The first plan leaned heavily in Croly's direction. It involved finding enough money for a well-balanced research faculty, whose aim should be to develop the potentialities of mature students, men and women from business and the professions, who had through years collected information but needed guidance to focus their experience creatively. The plan would trim down the general lecture courses to the minimum needed for recruiting students for advanced work. My second plan leaned toward Robinson. It proposed to develop the lecture courses still further, deliberately following the principle that nothing human was alien to us. But inside this lecture program I would maintain a small nucleus of trained research teachers, to take care of the occasional adult who needed guidance in working out an essay or a book.

At the meeting I presented first the plan designed to satisfy the

Croly faction. Some of the other faction voted for it. It would have been adopted if the Croly faction had not voted solidly against it, as they did against the other plan, which, however, carried. It had been their purpose to kill both plans and so put an end to the school. Not succeeding in this, they resigned from the board.

I thought the problem of the school had been solved. The remaining members of the board could work together and we could replace the secessionists with new members who were willing to work with us.

With the secession of the Croly faction we had lost our most potent contributors. We should have to work out new methods of raising money. The existing administrative staff had not been trained for this task. The surviving members of the board insisted that the business manager and the secretary should be replaced by a staff that would cooperate more efficiently with the money-raising efforts of the board. I didn't like the job of breaking the news of the reorganization to Robinson and Beard and the staff. But the business manager and the secretary were able persons and could easily find other employment.

When Robinson heard of the plan he called me on the phone.

"Johnson, will you be in your office this evening? I want to talk things over with you."

At eight he appeared, with Emma Smith, the secretary.

"Johnson, I'm quitting. I'm tired of the vexations the board has put me through. We were to be free; no interference in academic matters by the board. I've had to suffer more interference in these two years than in my entire career in the conventional institutions. I'm through."

"Beard is leaving too," said Emma Smith. "So that's the end of the New School."

"Oh, I don't know," I said, trying to sound calm.

"Whom will you get to run the school?"

"If I can't get anyone else, I'll run it myself."

In old times, when a Viking chief saw his end coming, he sailed his ship out to the horizon line and set fire to it. If he could sail the ship no longer, no one else should sail it. I think Robinson would have been happier, at first, if I had let his ship go down with him.

I have given here the whole story of my election to the headship of the school. It did not occur to me to ask for a vote of the board or the faculty.

I was far from rejoicing in my prospective office. To begin with, the ship I was seizing was not at all seaworthy. I had found that the maximum contributed income I could count on was twelve thousand five hundred dollars; the minimum to which expenses could be cut was thirty-five thousand. Tuition receipts had run about ten thousand. But three-fourths of the attendance was in courses of Robinson and Beard.

It had been one of my practical principles that any American could measure up to anything he had to do. The job before me involved administration and fund-raising, of all jobs the least suited to my temperament and abilities.

On my way home for the night pessimism came upon me in successive waves. But it is old habit with me to appeal from the pessimism of night to the optimism of morning. At daybreak I was out of my bed, prepared for anything. I'd try to get someone to do the educational administration, with myself discreetly behind his chair. Our best agents for recruiting students should be the students already familiar with our work. How could I get in touch with the students and stir them to cooperate?

That was a problem, like so many others, that settled itself. There had been much concern among the students over what looked like the impending closing of the school. A committee of the student body, Clara Woollie Mayer, W. W. Norton, and Mary Ely invited me to meet them for tea. They were confident that there were rich resources for the support of the school in the student body. They could not only recruit new students; they could also help in raising funds.

The meeting gave my spirits a great lift. It had been my dream, from the time of the launching of the school, that the students should be enlisted not only for the promotion of the institution but also for participation in its government. As a first step in this direction I had the board elect Clara Mayer to its membership.

I could write a whole chapter on C. W. M., as she appears on reams of New School stationery. She was the youngest member of a large and powerful family, and she won for us the support of her father, a solid and significant businessman, in whose memory the auditorium of the New School is dedicated. She won us the support of her mother, who had been an educator in her early life and remained a true and energetic educator to the end. She won us the support of her strong brothers and brave sisters. It would have been hard for the New School to survive without the true friendship and the staunch support of C. W. M. and the Mayer family.

One asset the school had that was not working, the intellectual power and towering reputation of Thorstein Veblen. I was convinced that scores of people would like to hear Veblen, if only they could hear him. But in his lectures he affected a voice so low that only the two or three students seated directly before him could hear him at all. I was so ungenerous as to regard this expiring voice as an affectation, for I had heard Veblen's strong, clear voice through the eucalyptus grove on the Stanford campus.

Among the students who had tried to hear Veblen was an able intellectual businessman, Daniel Cranford Smith. He proposed to supply our auditorium with loudspeaking apparatus. Another student, Helen Slade, undertook to recruit students from the graduate departments of Columbia. Here was this very great man, she argued, who might have to retire for reasons of ill health after a year. Could the Columbia students afford to miss this opportunity?

Helen Slade was so good a propagandist that Veblen found himself facing eighty students at the first lecture. As usual, he began by breathing the statement, "It is said that economics is a science." The loudspeaker roared, *It is said that economics is a science.* Veblen looked about him in astonishment and continued, "There are two questions: what is economics and what is science?" Again the loudspeaker roared out his statement. Then he became aware of the microphone, picked it up, and deposited it upside down in the wastebasket at his feet. He continued his lecture in a voice barely audible to the three students just in front of him.

The rest never came back.

A few days later, encountering Leo Wolman, Veblen said, "Johnson thought he would make me popular. But I fooled him."

If the New School had been an established success it would have been easy to find a director with better administrative capacities than mine. No established scholar was willing to consider so precarious a venture. But I thought I had found the man. Clark Ansley had been a professor of English literature at the University of Nebraska, and an extremely good teacher. In the course of an academic row he had left teaching and betaken himself to a farm in northern Michigan. He could afford the gamble of the New School, I thought, as he had nothing to lose. I invited him to join me. I'd hold the reins until he had got adjusted to the educational ways of the East.

Ansley could not adjust. His pattern of education was still the college. At the end of the year I had to bid him farewell and take over the job directly.

In making myself officially the director of the New School in 1923

I was running into grave embarrassment at the *New Republic,* where I still occupied my old post on the editorial staff. Croly continued to detest the New School—a failure, he regarded it, a pernicious failure. My position was becoming untenable. I picked a quarrel with Croly—a quarrel in which I was in the wrong—and resigned. Croly was glad to replace me with George Soule, a talented young economist whose economics suited Croly better than mine. For Soule carried the tradition of the London School, while my tradition was that of Columbia, Harvard, Chicago, Cornell.

Meantime the New School was steadily growing stronger. Attendance at the courses by lecturers who remained with us increased notably, and new lectures by John Watson, behavior psychologist, and W. I. Thomas, sociologist, brought us shoals of students. Attendance the first year, under the new regime, was nearly twice that of the last year of the old regime. More important still was the activity of the students in organizing and promoting courses and in working for the school as a whole.

One group petitioned me to invite Dr. Sandor Ferenczi to come over from Budapest to give a systematic course on psychoanalysis. Dr. Ferenczi was regarded as second in command after Freud in the psychoanalytic camp. The petition came to me as a sort of shock. I had held myself aloof from the psychoanalytic concepts that were floating around liberal New York. Robinson and Alexander Goldenweiser had drawn heavily on psychoanalysis in shaping their interpretations of life. Robinson used to say that he had learned from Freud that human action, even when it purports to be noble, is fundamentally dominated by "the meaner motives." If I thought otherwise, Robinson judged that I was addicted to wishful thinking.

Anyway, Ferenczi proved to be a most charming, cultivated gentleman, and his course drew such a fleet of limousines to Twenty-third Street that the local police captain felt called upon to investigate. He was an upstanding young fellow, attended by half a dozen ordinary cops. He explained to me that, seeing such a lot of limousines, he wanted to know what was going on, perhaps a lecture on physics or—or—

"Birth control," I suggested.

"Yes, that is what I suspected."

"Well, it's nothing of the kind, but a lecture on psychoanalytic psychology. Come in and hear it."

Soon the police captain and his squad retired to the door. "Pity that old boy can't speak English. I couldn't understand a word he said."

That was the only encounter I had with the police, except one other.

My friend George W. Bacon was trying to train me in money-raising. It wasn't clear to me whether he was making a silk purse out of a sow's ear, or a sow's ear out of a silk purse. Anyway, it was a difficult job.

Bacon organized a little dinner of businessmen at the school for me to cut my money-raising teeth on. A few days before the dinner he called me up and said the guests would expect liquor. I'd have to get it because he knew nothing about liquor, having been a total abstainer all his life.

It was in the time of Prohibition. I took the law seriously, but necessity knows no law. Where could I find liquor? A wise friend recommended me to a literary man uptown, who said over the phone that if I'd send him a list of what I wanted he'd see that it got started on its way.

Two days later my secretary came to me in a panic. There was a motorcycle policeman in the reception room, inquiring for me.

So my sins had found me out, I thought. I tried to remember the penalties. Fines? Jail? Well, everybody ought to have a term in jail, to know what life is really like. I asked the secretary to send him up.

He was a tall fellow with a businesslike air. "Doctor Johnson, you ordered some liquor."

"Yes," I said feebly.

He took the list from his pocket. "X bottles of scotch. X rye. X gin. Bitters. Bottle of Courvoisier brandy. That right?"

"Yes."

"I've got the package on my cycle. I'll bring it up."

He brought the package and opened it, asking me to verify the contents. He thrust the bill into my hand. I gave him the money and five dollars besides. He handed the five dollars back.

"No, thank you. The police don't take tips."

Of course, this was in the good old days.

To return to the activity of the students. A committee called on me to urge an invitation to Alfred Adler, then in the country. He too gave a course that was immensely popular, the attendance consisting largely of teachers and social workers. Another committee asked me to bring over Leo Stein to lecture on art. An enterprising friend of the New School, Mrs. Otto C. Sommerich, proposed a series of lectures

on modern art, poetry, music. I hesitated, because the course would
cost a lot and I did not know where to find students. Mrs. Sommerich
proceeded to find students enough to make the course a great success.
This was the beginning of the New School series of lectures and per-
formances in painting, poetry, music, the dance, the theater. Lewis
Mumford organized a group to bring Patrick Geddes, the father of
city planning, to the school.

In the last years on Twenty-third Street the New School was exactly the kind of institution I had dreamed of. We had an active board
with not a rift in its harmonious unity. We had a stimulating and
eminent body of lecturers, with no strife among them within our
walls, although outside of our walls the psychoanalysts and the Individual Psychologists detested one another; the lovers of classical
music ranted against the ruthless fury of the music of Varèse and
Henry Cowell. But our warring friends stacked their arms outside the
New School.

We had a large and increasing body of students, not an inert body
waiting for such educational fare as the school authorities might supply, but participating actively in curriculum-making, in recruiting
students for the classes they wished to organize, and in case of need
helping to raise subsidies to take care of any course deficit.

The New School was still far from self-supporting and had to raise
considerable sums through contributions. But we had generous friends
who saw to it that we made ends meet.

We tried very hard to make up advertisements that would draw
students from additional circles in New York. But I believed that the
most important force for bringing new students was the spontaneous
propaganda carried on by those who had found satisfaction in our
courses. To confirm their interest I launched a bulletin, with announcements of events but also with editorials presenting the case for
adult education. Mary Ely, of the American Association for Adult
Education, collected some of them for publication under the title,
Deliver Us from Dogma, and handed me the manuscript for my signature. It was the easiest way I ever encountered to get credit for a
book.

President Keppel of the Carnegie Corporation was deeply interested
in adult education. As he saw it, the crucial problem lay in the supply
of teachers. He proposed to me that the New School set up a group
of courses that would train for the teaching of adults. He would find
ten thousand dollars for the purpose.

My attitude toward Keppel's proposal, particularly the money part of it, was very friendly. But I thought I had found a better way to promote adult education. Most Americans are visual-minded. Why should we not search through the several hundred thousand films lying around New York in uncatalogued storage and piece together films of American geography, agriculture, industry, anthropology, sociology, hygiene, child care, and the like? Supplemented with appropriate literature, such films could offer realistic adult education to the millions. What outlets for the films could be found? The public libraries. I had already begun to speculate on the marvelous possibilities of the public libraries as educational institutions. (Some years later I went on a second pilgrimage through the libraries and came back with a manuscript the American Association for Adult Education published under the title, *The Public Library: A People's University.*)

In revolving my film project I saw that only if I could set up a committee headed by a great figure in the film industry could I hope to overcome the inertia that has delayed every form of educational project for decades and generations. I could not find a way to approach the big figures in the commercial films. But why not Thomas Edison? The basic work on the cinema had been done in his shop. The profits had slipped away from him, but possibly he would have enough pride in his invention to lend his name to our project.

I realized that the movie might be a sore point with Edison. His original work had taken two directions, one leading to the disk and another to the film. The disk exhibited clear-cut figures, interesting if narrowly limited. The film exhibited a succession of blurred figures shot through with eye-blinding bright spots. Edison made up his mind that there was nothing in the film. He would not patent it nor let the inventor patent it in his own name. In the sequel, the disk cinema became a museum curiosity. Out of the film, patented by others, came the gigantic movie industry.

The chances of interesting Edison in my visual-education project were not brilliant. But I got an effective introduction and wrote Edison about my plans and asked for an interview. My request was granted, and I went down to Menlo Park. Whether I succeeded or not in interesting Edison I'd have the honor of meeting a very great man. And I was still, and am still, child enough to be excited by human greatness.

At the door I was put into the hands of a short, round, middle-aged man, with an intriguing expression of benevolence combined with anxiety. He led me into a great hall, heavily cluttered with machinery, mostly obsolete. In an open space at the center of the hall sat the Wizard, incredibly long, in an incredibly extended, weather-beaten Morris chair.

The secretary shaped his hands into a conch and funneled into Edison's ear: "Doctor Johnson."

Edison offered me his long, bony, creative hand and looked at me with quizzical, half-shut eyes. "Let me introduce my temporary secretary," he said. "Meadowbrook. He has been my temporary secretary for forty-two years. Sometimes I think I ought to give him a permanent job."

I reminded Meadowbrook of my business. He funneled my request into Edison's ear.

"Oh, the movies! I invented the movies. And what did I get out of them? Nothing. Who got it? Hollywood.

"You want the movies for education. They could be educational. But Hollywood has ruined all that. Take a word of advice from me. Forget the movies. There could have been something in them, but there isn't."

With that he again offered me his hand. The interview was over.

Browning apostrophizes someone who "had seen Shelley plain." I had seen Edison plain. For me, personally, that was enough. But for my project, visual adult education, it was a defeat from which I have never succeeded in recovering.

Whatever my disappointments, the late twenties were the Golden Age of the New School. But no Golden Age lasts. A mighty builder bought the London Terrace estate and pulled the ground right out from under our houses. We should have to seek new quarters, with all the losses this implied. But we had a life of our own that did not depend on location.

TWENTY-EIGHT

Adventures in Land Reclamation

Elwood MEAD was a son of the high plains and the mountains. As state engineer of Wyoming, from 1888 to 1899, he had ridden through every river valley and over every grassy mountain slope in the state. He was intrepid, and took it as part of the day's work to gallop down a canyon with his gang of surveyors, pursued by giant Arapahoe Indians, the Hole-in-the-Wall brigands galloping up the canyon from below. There are always swamps along a canyon river, with willows and aspens where men and horses can hide. When pursuing horsemen galloped by on the road, each man was prepared to give a heavy blow on his horse's cheek if the horse opened its mouth to neigh.

Like so many men of our high Western country, Mead was interested most of all in water. It was said of him that he had water on the brain. Naturally; for in that huge square State of Wyoming there is not one acre that receives enough rainfall to grow a crop of wheat, although the wheat plant is very moderate in its demand for water. Wyoming doesn't look like an arid state. Drive along the Sweetwater, from its upper reaches where the Tetons are in plain view, down to the Pathfinder Canyon, now blocked by a great dam: at your left you see a jagged barrier of miniature mountains, but at your right a deliciously green slope rises to a modest mountain with top that parallels your road for scores of miles. The grass seems good, but not a cow or sheep is in sight, only little antelopes hopping about like mechanical toys. There is indeed one ranch house in the hundred miles, but I think it makes a living by keeping an emergency store of gasoline and a stock of highly emergency sandwiches.

If you are from the East you are surprised to see such illimitable grassy slopes without cows and picturesque real cowboys. You will be told that it takes a hundred acres to graze a cow, and there isn't much thrift in a cow who has to skim the thin grass off a hundred acres. Besides, cows are slow and thirsty animals and can't go far from water. Two miles to water is about all a cow will tolerate. An antelope thinks nothing of forty miles. Since a sheep does not perspire it can get along without drinking water if it is routed out early in the morning to graze on the dewy grass. With binoculars you might make out, high up the mountain slope, hundreds of sheep scattering around a sheepherder's wagon.

There are indeed rivers in Wyoming, fed by the melting snows of the high mountains. Anyone would dream of taking the water out of the rivers to irrigate the plains now covered with sagebrush, all uniformly six feet high. But the flow of the rivers is very irregular. Water is most abundant in the months when it is least needed. And so a first step in practical irrigation is the construction of storage dams. There are now a lot of them in Wyoming, some more than two hundred feet high and adorning the canyons with lovely lakes that dwindle to ponds when the water is drawn off for the fields in the midseason.

Mead's early career was one of surveying sites for dams and contours for the main ditches. He won so imposing a reputation that the Australian State of Victoria borrowed him to develop irrigated farms for the landless on the Murrumbidgee River—wherever that may be. After his return to America in 1915 he persuaded the State of California to develop two projects of irrigation and land settlement, one at Durham in north-central California and the other in the southern part of the state. The latter was a failure from the outset. The soil wasn't right. The Durham project also failed, partly because Mead miscalculated the alkali content of the soil and made no provision for draining off the seepage, but mainly because a cooperative agricultural settlement patterned on Danish methods had to be planted with settlers having none of the patience and cooperative spirit that have made Danish agriculture the finest example in the world of a prosperous way of rural life.

Mead was a passionate admirer of the Danish farmer, and so was I. He had seen more of Denmark than I had, but the evolution of Danish rural life had been a staple interest of my family. When my father left Denmark in 1849 rural Denmark was about as backward as any part of Europe. There were noble estates, church estates, estates pieced together by skinflint peasants, and wretched little tenant holdings, thatched huts with dwellers always near starvation. All but a tithe of the country population dreamed of emigration to America, but wages were too low to enable any but a few to accumulate money enough for steamship tickets. Three-quarters of a century later the noble estates had been broken up, the noble castles had become schools or museums. The church estates had been liquidated, and the typical farmer had his twenty or thirty acres, all paid for or financed by a long-term, low-interest government loan.

The urge to emigrate disappeared. A friend of mine who wished to set up in North Carolina a dairying community patterned after the Danish sent an agent to Denmark to induce a few Danish farm families to come to America. The agent spent six months in Denmark, going from farm to farm, offering extravagant terms. Not one Danish farmer could be induced to leave his own community, which afforded him all the happiness and security he required.

I first met Mead in San Francisco in 1916, presiding over a meeting of citizens who were organized to push the project of Boulder Dam. The problem of Boulder Dam was not a matter of engineering. The Reclamation engineers had picked out a site where there could be no question of the faulting of strata, which has ruined so many great dams constructed by private interests or municipalities. The Reclamation Service knows how to build dams. Not one of the hundred and fifty and more then standing had developed a single crack. Mead, who was leading the movement for Boulder Dam, had laid down the principle that there should not be a single stroke of a pickax before the engineers found sufficient deposits of round pebbles, granite or marble, for the huge dam. Mead would not hear of crushed rock, subject to further crushing as the masonry grew to imposing height.

Neither was the problem one of economics. The impounding of the Colorado River would remove forever the menace of the river breaking through the dikes of silt it had created and drowning out the Imperial Valley, as it started to do in Theodore Roosevelt's administration. The security of the Imperial Valley was alone worth the cost of the dam. The stored water, applied to irrigation, would be sufficient to pay for the dam in half a century. The hydroelectric power generated would pay for the dam in sixty-five years.

Economically the Boulder Dam was a triple gilt-edged investment. Just for that reason the electric light and power companies throughout the country fought the project tooth and nail. The public might form illusions as to the cheapness of power and demand reductions in rates. In the end Mead and the people won out, and the tourist may behold the most majestic dam in the world, holding back a beautiful lake, to be known forever as Lake Mead.

As Commissioner of Reclamation, a post to which he was appointed in 1924, Mead usually went out in summer for a quick survey of the Reclamation projects, particularly those that were "sick." On several of these expeditions I accompanied him, under the title of economic expert.

Our expeditions were mostly confined to the highlands of Wyoming, Montana, Idaho, the Dakotas, and Nebraska. This was the region in which Reclamation settlements were likely to be in distress. Both altitude and latitude were against them. In the Arizona and New Mexico projects it was possible to count on ten or more frost-free months; any crop, however long its season, could be grown, or a succession of short-season crops. The farmer on the Milk River in northern Montana could count on only three frost-free months. That was a sufficiently long period for spring wheat, and the Indians had grown a short-season type of corn, mixed blue "squaw" corn and flint. The yield was low, and no farmer could make such corn pay. Alfalfa thrived, but only two or three cuttings a year could be expected, as against eight or nine in Arizona.

The experts of the Department of Agriculture in the northern region pinned their faith on the sugar beet. The long hours of bright sunshine were said to encourage rapid growth and produce roots with high sugar content. This may be true. I had acquired from my Reclamation friends a healthy skepticism of the Department of Agriculture and all its works. I had another theory. In humid-land beet fields you will see a lot of stunted plants. Pull them up and cut open the roots; you will find them drilled through by nematodes, primordial worms. There were no nematodes in the Reclamation beet fields. Every plant produced its giant root if the ground had been properly fertilized and tilled.

The farmer got five dollars a ton for beets delivered to the sugar mill. If he produced twelve tons to the acre he only broke even; twenty-two tons gave him a net of fifty dollars an acre, plus five or ten dollars for the tops, for fattening sheep. On forty acres the farmer could make over two thousand dollars, real money in those days.

Nevertheless beet culture was an economic parasite. That five dollars a ton was payment for three hundred pounds of sugar, at a cent and three-quarters a pound—just the excess over the world price that the consumer was compelled to pay by the tariff. Without the import duty, not a beet could be grown.

This was not the whole story of the beet's parasitism. It was necessary to bring in Mexican families from the border to thin and hoe and harvest the beets. A Mexican with a likely wife and three or four half-grown children could care for ten acres of beets. At the time I visited the Reclamation projects the Mexican family was paid fifty dollars an acre, an annual family wage of five hundred dollars. No Nordics except Mormons would have touched the beet for such compensation. Mormon families took care of their own beets and prospered exceedingly.

All through that country sheep-raising was the staple rural enterprise. For the winter the sheep were folded in low valleys, feeding on salt sage and grasses cured by frost into a rich hay. In the spring after the lambing, flocks of seven or eight hundred would be put under a sheepherder, who would lead them slowly up the grassy mountain slopes, a mile a day at first, then two miles, and later a little more. As the year began to verge toward frost, the sheepherder and his flock would creep back to the valley, where the grasses had grown untouched, for the winter's feed. The lambs not needed for breeding would be sorted out and either fattened on the spot with corn imported from the East or shipped down into the corn country, to be fattened for market.

There was something absurd in the economy of the country. The sheep men were paying a dollar a bushel for corn; the beet-growers were getting five dollars a ton for beets. But there is as much fattening capacity in a ton of beets as in ten bushels of corn. I suggested to some sheep men that they buy the beets and slice them over chopped alfalfa for sheep feed.

It is hard to get an idea into the head of a sheep or a sheepman, but my idea was beginning to penetrate. I was waited on by an agent of the Department of Agriculture, who informed me that the sugar mills had heard of my propaganda and were preparing to demand my recall.

In the Milk River country of northern Montana the Reclamation projects were hard pressed by the competition of the farms on the limitless prairie lands beyond the areas that can be reached by irrigation but which at the time had natural rainfall. But there the climate is markedly cyclical. At the wet end of the ten- or eleven-year cycle there is plenty of rain on these high prairies to make a good wheat crop. The wheat-grower may lease as much land as he pleases and turn it under in the fall with gang plows. In the spring he sows with gangs of seeders, harrows in the seed and waits for the harvest, to be done with huge combines.

I met a family of three persons, father, daughter of twenty-one, and son of eighteen, who were handling two thousand acres without a day of hired labor. They were harvesting. The father ran the combine, son or daughter followed with a truck to take the wheat as it flowed from the machine. As soon as one truck had a full load the other truck came up, and the first drove off to the elevator. Those three people harvested more than sixty thousand bushels, wheat enough to make a year's supply of bread for a thousand people.

How could the little Reclamation farms compete with anything like that? Settlers, collected by Reclamation at great expense, were steadily deserting. They lusted for dry farming. For had not the climate changed since the years when the upland was dust?

Three years later I again passed through the region. My sixty thousand-bushel family, after living high for a year and well for another year, were now on relief.

The American white man, of whatever class, is religiously intolerant of any suggestion of cyclical changes in rainfall, though he accepts eagerly every suggestion that the climate is changing for the better. Anyone can read the record of cyclical changes in the varying growth rings of old trees, or in the changing depth of water in Great Salt Lake or Lake Superior. But he refuses to read the record. Professor Ellsworth Huntington of Yale collected oceans of data on climatic cycles and elaborated theories that explained the apparent anomalies of excessive rains in some places at a time of general drought. The theories fit the facts as well as theories ever do. But every essay or book Huntington published was greeted with such a clamor of criticism that he was forced to turn stone deaf in self-defense.

The Indians knew the cycles and were prepared to follow the buffaloes in their shift toward the more humid East as the cycle developed toward its dry end. When the Salt Lake and Los Angeles railway company laid down its tracks around the southern end of Great Salt Lake the local Indians asserted that in five years the lake would be back, deep over the tracks. So it proved, and the railway company lost a lot of money moving the tracks to a higher level.

The white man is a glutton for easy explanations. We all were eager to believe that it was "the plow that broke the plains" that gave us the dust storms of some years ago. But the soil of eastern Nebraska, more than a thousand miles from the dust bowl, is loess, sometimes two hundred feet deep. All this loess originated in dust blown in from the southwest eons before Tubal-cain invented the first plowshare.

Roy O. West, Secretary of the Interior in the last year of the Coolidge administration, decided to accompany Mead on one of the summer visits to the Reclamation projects. We were all to meet in St. Paul. Besides Secretary West, Mead, two of his Washington staff, and myself, a New England congressman, known as watchdog of the Treasury, was of the party, together with two or three men from Montana and Wyoming, representing, I suppose, local interests.

At the hotel where we assembled we were greeted effusively by agents of the Northern Pacific and the Great Northern, who informed us that the railways had put a private car at our disposition. For once, I thought, I'll travel in style. But the incorruptible Secretary West turned down the offer. It wouldn't look right for a government body to travel as guests of the railway. All he would accept was the help of the agents in selecting Pullman berths.

But the private car hooked itself to whatever train we were on. We ate Pullman fare sparingly, and after the Secretary had retired to his drawing room we irresponsible members of the party made our way to the private car and were regaled with dinner by a chef who deserved a prize for pre-eminence in his noble art.

The Secretary decided that we had to go to Glacier National Park and view St. Mary's Lake, which regulates the flow of the Milk River. Mead had put a map before the Secretary, which exhibited a pleasant instance of international cooperation. The river, rising from the glaciers of the park, flows straight north, deep into Canada, and then returns to Montana. Canada had agreed not to divert the water we accumulated at St. Mary's and wished to send down the river to our projects. Secretary West felt that it was his duty to inspect the lake, although there was nothing that needed to be done about it.

St. Mary's is a charming lake, equipped with a comfortable inn, where we rested over Sunday. In the evening we sat out on a balcony over the lake, looking across to a mountain which in the moonlight seemed clothed with human kindness.

Then we went on to the Blackfoot Indian Reservation, an area, I should judge, about the size of the State of New Jersey, extending from the Continental Divide far out into the rolling prairie. The Blackfoot Indians were no part of our business as a Reclamation Committee, but I was delighted with the opportunity to see something of so famous a tribe. The superintendent, assuming erroneously that I stood in some close relation with Secretary West, worked strenuously to make me well informed on the Reservation conditions.

The superintendent was a hearty, energetic Scotsman, who was convinced that Blackfoot Indians were fundamentally like the Highland Scots. As the Highland Scots were kept under control by petty chieftains, so the superintendent was trying to mold the Indian character to look to chieftains for their rules of conduct. The Blackfoot Indians lived in small communities where the grass was good—generally in long, winding valleys. For each community or group of families the superintendent picked out the most venerable man to be president, the most literate to be secretary, the most reliable to be treasurer, and the most truculent to be sergeant-at-arms. If an Indian in any group misbehaved, the superintendent submitted a complaint to the president, who was prompt to send the sergeant-at-arms after the offender, have his misdeeds recorded by the secretary, and have the treasurer levy a fine, usually a pony or a dog. I saw a treasurer's premises, awfully cluttered with fines.

The system worked—and there was need of a workable system. For the Blackfoot country extended far into Canada and served as a pipeline for liquor, then banned by Prohibition. But the seepage in any two-hundred-mile pipeline can be serious; in this liquor pipeline it was disastrous. Hardly a drop got through to irrigate the parched white throats at the southern end of the Reservation.

It was the ambition of the superintendent to make a tribe of sheepherders out of the Blackfoot Indians. The grass was just right for sheep, short and nutritious, and the government was ready to give any Indian family two hundred sheep as the start of a flock. Unfortunately the valleys and hill slopes were grazed bare by the innumerable Indian horses and ponies. In the matter of horses the Indians never interfered with the course of nature. Every mare foaled freely and kept her young blood with her. You'd see an Indian going visiting, himself on the biggest horse, his wife on one less imposing, the children on ponies. Forty other horses and ponies and colts would follow after. Even a short visit of such a family would lay the grass waste for a mile around.

Paleontologists have proved that the horse, indeed, the whole equine genus, originated in Montana. The four-toed Eohippus, finding the grass right, proceeded to evolve in many directions, to become true horses, asses, donkeys, quaggas, zebras. In some period of heavy glaciation, when the ocean was sunk several hundred feet to provide the three-mile-deep ice sheet, a fraction of the equine genus walked with dry hoofs across Bering Strait and made their way as far as

South Africa, occupying always the short-grass country. The short-grass areas are determined by low and irregular rainfall. When it does rain, the grass makes haste to put away in its blades and stems all the nutriment it can get. It is therefore rich grazing, something very necessary for the horse, an animal with a small stomach as compared to that of the cow and other ungulates.

Besides, the short-grass country is devoid of bushes and coppices where the great carnivora may lurk. The horse can see the whole horizon round and can detect any possible enemy at a good distance. For that reason the horse in the short-grass country exhibits none of the nervousness of a horse ridden through woods. You can ride all your life without accident in the short-grass country. A horse has to be specially trained to throw its rider. Ride in the woods, and you may count on broken collarbone or ribs.

Something happened—perhaps a malignant disease—to exterminate the whole equine race in America. But when Spanish horses made their way to Montana they realized that they were at home. They are much more at home than the elk and deer, later intruders of ten thousand years ago. A bad sleet storm will decimate the deer and elk, but no horse perishes because the grass is covered with ice. He gallops to the other side of the hill, where the sleet may not be so thick, or resorts to the aspens along the streams and feeds on their bark.

The superintendent imagined that he had a solution to the superfluous horse problem. Get the Indians to eat them. There is no dog problem among the Indians. A fat dog makes toothsome eating. Why not a nice young filly?

The white races do indeed have a tabu on horseflesh. The mythical heroes from whom we derive our tribal origin prided themselves on their equine ancestry: Philip, son of a horse in Greek; Centaur, son of a horse in Thracian. Were not the Anglo-Saxons led to Britain by Hengist (stallion, in Low German) and Horsa (stallion, in Jutland Danish)? How could we eat our totemic ancestors? But the Indians never conceived of the horse as a totemic ancestor.

At a time when meat rations were short among the Indians the superintendent organized a sandwich feast. He slaughtered a fat young horse and a three-year-old steer and ground them up into hamburger. Each guest, including all the white staff of the agency, was given three sandwiches, one of horse and the other two of steer, or vice versa. Prizes were to be given to those who guessed correctly what they were eating. Hardly anyone won a prize; indeed, correct guesses fell far short of the law of chance.

The chronically meat-hungry Indians began to look greedily at their horses. But the Indian Rights Association sent an emissary from the East to warn the Indians not to touch horsemeat. It was carrion. The horsemeat scheme was a diabolic machination of the government, which wished to repudiate its obligation to feed the Indians adequately. And so the superintendent's dream of reducing the horse population and reserving the grass for sheep failed utterly. Whatever grass grows on the Blackfoot domain still goes to feed superfluous horses.

We could not dally long among the Blackfoot Indians, for there were a lot of communities we had to visit. Each one hoped to get something out of Secretary West. In those days the highland states regarded the United States Treasury as a great natural resource, comparing favorably with the grass lands, the precious waters, and the mineral deposits.

Secretary West was an early riser, and so was I. We both liked to take a walk before breakfast and soon developed the habit of walking together. The Secretary expected me to know what the next community wanted of him and whether its claims were justified or not.

There were indeed a lot of just grievances. The government sold the raw land in a project to the settlers at cost. But the expense of constructing a beautiful dam and then carrying the water, perhaps a hundred miles along contours, tunneling through spurs, siphoning under gullies, supplying concrete linings where the canal crossed stretches of sand, ran the cost to high figures per acre. True, the government juggled the figures somewhat, to keep the cost down to something like a hundred and fifty dollars an acre. Also, the government offered part-payment plans without interest. At first the payments were fixed at a certain percentage of the cost. This percentage was cut several times and was finally superseded by a percentage of the product, again successively cut, until in the late 1920s there were contracts that would not wind up the payments due short of a hundred and sixty years.

The raw land that the settler acquired was a laborious asset. You look at a stretch of sagebrush land tilted just enough for a good flow of irrigation water. It is no great problem to get the sagebrush off, but then you find that you have by no means the even gradients you inferred under the sagebrush cover. There are hummocks and depressions that have to be ironed out. And you can't just throw the superfluous soil of the hummocks into the depressions. This would be to waste the topsoil that the sagebrush built with decaying roots through many millenniums.

What needed to be done was to cut through a depression and throw the topsoil to the side, cut through a hummock and throw back the topsoil, fill the depression with the underlying dead clay of the hummock and put the topsoil back over all. I inquired into the cost of such an operation, of Comstock, superintendent at Riverton, Wyoming, an engineer who kept turning down offers of fifty thousand dollars a year, preferring to operate as a community satrap under Uncle Sam at seventy-five hundred a year. For the government engineering staff to put the land into perfect shape to take the water would cost thirty dollars an acre. For the settler to do it with his mules, plow, and scraper, his guesses for instruments, his hopes for plans, it was a matter of a year of life for five acres, ill graded at the end.

In some projects the first settler did his best, broke down, and quit. The second settler took what the first had done, did his best, broke down in turn, and quit. The third settler took the work of the first two, added of his life, broke down, and quit. But the fourth settler succeeded. And so the principle: three strata of settlers plowed under for fertilizer that the fourth might succeed.

When I went around with the Secretary I would point to spots in the beet fields with plants fit for nothing but salad. The farmer was trying to grow beets on the underlying clay that had been substituted for topsoil by inexpert grading. That clay would hardly take water and would not hold it. For thirty dollars an acre this could have been made a uniformly good field. The Secretary would shake his head. "We can't add thirty dollars to the hundred and fifty we have already put in."

At first I had a liberal's snootiness toward this politician who didn't know a beet from a Jimson weed, this excessive Christian who had callouses on his knees from frequent and prolonged prayers; this man in his sixties who was sunk in depression if he failed to receive every morning a long telegram from his maiden sister, also in her sixties. But in the course of miles of walks I developed another feeling for Secretary West. He was indeed a party henchman, elevated to a position for which he was ill-equipped. But for purity of public spirit the Secretary had a right to a place among the best.

We visited a town that was bent on having the government set up a Reclamation project of twenty thousand acres. A splendid dinner party had been arranged for us; one of the senators was to be present, two congressmen, the mayor, and the members of the Chamber of Commerce. In the afternoon the local committee proposed to take the Secretary around the project, but he was tired and had me go out as his substitute. As I had been introduced as "Professor" my guide assumed that I wouldn't know anything about land and boasted of the natural fertility of the soil, rich in phosphates and potash, needing only water and tillage to yield abundantly. But the sickly leguminous weeds testified to the absence of phosphates, the stunted oaks and diminutive ground cherries proclaimed the scarcity of potash. Of course these constituents of fertility could be supplied. What was really important was the texture of the soil. It was too sandy to hold water well.

Important, too, was the shape of the land. It was billowy, with swales and depressions too pronounced for economic leveling off. Not more than ten thousand acres could be put in condition to receive water. As the estimated cost had been divided by the whole twenty thousand acres, to arrive at a cost of a hundred and fifty dollars an acre, the actual cost per usable acre would be three hundred dollars. No crop could be grown that would yield a fair return on any such cost figure.

I reported to Secretary West on the economics of the project. But I urged him not to let any such calculation determine his attitude. From the conventional economic point of view, not one of the projects we had visited was a sound venture. But just as in the East we liked to interrupt extensive arable areas with parks, regardless of the expense, so it might be wise, in these vast grazing areas, to develop charming oases of tillage. And though beet-growing was parasitic, it taught the farmer the secrets of intensive culture, which might later be applied to crops that were not parasitic. Some communities were already beginning to produce garden and field seed, to supply the East. The conditions for seed production were uncommonly good: no local weeds to corrupt the product, uniform ripening after uniform and adequate watering.

The Secretary listened gravely to my argument but objected that if reclamation was justified on the grounds I advanced, these were not the grounds that had been presented to Congress. He proposed at the meeting neither to approve the project nor disapprove it.

At the meeting the Secretary's speech was a masterpiece. So was Elwood Mead's. They left the community with just the mixture of

hope and disappointment that constitutes the Western spiritual standard of living.

The Secretary returned to the East; I went back to Riverton, to see
more of a project Comstock was planning. Comstock had under his
hand a beautiful tilted plain, covered with thrifty sagebrush. Water
could be had in abundance from the Shoshone reservoir. All Comstock needed was an appropriation, to create what would certainly
be one of the most productive of Reclamation projects. But Reclamation funds were scarce. Their source lay in the payments from settlers
on going projects, and the settlers were slow pay.

Comstock was under instructions to deliver me at North Platte,
Nebraska, about two hundred miles away. He had a Model T Ford,
capable of negotiating anything in the terrain which fell short of the
perpendicular. We zigzagged about for an hour or two and came to a
wide plain rising to a long mountain barrier.

"You see where the mountain drops off?" Comstock pointed.
"That's where the road gets around it. But see that notch in the mountain? If we could get through that we'd save forty miles. We'd cut
straight through the sagebrush. It makes a good tread."

"But aren't there any canyons hidden in the sage?"

"No. There never has been any rainfall here to cut canyons. Want
to try it?"

"Sure."

Comstock drove straight for the notch in the mountain. The sage
crushed down by the wheels made excellent footing for the car. In an
incredibly short time we reached the mountain notch, where we found
cattle paths the car could use in ascending. Nothing else but a cat
could have climbed that slope. The descent on the other side was
simple. All we needed in the way of power was gravity, and we had
plenty of that.

It was one in the morning when we drove into North Platte. "We'll
go round to the office," said Comstock, "and see if anybody's in."

"What!" I said. "At one in the morning?"

"Oh yes," said Comstock. "Did you see the weather report? There
may be a flash flood tonight, and the office has to be ready with the
trucks of sandbags, to fortify the ditch against a torrent from the upland."

The torrent hadn't come, but there at one in the morning was the
superintendent and all the personnel he needed for an emergency.

I do not know what the Reclamation personnel may be like today. But at the time of which I am writing it was unlike anything I have experienced, heard, or read of in the world of officialdom. Those Reclamationists were devoted men. They gave not a hoot for their time, their convenience, their family interests, their salaries. They were doing a job they believed in. They were giving their best. Who is there among the sons of earth who prays for more than this: "O Lord, permit me to give the best I can give; and record it yourself."

My immediate business was to study and report on a project on the North Platte that wasn't doing too well.

The North Platte River, coming down from the west, flows through sandy bottom lands in Nebraska. Private irrigation companies, as a rule badly managed, had put the easy bottom lands under water. But the government, with its Pathfinder dam, had impounded an immense volume of water that had formerly run in flood down the river. There was water enough to add irrigated lands on the slopes above the bottom. The project I was to examine was one of these high contour developments.

Western Nebraska is a strange tract of country to one who does not look into the fairly recent history of the world. It is a land of modest sand hills, lying in long arcs from north to south. Behind the hills lie ponds and lakes. Although the climate is semi-arid, there are more lakes and ponds in western Nebraska than in any other state of the Union.

They are fresh-water lakes, although they have no outlets. They fill with water in the rains, but before ever the water rises to the edges, to cut a way through, it seeps out through the sand. The surface of the dunes is covered by grass, which remains luxuriant even in drought, for it has deep roots to catch the seepage from the ponds and lakes.

In remote, though not the remotest, known geological times, America harbored an inland ocean from the Appalachians to the Rockies. Like all oceans, this one beat the rocks into sand and threw up the sand on the western margin. To this day you will see on Wyoming mountainsides what looks like snow. It is a sand dune, beating about as the dunes do in Frisia or Long Island.

This primordial ocean backed up by stages, leaving arc after arc of sand dunes. These are the sand hills of western Nebraska. The North and the South Platte Rivers cut through the dunes and created wide sandy bottoms. Well watered, they are fruitful, for the sand was largely made of stratified rock, not, as on our present ocean beaches, of granite and gneiss, infertile quartz, hornblende, and mica.

The project I was to study lay on the slope from the characteristic sand dune upland to the river bottom. The land had produced good grass. The original topsoil had been a sandy loam, primordial sand enriched by the decaying roots of the grass that had grown there for a million years. It was a soil that should never have been broken up. Reclamation had broken it and was trying to make it over for sugar beets.

This, anyone could see, was a mistake. Under beet cultivation the vegetable matter in the soil would promptly weather away, leaving sand one would vainly irrigate, for the water would sink below the reach of the crop roots. But fine crops of grasses could be grown, and alfalfa would do superbly.

I found, in surveying the project, that all the farmers realized that the only possible future of the project lay in forage and dairying. But the farmers had no resources for the purchase of cows. The government lien was a hundred and sixty dollars an acre, payable under contracts, without interest, in a hundred and sixty years. The land was not worth that sum per acre, and no bank would lend a dollar on it.

I called on a local bank and had the cashier figure for me what such a contract was worth in present values. Assuming interest at four per cent, it was worth about seventeen dollars per acre. I put the question: If the government would substitute a contract of twenty-five dollars an acre, with interest at four per cent—which would give the government eighty per cent more than the value of the existing contract—would the bank lend money for cows? Certainly, up to a cow an acre. I went to the Kraft organization, which was developing a cheese industry in the area. What would they pay for milk? They were prepared to make a long-term contract for all the milk the farmers could produce.

Then I got the farmers together. Suppose I can get the government to change the contract to a straight interest-bearing loan of twenty-five dollars an acre; suppose I can get the bank to lend you money for cows up to the cost of a cow per acre; suppose I can get a five- or ten-year contract from Kraft for the milk. Will you play? The unanimous response was that such an arrangement would be the salvation of the community.

I hurried back to Washington and presented my proposals to Mead. He was wholly for them and passed them on to West, who was interested but frightened. I never found out who it was that vetoed my proposals, but Mead reported to me, regretfully, that my proposals had been turned down as socialistic.

"Socialistic," when they fitted letter for letter with rational capitalistic theory. Well, my proposals had been turned down. The settlers continued producing beets, leaving the soil without cover to weather away its hard-won stock of humus. In the dust-bowl years the soil and the farmers blew away.

A prophet counts for naught in his own country. While I was chewing the bitter cud of disappointment over North Platte a handsome French official called on me, with an introduction from Mead. He was representing a great reclamation project in southern Algiers. Would I entertain an invitation from the French government to head the economic and settlement phases of the problem? If I would accept, he could assure me, such an appointment would be forthcoming.

Was I tempted? Of course. What live Nordic is there whose deeper urges are not drawn to Africa, dark, dangerous, mysterious? But I had two jobs on hand: the resettlement of the New School and a project, on which I had associated myself with Professor Seligman, to get out an *Encyclopaedia of the Social Sciences*.

I had to forego Algiers, and the fascinating problem of making Christians and Moslems work together, of building an agricultural economy that could survive the handicap of workers who for one month every year could barely get up energy to breathe, the month "hunger-stricken Ramazan." But there could be no Arabian Nights romance for me: I had my job to do at home.

TWENTY-NINE

The "Encyclopaedia of the Social Sciences"

FOR a quarter of a century, at every annual meeting of the social science associations, the project of an encyclopedia had been discussed. As I had had much experience with the *New International* and *Nelson's,* I always participated actively in the discussions.

It was the unanimous opinion that our sciences needed an encyclopedia. The several social sciences had fought vigorously for scholarly autonomy through the last decade of the nineteenth century and the first decade of the twentieth. But an ever-increasing proportion of the personnel of the social-science professions were coming around to the view that the sciences would have to join forces and work cooperatively if they were to deserve a voice on practical issues. An encyclopedia covering the whole ground would act as a powerful force for unity.

Still more important, a properly constructed encyclopedia would offer a conspectus of the actual position of the several social sciences, showing not only where they were strong but also where they were weak. In every science some problem rises up to attract to itself the best abilities in the field; other problems that may be just as significant are neglected. A graph of the actual distribution of interest in a science would exhibit mountainous heights and Dead-Sea depths side by side. Equipped with a comprehensive encyclopedia, the young scholar would be less likely to throw his energies into overexploited areas and would be drawn to those that are neglected.

And finally, an encyclopedia could save months of time for students working toward higher degrees. Again and again one encountered graduate students who had worked a year or two on theses that looked new, only to find that some obscure Englishman or Frenchman or German had exhausted the subject. There were indeed reference works that were of some help—Palgrave's *Dictionary of Political Economy,* Lalor's *Cyclopaedia of Political Science,* Bliss's *Encylo-*

paedia of Social Reform—but these had been long out of date. Something also was to be gleaned from the general encyclopedias, but their interest in the social sciences was limited.

Thus there were three reasons for launching an encyclopedia of the social sciences, any one of which was sufficient. But such a work would cost a lot of money, and there was no hope that the cost could be recovered through profits on sales. And our ardent groups of encyclopedia promoters knew of no way of finding the money.

In the middle twenties Alexander Goldenweiser, of the New School faculty, organized a series of meetings of the social scientists of the vicinity to discuss plans for launching an encyclopedia. I attended the meetings, although my ardor had been cooled by twenty years of meetings that had proved to be only meetings of mice to bell the cat. But Goldenweiser won to the plan a mighty force, Professor Seligman. With Seligman in our movement there was a chance for us.

Seligman had tremendous prestige, in America and abroad, as a scholar with a cosmic range of interests. He had collected a library of economics and social science which, after the break-up of Foxwell's library in England, was the finest private library of social science in the world. For any topic in the history of doctrine the Seligman library was richer than any of the great university libraries. Seligman's political and social stature was such that he could talk man to man with the presidents of the great foundations, figures of such dignity and power that ordinary scholars could never get near them. With Seligman as our champion, money could be had.

But what kind of encyclopedia were we to launch? Was it to be a work of multitudinous topics or of great, comprehensive articles like the mid-nineteenth century *Encyclopaedia Metropolitana,* now nowhere to be seen except in Seligman's library. Goldenweiser favored the latter type. He wanted to write an article of three hundred pages on anthropology, and he wanted Seligman to write four hundred pages on public finance. He offered me two hundred and fifty pages for a history of economic theory. Such articles could be sold as separates, like Nassau Senior's article on political economy written for the *Encyclopaedia Metropolitana,* Senior's one title to undying fame.

To me an encyclopedia with such colossal articles would be merely a library, the various treatises bound together to create the maximum inconvenience. Seligman listened patiently to our arguments and brought forth his favorite maxim, "There is something to be said on both sides." He had the practical gift to postpone to the future problems that could be solved only in the future. "Let us see whether we can get an encyclopedia. Then we can consider what we will do with it."

First things first. Seligman sounded out the Rockefeller, the Carnegie, and the Russell Sage Foundations. They were interested. Then he proceeded to build a board of directors, academic and lay—the former, outstanding scholars, the latter, outstanding businessmen. Next he set up a body of advisory editors, American and foreign, and a joint committee, consisting of representatives of the ten associations in the field. With this huge apparatus he got the Foundations to agree to subsidize the venture, to the amount of six hundred thousand dollars. I protested that this sum would fall short by one-third. Seligman dismissed my objection. We'd go ahead, and if we ran short of money we'd ask for some more.

Seligman next negotiated with a publisher, the Macmillan Company, and arrived at a highly favorable agreement. The Macmillan Company stipulated that our organization should buy fifteen hundred sets for free distribution among members of our constituent learned societies. This would absorb nearly two hundred thousand dollars of the six hundred thousand the Foundations and members of the board were to supply.

I had another friendly quarrel with Seligman over the inadequacy of our finances. We were counting on a work of one million words. We would pay the authors two cents a word. That would come to two hundred thousand dollars, leaving another two hundred thousand for editing. Surely, Seligman argued, that would be sufficient. I demurred. It was my experience that editing encyclopedia articles takes three times the effort of writing them. We would need four hundred thousand for the editing. Seligman laughed joyously. I was contemplating a great work at a dollar a word, as costly as the most portentous articles in the *Saturday Evening Post*.

Down to this point my relation to the project was that of an intensely interested adviser. I did not expect to take part in the actual editing of the work. I had my hands fairly full as director of the New School, and I foresaw much greater demands on my energies when the time came for the school to find new premises. Besides, I had planned a three-volume novel, tracing the development of a personality through the social-political phases of ardent though immature radicalism, doctrinaire liberalism, and ripened liberalism based on an honest endeavor to know the real interest of the people. I had in my odds and ends of time finished a first volume, which I entitled *Spring*

Storm. I showed it to my friend Clarence Day, who liked it and got Alfred Knopf to publish it.

I had assumed that Seligman would take Goldenweiser for his second in command. I did not consider the choice a good one. Goldenweiser was a man of immense scholarly reach, but he was extremely idiosyncratic. He could see his own position clearly, but he refused to see at all clearly the position of men in other scientific camps. As I conceived it, the position of editor is that of servant of his constituents, not their master. Goldenweiser would have gone to any lengths to enforce his own views. But I kept my opinion of Goldenweiser to myself. After all, it was he who had taken the initiative that had led to the launching of the encyclopedia.

Seligman, however, informed me that whatever his merit Goldenweiser was out of the question. The profession regarded him as too erratic. Seligman tried to get Allyn A. Young as his associate, but Young had no stomach for the job. Finally he asked me to join him. There was a twinkle in his eye when he told me he was asking me at his own risk; for there was a current notion that I was insistent and resourceful in gaining my own way. I replied that some of my friends had advised me not to touch the project, for Seligman always insisted on absolute control over anything he was connected with. So we were even; we could wait to see how things worked out.

They worked out well. In the seven years of our association on this project there was never a rift in our mutual understanding, never a cloud on our friendly relations. Without any formal agreement we divided the responsibility, Seligman undertaking the "foreign relations"—negotiations with the Foundations, with the constituent societies and the Board of Directors, with the European universities, where he was as much at home as at Columbia. I assumed charge of "internal affairs," laying out the contents, building a working staff, selecting contributors, editing the copy, and putting it through to the publisher. My function involved much more work than I had counted on. But I meant to build an able staff and shove off much of the responsibility on them.

We decided that Seligman should go to Europe and cultivate interest in our project all the way from Helsinki to Madrid, a task he performed so brilliantly that all the universities dismissed the notion that our encyclopedia was a local American affair. It was recognized as an enterprise of world scholarship, and we could count on the full cooperation of the European faculties.

Experience with the *New International Encyclopaedia* had taught me to steer clear of a staff of disappointed men and women who had worn out their energies on other works of reference or who nearly but not quite had established themselves as professional writers. I wanted to make up my staff of young doctors who would easily adapt themselves to the job.

My friend Walton H. Hamilton, then professor of economics at the Robert Brookings Graduate School of Economics and Government, sent me one of its new doctors. He was of a slight, brief figure, so deeply enveloped in a coonskin coat one saw hardly anything of him but eyes of brilliant intelligence: Max Lerner. I engaged him on the spot. I enlisted more young scholars, and we were ready to start compiling a list of topics, drawing on all existing encyclopedias and works of reference. Our lists had to be extremely detailed, for I had laid down the arbitrary principle that there should be no articles exceeding five thousand words in length. Of course I had to grant exceptions, later. But nobody who looks for a topic in the *Encyclopaedia* has to dig it out of some long-winded treatise.

Although my staff made a very thorough search for topics, we could not be sure that we had all the relevant ones, nor that some we had were of value. We had our board and advisory editors, an imposing array of abilities to draw on, but we decided we needed a wider range of advisers. There might be fifty or more scholars, in America and Europe, doing important work in public finance. We mimeographed our list of public-finance topics and sent it to all fifty, begging for supplementary topics and suggestions as to writers. We consulted some six hundred scholars, of whom only one refused to cooperate.

Two serious difficulties beset the encyclopedia editor. One is the disposition of the scholarly writer to run off the boundary of his topic on forays into neighboring topics. The other is the extreme willingness of scholars to promise articles, and their extraordinary capacity for repudiating their promises when the printer is at your heels. I saw a way of killing two birds with one stone. Make an outline of every article you want, noting also the topics adjacent. Of course some scholars will write with indignation that your outline is all wrong. The proper outline should be such and so. You write with humility, thanking the scholar for his improved outline and begging him to execute the article. He does.

I had tried this plan in the last volumes of the *New International* and knew it would work. What makes a scholar delay in writing an article is his aversion to working out an outline. You can't write a scientific article without an outline, so you keep postponing the writing. Under our plan the articles came in with admirable promptness. When we were ready to publish, we put out our huge volumes, with hundreds of contributors, with the regularity of a quarterly magazine.

This procedure meant an enormous amount of work for the staff. Sometimes they showed signs of balking. Was I not requiring an assistant editor to do so much preliminary work on a topic that he could write the article himself? True; but that work fitted him to edit the article when it came in. If the article we ordered failed to come in, the assistant editor would be qualified to write it.

Much of the writing for the encyclopedia could have been done in the office. But it was our business to have the writing done by the whole body of the professions. I indulged the staff in one signed article each per volume. I meant to run no articles over my own signature, and only made a few exceptions to the rule, to fill gaps occasioned by a belated letter of regret from the scholar who had held the topic in his pigeonholes for two or three years.

I'd like to be able to say that the relations between my excellent staff and myself were always harmonious. But nothing human is perfect. We never could agree entirely on the limitations of the fields we proposed to cover.

Sociology flows over into ethics, ethics into religion, and religion tails off into philosophy. Statistics cottons to mathematics and penetrates to logic, which insists on dragging metaphysics along. A line had to be drawn somewhere. After listening to the arguments of the staff I'd draw the line, with a pencil too authoritative except for the urgent necessity of getting on with the work. The editor defeated in his argument would keep reopening the case until I found it necessary to fire him. He'd cool off and return, prepared to listen to "right reason"— my reason, of course.

The assistant editors and I were of different academic generations. Naturally the younger generation regarded mine as reactionary. Karl Marx had come into vogue among graduate students, especially among students of philosophy and ethics. Marx was an intellectual convenience. He absolved the student from the necessity of attending to the problems of the actual economic system. Protection and free trade, the incidence and shifting of taxation, the development of standards of living, monopoly and competitive pricing, and the scores of other problems that occupy the "bourgeois" economist presented no difficulties to the Marxian disciple. To him there was only one problem: how to get on with the revolution.

In enlisting assistant editors I forbore all inquiry about infection with Marx. Like the common cold, Marx was in the air, sometimes cutting editorial efficiency, but not irremediably. Although I have always regarded myself as a self-effacing scholar, I meant to keep the encyclopedia under my hand. The assistant editors were to draw up the outlines for the topics, but no outline was to escape my examination. They were to prepare lists of possible contributors, but none could be accepted without my knowing what manner of scholar was proposed. When an article came in I read it before turning it over for editing, and I read the edited version before it went back to the author. If the article was written in a foreign language, as some twelve per cent were, I read it before assigning it for translation. Fortunately for me, I could read economic material in any European language except the Slavic, Finno-Ugrian, and Lithuanian, and persons to whom those languages are native wrote as a rule in French or German.

In comparing the translation with the original I sometimes experienced disagreeable surprises—especially with the German. I'd read an article that looked good in the original. In the translation there was not a thing in it. I would compare the original and the translation, sentence by sentence. The translation had been faithful. And my respect for the German would rise. With that wonderful language you can make something out of nothing.

I had two assistant editors who asserted that they were Socialists. That was nothing to me; they were good and faithful workers. And one was so considerate of my reactionary bent as to inform me that a new editor I had taken on was a Communist. I sent for him.

"Yes," he said. "I was once a Communist. The name by which I go is not my real name." He gave me his real name, which had figured in press accounts of rows in the Communist party.

"And so," he said, "you are going to fire me."

"Certainly not. You are here to do a specific editorial job. Your private political views are your own business. You can't import them into any work you do for me. But you exhibit the frankness of a gentleman and a scholar. All I ask of you is that if ever you feel it your moral duty to slap a little Communist color on your work, you will resign."

That he promised, and he kept his promise. He is now a respected college professor, anti-Communist, but making neither a secret nor a parade of his early affiliation.

Those were tolerant days. Intelligent Americans were no more hysterical about Communists than intelligent Europeans are today. We had not formulated the principle, "Once a Communist, always a traitor." We overlooked, with a smile, the excesses of the false spring of ardent youth. And a lot of crocus Communists developed into sound and reasonable scholars and businessmen, now a bit apprehensive that the McCarthyite goblins will "git them ef they don't watch out."

One might think that the job I laid out for myself would break any back. It was to be distributed over seven years from 1927 until 1934. I knew that all one could expect of an assistant editor was that he should put over the dam every week three thousand words of finished copy, verified as to fact and bibliography, returned to the author with queries, revised and rerevised. With ten assistant editors—the maximum number I contemplated—I'd have thirty thousand words to read in the original draft, in revision, in the author's approved final text. What are thirty thousand words a week to a seasoned editor?

When Seligman returned from Europe after four months he was astonished to see what an editorial structure had grown up. His first comment was, "Well, we haven't anywhere near enough money. But we'll find it somehow."

To do a really sound encyclopedia job you not only have to have your list of outlined topics and your selected contributors. You have to be prepared to study every article that comes in, cut it back to space, verify every fact and every bibliography item, supplement and rearrange the bibliography. Then you make a clean copy and send it to the author for his correction and approval. As it comes back, you send it to the printer. You wisely avoid sending proof to the author, but this means you have to be extremely responsible in proofreading.

When we were fully under way we made up a staff of fifty-five persons, all overworked.

Seligman had forgotten any inclination he may have had at the outset for the comprehensive article. But he informed me that he had made a commitment to Goldenweiser, promising him the first volume for a philosophic handling of the social sciences.

A commitment is a commitment; but I didn't want any such volume. I proposed instead that we find space for two extensive articles, one on the "Development of Social Thought and Institutions," the other on the "Social Sciences as Disciplines." I was willing to turn those sections over to Goldenweiser, although I doubted that he would have time to do the job, and as matters developed he never found the time to make any progress. He had accepted an appointment as professor at the University of Washington, and what with books he had contracted to write he had his hands more than full. We had to make up in the office the plans for the articles and find contributors.

Even a seven-year job comes to an end. We read the last pages of proof, sent a truckload of correspondence down to the publisher's offices, and disbanded.

We were content. We looked at our work: some errors had crept in, but on the whole we counted it good. We had gained a high esteem for the body of social-science scholars. Of the hundreds who contributed articles, not half a dozen supplied unusable material. Probably some were a bit shocked by our drastic editing, but no one of them proclaimed himself our enemy. Nor did the reviewers treat us badly; and the complaints that kept coming in from the libraries on the cost of frequent rebinding added to our satisfaction. The work was being used.

Professor Seligman and I cornered most of the credit for the achievement, as is the custom of the trade. The merit for going through with the work rests with the assistant editors and the faithful secretarial staff.

The *Encyclopaedia* was an expensive venture. At the outset Professor Seligman calculated the cost at six hundred thousand dollars; I calculated it at nine hundred thousand. The actual cost was eleven hundred thousand. There must have been some waste. I think we might have saved fifty thousand if we had been as efficient at the outset as we became later. In our fifth year the publisher and the Foundations sent in a high-class business expert, Mark Jones, to find out whether we were wasting money.

When he appeared he informed me that he had been sent up to find out just what it would cost to finish the work. I told him our house was open to him, our books were before him, every one of our fifty-five personnel would gladly answer any questions. But, I said, I already knew what it would cost to finish the work. It would cost four hundred and thirty-four thousand.

Mark Jones lived with us for six weeks. I was eager to hear what he had found.

"Doctor," he said gaily, "you are wrong. It won't cost that much to finish the encyclopedia. It will cost three hundred and ninety-four thousand."

I was a bit shocked. I had figured very closely. I was prepared for five or ten thousand of cheese parings, but forty thousand looked like a disaster.

"Where the devil can you find forty thousand to cut?" I demanded.

"I've persuaded Doctor Seligman to forgo his salary. He's a rich man and doesn't need it."

I made a swift calculation. "Is that all you found?"

"Every cent. I couldn't find you are wasting even paper clips. And you are to sign a guaranty to finish the work within that amount."

I signed the guaranty, for what my signature was worth. I had bad luck; some of my most efficient assistant editors and secretaries left for other jobs before we were through. I worked hard to keep within the limit nevertheless, but I overran about three hundred and fifty dollars, which I'd have paid if I had been asked for it.

Perhaps the Foundations would not have come in if they had known how great the cost would be. Seligman's technique with them made me think of the Santa Fe expedition in the Mexican War. There were more miles of desert to traverse than the commander had calculated. The water ran out; thirst became so intolerable that the soldiers were on the point of fainting and dying. The commander would send a rider ahead who would gallop back with the news: "A great spring of water just over the hill." That device was repeated three times and was losing its potency. But the fourth report was true.

Nearly twenty years have passed since the last volume of the *Encyclopaedia* appeared. They have been years of revolutionary changes in social and political institutions and in theory. There is a crying need in the universities for a revision of the *Encyclopaedia*. In the last few years letters have come to me from scholars throughout the country, and from France, Japan, and India, urging a revision. Librarians have given me estimates that indicate there are at least half a million consultations of the *Encyclopaedia* every year, in spite of the fact that it is out of date.

The impact of the letters has forced me to make some calculations. Five-sixths of the text of the *Encyclopaedia* is still good, but the other sixth spots around in such a way that it would be cheaper to reset the whole work than cut the plates. I have a figure from Macmillan of two hundred thousand dollars, for revising the work and enlarging it by nine thousand words—my estimate of what is required. I have set up in my mind an editorial staff that could do the work of revision in three years at a cost of three hundred thousand dollars.

If my beloved E. R. A. Seligman were with us I have no doubt he could enlist all the support needed from the Foundations. It would not be necessary to play them along with the hope of water over the next hill, for the water would actually be there. Alas, Seligman has gone to his reward, and there is no man living who can take his place.

THIRTY

The New School Building

T HE school year 1928–29 brought a crisis in the affairs of the New
School. We had to vacate our Twenty-third Street quarters and find
a new home.

We had known when we acquired the houses in London Terrace
that we might not be able to renew our ground lease at the end of ten
years. But the ground was held by one of those dead-hand estates to
which time is as nothing. The estate was waiting for a builder powerful enough to take over the whole block.

In 1918 the appearance of any such magnate was unthinkable. But
1928 was a flush year, with grand enterprise the rule in the building
industry. We received notice to remove ourselves in the autumn of
1929, accepting the stipulated depreciated value of our improvements.
That figured out to twenty-three thousand dollars.

West Twenty-third Street was not an ideal location for such an
institution as the New School had become. It had been entirely accessible to the students we attracted in the first years, many of whom
came in their own cars, many in taxis. But as we became a real school
of higher adult education we had to draw upon the population that
used the subways, elevated lines, and surface cars. The Ninth Avenue
Elevated and the Twenty-third Street surface cars were our principal
transportation resources.

Students could indeed come by way of any of the rapid transit lines,
changing over to the crosstown. New Yorkers on pleasure bent will
stand any kind of traffic difficulties. Not so New Yorkers bent on education. A survey of the domiciles of our students, made by the firm of
Ford, Bacon and Davis, showed heavy concentrations along the Ninth
Avenue Elevated and the crosstown, which brought students from the
Hudson ferries and from Brooklyn. Vast areas of the Greater City
were desert, as a source of students.

Nevertheless attendance was growing rapidly toward the twenty-five hundred we recognized as the maximum our building could accommodate. It was an eager and resilient body of students, and the faculty exerted itself to make every course interesting. I instituted the plan of publishing in the catalogue detailed descriptions of courses, lecture by lecture. This gave the student a clear idea of what he would get and saved the teacher from the common academic vice of desultory meandering over an indefinite field.

I was convinced that our type of adult education answered a pressing need in American social life. I was also convinced that the institution could finally become self-supporting if it covered the field with well-organized, well-taught courses. But we should need an adequate plant and an accessible location.

My friend and fellow trustee, George H. Davis, prepared for us a chart indicating the possible locations suitable for our institution. There are two important transit ganglia in New York, one centering at Fifth Avenue and Forty-second Street, the other at Fifth and Fourteenth. We agreed that we should look for a site within two blocks north or south, east or west, of these centers.

As we had hardly any money it seemed best to look for space we could lease. We explored both areas, but found that rent in the Forty-second Street district would be prohibitive, and even in the Fourteenth Street district would come very high. To take care of five thousand students, our new goal, we should need between forty and fifty thousand square feet of floor space. There was no desirable space to be had for less than a dollar a square foot, and in buildings with evening heat and elevator service the best we could do was a dollar and a half, with a short-term lease that would expose us to another removal within five years.

I hated the idea of leased premises. How could we possibly develop institutional personality in forty thousand square feet of space in an office building? I consulted some of my friends expert in the building industry. Land could be bought in the Fourteenth Street section and a building with forty or fifty thousand square feet could be erected at a cost of three-quarters of a million; better, with another hundred thousand for leeway.

Those were flush times, and three-quarters of a million didn't loom so large then. I presented my idea to the board, who were not in the least horrified; the idea of a three-quarters-of-a-million building, to rise out of the twenty-seven thousand in our treasury, looked too fantastic to inspire horror.

It was the last meeting of the spring of 1928. I asked the board to
let me have a committee of three, George H. Davis, engineer and man
of large affairs, Joseph Milner, an able real-estate operator, and myself,
with authority to acquire the necessary land, if we could, get an architect to prepare plans, if we could, and set up a workable scheme of
financing, if we could. The board voted me the subcommittee with
authority. But what they thought of it was voiced humorously by my
friend Maurice Wertheim.

"You can't do it, Alvin. But if you do succeed, you'll belong either
in the penitentiary or in Wall Street."

The next day I went down to Twelfth Street, to call on Daniel Cranford Smith, a partly retired businessman, a passionately loyal friend
of the New School. Uncle Dan, as we called him, had attended courses
assiduously since the first year, had subsidized courses, organized discussion groups, and had made a second home for himself out of the
New School.

"Uncle Dan," I said, "I've given up the idea of another rented home
for the New School. We have to have a building of our own."

"That's what I always thought," said Uncle Dan.

"The board has given my committee authority to acquire a site, get
an architect to make the plans of the building, and work out a scheme
of financing."

"Good."

"And so we are commandeering your three houses."

"My three houses?"

"Yes. You see, the location is right."

"Yes, but—"

"You see, Uncle Dan, you bought this house to live in, and one on
either side you bought for protection. Now we propose to erect a
seven-story building and will give you the sixth floor at modest rent
for life. You'll have all the space you have here, and you'll have the
protection of being over the housetops.

"You try to grow flowers down here in your shady and moldy back
yard. Up there you will have a wide balcony facing the sun, where you
can compete with any greenhouse. You and your wife are continually
taking cold down here. Up there you will be in much better health
and you'll live much longer. You will have a spacious living room,
to hold your discussion groups. Down here the room is so narrow you
just about have to seat your guests in a row.

"We haven't any money to pay for your equities. But we will agree on an honest appraiser, and whatever value he fixes we'll cover with bonds of the New School. They won't be a gilt-edge investment, but neither are your real-estate equities.

"You get rents now on your two extra houses. But by the time you've paid interest on the mortgages, taxes, insurance, repairs, you haven't much left. Up there you will be tax free, with heat supplied by the institution."

Uncle Dan chuckled. "Doctor, you should have gone into real estate. But I'll have to talk it over with my wife."

The next day he called me up and said that his wife was enthusiastic about the plan. She thought, however, he was driving too hard a bargain, and to appease her he had agreed to cut twenty-five thousand dollars off the appraised value.

I must pause for a few moments to record my devotion to Uncle Dan and his sweet wife. Daniel Cranford Smith was a man who knew how to make money and how to use it. How many good causes he promoted I can't say, for he never boasted of his philanthropies and I heard of them only by accident. I did hear that Booker T. Washington was deep in Uncle Dan's debt. He was mainly self-educated, and this means efficiently educated. He came to the New School not to repair a neglected education but to carry forward the wide-reaching education he already had.

Eventually, when he occupied the sixth floor of our building, he was, I think, more at home than he had ever been. He developed a wonderful garden on the terrace. You almost expected to see little South American monkeys in his flowering vines. He held intellectual court in his living room, attended by the finest intellectuals there are, like Eduard Lindeman. He was happy, and his happiness was a glow of sunshine upon the face of his sweet wife. The end came, after many years, but I do believe he had ten years more than he could have had at the street level.

I made haste to get my committee together to consider the arrangements I proposed to make. We visited the site. Three houses made a rather narrow front, but fortunately the next house east was for sale. We got a local broker to negotiate with the owner, who was willing to accept twenty thousand for his equity, a sum we lifted from the vanishing New School treasury.

So we had our eighty front feet nailed down. Like all real estate it was a tissue of equities and mortgages, but we had among our friends

Joseph Milner, and Charles and Albert Mayer and William Korn of the Taylor Construction Company, among the most experienced and resourceful real-estate operators in New York, who could be counted on to get us clear titles and weave the existing mortgages into a legal unity. They could amplify the credits through a building loan which would help to finance us. For the additional funds needed I proposed to float bonds among our friends. This was my plan of financing.

The next urgent problem was to find an architect who would give us plans so seductive that they would draw our friends to help finance our building. I had long since become an addict of modern "functional" architecture. I could hardly refrain from laughter when I passed a savings bank with the façade of a Greek temple or a college library of colossal masonry with deep-set narrow windows for the light to look in furtively.

My mind was fixed on two architects, both probably out of my reach, Frank Lloyd Wright and Joseph Urban. They were both geniuses: Wright the most powerful force in American architectural design, Urban an artist of universal talent. He had been trained as an architect in Vienna and had designed palaces in Egypt and castles in Hungary, but as a master of design and a magician in color he had been drawn away from architecture to glorify the stage of opera and theater.

I admired the work of Frank Lloyd Wright, and I admired his personality more intensely. He was bold, free, creative, uncompromising. The last quality gave me pause. He would give us a building to his mind, not to my mind. It would be "functional," but function is a relative term. To me it meant the expression of the needs and spirit of the individual enterprise. To Frank Lloyd Wright it meant the expression of the needs and spirit of the new time, as he foresaw it prophetically.

Urban's conception of functionalism was essentially the same as mine. But how could I win even the attention of a world-renowned artist, whose shop was full of orders reported to yield a hundred and fifty thousand a year? Imagine my delight when Charles Mayer said one day, "Would you like to meet Joseph Urban? I could arrange a meeting at the City Club."

I expected to be struck dumb when face to face with the great man. But with all his visible power, he was so understanding, so charming, that I found myself almost eloquent in describing the New School, its character, its aspirations, its meaning for education and for society. I dwelt on the imperative need of a building that should express the ideals of the school, give visible form to its personality.

Joseph Urban let me go on to the end of my discourse. "I'm sold," he said. "When do we start?"

"But, Mr. Urban, we are very poor, and your fees are said to be very high."

"Oh, I don't know. What did you expect to pay?"

"The regulation six per cent."

"For interiors too?"

"Yes."

"All right. When do we start?"

"But an architect has a right to fifteen per cent of his contract in advance. Our treasury has nothing in it but cobwebs. And there won't be any money unless the building plans appeal to our friends."

"All right. We'll design the building. If we can't find any money, we'll forget it. Let's start tomorrow. Will you come to my studio at eleven?"

My committee was astonished. They could not imagine how I could have prevailed on Urban to do the work at all, and on such terms. For it was rumored that his regular fee was fifteen per cent for a building and twenty-five per cent for interiors.

Later, over a table at the Plaza, Urban explained away the anomaly. When Charles Mayer had suggested that he should design a school-building he had laughed. But Mayer insisted that if Urban would see me he'd find that the New School was something he'd find interesting, if he'd let me put the case for it.

He had come to feel that the sand in his life glass was running low, and he wanted to present the future with an example of the art he had loved most, architecture, from which he had been drawn away to the ephemeral splendor of the stage.

To me the New School building is sacred to the memory of Joe Urban. For good practical reasons some changes have been made in the layout since the building was erected, but I must confess that every one has caused me acute pain. The most important was the removal of the noble stairways from the lounge floor to the library floor, and the closing of the well between the floors. This was necessitated not because of any flaw in Urban's functional conceptions, but because of a shift in the functional requirements of the Graduate Faculty and its students, which could not have been foreseen when the building was designed.

We had planned the fourth and fifth floors together, as the social home of the students. The adult student has little time for library work. In the old New School buildings we had a small library in an isolated room. It was visited very rarely by the students. What we had in mind in planning the floors was a delightful reading room, which would draw lounging students down the stairs to magazines and new books when conversation ran thin.

After the establishment of the University in Exile during the Second World War full-time graduate students multiplied. They needed a library where they could work undisturbed by the murmur of conversation in the lounge above. To provide it, we had to abolish the stairways and the open well.

That summer is memorable to me for my close association with so infinitely interesting a man as Joseph Urban. Very soon he had the general scheme of the work outlined; but each detail had to be considered and reconsidered in relation to other details. I'd produce the probabilities as to the use of a particular room. Then the color scheme would need to be established; also the color scheme of everything else on the floor. And this meant a lot of adjustments, for Urban did not like all the walls of a room to be of the same color. They never can be, for the color changes subtly with variations in the light. And the eyes of the audience, unconsciously following the half-perceptible nuances of color, begin to blink. But if the eyes flit from one strong color to another the audience is wakeful to the lecture.

After working two or three hours we would go over to the Plaza and settle down on the comfortable cushions in a retired corner. The resourceful waiter Caesar would suggest a delightful menu and bring up from Urban's locker a bottle of rare wine. Urban would relate fascinating stories of his career, going back to the time he went to Egypt with the young Khedive, who couldn't endure the thought of living in musty old Arabian Nights palaces and so was going to build new palaces, fresh and gorgeous. Urban and the Khedive would work on plans all day and in the evening float on the Nile in the royal barge, with wonderful music and dancing, a tradition that went back to Cleopatra and beyond.

Or we would compare our experiences and impressions of Florence, Rome, and Athens and discuss ancient and medieval civilizations. We agreed that even in the classical period Greek art could not have been so cold as it appears in the British Museum, for on the Acropolis of Athens you have only to turn over some of the multitudinous fragments of columns and statues to find vestiges of the splendid colors with which the Greeks clothed their white marble.

We were agreed in liking the Neo-Hellenic better than the Hellenic. We liked Sappho and Anacreon better than Tyrtaeus and Pindar. We would have preferred plays by Menander and Demiphon to the lofty, god-inspired tragedies or the flip comedies of Aristophanes. We preferred the Hellenistic sculptures to the works of Phidias and Praxiteles. For in the post-classical and Hellenistic world man was the measure of all things. Literature and art left the gods to sit at ease on Olympus and addressed themselves frankly to man.

We discussed the use of every available bit of space in the New School building. The basement, I had assumed, would be a large, dim space, to house the tons of letter files, reports, and bulletins every educational institution accumulates for lack of resolution to throw useless things away. Urban had an infinitely better idea. He would develop the basement as a dance studio.

According to Urban, in the periods of history when the dance really meant something, religiously and socially, the dance floor was a circle with space for the spectators to sit or stand all around. The spectators felt themselves part of the performance; often a spectator would be inspired to join in the dance, or groups would dance in circles adjacent to the central circle. A decadent aristocracy thrust the dancers up on a stage, with the spectators viewing them from below, fixing their attention on a show of legs no more edifying than the trays of frogs' legs in a fish market. We would sink our dance floor instead of elevating it, and the spectators, seated or standing, would get a sense of the grace and beauty of movement of the dancers' whole bodies.

Our most serious problem of construction was presented by the auditorium. I wanted to have it shaped like the inside of a half-eggshell, with the rostrum at the small end of the egg. I hate a large quadrilateral room, like a Masonic hall. A shy lecturer—and most lecturers who have anything to say are shy—is embarrassed by the huge empty space overhead and by the audience groups scattered in the near and far corners. If the capacity of the room is six hundred, the audience looks enormous, formidable; if there happens to be a small attendance—say, a hundred—they scatter about in small groups or as individuals, *rari nantes in gurgite vasto*. An oval room tends to draw the audience together. A hundred hearers do not seem few and six hundred do not seem distressingly many.

Urban said nothing when I suggested the eggshell. He put his palm to his chin and the glow in his eyes turned inward to thought. He would encounter acoustic problems, and he would be pounded by the cub architectural critics for designing a nonfunctional room. But a few days later he said, "You shall have your egg."

When the drawing of the room was circulated among our friends some of them cried out in horror. The acoustics would be terrible. One of my friends sent me two acoustic engineers, one from the telephone company and one from radio broadcasting. Both assured me that the form would never do. If I liked, they would make a miniature hall of that shape, with mirrors distributed along walls and ceilings, and with candles to show me just where light would concentrate. Sound would concentrate in the same way. There would be two spots where the lucky listener would hear two lectures at the same time, not quite synchronous, and large areas where hardly anything could be heard because of the bumbling echoes.

I was not convinced. I knew a little about sound, enough to know that its behavior could not be deduced from the behavior of light. But I reported the engineers' opinion to Urban.

"Umm. There is an old fellow at the University of Illinois, Professor Phillips, who really understands acoustics. He is lecturing in Philadelphia next week. Suppose we ask him to come over."

Professor Phillips was a spare, brisk man with an air of eagerness for problems. His face lighted up as Urban handed him the drawing. "Ah! An interesting problem in acoustics."

"Yes," I said. "We have consulted two Massachusetts Tech acoustic engineers. They agree: we have to square the room to make it acoustic. But Urban says you are able to make any room of any shape acoustic."

The professor smiled. "I wouldn't claim that. But we have made an experiment that shows that if ten per cent of a surface consists of perforations, eighty-nine per cent of the sound wave striking it goes on out. You see, the sound wave funnels."

"And what becomes of the sound when it has funneled through?" I asked naïvely.

"Oh, it gets demoralized in funneling. And a demoralized sound wave, you know, is no sound at all."

We had our answer. Urban made our ceiling a plaster grill, with perforations amounting to fifteen per cent of the surface. Not a single sound wave bumbles back from the ceiling.

We do have minor concentrations from the curves of the solid side walls. We could easily eliminate them by acoustic plaster or hangings.

When we had finished the design Urban said, "There is one room I haven't discussed with you—your office. I know you better than you know yourself, and you'll have to accept my judgment."

I was perfectly willing to do so. The room, a corner office, had a large window that would be on the left of my desk. Behind me would be an alcove with the walls curving to a half-circle; at the axis of the circle there was to be a beautiful overhead light. The walls were to be painted Byzantine red.

"And under the light there is to be a copy of an antique statue, in white marble."

I had to protest. "I'm sorry, but the finances of the school can't stand a marble statue."

"The New School and the finances have nothing to do with it. I'm giving this statue to you personally—on condition that you will never let it go out of your possession." Then he chuckled. "That statue will be happy with you."

He showed me a photograph. It was of the Aphrodite of Cyrene. I was overwhelmed.

The Aphrodite of Cyrene had been found early in 1914 by Italian soldiers digging a ditch on the site of ancient Cyrene, in the fourth century B.C. a great center of commerce and culture. Kept underground during the First World War, the statue was set up after the war in a special alcove of the Museo delle Therme. I saw it and regarded it as the most beautiful of all the Aphrodites. I tried to get a good photograph but was not successful. The same year Mr. Urban saw it, and he too thought it more beautiful than any other Aphrodite. He went to the museum chief and asked for permission to make a plaster cast of it. This was refused; the museum also refused to let him make a copy in marble. Urban went to Mussolini, who gave him an order to the museum, authorizing him to have a copy made in Carrara marble by a sculptor to be selected by the Academy.

That is my statue. When I gave up my office in the New School building I took the statue to my house in Nyack. For these many years the statue has been a part of my life. In the presence of the statue I have a serene sense of the values that endure.

In September I laid before the board a report of progress under our committee. I presented Urban's exquisite drawings of the façade and the interiors. At first all the members hesitated to express either approval or disapproval. But Mrs. Putnam, our recognized arbiter of good taste and good sense, declared, "I like this building. It is chaste, dignified and beautiful. It meets our needs fully, generously." All the board agreed, at once.

There was more discussion of the plan of financing. One member pronounced it utterly unsound. We should not build until we could pay the full cost in cash. To me that meant never. The member, a corporation lawyer of distinction, resigned when the other members voted to approve the plan. In parting he warned us that the money invested in loans to the New School would be lost. Much of it was indeed finally lost. So was most of the money invested in our seceding member's corporations. Neither the New School nor the corporations foresaw the financial disaster that was to shake our economy to the roots.

"Well, Alvin," Maurice Wertheim said as we left the meeting, "I said you couldn't do it, but you did it."

"And so I go to the penitentiary or to Wall Street?"

"I condemn you to Wall Street. It's the heavier punishment. Bernie Baruch says we are all going to be skinned alive down there."

I knew what my admired chief Baruch meant. I had had the privilege of dining with him and Straus of Macy's. I had ventured the assertion that we were approaching the most terrific crisis in American history. We had built up a towering structure of cards, on installment sales, equivalent to an enormous issue of fiat money.

"Professor," said B. M. B., "sometimes an economist is right."

I thought, however, that Hoover's two cars in each garage might hold up for two years longer. In two flush years I'd collect the money to wipe out our debts. I was wrong, wrong as Hoover, and wrong as all the highlights of finance. But what was wrong with an educator and economist being wrong?

We had just got under way with our fund-raising when the depression struck its first savage blow. The financial structure of America reeled, but recovered its footing, after hundreds of millions in losses. Wertheim advised me to put off the campaign. I refused. There was still money to be had while the wounds were bleeding. If we waited for them to stiffen we'd be lost. Later he admitted I was right. If I had followed his advice, he said, it would have been years before we could build, if ever.

However painfully the financing dragged along, the construction proceeded with tremendous speed, under the Taylor Construction Company, Charles Mayer, construction engineer, Albert Mayer, builder. They built soundly and with great economy. To outsiders it looked as if an Urban building would be erected at extravagant cost. That was not true. The cost per cubic foot, including the fixtures, was sixty-seven cents. Conventional college buildings erected at the same time were costing a dollar and a half or two dollars a cubic foot.

As the building progressed a new problem arose. We were to have two large, square rooms, on the third and fifth floors. Urban pointed out that they would be good rooms for mural paintings, not subtle decorations on the wall, like the murals of Puvis de Chavannes, concessions to the architects who wished to enclose the occupier entirely in the measured space, but paintings that enticed the mind abroad, like windows looking out on real life.

Alma Reed, agent of José Clemente Orozco, called on me with the astonishing proposal that Orozco would contribute a mural painting gratis as a tribute to the ideals of the New School.

For years I had been an addict of the new school of Mexican painting, of Rivera and, above all, Orozco, the most authentic genius rising in Mexico. America had produced great civilizations in Mexico, Yucatán, and Peru. Before Columbus the American peoples had carried their civilizations to heights comparable to the highest in contemporary Europe, in architecture, sculpture, and mural painting. I had learned from Carlos Chavez that they had also developed a music, weird to my conventional ears, but fascinating. They had developed lyric poetry, mostly to be recited at folk gatherings, as poignantly tragic as the Greek epitaphs in the Kerameikos. And all this had been suppressed through four hundred years of Spanish colonialism.

The spirit of autochthonous American civilization was now rising out of alien oppression. The most versatile exponent of the new American freedom of creativeness was Rivera, but his art was corrupted, I felt, by the impulse to cross ancient American art with the art of Italy and France. Orozco scorned Italy and France and painted out of his Aztec-Basque soul.

I am an economist. Art is no business of mine. But how could I fail to see that Orozco and Rivera had lifted the oppressed historic American culture into the light of contemporary civilization, now at last beginning to realize that the narrow channel of art, from the Greeks through the Romans, the Renaissance, the French, did not carry the whole of human art? We were beginning to acknowledge that there was a period of Chinese art as exquisite as that of the Renaissance; we were growing passionate about the miniatures of Iran; even the Congo figurines, one-third devil, one-third piety, but the last third man, were

gripping us firmly. Art, like a morning star, was beckoning us forward
out of the egoistic white-race murk to the wide white light of all humanity.

Then what could have been my feeling when Orozco, the greatest
mural painter of our time, proposed to contribute a mural to the New
School? All I could say was, "God bless you. Paint me the picture.
Paint as you must. I assure you freedom."

It was noised about that I was having a mural by Orozco. My friend
Ralph Pierson, six feet and a half tall, acrobatic, hundred-per-cent
American, artist of angular and athletic drawings, a great teacher, a
great man provocatively, came to me in indignation. I was commission-
ing an alien to do a mural when Tom Benton, an authentic American,
whose grandfather had dueled with Andrew Jackson on an island in the
Mississippi and had caused President Andy to limp for life, this authentic Tom Benton, trained as a mural painter in France and Italy,
could never find a wall and had to live on easels at about five hundred
dollars a year.

"Ralph," I said, "come down off your high horse. I know something
of Tom Benton. I could give him just as good a room as I'm giving
Orozco. But on the same terms. No pay. And he can't afford it."

The next day Tom Benton appeared. He is a delightful fellow, frank
and free, possessed of an Italian wife, replica of the beautiful lady you
see in one of the charming frescoes of Pompeii.

"Sure," said Benton, "I'll paint you a picture in tempera if you'll
finance the eggs."

The two great artists, Orozco and Benton, left it to me to set up the
general themes on which they were to work. A mural painting, I
thought, should express a great idea. It could not today be a religious
idea, but it could be a social, humanistic idea. I asked each painter
what he considered the most powerful living movement of our time.
Benton fixed on the gigantic technological urge that was remaking the
economic center of the world. Orozco fixed on the revolutionary movement stirring all around the periphery of the technological center.

The themes looked magnificent to me. They look more magnificent
to me on the walls. One may like the pictures in detail or dislike them.
But every fair-minded critic must agree, it was an achievement to lift
painting out of the modern rut of inconsequence and give it the rightful
place it has held in every vital civilization—that of expressing ideals
and prophecies.

I knew well I was destined for difficulties about those paintings. I anticipated less difficulty from Orozco, because few people would understand him, and Americans are a people who value most what they can't understand. They would understand Benton, with his realistic pictures made up from thousands of drawings from real industrial life.

"I have to get into a modern steel mill," Benton told me. "Steel is the very focus of my picture. But those babies won't let me get near steel. 'An artist! What the hell does an artist want with steel? Out with him; must be a Communist.' "

One of my good friends in Wall Street got entrée for Benton to the Sparrow's Point plant in Maryland. You can see the hot center of the plant on the New School wall.

I got a loft floor from a friend to serve Benton as a studio. I'd go to see him almost every day. He'd piece together scores of drawings, tentative setup for a panel, and then do a little garden of the needed solids in clay and study it painfully, to determine the proportions and the color scheme of darks and lights needed to create plastic form. He had a color table, black at one end, white at the other; red was such and such a percentage of black, yellow was such and such a percentage of white. With the right relations of darks and lights, plastic form is inevitable.

All the esthetic spade work done, Benton proceeded gloriously with a panel, bankrupting me with the dozens and dozens of eggs needed for tempera.

One critic, on seeing the first panels, complained to me that Benton had no social philosophy. He depicted the gigantic, inhuman machinery of industrialism with never a pathetic note for the wage slaves operating it. Indeed, the operators do look triumphant. Too bad. But I too have seen the men in industry operating thousand-horsepower machinery. They look triumphant, they feel triumphant, they *are* triumphant. And what are we to do about it?

Benton told me, with a humorous twinkling of his dark eyes, of an exquisite critic who had complained that though his work was strong it was coarse. And I quoted to Benton, from my capacious though inexact memory:

> *"Doch die Kastraten klagten*
> *Als ich meine Stimme erhob.*
> *Sie klagten und sie sagten*
> *Ich sänge viel zu grob."*

Orozco was exciting to watch but hard for me to understand. His English had not advanced far beyond that of Adam. He didn't work, like Benton, from realistic sketches, but from cartoons he had worked out, on the dynamic symmetry principles of Jay Hammidge, which the Devil may understand.

Orozco would chalk with his one arm (he had lost the other in a childhood accident) an area of rough plaster he wanted covered with a final coat, on which he would work with his little hair brush, with pigments, while the plaster was dripping wet. I was fascinated. There had never been, so far as I knew, a piece of true fresco in all the United States east of the Rocky Mountains. Here a true fresco was growing under my eyes.

I watched with sympathy, almost passion, the picture of India going forward: primordial slavery, the fat pale slavery of the *bunnias,* the slender slavery of the white-collar crowd, the whole mess protected by a gorgeously inhuman Scottish officer and beautiful Sikh soldiers against the force of an emaciated Gandhi and a woman void of all character but that of woman, Mother India.

As an amateur anthropologist I had learned that in pre-Columbian America, from Point Barrow in Alaska to Tierra del Fuego, shivering under the Antarctic, red is a sacred color. All indigenous American art builds on reds, from light pink to dark, foreboding red, ranging from the lightest to the darkest with the evolving of passion. I knew how the Renaissance and Benton could get plastic form out of darks and lights. How could one get plastic form out of the religion of reds? Orozco was doing it.

When the picture was nearly finished a great French critic of art came to see us. "Look at that woman's leg," he said. "It is heavy for a lover to carry. By what means did he make that leg? Darks and lights? No. By magic.

"He's crazy. I cross the Atlantic to see his picture. Bah! The terrible Atlantic! I would cross the Pacific, too, to see this picture. The only great picture in the whole history of the United States of America."

That sounded good to me. But who are the French? A queer people. The critic told me, if this picture were shown in Paris, the very street sweepers would crowd to see it, in the lunch hour, and debate Orozco's devices for attaining plastic form.

But, alas, we are in New York, not in Paris; in New York, where the men of light and leading, and the sum of these, money, do not have the artistic sense and imagination of the Paris street sweepers. Art to us is just illustration and moral propaganda, Mother Goose well illustrated. And I knew, when Orozco had finished painting the revolution in Yucatán, with the poor dumb population held down by a poor dumb soldier, but with the grand revolutionary figure of Carillo Puerto rising high above, alongside the pyramid of ancient greatness—I knew this would do, for what New Yorker had any sense of Yucatán, or had ever heard of Carillo Puerto or of the pyramid?

But then Orozco's picture leaped over an ocean sunrise to Russia. After days in my garden at Nyack I came down to see what Orozco had been working at. There was the old Red army, led by a poster of Lenin. The army was in grays, signifying that it was of the past; but its bayonets had been done *con amore*. Twelve different whites had gone into those bayonets. After the triumph of revolution, a file of men going out to work, each with a conventional sculptor's work tool in his hand. And at the head of the file a figure that looked like Stalin.

As I looked at the picture, my liver, to use the Homeric expression, dissolved to water. My God, what trouble was in store for me! My beloved country had not at that time sunk so low, esthetically and intellectually, as it has sunk since. But even then it conceived of pictures as propaganda, good or bad.

Orozco scanned my features, congenitally inscrutable. "A reporter of the *New York Times*," he said, "told me this picture will make much trouble for Doctor Johnson. I do not want to make trouble for my friend Doctor Johnson. I am willing to knock the picture out and put something else."

"Señor Orozco," I said. "You painted this picture on my promise that you should be free. If you know of some other picture that would better express your idea, we will knock this one out and substitute the other. But not on account of any trouble to Doctor Johnson. For Doctor Johnson, as man, is of few days, and full of trouble."

A faraway, prophetic look came over Orozco's face. He offered me his creative hand—his true, sincere hand. Its pressure was the highest tribute that has come to me in all my life.

THIRTY-ONE

The University in Exile

THE New School resumed instruction in its new building in February 1930. The auspices were not of the best. The economic crisis was proceeding remorselessly. One financial structure after another toppled. Unemployment was growing distressingly. Hundreds of persons who in normal times would have registered for courses hesitated to commit themselves even for modest fees. They could not know whether or not they were destined to join the army of the unemployed.

It may be true, as the moralists say, that a crisis brings out the best there is in an individual, but that is not true of a community, a nation, the world. Much of the worst was coming up from below. Ulcers of intolerance, particularly antisemitism, were spreading their noxious structures on the face of the American body politic. Pygmy Mussolinis were cropping up all over the country.

I was not greatly disturbed about America. Our history shows that while our society is extremely susceptible to infection and we may run high fevers, our Constitution is robust enough to throw off disease. But I was deeply worried about Germany, where Hitler with his poisonous propaganda against the Jews, the Allies, and peace appeared to be gaining ground.

I had made several visits to Germany after the First World War. On my first visit, early in the twenties, I was shocked to discover that order, the crowning virtue of the vanished empire, had turned into a disorder uglier than anything we had ever known in America. Assassination was proceeding with virtual impunity; robberies were executed with cynical boldness. While I was at the Adlon in Berlin a disheveled citizen came in; his house had just been robbed. A band of twenty young men, probably war veterans, had driven up in a truck, broken in his door with a sledgehammer, and collected his Oriental rugs, the clothing in his closets, and his silver. They had pushed him around like an inert piece of furniture and then driven off. He had called up the police, who had shrugged the incident off.

I went out to Wannsee to call on Bernhard Dernburg, former Colonial Secretary, whom I had met in Washington when he was trying to keep us out of the war by methods that enraged us. Dernburg had a pleasant house, enclosed by a tall spiked-iron fence; armed guards cautiously opened the gate for you, examined your letter of invitation, scrutinized the signature of Dernburg, right side up and upside down, then led you to the great man.

Dernburg was one of the most intelligent men in Germany. Of rather forbidding appearance, his address was frank and engaging. I wanted to know his judgment as to what was coming out of the German situation. His views were not reassuring.

Germany had been a land of perfect order. Almost every man had had an established place: laborer, peasant, artisan, small merchant, engineer, teacher. Everyone knew where he was going, since he was going to stay just where he was. If he had low wages, he had long since adjusted his standard of living to them; if he had a comfortable income, he had adjusted his social life to it. Everybody looked to an efficient police to protect him against violence at home, and to a powerful army to protect him against invasion from abroad.

The army was gone and the police morally shattered. They no longer offered the peaceful citizen protection, and the citizen had never learned to protect himself. In America, Dernburg said, the army had never figured in the citizen's mind. Americans had never had much confidence in the police. They trusted more to the guns in their closets. And so, Dernburg said, when disorder becomes a serious problem in America, we organize vigilance committees, "citizens' committees," hang freely, set up "bull pens," and do what else we think necessary for our protection. Germans could not do that. They were defenseless, crippled by their long dependence on efficient government, police, and army.

Anything could happen in Germany. And what would happen was likely to be terrible.

From Dernburg's library I looked out through french windows at a wonderful garden, set with noble trees. The ground sloped down to a little river or canal. I suggested that we might lift the gloom a bit if we took a turn in the garden. Dernburg went cautiously up to one of the windows and studied the landscape intently. Then he said, "I wanted to see if there were riflemen on the other side. I don't see any. You might go down there, to the right, and pick yourself a bouquet of those red roses. They are fine today. Here's a scissors. But don't be long. They might shoot you by mistake."

I got the roses very quickly.

In the late twenties I was again in Germany. Assassination was still going on, and the government wasn't doing anything about it. But the spirit of the country seemed a little better. After the terrible inflation the government had created a new currency, the Rentenmark, secured by a mortgage on all the real property in Germany.

I was on a train from Berlin to Munich. A stout, pugnacious German sat next to me. After scrutinizing me for a while he asked if I understood German. I did.

"You are English?"

"No, American."

"You ruined Germany. But now she is coming back, thank God. Now we have a sound currency at last."

I said nothing, as I had no desire for an argument, in my imperfect German.

"You know our Rentenmark is sound. Secured by all the real property in Germany."

Still I said nothing.

"If the paper depreciates, we take the real estate."

"Who takes it?" I asked.

"Why, the government."

"Oh," I said.

"Yes, the government—if we had a government, instead of those Weimar cowards."

I said nothing. Apparently in Germany silence is a devastating argument. The German seemed to collapse morally, as if totally defeated in his hopes.

"Listen," he said anxiously. "I made two fortunes. One I lost by the war, when your government looted the alien property. Another I lost by the inflation. I've made another fortune, a small one. If I lose that, I shoot myself."

He brooded a while in silence. "Listen," he said. "You will stop at Munich a day or two? Let me bring you fifty thousand dollars in a bill of exchange. You deposit it for me in London or New York."

I stared at him. "You don't even know my name. If you gave me that bill of exchange, how can you be sure I wouldn't keep the money?"

"I can't be sure. The world is full of scoundrels. But I'd take my chances with you."

"But I won't take chances, smuggling exchange out of Germany. I have no stomach for your penitentiaries."

"They wouldn't search you."

But I was obdurate.

Americans had enough to occupy their minds at home, with the deepening depression and the bold experimentalism of President Roosevelt. To study the situation more systematically I organized at the New School a discussion group which I called "the Unpublished Review." The two most active students in the group, William Mc-Chesney Martin and Joseph Mead, got together funds to put out a quarterly, *The Economic Forum*.

It was my belief that the depression could be checked in its course by a joint effort of the principal economic powers: the government, the banks, the great industrialists, the railways, and labor. On the War Industries Board I had observed the power of the combination of great interests working together for a common cause. I wanted President Roosevelt to set up an organization, not of advisers, but of men carrying the power of the interests they represented. If there was a project on the margin of feasibility which would make employment and take its place later in the national productive equipment, it could be made entirely feasible by lower interest, cheaper steel, adjusted railway rates, full labor cooperation.

President Roosevelt regarded my proposal as reactionary. He liked better the suggestions of Keynes, to cope with depression by increase in government spending, although Keynes' estimates of the amount of spending required looked to Roosevelt too much like an exercise in higher mathematics.

In the meantime nazism in Germany was rapidly gaining strength. It was hard for me to believe that a people we had always regarded as standing in the forefront of culture could choose to be governed by an ignorant demagogue, drawing his moral sustenance from poisonous hatred. But we had seen Mussolini, with the slenderest following, take over and hold the government of Italy. Germany, to be sure, was not an Italy, but, like Italy, she had made the mistake of patterning her constitution on that of England, a constitution under which government can work only if political life is organized on a two-party system.

It had taken more than two hundred years of trial and error, of statesmanship and the bold employment of bribery and corruption, to make the English parliamentary system work. Germany had no two hundred years to spend.

In our search for contributors to the *Encyclopaedia* we had become very familiar with German academic personnel. We knew what professors were marking time and what ones were forging new and interesting ideas. In the political sciences the scholars we regarded as most promising were those who drew their inspiration from Max Weber, the most creative thinker of our time. In psychology we rated highest Max Wertheimer and his associates in the Gestalt school, Wolfgang Köhler and Kurt Koffka. I had corresponded with many of these men and regarded them as my personal friends.

In the summer of 1932 I again visited Germany. Conditions appeared to have worsened. Violence was gaining headway, especially among the young, for whom there appeared to be no place in a system of employment that gave at least a semblance of security to the older workers but left the young out in the cold. Soon after my arrival in Berlin, when I was walking in Unter den Linden, a street then sadly decayed, a group of a dozen or fifteen young men surrounded me and demanded a dollar. Their spokesman was movingly eloquent. They had no work; however willing, they could get none, for the jobs were monopolized by the older men. They had to live on their families, which grew more and more impatient under the burden. They never saw any money, not even the few pfennige that would let them take their girls to a dance *Lokale* and treat them to a beer or an ice.

Where was the money? They suggested that I go in the evening to the Kurfürstendamm. There I would see money thrown around like trash. By whom? By the Jews, who guzzled and gobbled and danced. But their time was coming.

I surrendered the dollar and was glad to get away. I'd have been willing to take on two of the youths, but not the dozen or fifteen, behaving menacingly, and no police in sight.

I called on my old friend Professor Moritz Bonn at the Handelshochschule. Hitler, he said, would win. He had not, and never could have, a majority of the people behind him. But the active opposition was split between the Communists and the Social Democrats, who would never be able to agree on a common policy. For himself, he meant to go to England as soon as the government fell into the hands of Hitler.

Bonn invited me to his seminar, where I met a man I had long wanted to know, Werner Hegemann, an extremely distinguished city planner, who had worked for long periods in America and was more American than German. He too meant to get out of Germany at the first news of Hitler's triumph.

The man I most wanted to meet was Professor Emil Lederer. By birth and upbringing Lederer was Austrian, well imbued with the old Spanish courtesy of the Hapsburg Empire, with a subtle and extraordinarily enterprising mind. He was a distinguished economist, but his mind ranged freely over the whole political and cultural field. He too was convinced that Hitler would get control of the government. His regime would be mob rule, the most terrible in history. Hitler would egg on the mob to commit outrages against liberals and Jews, outrages at first limited to beatings, mutilation, sporadic assassinations, developing rapidly toward massacre. Finally, war and the ruin of Germany.

I asked him whether he was not perhaps painting the picture too black. Was it not the rule in history that responsibility sobered even a leader who had climbed to power by the most abominable means? Power, Lederer said, did not sober Nero. He was a madman. Hitler was madder and more cruel than Nero.

Within a few months Hitler came into power. Mussolini had won power by marching on Rome, with a force that a regiment of loyal soldiers could easily have dispelled. Hitler won power quite legally under a constitution that made legality an empty form. Very soon the proscription of professors began. Two lists were published, containing the names of nearly all the social scientists who had any creative spirit in them. The positions thus vacated were promptly filled with Nazis whose intellectual qualifications consisted in their fervor in parroting Hitler's ignorant mouthings.

I was deeply distressed, not only for my friends who had been cashiered, but for an institution which had stood out before the world as the most secure fortress of intellectual freedom, the German university. The imperious Hohenzollerns had never laid an impious hand on the university; Bismarck, who respected, as a rule, nothing that might stand in his way, respected the universities. Even the disastrous World War had left the universities fundamentally unscathed.

Of course I signed circular letters of protest but begrudged the waste of ink; nothing could come of mere protests. It was incumbent on American scholars to make their protests real through action. Invitations to the displaced professors to join our American faculties, I felt, should be forthcoming straightway. I carried on an urgent correspondence with friends in the universities. They agreed with me in principle; but university budgets were suffering severely under the depression.

At least, I thought, I could make a place for Lederer in the New School. Our budget too was feeble, but I set out to raise contributions. In three weeks I had pledges amounting to four hundred and fifty dollars. But for Lederer I needed five thousand dollars a year for two years.

Reflecting on these disappointing results, I began to cudgel myself for my stupidity. This is New York, I said to myself, and New York can't see anything so minute as the fate of a single man, however great a man. If I had set out to finance a whole faculty, New York would at least have taken note of the fact.

The idea excited me.

If I only had a name for the idea! The "New School Faculty of Political Science" wouldn't do. There was no barb in that hook. A "Faculty of Exiled Scholars" wouldn't do. That would be a hook with a broken point. My mind flitted around among names of institutions memorable to me. Saint Peter in Chains in Rome; who that ever saw the church could forget *in vincolis?* A "University in Exile"—that sounded good. For it was the university itself that was being exiled from Germany.

Could I raise sixty thousand a year for a two-year initial period? That would give me fifteen scholars at four thousand dollars, or twelve if it were wiser to fix the salaries at five thousand.

I kept my idea to myself the rest of the day, to examine its implications.

It would be possible, I thought, to raise some money to support a number of proscribed professors for two years. But a University in Exile, like Saint Peter in Chains, looked to permanence. Only under the condition of permanence could the best brains of Germany be drawn together.

But permanence meant financial commitments for the indefinite future. It had been my dream that the New School, as an institution of higher adult education, could eventually become self-supporting. A University in Exile, a faculty devoted to graduate instruction, could never be. How many graduate students can a professor teach and direct efficiently? Possibly ten full-time students. Can ten graduate students pay tuition enough to support a professor? Experience shows they can't, or they won't.

My project meant a permanent financial burden for the New School. Had it anything to give that would justify the cost? Here there could be no question. Certainly it had something to give.

The New School was operating on the theory that the continued education of the educated is a vital national interest. Nicholas Murray Butler, with a true poet's sublime arrogance, had called America the "best half-educated people in the world." The illiterate South Atlantic mountaineers are no menace to America. The somewhat literate McCarthys are a desperate menace. If we can't set up a scheme for educating the half-educated we shall have to fall back on illiteracy or semi-illiteracy for our salvation.

The New School had proved that the intelligent layman can be drawn to serious lecture courses. He can be enlisted in discussion groups. We had also discovered that many of those who came to us had intellectual projects of their own: young lawyers who had grand juristic ideas, young bankers who had something to say about finance, young industrialists who knew where the king pinions of industry were located. These men had something important to say but did not know how to say it.

It had been a conviction of mine that we could mobilize the disorderly mass of lay ability if we had a group of graduate instructors, with the power to grant degrees, therefore the power to discipline the spontaneous abilities emerging in the lay public. I hate the institution of degrees. My conscience smites me because I could not suppress the pleasure I got out of honorary degrees, particularly one from the Free University of Brussels, with true ermine I'll never know how to wear.

To achieve its true and vital purposes the New School needed a graduate faculty.

Every great nation develops a university mind peculiar to itself. An Oxford professor is not just a Harvard professor with a quaint British dialect. His handling of the material of his science is peculiarly Oxonian. This is even more true of French scholars, of German scholars. To function perfectly in an American institution, the foreign professors have to go through a process of assimilation. But assimilation by individuals, in America, has always involved much amputation of virtues as well as vices. A coordinated faculty of German scholars would adapt itself to America, but as a group, retaining in its inner structure the strength of its original discipline.

A University in Exile had to be conceived from the outset as a permanent institution. And this meant committing myself for life, and my successors in the presidency of the New School, to a grave recurrent financial problem.

As night came on the idea of a University in Exile looked less seductive to me. But I prorogued any decision on it till morning. And on waking I found myself burning with excitement. At the earliest reasonable hour I called the members of the board to a special meeting, laid my idea before them, and asked their approval, assuring them that I did not expect them to contribute or to solicit contributions. The board approved my proposal without a dissenting voice and granted me permission to go ahead alone. But one member whose good works would fill an encyclopedia volume, Mrs. David M. Levy, made one of the first substantial contributions to the enterprise.

My plan of financing was homemade. I set forth in a one-page letter to my old chief, Professor Seligman, the essentials of my project, how it would be organized, and what it would accomplish morally. I asked him to let me make a hundred original signed copies of this letter, to be sent to a hundred influential friends with a covering note from him, endorsing it. Within a week pledges began to come in, a thousand dollars, twenty-five hundred, five thousand. To my mind the campaign was going splendidly.

One day a strong, pleasant voice came to me over the phone. "Doctor Johnson, you don't know me. I am Hiram Halle. A letter you wrote to Professor Seligman has come into my hands, about a University in Exile. May I ask, how much money have you got pledged?"

"Twelve thousand," I answered proudly. For less than a week had gone by since I wrote the letter.

"I am surprised that it is so little," said Halle. "But I will say something that may interest you. I am prepared to guarantee the sixty thousand a year for two years, so that you can go ahead at once."

All things are possible, but such a piece of good fortune looked incredible. I rushed downtown to the office of Frank Altschul, to find out more about Hiram Halle.

Altschul did some telephoning. "Hiram Halle's signature on a check for a million dollars would be accepted by any bank in New York. But we'll keep his amazing offer under our hats. Nobody will contribute if he knows Halle is ready to carry the whole load."

The next day I called on Halle in his office. He impressed me powerfully. A man obviously of great strength of will, of the keenest intelligence, of seasoned humanity, he was among the rare personalities you enroll at first sight as treasured friends. I count my long association with Hiram Halle as one of the great privileges life has accorded me.

About a week later Morris Cohen called me up to congratulate me on having sixty thousand dollars a year for two years. I assured him that he was in error. I had only twenty-two thousand pledged.

"But you have Hiram Halle's guaranty."

Lord! I thought. How did that get out? Only my wife, my secretary, and Frank Altschul knew about it besides myself. None of us could have let it leak.

A few hours later my anxiety lifted. Another friend had been at a meeting of forty men assembled to raise money for a good cause. Halle had explained to Felix Warburg, who sat next to him, that he could not make any material contribution as he had guaranteed the sixty thousand a year for two years for the University in Exile. Warburg insisted on his stating the fact to the meeting. It would stimulate their giving to the other cause. The forty men present were pledged to keep the information confidential. Of course within a week forty thousand persons had the secret.

To an outsider my problems seemed already solved. I had the authority to set up a graduate faculty of the social sciences. I had the money to support it through the critical two years of launching. I had a marvelous panel of abilities to select from. But to the insider no action is free from problems that must be grappled with resolutely.

The expulsion of professors from the German universities took place in the late spring. I meant to have my faculty assembled and entering upon the work of instruction by the opening of the fall term. To scholars experienced in the dilatoriness of academic decisions, such haste seemed unreasonable, perhaps undesirable. Would it not be wiser for me to allow myself time to mature my plans, to lay out a really sound organization?

I wanted to get my future colleagues across the Atlantic and at work before the outrage of expulsion could grow fast in their spirits, to cripple their initiative and gnaw away at their energies. But there was a less obvious reason that made speed urgent.

A lot of talk was going around about the novel enterprise of a

University in Exile. Talk is a perishable commodity: if it is not consumed in action it spoils on your hands.

Would such a group of aliens be able to adjust to American life? Would not the assembling of a faculty consisting mainly of Jews give impetus to antisemitism? This question was put with especial intensity by some of the most distinguished leaders of the Jewish community. A great Jewish lawyer I tried to interest in the project wrote me that there were three reasons against it. First, these scholars could not be got out of Germany. Second, they would not be admitted to this country under the immigration laws. Third, the University in Exile, if ever it became a fact, would be regarded as a little intellectual Ghetto, to the injury of a people already suffering severely under growing prejudice and discrimination.

There is a current saying that excites the ire of Jews whenever they hear it. "Some of my best friends are Jews." I mend the rhetoric in the interest of truth. "The Jews I know are among my best friends." My exiled scholars needed only to be known to be accepted in the category of best friends.

Talk turning rancid would not, I felt, be confined to our local community. It would also affect the responses of the scholars I wished to enlist. What sort of institution was the New School? Could one accept a position in a school of higher adult education, paralleled in Europe only by Social Democratic Urania—essentially propaganda institutions? Would one's standing as a scholar be compromised? And as to security, what endowment did the New School have, to assure permanence?

Immediately upon receiving Halle's guaranty I wrote Lederer, explaining the whole situation and begging him to join me and assist me in assembling a faculty. I enclosed a tentative list of scholars I'd like to see on the faculty.

Lederer's reply was encouraging. He suggested that I send immediately to London a representative who could answer any questions that might be raised. There were three of the scholars on my list in London, Karl Mannheim, Adolf Lowe, and Jakob Marschak. If I could win them the rest would be simple.

I sent my *Encyclopaedia* colleague, Edwin Mims, Jr., to London. Eddie was profoundly impressed by the charm and intelligence of the three scholars and did his best to win them. They held back, and Eddie came home, discouraged. I cabled Lederer, asking him to come to New York at once.

Lederer was a most courteous gentleman, and as shrewd as a Spanish diplomat. He inquired penetratingly into every phase of the problem, the independence of the faculty from the general New School, and from me; the present finances and the prospects for the future; the attitude of the great universities and the local community, particularly the gentile part of the community, for he suspected that the leading Jewish intellectuals would seriously question our project.

He was satisfied and told me he was turning down an offer from the University of Manchester. We went over the whole list of expelled professors and made up a new tentative list. It included Eduard Heimann, Lederer's old rival for honors in economic theory; Arthur Feiler, splendid combination of scholar and journalist; Max Wertheimer, the greatest of the psychologists; Arnold Brecht, a powerful jurist and parliamentarian; Frieda Wunderlich, authority on labor; Albert Salomon, sociologist of the Max Weber school; Hans Speier, a sociologist with passionate literary interests; Karl Brandt, agricultural economist; Hans Neisser, mathematical economist; Gerhart Colm, expert in public finance; Hermann Kantorowicz, jurist and historian. We did not get Hans Neisser at the time, for Joe Willetts had him committed to the University of Pennsylvania.

Later Max Wertheimer stipulated that we invite also Erich von Hornbostel, the greatest of all musicologists, who had collaborated with Wertheimer on problems of musical psychology. And later in the summer I added Max Ascoli, the most brilliant of the younger Italian political scientists, who was completing his second year as a Rockefeller fellow. I also added Horace Kallen, who had been with the New School from the beginning and whose profound knowledge of philosophy, particularly American philosophy, would be invaluable.

I wanted to add Werner Hegemann, city planner, but Lederer felt he would not fit into the family. So I invited Hegemann to join the New School faculty, where he would find students deeply interested in city planning.

While Lederer was carrying on negotiations with the scholars we wished to enlist I visited London, where two of the future members of the faculty, Albert Salomon and Hans Speier, flew over to see me. I also met Kantorowicz, who explained that he could join us for only one year as he had an appointment at Cambridge. I also met Mannheim, Marschak, and Lowe.

I met Lowe at a time when it still looked uncertain whether we should be able to assemble a satisfactory faculty. I was somewhat bitter about the resistance of the three professors, which I felt then might compromise the future of an institution that could do important service for the exiled scholars. I was feeling down on my luck, a feeling not natural to me and therefore likely to impair my manners. But if I reproached Lowe he has forgiven me, and for the last dozen years has been one of my best-loved and most highly valued colleagues. In 1943 he led a movement of the faculty to set up an institute devoted to long-run studies of world affairs.

While in London I met a charming and energetic lady, sister-in-law of Hans Staudinger, whom I knew of as an admirable economist and a high official in the German government service. Word came that he had been arrested, and she flew back to Germany to deploy whatever influence she could command to get him released. I made up my mind then to try to get Staudinger for my faculty.

Not long after I had announced my plan for a University in Exile, Stephen Duggan, of the Institute for International Education, invited me to lunch. He told me of a plan he was working on to place exiled professors in the universities and colleges throughout the country. He hoped to raise large funds for this Emergency Committee, so that he could offer the several institutions the gift of a displaced professor with a two years' stipend.

It was a grand plan, and I approved it with all my heart. But Duggan proposed that I give up my University in Exile and throw in my resources with his plan.

I could not. I pointed out to Duggan that whatever resources I had were given specifically for the establishment of a permanent faculty. We could never hope to have resources comparable to such as he would be able to raise, for the great Foundations regarded me as an educational adventurer. But what resources we had were extremely mobile.

The contemplated Emergency Committee would not be able to act before some university or college decided that it wanted to add a certain scholar to its faculty. Universities and colleges dislike commitments and are slow to act. While the Emergency Committee would take care of the stipend for a certain time, the college would be under a moral obligation to continue the scholar's tenure at its own expense.

I put the case of a scholar just one lap ahead of Hitler's hounds. What would the Emergency Committee be able to do for him? Recommend him to a college, where he would have to be approved by department, dean, college president, perhaps a committee of the board.

In the meantime Hitler's hounds would have got him. My institution could make up its mind in an hour and send off a cable carrying the privilege of non-quota immigration for the professor, his wife, and minor children.

In such an emergency an Emergency Committee would have to turn to the University in Exile. We would always be ready to cooperate, but we could not merge.

In the summer of 1933 the members of my new faculty were arriving, ship by ship. It was exciting to wait for them at the foot of the gangplank and pick them out from among the hurrying passengers. The men appeared grave and resolute, their wives with anxious faces, their little children shy but tripping blithely.

Kantorowicz was delayed a few weeks after the opening of the term by lecture engagements in England. Arnold Brecht was delayed for several months, conducting the legal defense of the Social-Democratic leader Carl Severing, at great risk to his own liberty. Salomon was re-educating his body after a crippling attack of poliomyelitis and felt that he needed to remain in Germany for some months, to be treated by his trusted physician. Fortunately he got away before Hitler's madness evolved to mass murder.

Early in September we had our first faculty meeting. I imposed on the faculty an institution novel to them—and to me—a general seminar, in which the professors would present papers before the faculty, the students, and guests. This meant a heavy burden on scholars new to their positions. But I had three objects in view that I considered compelling. First, the plan would promote the unity of the social sciences within our faculty. Second, the several members would appear repeatedly, not only before their colleagues as in faculty meetings, but before a public including professors from other institutions. Thus they would come to be known to an expanding circle of Americans and would soon feel at home.

My third object I did not expatiate on. Friction inevitably develops in every faculty group. Strong characters are prone to doctrinal disagreement, and these exiled professors were all strong. In most universities professors criticize one another severely in their offices and more or less furtively in their lectures. By the institution of a general seminar disagreement and criticism would be drawn out into the open.

The institution of a general seminar survives to this day. And while it has not produced harmony of opinion, it has created an atmosphere of frank exchange of views, which has made of the Graduate Faculty the most unified educational body I have ever participated in, except for the Columbia School of Political Science in its early years, which served as my model. Equality, academic freedom, autonomy, have been the principles of the Graduate Faculty for the eighteen years of its existence. But I did not dare to establish the principle of unanimity; for we had no nuclear group, like Dean Burgess and his lieutenants, who carried in them the tradition of liberty that had been slowly worked out from Runnymede down. German scholars did indeed enjoy academic liberty, down to the time of Hitler, but it was liberty conferred by enlightened royal grant, not won in the face of authority through a persistent will to be free. Our New School constitution works well, but not so smoothly as that of the Columbia School of Political Science.

The faculty was more disturbed by my proposal to launch a quarterly magazine in the middle of the year. Lederer remarked gently that it had taken his group in Berlin six years to prepare for the launching of a new quarterly. I said we hadn't any six years at our disposal if we wished to become known to our American colleagues as a creative institution. We launched the first issue of *Social Research* in the spring. The magazine was at first a terrible burden on the faculty. Most of them fell short of perfect command of English. Severe editing, often painful to the contributor, was necessary. Today our faculty members write well, and we have no lack of contributors from other institutions.

The following year we planned to expand the faculty by the enlistment of new members who should broaden our range. Lederer drew up a list, including Hans Simons, Alfred Kähler, Fritz Lehmann, and Erich Hula. Lederer asked me, if I had a free choice, what German scholar in addition I would take first. I replied, Hans Staudinger, but we couldn't get him. We could, said Lederer; should he cable him? Sure. And so we annexed one of my most dynamic colleagues.

Erich Hula refused. He was in Austria, still an independent country, and he considered it his duty to stand by. Later, when Hitler broke into Austria, we invited three Austrians, Fritz Kaufmann, Erich Hula, and Karl Winter, who accepted.

In the normal course of our expansion we annexed to the faculty Carl Mayer and Leo Strauss. We also added Julie Meyer and Abba Lerner; two Italian scholars, Alexander Pekelis and Nino Levi. After years in England, Adolf Lowe and Jakob Marschak joined us, and

Hans Neisser from Pennsylvania. On the collapse of the Spanish Republic we won to our faculty the incomparable Fernando de los Ríos, and not much later the great German philosopher Kurt Riezler. With Riezler the roster was closed, for the period of my headship of the school; but the institution continues to draw in new blood.

We had losses too. Karl Brandt left us for Stanford University, Marschak and Leo Strauss for Chicago, Gerhart Colm and Hans Speier for positions in the government in Washington. And, tragically, our numbers were thinned by deaths. Pliny remarks somewhere that the most serious penalty upon long life is to see one dear friend after another carried off by death. I have mourned much.

The University in Exile, later known as the Graduate Faculty of Political and Social Science, promptly took its place among American educa‎tional institutions. This was due in no small measure to the signal generosity of our American colleagues. In the first years the political science faculty of Columbia joined with us in a series of regular dinner meetings for the discussion of scientific topics. The national associations gave the members of our faculty a number of places on their annual programs quite beyond our reasonable expectations.

In setting up the University in Exile I conceived that while the faculty as a unit would become assimilated to American conditions, the group organization would protect the individual member against the conventional mutilating process of individual assimilation. I hoped that these European scholars would retain the values of the European university discipline.

Philosophy lay at the center of that discipline, philosophy extending to the state and society. There was indeed intense specialization in the German university, but the specialty was conceived of as a branch of the philosophical tree, not as an autonomous growth. The scholar, whatever his branch of the social sciences, felt himself responsible for the whole cultural system. And this gave the scholar a mission. Particularly after the debacle of the First World War, with the restlessness and disorders of the times, the scholar felt the obligation to help the student to think his way through to an inner order of mind.

A teacher with a mission is a good teacher, whatever method he employs—lectures, class discussions, textbook drilling, syllabi of readings. The teacher with a mission imparts the sense of values without which study is a dull grind.

Our exiled professors have proved good teachers. There is no grumbling among them over the tedium of teaching. They are interested, and interesting. I have never known a graduate faculty so uniformly interested in their work, so ready to give all the time they have to meet the needs of the students.

In recent years American scholars have been steadily infiltrating the Graduate Faculty. In the course of time the institution will become wholly a faculty of the native-born. But our American recruits are developing in an atmosphere of coordination of the social sciences animated by a philosophy of life. The spirit of the University in Exile will long survive.

THIRTY-TWO

Puerto Rico

S INCE my student days in Nebraska I had been deeply interested in imperialism and in the conditions of living in subject colonies. The whole system was obnoxious to my democratic principles. But democracy could mean little in a region infested with headhunters, or with tribes that made their living, as the Masai did in Central Africa, by raiding the peaceful villages at intervals long enough to allow a new crop of loot to grow. If imperialism brought order and security it might be justified, provisionally, as a stage leading up to democracy.

I had always been troubled about Puerto Rico. Here was a people whom we had liberated from Spanish rule, at the time not a very oppressive rule. The Puerto Rican way of life was as peaceful and orderly as that of any Latin-American republic. Indeed, it was more peaceful and orderly than some parts of the United States. Yet we held this people in colonial bonds.

We tried honestly to make the bonds as silken and humane as possible. We gave the Puerto Ricans the privileges of American citizenship with the right to trial by jury and the writ of habeas corpus, free movement to the United States, free trade with us. In late years we went farther and turned into the Puerto Rican treasury all the customs and internal revenue taxes collected in the island. Imagine how the State of New York would swim in cash with the same privilege! And while Puerto Rico was not represented in Congress, it could maintain legislative delegates in Washington who, though having no vote, had exceptionally potent voice.

Yet murmuring in Puerto Rico was chronic. Most frequently the object of discontent was the educational system. What should be the role of English in the schools? Should it be the medium of instruction or should it be treated as a foreign language, perhaps required of all pupils? At one extreme were the Americanizers, who would have liked to make an English-speaking island of Puerto Rico; at the other

349

extreme, the Independentists, who clung to Spanish and begrudged even the modest hours given to English as a foreign language.

In the early part of the Roosevelt administration strident cries were going up from the Puerto Rican delegation in Washington over the arbitrary and brutal management of the schools under a commissioner Puerto Rican by birth but educated in American universities. There was said to be a conspiracy under way to assassinate him.

It seemed worth while to President Roosevelt to send down a commission of educators to face the problem on the spot. He appointed as chairman Isaiah Bowman, geographer and president of Johns Hopkins, who selected for his fellow commissioners the president of the University of Hawaii, the dean of education of the University of Illinois, Max Radin, political scientist from the University of California, Frank P. Graham, president of the University of North Carolina, and myself. We had attached to our group two officials from the Washington departments, who knew their way around in Puerto Rico.

Isaiah Bowman proved a most efficient chief. None of us had had a very clear idea as to what we could do with that island, which looks bigger the nearer you approach. We boarded our ship, the Coamo, and had hardly found our staterooms and deposited our bags when Bowman summoned us to the lounge, to lay out our plan of work. We were deep in planning by the time our ship passed Ambrose Light and met the swells of the Atlantic. The Coamo, built to take on the maximum cargo of sugar, had no freight on this voyage except a few baby carriages and some gross of cigarette cartons. It pirouetted about on top of the waves like a tap dancer. We promptly got seasick, every one of us, including Bowman, who suppressed a paroxysm long enough to request us to reassemble in an hour. We did, chastened in spirit and prepared to meet Puerto Rico and its problems with due humility.

The job assigned to me was to make a quick survey of the economic condition of the island, in its bearing on education, public health, and social welfare. There were enough statistical reports available, but Bowman, as a geographer, felt that statistical reports become more illuminating when you have seen the terrain. The assignment suited me exactly. I'd have a car and a guide at my disposal and would be able to explore the whole island, by true report an exquisitely lovely island.

For some days I hung around our hotel, the Condado, gathering information on the social-political structure of Puerto Rico and observing the methods of inquiry of my colleagues. The main case against the Commissioner of Education was that he had summarily dismissed a teacher, according to some witnesses, because the teacher advocated independence; according to other witnesses, because he was dead against independence. Frank Graham was our chief inquisitor.

Before beginning his inquiry Graham had sent for the teacher whose case was to be reviewed. The teacher had never been fired at all but had been promoted from a lower position in a small village to a higher position in a large one. But Graham continued his inquiry, listening to the witnesses' lying without a shadow of disdain on his face. The outcome of the inquiry was the complete vindication of the Commissioner of Education.

Frank Graham is my ideal of the American diplomat. He combines high moral purpose with the most penetrating intelligence and the most charming courtesy. It is a striking instance of the luck of the American people that he is now serving as Ambassador to Pakistan, the most difficult post in our whole service.

To Graham there is always a vestige of truth in a liar, of mercy in a murderer. And it is incumbent on the honest investigator to discover these vestiges. They may mean more than the patent facts. Out of the mass of false testimony he elicited much information on the whole educational system of Puerto Rico.

It was a wonderful opportunity for me. With a succession of college-educated young Puerto Ricans serving me as chauffeurs and guides, I was privileged to visit the whole island, from east to west and across, the remote valleys and far into the dark rain forest. I could stop anywhere to look at the scheme of Puerto Rican life, the great sugar plantations operated by Americans, the peasant-held sugar land, the decaying tobacco districts, the hill slopes of coffee ruined by a hurricane which had uprooted the shade trees indispensable to the modest coffee tree.

I could stop to watch the workers cutting down and stripping sugar canes thick as my arm. For a few minutes I borrowed a machete and cut cane myself. What hard work! Those Puerto Rican workers kept it up from dawn to sunset.

There is a comfortable delusion in America and northern Europe that in southern Europe and all lands of mild climate men are lazy. After seeing men at work in Italy, I had doubted their laziness.

I doubted still more, when I saw these Puerto Ricans with their machetes leveling acres of cane.

I had been contemptuous of ox culture. In my youth, horses were traction, and later, the Fordhook tractor. There in the fields of Puerto Rico you would see men loading into trucks four tons, five, six of cane. Nothing short of a twenty-mule team or three Fordhook tractors in a string could have drawn such loads out of the field soil, with wheels sinking halfway to the hub. The Puerto Ricans brought a span of white oxen, heavy horned, beautiful, like the bulls in the ancient pottery paintings of the Suovetaurilia. Those noble white oxen, with a bar from the brow of one to the brow of the other serving for yoke, would put their heads to a low level and draw and draw until the truck responded as to a geologic force. You watched open-mouthed until the load was drawn out upon the hard-surfaced highway.

My guides also took me into the huts to see what these hard-working Puerto Ricans were eating. A little fried yam or plantain— a sugarless banana; a little dried codfish stewed in water; coffee. What had they had for breakfast? Two cups of black coffee and nothing else. What would they have for supper? A little rice, a little more codfish. All told, they were getting one-third of the calories supposed to be necessary for heavy work. They came back to their huts, tired and burned out by the sun, to sit on their steps with cocks in their arms, gamecocks, their love and pride.

The Puerto Rican does not have a chicken in the pot on Sundays or any other days, save when a cock has been slain in fight. Puerto Rico is infested with snails that harbor a parasite which must realize itself in the entrails of a bird. Birds in Puerto Rico sing sadly, with gnawing worms in their interiors. Chickens are reduced to bone, feathers, and faint squawks. But the chicken destined for Homeric battle is grown on the floor of the hut, away from the fatal snails. He is fed out of the worker's scant bounty. He may grow up to lord it over the village cocks, the cocks of the province, of the nation. But sooner or later he goes down in battle, to be stewed and eaten by his friend and master, 'mid tears.

My guides stopped to let me visit a little ménage on a mountainside. You dug your toes in and plodded up a slope of about sixty degrees, until you came to a clearing on soil lying at an angle of about fifty degrees, well planted with beans, yams, and a few plantains around the thatched hut. The bulk of the cleared slope was in tobacco, which the husband would carry half-green down to the store—for not even a donkey could negotiate the slope—and bring back rice, codfish, and lipstick.

The husband was eighteen, the wife sixteen, and they had two little almost spherical children. Looking at the dizzy slope below, I felt, if these babies started to roll, they'd roll half a mile. But the babies, like their parents, knew life and what to do with it.

The boy-husband and girl-wife had not been married. To get married you had to accumulate a capital of a dollar for priest and public clerk, and what ardent Puerto Rican lad could wait till he had accumulated a dollar? After all, if it was only a dollar that stood between him and happiness, to the devil with the dollar. And you could wager all you had, that boy and girl would stick together to the end.

From what I saw of it, I came to love the Puerto Rico population—not the population of the slums of San Juan, almost as abominable as the worst slums in New York or Chicago, but that of the little, compact towns of Old World character, the small farmers wresting their living from little, irregular plots of ground, mostly clinging to hill slopes. I think those brave farmers were Basque in origin. They didn't have the high, narrow heads of Castilians. There were gray-eyed blonds among them reminiscent of the Visigoths. And there was some African admixture, especially in the approaches to the lowland and the cities.

One saw more of the African admixture at the university. There you saw groups of young men with a contingent of Negroes or mulattoes among them; also, mixed groups of young women. I tried to find out whether race prejudice corrupted this charming group life that I saw. I could get no data to confirm the Southern principle that black and white can't mix, except immorally.

I visited schools, primary schools with the loveliest children, white Basque sprinkled with light and dark brown coffee, taught by charming ladies whose imperfect English was lovelier than English in perfection. The grade-school children loved their English lessons and were very proud to enter into a question-and-answer session with the formidable foreigner from the States. But the high-school boys and girls, though much more proficient in English, appeared to dislike the language. They were passionate about their Spanish heritage.

I asked myself, why, in all these years since we seized Puerto Rico in 1898, have we made no progress toward transforming the Puerto Ricans into an English-speaking population? The Romans made Latin speakers out of the inhabitants of Gaul and Spain and the Danube territories that became Rumania, but perhaps it was because those regions had no written language except among the priests. The Romans never succeeded in compelling literate peoples, Greeks, Hebrews, Egyptians, to speak Latin. The mighty U.S.A. will never be able to compel any Spanish-speaking population to come over to English. Thank God, for Spanish is a noble language, fit instrument for the explorations of the human mind in the world of the future.

From my guides and from my university friends I learned much about the social constitution of Puerto Rico. At the top of the social ladder was a group of families established in Puerto Rico in the era of Latin-American revolutions. From their South-American homes they took what they could of their substance and fled to Puerto Rico, as our own Tories fled to Nova Scotia and Canada. These Tories were still nostalgic for the imperialism of Old Spain. One of them, my host Señor Gonzales of the Hotel Condado, had sent a gift of a hundred thousand dollars to Franco.

But since Spanish imperialism was finished, these loyal Tory souls were for American imperialism. They had wealth and power. They could draw our satraps into their net. They could name the delegates to Washington and largely determine our policy toward Puerto Rico.

President Soto of the University of Puerto Rico staged a party, mainly of young Tories, in the courtyard of his residence. Under a full white moon these slender young gentlemen and graceful young ladies danced beautiful, civilized Spanish dances to music that made one nostalgic for Old Spain. A more handsome and beautiful party of young adults I never saw in all my life.

Most of the sugar was produced on plantations owned and operated by Americans, with native labor. The plantation owners and their higher employees were dogmatically pro-American. So also were the rum distillers. But the rest of the population, while not as a rule severely critical of our colonial administration, harbored yearnings of national independence in their breasts.

I would argue with my guides. How could Puerto Rico afford independence? The most important economic asset of the island was sugar. The export of sugar to the United States brought back a quarter of the food needed to keep the Puerto Ricans alive. But sugar could not be produced so cheaply in Puerto Rico as in Cuba, Jamaica, and many other regions washed by the Caribbean. Puerto Rican sugar could live only by grace of the free American market, protected by a heavy duty against foreign sugars. Impose even the preferential Cuban duty on Puerto Rican sugar, and the Puerto Rican industry would perish.

But could not the sugar land be converted to direct production of foodstuffs? The product of an acre of sugar could bring into the country by way of exchange eight times the amount of food that could be produced by an acre of corn, rice, beans.

Independence, and the loss of the sugar market, would mean starvation for a large fraction of the population, already living at the minimum of subsistence.

My Puerto Rican friends did not question the validity of my economic argument, but they asked, why should America not grant to an independent Puerto Rico free access to our markets? Had not England, under the Methuen Treaty, granted Portugal virtually free access to the British market for wines ever since 1703?

I could only reply, my Puerto Rican friends did not know the sugar beet and its ferocious jealousy of the far more productive sugar cane. They did not realize that the distribution of beet culture in our sparsely peopled mountain states, each with two senators, gave more political power to a single Wyoming beet than to ten New York citizens. But it was of no use to talk beet sense to those idealistic Puerto Ricans. If independence meant starvation for some hundreds of thousands, well, hundreds of thousands had died before for freedom and independence.

Perhaps my failure to convince was due in some measure to my inner conviction that the Puerto Ricans were right. The island should have been declared an independent state when we took possession of it in 1898. But we were romantic children then. We were readers of Kipling and envied the British their dominion over palm and pine. We had acquired the Philippines and Puerto Rico; only the fierce opposition of the Boston anti-imperialists had kept us from annexing Cuba. We looked to the death of Díaz, the strong man of Mexico, for a chance of splendid imperial enterprise.

We have grown up, and imperialism has gone out of fashion. Already yesterday's pomp of the British Empire is one with Nineveh and Tyre. The one great gem in our late-purchased imperial crown, the Philippines, we have cheerfully given away. We have gone a long way toward Puerto Rican independence in making the governorship an elective office, and, recently, in approving a Constitution that falls very little short of independence.

Imagine what it would mean in our Latin-American relations if we proclaimed full Puerto Rican independence, asserting, however, our right to grant Puerto Rico in our markets every special privilege she had ever enjoyed as a colony. And imagine, too, the effect on all Latin America if by government grant or private philanthropy we set up the University of Puerto Rico as the premier university of the American continents, gentle interpreter of the two great civilizations of America, the English-speaking and the Latin-speaking half-worlds.

A dream. I did not incorporate my dream in the report of our Commission, for filing in Washington. But I still dream.

THIRTY-THREE

Van Eeden

ANTAEUS, mythology tells us, was the son of Mother Earth, and so long as he kept in contact with Mother Earth he was sound and strong. I think some genes of Antaeus have come down to me, through the ages. For I have never been able to overcome entirely my yearning for the soil and its growth. At my home in Nyack I work a vegetable garden, on thin soil that becomes more fertile, year by year, under my hand. But that is only a sop to my soil hunger.

The one growth of the soil I most cherish is the independent small farmer, or, to use the European style, the peasant. He is my brother, and his historic fate is mine. What characteristics he has, I have too. After I set up the University in Exile its most literary member, Max Ascoli, wrote an article about the institution for an Italian journal. His judgment of me was that I am a Danish peasant type.

I do not depart from the type in my love of the soil, or in my delight in its good fruits, my vivid interest in weeds, pests, mosaic diseases. But as economist and political scientist I have borrowed or created for myself theoretical social-political structures, as moral growths of the soil. For farming as a way of life I have passionate respect. But for farming as a way of making money enough to retire from farming I have only regretful toleration. It is in harmony with our age but out of harmony with nature. In most instances it wrecks the soil that feeds it.

I am not dogmatically equalitarian in my devotion to the soil. Mostly I approve the modest holding worked by its owner. But the "gentleman farmer," the true improver, has his place in my heart. On one of my trips to Denmark I took great satisfaction from true peasant farms, talking with the extremely intelligent and well-read peasants, looking over their library shelves with useful books in Danish, German, French, and English, all easily understood by the peasant. It gave me pleasure to meet the peasant's wife, blue-eyed, blond, rosy-cheeked, and his delightful little children. But I also found pleasure in a fine experimental farm, whose owner explained everything about it except that he was a prince, son of the reigning king.

Where the peasant owns the land and is married to it for life, the ups and downs of the commercial world are not vital to him. His acres feed him and his family, whatever the economic weather. But if the cities ask him to supply them with food he expects something in return. He will not take worthless paper. Nor can he be fobbed off with tax receipts. If the cities have nothing to give him for his wheat, he will feed it to his pigs. If the city will give him nothing for his pigs, he will slaughter them, smoke the meat, and await the city's recovering its good sense.

The Communists seem rational in their policy of displacing the peasant and organizing agriculture in collectives, where the worker has his bread handed down from above. For propaganda purposes the Communists stress the great advance in efficiency that results from large-scale operations. Anyone who knows the soil knows that this is propaganda bunk. Labor is not half so efficient, nor costs half so low, in any collective in the world as on the individual peasant farms of Denmark. But where the land is operated by free peasants, the artisan or the manufacturer must be free to produce the goods the peasant will accept, and free to bargain as to terms. And this means there can be no absolute Communist state where the peasant controls the land.

The peasant holding, the small farm as a way of life, is a bulwark of liberty. Loving liberty more than life itself, I have naturally attached myself to every movement for establishing small farms. This it was that drew me into Reclamation.

A valley in the mountains, with a silver stream that, dammed and controlled, could turn five thousand acres of desert into a hundred small farms, even at costs the farms could never support, looked worth while to me. But I could not put it out of my head that from Maryland and Virginia in a great arc ending at Brownsville, Texas, there are thirty million acres of land, in scrub trees and bush, in savanna and swamp, sandy land, muck land, but essentially better land than that which lies at the base of the brilliant Danish agriculture. Denmark suffers from slightly inadequate rainfall; our great southern arc has slightly too much rainfall. Denmark is cold; there is no month of the year when you may not have night frosts, and the season of open pasturage is short, of expensive barn feeding long. In our great arc there are nine frost-free months in the most northern sections, and at least eleven months in the greater part of the area. Much of the thirty million acres have too much water. They need drainage. And drainage often requires large-scale engineering. But the acre cost of drainage would seldom equal the acre cost of putting water on the land in the mountain valleys.

Denmark built a great dairy industry, supplying butter and cheese to England, the Kameroons, and Tierra del Fuego. This Denmark could achieve on its brief summer pasturage. What could we not do in our great southern arc, now waste land but quite capable of maintaining a million farm families?

To settle reclaimed land in the Mountain States, it had been necessary to seek farm families from localities in the Middle West, sometimes a thousand miles away. The South has a great overpopulation of farm families, starving as sharecroppers on small, worn-out plots of ground.

The chief obstacle to the development of the waste lands of the southern arc is political. The dominant classes in the South are indifferent to the possibilities of waste-land development. Most well-to-do Southerners are content with conditions as they stand. Where the land is rich, the plantation system yields good revenues, thanks to the superabundance of reliable Negro labor. Where the land is poor, a fair revenue is still to be had out of sharecropping, with the landlord-owned store to skim the cream off the tenant's share. No one defends the system as making for a contented rural population. But the system operates somehow, for the day.

In the Mountain States the senators, congressmen, governors, the chambers of commerce, the press all work together to promote reclamation. In the South there are no political forces working toward similar ends.

I joined an informal organization, in the twenties, to agitate for reclamation in the South. At our head was Elwood Mead, Commissioner of Reclamation. Hugh MacRae of Wilmington, North Carolina, David Coker of Hartsville, South Carolina, Matthew Hale of Boston, and I formed the core of the organization. We enlisted influential Southern friends, like Congressman William B. Bankhead of Alabama and Daniel C. Roper, who had held various high offices in Washington and was destined to be appointed to the Cabinet in 1933.

MacRae was a North Carolina businessman of far-reaching interests, in real estate, lumbering, coal, in the development of the summer resort Linville on the shoulder of the Grandfather Mountain, which he then owned. But his heart was deepest in two projects, not unrelated, the development of dairy farming on his place, Invershiel, not far from Wilmington, and the development of communities of farmers on small acreage devoted to intensive cultivation. He had established two successful communities, at Castle Haynes and St. Helena, some thirty miles from Wilmington.

The success of MacRae's settlements began with the initiative of a Dutchman, Ludika, who had come South because of his weak lungs. Ludika carried under his hat the encyclopedic knowledge of gardening that the Dutch had worked out since Roman times. When I first visited Castle Haynes, Ludika was cheating the box plant into making a better show of itself. The box is valued according to its height, a dollar a foot. Ludika put a lattice over the heads of his box, to make them think they were in a forest and had to reach up for sun. In five years they were as tall as they would have been in seven years out in the open. True, they were somewhat spindling. But in the fifth year Ludika put them out where the winds would twist them. They thickened; and Ludika had good seven-year box at a cost of six years.

I haven't space to go farther into Ludika's Dutch magic. It worked in a thousand directions; it inspired his fellow-settlers on ten-acre farms of land that had been waste. Twenty years later I was coming north from Wilmington on a so-called express train. The train stopped at the siding of Castle Haynes to take on a refrigerator car of cut flowers. I twitted my conductor about an express train's dropping its schedules to take on vegetation. Said the conductor, "That dinky little community of Dutchmen gave us six million dollars of freight last year. And you know what the post office says? They sent three million packages of bulbs, to every darn post office in the United States."

Contrary to the conductor's notion, this community was very little Dutch. The farmers were mostly Americans who had learned from Ludika the mystery of the green thumb. At the newer settlement of St. Helena there were some couples that had been boys and girls in Castle Haynes, but mostly the settlers were recruits from outside. One who particularly interested me was a Russian, who didn't know himself whether he was red or white, blue or green, who knew no English, bumbled sounds intelligible only to his horses through his colossal beard, learned only through his eyes, but managed to make a lot of money on his ten sandy acres. After five years he wanted to bring over his wife and children, but he had to be a citizen to do it. MacRae pro-

ceeded to make him a citizen. The Russian was to appear before a judge
who would ask him questions. MacRae had managed to convey to the
Russian that when MacRae's secretary, seated behind the Russian,
pinched him, the Russian was to say yes.

The Judge, in his rich orotund voice, declaimed, "Have you read the
Constitution of the United States?"

A pinch from the secretary. The Russian jumped. "Yaw!"

"Do you swear to be loyal to the principles of the Constitution of
the United States?"

Another pinch. The Russian jumped again. "Yaw!"

"Well," said the judge, "that is sufficient. His petition is granted."

"But, Judge," cried a busybody, "how can you make this man a citizen? He doesn't understand a word of English."

The judge said calmly, "Some of the best men that ever lived did
not understand a word of English. Isaiah, Josiah, Saint Paul—they did
good work. This man, I have learned, is a good farmer. He wants to
bring over his wife and children, to maintain his wife and bring up his
children in the fear of God. No harm can come to the United States
from a citizen like that." I'm sorry I never learned the name of that just
judge, true American, whose spirit rises in my memory like a tall pillar
of flame above the ruck of cheap and strident Americanizers.

MacRae's other project, his farm Invershiel, was devoted to the
principle of continuous pasturage. Our usual American practice is to
allow five acres for pasturing a cow. We turn the cows into a large
lot; they eat the grass that suits them best. Most of the grass gets too
old for satisfactory grazing, and the cows have to be fed on grain or oil
cake if they are to yield milk. MacRae cut his ground into small lots
and kept the cows in a lot till they had eaten the grass to the ground.
Then he moved them to another lot, plowed up and resowed the first
with a later season grass. Thus, with a dozen plots, MacRae could keep
his herd in continuous pasture, even in the winter, for rye and burr
clover care nothing about the light frosts of North Carolina. And
throughout the year he combined one grass rich in protein with one
rich in carbohydrate.

The point of MacRae's experiment was to prove that on any properly handled farm milch cows could be maintained one to an acre. In
Denmark twenty cows were all the individual farmer cared to handle.
On our thirty million acres of waste land in the great southern arc, the
greatest dairy region in the world could be developed.

David Coker was another admirable Southerner. He was a handsome man, physically patterned on the great Elizabethans, bold, straightforward, human, and true. The Coker family dominated and adorned Hartsville, South Carolina, where they set up a charming college for young girls, Coker College.

Coker was a distinguished plant breeder. He had bred up the upland cotton until it approached Egyptian cotton in length of fiber. The government had introduced in its experimental stations a magnificent Italian rye—Abruzzi rye—which made a good third more growth than the common varieties, a point of great importance where rye is employed for winter grazing. But the imported plant was subject to rust and other local diseases; it did not stand dry spells well and it was likely to go down flat with heavy frost. Coker bred the plant until it was immune to rust and could stand being frozen solid without perishing.

Both Coker and MacRae were successful businessmen; both were ardent for the development in the great arc of a thriving and contented population of independent farmers. Coker's plant breeding and Mac-Rae's experiments in continuous grazing were designed to supply technical processes that would help the small farmer to succeed. The two men were regarded as cranks by the local businessmen and plantation owners. But the Southern gentleman is humorously indulgent toward the crank, so long as he is not a bomb thrower.

In the desperate years of the depression the country population in the South suffered severely. The typical white sharecropper produced no food, only cotton or tobacco, and when there was no market for these he starved. The Negro sharecropper fared a little better. His native food instincts were better. While the white sharecropper lived on store flour, denuded of all life in the milling, or commercial cornmeal, equally innocent of vitamins, and store bacon and fat pork, the Negro managed to grow somewhere on his farm vegetables and greens. And if the landlord insisted that every foot of field be put into tobacco or cotton, the Negro tenant knew fifty different kinds of weeds that would make greens. You saw the Negro tenant, upstanding, clear-eyed, though not comfortably fat. You saw the non-greens white sharecropper, skinny, restless-eyed, dyspeptic, embittered.

We cranks knew that there is liberty and health in the small farm, but only if it is devoted to food production. Cotton and tobacco are noble crops, but they never bred a free man.

The first object of our group was the setting up in North Carolina of three farm communities, each of about a hundred families, two for white farmers and one for Negro farmers, all converging upon a common cooperative center. We had perfectly good public opinion behind us in North Carolina. There were reservations about the success of the white colonies. The white sharecropper had dropped overboard too much of rural lore and rural arts. But nobody doubted that the Negro colony would be a success. And many good Southerners thought that the successful Negro colony would put the white colonies on their mettle.

The election of Roosevelt gave us high hopes. Roosevelt was ready to try anything once. Why not our tripartite colony? It wouldn't cost a mint of money; its development would give a lot of employment in an area of ghastly unemployment.

The group left it to MacRae and me to push the project in Washington. MacRae would wire me to meet him at the Hotel Washington; we'd get to some Southern senators. They were blandly kind and urged us to cultivate Miss Le Hand, channel to Roosevelt. We did. Miss Le Hand was kind, but communication with the President met too much resistance. We forced our way into the office of Secretary Ickes, but that great official had slept badly the night before and was unusually curmudgeonly.

In the end we got one colony, of course a white colony, Penderlea in MacRae's county of Pender. It is settled by good people, and it has wonderful schools. But as one who loves the soil I could cry over its agricultural ineptness. The tripartite colony scheme had to be given up. The Negroes of New York and Washington could not tolerate the idea of a farm settlement for Negroes only, even if it were woven into a cooperative setup with white colonies. And so the Negroes got nothing. It was hard on me to have to face some of the finest men I knew, Negroes, and say, "We can't do anything for your group. They say it would encourage Jim Crowism." My Negro interlocutor would laugh a hearty, musical laugh. "Encourage Jim Crowism. As if it wasn't everywhere already."

I doubt that there is anyone living who detests Jim Crowism more than I do. We do terrible injustice to the Negro and great wrong to ourselves by segregation. I would like it best if I could see good Negro farm families and good white farm families planted side by side. But I can't unmake history. Inside the barriers of history, which must in the end fall, it would be possible to plant integrated Negro groups alongside integrated white groups, to promote the march of anti-discrimination. But that is probably not for my time.

New York was filling with Jewish refugees from Germany. There was no employment for them, and more and more of our humane congressmen were urging that we close our doors.

If a start could be made toward planting refugees on neglected soil, what American could fail to approve? MacRae had a tract of land near Wilmington which he had once planted with some Dutch families under the leadership of a Herr van Eeden. Van Eeden was a gentleman, not a farmer, and the colony petered out. A single settler survived.

The land was a drainage problem, and local authorities asserted that it could never be drained, because it lay below the level of the surrounding territory. I knew that was untrue. There was a ditch out of the property, and I had followed it through brier and bramble to the swift descent of the water to a level twenty feet below.

And the soil—no son of Adam ever touched better soil. Sub-sandy, therefore easy to work, with free access for the plant rootlets. In the Salinas district of California, which produces the bulk of our iceberg lettuce, big capital has to take over the soil, plow it two feet deep, fill it with a foot of high-priced water. In Van Eeden—the settlement was so called—I've seen as fine iceberg lettuce, the plants stuck into the ground by an amateur who didn't know what he was planting.

I had devoted much time to my siege of Washington departments, trying to set up a scheme for the utilization of waste land and waste human abilities. Why not try to do something myself? I had good friends, Charles Liebman and Bernard Flexner, salt of the earth, who operated the Refugee Economic Corporation. They were financing refugee settlements in various quarters of the globe.

I persuaded them to back me up in establishing a refugee settlement in Van Eeden. We formed a corporation, which for want of a satisfactory name we registered as the Alvin Corporation. The Refugee Economic Corporation gave us a generous grant, and a number of individuals gave us additional money. We purchased Van Eeden from Mac-Rae, a hundred acres suitable for ten market-gardening plots, with a hundred acres of woodland for reserve. I selected an agent to go down and see to it that we had housing for ten families. There were old three-room cottages on the place that would do if the roofs were repaired. And we built some new four-room houses at extraordinarily low cost.

I proceeded to enlist settlers. There was no dearth of fine, eager families, but they were all of urban experience except one. Wolf had got into dairying in Germany by way of the traditional Jewish cattle trade.

I had never believed that one has to come directly off the soil if he is to know the soil and love it. We are all sons of Adam; his hoe is on our shoulders. But the complete lack of soil consciousness in my candidates disturbed me somewhat. So too did the lack of any sense of refugee solidarity. When I explained that I was counting on them to pioneer for other refugees to come their enthusiasm was not in the least touched. They were concerned about themselves.

One set of applicants consisted of a bookkeeper from Vienna and his charming young wife. I meant to dissuade them. I urged that in their evening promenades around the Ring in Vienna, they had had no occasion to learn the difference between a vegetable plant and a weed. Besides, they had no children, and there is no thrift in a farm family without children. The wife colored a bit and said it was with the hope of a child she wanted to go on a farm. I accepted the couple. They were my best settlers, except for the experienced Wolf.

If I could have lived with the community I think it would have succeeded. Success on the soil depends on your quickness of reaction to losses. Your lettuce crop fails, or is too late for market. Plow it down and plant sweet corn; if you can't sell that, can it for winter's use. Your cucumber vines have stopped yielding. Pull them up and plant fall cabbage. My settlers accepted loss or overmaturity inertly. I could come down only at infrequent intervals, and when I came I was desolated by gardening tricks the settlers had missed.

We kept the settlement alive for some years. But the era of unemployment was closing. One settler after another found a more congenial job. Finally we had to liquidate the enterprise and the corporation, taking our losses.

The losses did not weigh us down seriously. After all, there were some fifty souls for whom we had provided a refuge through the period of unemployment.

THIRTY-FOUR

More Refugee Problems: The Ecole Libre

B Y THE time Hitler invaded Czechoslovakia in 1938 most of the proscribed German scholars had found their way out of Germany,
or had perished, or were perishing in concentration camps. Some
had taken refuge in Poland, many in France. The position of the
refugee scholars in Poland looked particularly grave. Where was there
a way of escape? The refugee scholars in France could not feel easy
either, but in 1939 Hitler's ambitions seemed to lie eastward, and
most people doubted that Hitler would expend his resources in an
attempt to breach the Maginot Line. Optimistic military commentators
raised our hopes by their discussions of the "phony war" in the West.

When the German military machine began to roll down through
Belgium, and the French Army collapsed, and the British achieved
their miraculous evacuation at Dunkirk, it became plain that it would
go hard with the refugee scholars in France, and with French scholars
of Jewish extraction or of prominence as liberals.

There was still time to get the imperiled scholars out of France, but
only a little time. The Emergency Committee worked valiantly to
secure invitations from American universities, but that was a process
that might take weeks, and the Germans were marching toward Paris,
twenty miles a day.

The New School could cable valid invitations, but it had no money
available, nor time to find money. I decided to go to the Rockefeller
Foundation and appeal for a grant. The Foundation had never been
very cordial to the New School or to me; but this was a matter of life or
death. The president of the Foundation, Raymond Fosdick, whom I
regarded as our foremost international educational statesman, would
at least hear me. I decided to ask for traveling expenses and a two
years' stipend for five scholars.

As I rode in the bus to Rockefeller Center, on a bright and hopeful
morning, I revised my ideas. I could get fifteen scholars as easily as

five. I revised my ideas again as the elevator shot me up to the Foundation offices. I'd ask for twenty-five.

President Fosdick was so cordial I found it easy to put my case. French liberal and Jewish professors, refugee scholars from Germany, were in deadly peril. Many of them had been engaged in research projects financed by the Foundation. Their fate was of profound interest to the Foundation. But the Foundation could do nothing for them, except perhaps supply them with money, which the Germans would grab. The New School, however, could issue invitations that would give those scholars non-quota visas to America for themselves and their families. Once in this country these scholars could be absorbed into the faculty of the New School, or they could be placed in other institutions, where, in the opinion of the Foundation and myself, they would be more useful. I knew the social scientists well enough to make good selections. But the Foundation knew the physical scientists and the scholars in the field of humanities far better, and I should have to depend on the Foundation for wise selections.

Fosdick heard me through patiently. "How many could you take care of?" he asked.

To my own surprise I answered, "It would not be worth while to go ahead with this project unless we are prepared to take care of a hundred."

"I shall have to consult my trustees," said Fosdick. "I can do it by telephone and give you an answer in three days."

But the next day he called me up. The trustees had approved and I could go ahead immediately. At once I began to sow cables, broadcast.

A group of these professors were assembled in a café in Paris, discussing desperately ways to escape their impending doom. Another professor came in and flashed a cablegram from the New School, offering a two-year appointment. The party scattered to their homes and reassembled an hour later. They all had similar cablegrams. Now, how to get out of France? The Channel was closed. There were still sailings from the Mediterranean ports, but the submarine menace was making them irregular. The safest way lay through Spain to Lisbon.

I referred the cables of acceptance to the Foundation, which promptly transmitted funds to cover the emigration. I went to Washington to petition the State Department to instruct the consuls abroad to handle the matter of visas with no waste of time. Nor did the professors delay. In an incredibly brief time groups of them were landing in New York.

Though speed was possible for the scholars in France, those who had been caught by the war in Poland encountered desperate difficulties. Russia was officially open to them, but the Russians would not lift a hand or abate a regulation to let them through. Many never got through at all. Their fate remains unknown.

A typical case was that of Dr. Turyn, classicist, caught in the section of Poland seized by Russia. His wife had managed to get to Athens by way of Rumania and Bulgaria. This road was closed by the adherence of Bulgaria to the Nazis. Turyn managed to get to a Black Sea port and find passage to Smyrna, where he was joined by his wife and son. From Smyrna the family proceeded by rail to Baghdad: then by plane to Karachi, where their traveling allowance gave out. The Foundation cabled them some more money, and they flew to Bombay, where they found the *President Roosevelt* just ready to sail for New York by way of the Cape of Good Hope.

Franco Spain was not too cordial to the refugees in transit to Portugal but presented no roadblock that a little grease on an official palm would not overcome. The French, after the full German occupation, were as helpful as they dared to be.

The gentle philosopher Jean Wahl had been arrested in the first days of the German occupation of France and thrust into a concentration camp, where starvation and despair soon reduced him to a skeleton. When my cable arrived the camp physician recommended the release of Jean Wahl to save the camp burial expenses. Wahl survived the trip to Lisbon and began to regain his health on shipboard. We assigned him to a position in Mount Holyoke College where in the kindly atmosphere of the college he recovered completely. He is now in his old chair in Paris, a philosopher much admired and deeply loved.

There was much romance, and often tragedy, in this flight of the scholars to America. To me it presented an infinity of detailed problems. The part of my job I liked least was besieging the State Department to expedite the granting of visas. The German sympathizers in this country, while without influence in the State Department, sometimes tried to put a spoke in my wheel by delation. There was the case of a young engineering student, held for months in Trinidad, because, as he was tall and blond, the Nazis could slip over the idea that he was masquerading as a Jew but was in reality an "Aryan," shipped here to make Nazi propaganda.

The State Department had set up a committee with representatives of the Interior, War, State, Justice, and Treasury Departments. I had to plead my cases before this committee.

Sometimes the questions they put startled me. One day I was urging the case of a political scientist. The Army representative asked me if I knew Christian Gauss of Princeton. Certainly I did. Did I consider him a competent political scientist? One of the most competent in the world. Then why did we need to bring in another political scientist? I swallowed my disposition to laugh and argued gently that the United States was too big a place to depend entirely on even Christian Gauss for its political science.

Above this committee of the Departments was a three-man appeals committee, with my old friend Fred Keppel as chairman. If the Departments committee turned me down I could appeal. But I never got turned down. I knew all about the scholars for whom I was appealing, thanks largely to the expert information supplied by the Rockefeller Foundation. I knew whether a man was Nazi or Fascist in his leanings —almost an excluded possibility—and whether he had been compromised with communism. I knew where he would find a post and that he could never become a public charge.

And so for the time I acquired the reputation of skillful negotiator in the cases of refugees needing to immigrate. My friends would bring to my shop cases that had nothing to do with the New School-Rockefeller program. I undertook such cases with reluctance, because I was already straining my welcome in Washington.

One day a Californian I did not know called on me to engage my interest in getting a visa for a German author stranded in Trinidad. The refugee was a great authority on the Dreyfus case. He had published two volumes and meant to write a third one on the experiences of Dreyfus on Devil's Island. He had got a visa for America and was on the Atlantic when the war broke out. For fear of German submarines his ship gave up its course to New York and sailed to the Caribbean, landing its passengers at Trinidad. There were no sailings for the United States in the next three months, and our refugee's visa expired. So there he was, marooned in the climate of Devil's Island, to get a more realistic sense of the sufferings of Dreyfus. He had been there three years when his case was called to my attention.

My Californian told me that Einstein and Thomas Mann were working to get a visa for the unfortunate author. He showed me their letters. All that the letters contained was the suggestion that he enlist the help of Alvin Johnson.

I was disappointed. I had hoped that those two mighty figures would go with me to the committee. We could easily ride down any opposition. And I saw legitimate grounds for opposition. The refugee was not a professor, entitled to a non-quota visa. I got his published volumes and read enough of them to assure myself of his political correctness. But the committee nearly always inquired about the possibility of an immigrant's making a living here. On this point I had no information. Still, a suggestion from Einstein and Thomas Mann was for me an order. I went before the committee.

They held me for over two hours, questioning me not so much on the case before us as on my whole philosophy of the cross-fertilization of cultures. When they excused me I was deep in doubt as to the fate of the refugee. But one of the commissioners followed me into the hall.

"Doctor," he said, "we often get bored on this job. We heard that you are a stimulating discussion group leader. You are. And we will cable the consul in Trinidad to give your friend a visa at once."

Like all other Americans, I used to make merry over the dusty mind of the bureaucrat. In my frequent appearances before the refugee immigrant committee I came to have a different feeling about bureaucrats. These men were faithful, painfully faithful, to their trust. They were of limited intelligence, but so are we all. Sometimes I had to spend hours to make my case, but I was finally successful because I never presented a case that I could not vouch for. I was just as anxious to keep Nazi and Communist propagandists out of the country as the committee was.

Perhaps one reason I came to feel that there is something to say for the bureaucrat is that I had a small adventure in bureaucracy myself. After America entered the war I was appointed to an enemy alien hearing board, with Maurice Davidson, chairman, and Joseph Leary Delaney. Case after case came before us, well prepared in advance by the FBI. After we had studied the record and had heard the FBI investigators, we would hear the accused.

Most of the cases were flimsy. A Japanese gardener from Westchester was brought before us. He was a hard-working, laconic person who had responded to a prewar order to report at the Japanese consulate. No doubt the consulate had suggested the patriotic duty of sabotage if war with Japan broke out; but what sabotaging could a gardener, an expert on lilies, find opportunity to do? We dismissed the case.

Or take the case of a young German woman whose inclinations toward matrimony had been thwarted and who had sidled up to the Bund and tried to comport herself as an antisemitic Joan of Arc. We interned her. She could not have done any real harm to the United States, but in the emergency of war it wasn't good to have such a fool at large.

I was particularly bent on interning Germans who had jumped ship. Under our Seaman's Act the members of the crew of any ship touching at an American port have a right to demand their pay, down to the day of landing, and leave the ship. The Germans packed their ships with trained Nazi propagandists, in the guise of extra stewards and deckhands. These supernumeraries were expected to jump ship and carry on propaganda and sabotage. Often a German seemed to make out a case of good faith in jumping ship. I didn't want to take chances and earned the repute with the FBI of "the hanging judge."

I had planned to organize the French and Belgian scholars as a faculty parallel with the existing Graduate Faculty. It had been my dream to build up in the New School an organization of international studies. The New School had never had resources enough to expand adequately the representation of foreign scholars of non-German origin. We had a sprinkling of Italian scholars, and Fernando de los Ríos, almost a faculty in himself, but that was as far as we had been able to go. Now the opportunity for a great expansion appeared at hand. French and Belgian scholars of great renown had come under the New School roof, Professor Gustav Cohen, Jacques Maritain, Henri Grégoire, Boris Mirkine-Guetzévitch, to mention only some of the stars of first magnitude.

Professor Gustav Cohen had another plan. With the refugee scholars at the New School and the members of the French departments in nearby universities, he proposed to set up a regular French university, with all the conventional faculties, using French as the medium of instruction, giving certificates that would answer the requirements for Civil Service positions in the great African areas controlled by General de Gaulle. We could not call the institution a university, as we could not qualify under the state educational laws (which required a minimum endowment of half a million), but we had as good a name— the Ecole Libre des Hautes Etudes. Professor Cohen had got in touch with General de Gaulle, who warmly approved the project and accepted the institution as the one Free French university then in existence. General de Gaulle also approved modest grants to the institution from his treasury.

I accepted Professor Cohen's plan with enthusiasm. I saw in it the chance to establish in America a permanent French university. Such a university would serve the needs of the thousands of students who were preparing for positions as French teachers in the high schools and colleges, few of whom would have resources sufficient for several years' residence in Paris. It would also serve as a liaison between the French university world and our own.

Our intellectual world has much to learn from the French. In France the integration between life and learning is complete. There is no classification of Frenchmen as highbrows and lowbrows, with good sense mostly on the side of the lowbrows. I have found that in traveling in Pullmans it does not pay to introduce yourself as a professor. I assert that my interest is in real estate, and get on famously. The French professor would never dream of hiding his light under a bushel.

Alive to his position of distinction, a French professor develops his lectures as an art. While the Ecole Libre was at its height you could hear there some of the most eloquent lectures ever given in New York.

There was intense vitality in the Ecole Libre. Its animating spirit was passion for the liberation of France and Belgium. The French professors in the American universities gladly gave their services. Most important was the cooperation of the great scholar Henri Focillon, who for a long period had served in alternate years as a professor at Yale and as a professor at Paris. Professor Focillon accepted the headship of the institution and gave it his invaluable support down to the end of his noble life. The institution profited greatly from the advice and support of Henri Bonnet, then an unofficial ambassador of Free France, now the official French Ambassador in Washington.

The Ecole organization still continues in existence, as an earnest of Franco-American cultural unity, but postwar French finances have not permitted the expansion of the institution to the position of a regular university.

We never attained to the full complement of a hundred refugee scholars, contemplated in the New School-Rockefeller Foundation project. But we rescued most of the gravely imperiled French scholars and a distinguished handful of Polish scholars.

With the return of peace, problems of the displaced scholars assumed a more baffling form. It was no longer a question of saving lives but of saving for civilization the abilities of scholars languishing in displaced persons camps or clinging to the edges of subsistence in the European cities. This was not the problem the Emergency Committee was organized to meet, and the committee, after its magnificent career in placing hundreds of valuable scholars in the American colleges and universities, liquidated its activities. I joined in the vote for liquidation. But there was no possibility of liquidating my own obligations to good scholars in distress. I joined with a number of the members of the Emergency Committee to set up another organization under the chairmanship of Nelson Mead to continue the effort to find positions for displaced scholars. We had very little money but we had an asset worth more than money, two devoted women, figuring as executive and assistant executive secretaries, but actually the organization. They were Else Staudinger, wife of my beloved and admired colleague Hans Staudinger, and Mrs. Henry Seidel Canby, wife of the distinguished critic. They organized relations with six hundred universities and colleges, winning the confidence of the presidents and deans by their sheer intelligence and spirit of enlightened humanity. They placed scores of hopeless scholars in positions potent with hope.

I had established a reputation for finding ways to bring over persecuted scholars, and one difficult case after another was laid upon my desk. There was Wilhelm Foerster, who had been editor of *Die Friedenswarte,* passionate German pacifist. In the days when all the world dreamed that lasting peace would come to bless us by way of the Briand-Stresemann negotiations, Foerster persisted in seeing behind the peaceful brow of affairs the hideous ghost of German militarism rising to the skies. He had been subsidized in his peace propaganda by the Carnegie Endowment for International Peace, presided over by Nicholas Murray Butler.

There had been an educational meeting in France, where Nicholas Murray Butler presided. Everybody talked peace, French representatives, German representatives. Butler expounded the glories of peace. Foerster sprang up. "You are under delusions. There is no peace in the present German spirit. If you want peace, you French, arm! Arm, in God's name!"

It was a shock to the assembly of educators, floating on soft dreams of peace. It was a terrible offense to Butler, brave champion of peace, true American victor over doubt. He would have no further truck with Foerster, and the whole meeting froze Foerster out. Such indecent German ineptitude!

When war came Foerster managed to get to Lisbon. All he needed was a little money to come to the United States. His friends put the obligation to find the money on me.

What could I do? I had exhausted all my approaches to money. I reflected: Nicholas Murray Butler still controls money. He had been offended by Foerster, and the offense must have been deepened by the event, for Foerster had been right. But I regarded my old chief as a modern figure of true Roman virtue out of Tacitus. I believed that I could get money out of him for Foerster, wrongly right. I appealed to Butler. God bless his memory! He granted the money immediately.

Then there was the case of Dr. Theo Suranyi-Unger, a professor in a Hungarian university, who had been equally vigorous in his condemnation of nazism and communism. The Nazis thrust him into a concentration camp, where they all but starved him to death. He was liberated by the American Army, which, after exploring his record, gave him the status of citizen of a liberated country and loaned him to the French Army to take part in its economic administration.

An officer of the American Army of Occupation presented the case of Suranyi-Unger to me. The Communist Hungarian government was demanding his return, with whatever object, known to them but very suspicious to us. It was important that Suranyi-Unger receive a call from America at the earliest possible moment.

I knew his work. Still a young man, he had written seventeen books on economics of which I had read two in English. He would be a valuable asset in our educational life. But where was I to find money for a two years' appointment at the New School? I needed a minimum of twenty-five hundred dollars a year besides the fees he would earn by lectures.

With the givers of philanthropic sums my welcome was exhausted. I decided to exploit the solidarity of scholarship. I composed a letter presenting the case of Suranyi-Unger, asking the recipient to join me in pledging twenty-five dollars a year for two years. I meant to send out a hundred copies of this letter and expected to get twenty favorable replies. Then I'd send another hundred letters and another, until I had the amount pledged.

I got tired of signing with the eighty-seventh letter and decided to wait to see how it worked. Of the recipients, eighty-four agreed to contribute. Immediately I wrote to Suranyi-Unger and invited him to join our faculty.

One of my correspondents, President Tolley of Syracuse, reflecting on the merit of Suranyi-Unger, asked me if I'd be willing to have Syracuse University take him on as an associate professor. Of course I was willing, even though I'd have been happy to have Suranyi-Unger on the New School faculty. Suranyi-Unger arrived at Syracuse in time for the summer term and made so good a teaching record that he was elected in the fall as full professor with life tenure.

THIRTY-FIVE

Anti-Discrimination

NATIONAL party politics in my youth was, or appeared to be, a matter of conflicting principles. The Republicans stood for a protective tariff that greatly enriched industry and left the farmer out in the cold. The position of the Republicans in the agrarian states was buttressed by a lavish pension policy. After 1896 they were the sound money party and the advocates of centralized banking. They could be described not unfairly as the party of big business and the industrial cities. The Democratic party, after the rise of Bryan to control, was definitely the party of the common people: low tariff, progressive income taxes, railway regulation, control of the trusts. When one voted as a Republican or as a Democrat, he had a fair idea of what he was voting for.

With the absorption of the Progressives into the Republican party this clear-cut distinction between the parties disappeared. No measure of any importance passed Congress without bipartisan support. By the time of the election of Woodrow Wilson the appeals to the electorate of the two parties covered practically the same ground, but of course with varying emphasis. National bipartisanship had come to mean mainly competing methods of attaining the same political ends.

With this change in the character of party opposition the grounds for an ordinary citizen's adhering strictly to one party were eroded away. I favored Theodore Roosevelt in the three-cornered fight that elected Wilson in 1912. In the second Wilson election I hesitated a long time in deciding whether I preferred Wilson to Hughes, and in the end I became an active supporter of Wilson. I thought nothing of Cox in the 1920 election, but less of the Harding-Coolidge ticket, nor did I vote for Coolidge in 1924. But I voted for Hoover in 1928. In the Hoover-Roosevelt election of 1932 I was all for Franklin Roosevelt.

In 1942 there were two candidates in the running for the Democratic nomination for governor of New York, James M. Mead and John J. Bennett, Jr., both excellent men, I believed; but Bennett, having the support of Tammany, did not seem to me to have the strength to resist Tammany's designs, as Al Smith, Roosevelt, and Lehman had done. Though the admired chief of my party, Franklin Roosevelt, accepted Bennett, I decided to vote for Thomas Dewey.

I had never met Dewey, although, as I learned later, he had attended lectures at the New School. But I had heard much about him from his political godfather, C. C. Burlingham. Charley Burlingham is an ageless kingmaker in politics. I had been told, though not by him, that it was he who bullied Dewey into accepting the thankless job of district attorney. Charley Burlingham's long head contemplated Dewey as a future governor, and perhaps president.

I had watched the work of Dewey as prosecutor, particularly in the cases of Lucky Luciano and Hines. Dewey had appeared to me a heady man, but tireless and relentless. I admired him more than I liked him.

One of my most valued friends, Edward Schoeneck of Syracuse, who had once been lieutenant governor and whom we always addressed as "Governor," called me up on the phone and asked me whom I was supporting. "Tom Dewey," I said. Would I come out for him publicly? No: I was an educator and an extremely private and anonymous voter.

Schoeneck was to be in New York a few days later. Would I have lunch with him? Certainly, with joy.

Schoeneck had arranged a party of four and introduced me to two young men who, I later discovered, were members of Dewey's staff. Schoeneck asked me to put on the table all the reservations I had on Dewey.

I had only two serious reservations. One was on labor. I had a distinct memory of Dewey's inveighing at some time against the CIO, which I regarded as a rising force, a tremendous force, in American life. My second reservation was on race discrimination. I had no factual basis to justify reservations on this score, but I knew a number of ardent Dewey supporters who asserted that Dewey would put an end to the system of Al Smith, Roosevelt, and Lehman, under which no question was ever raised as to race or religion and which threatened to flood the state service with Jews. These friends of Dewey had assured me that he would introduce a *numerus clausus*, keeping Jewish appointees down to numbers properly modest. But the *numerus clausus* idea is more obnoxious to me than unmitigated antisemitism. It discriminates with a hypocritical show of fairness. It is polite sin. I like better sin with a naked cloven hoof.

One of the young men asked me if I would like to meet Dewey. Of course I would; but Dewey couldn't afford to waste time on one single voter, particularly when he was dead sure of the election.

A few days later the same young man called me up, to say that Dewey would be glad to have me call at his suite in the Hotel Roosevelt at a certain hour.

I was all eagerness. I have found that if you can be with a man half an hour, with all your mind concentrated on him as a cat's mind on a thoughtless bird, you can know him, for life. I wanted to know Thomas Dewey. He was certain to be governor of New York, and that put him first in line for the Republican nomination for President.

In my conception of the role of political parties in present-day America, as competing servitors of American public opinion and interests, an alternation in power between the parties is essential. I was wholly for Franklin Roosevelt. I was for re-electing him as long as he could serve. But after Roosevelt I thought a Republican administration would be in the interest of America.

My first glance at Dewey won me to him. He was manifestly frank, candid, intelligent, incorruptible. For my own part, I could be entirely for him. He met my reservations in succinct statements, but I would not have needed them. His visible personality dispelled any idea that he might be an enemy of any body of labor that rose up within the law. It expelled more forcibly any idea that he might ever give aid and comfort to the polite *numerus clausus* crooks.

And yet when I came away I was a bit pessimistic about Dewey's future beyond the governorship of the State of New York. What filled me with doubt was Dewey's handshake. It was strong, vigorous, honest; but not magnetic, electric. It left you a free man, to struggle with your doubts.

As we were talking Mrs. Dewey happened to come in. Her handshake was quick as the flitting of a butterfly, but electric. I had a notion: if Dewey could borrow his wife's handshake he would surely be President.

So far as I know, American psychologists have entirely overlooked the great American institution of the handshake. The handshake may be limp and flabby; it may be strong and hearty; but these are not the essential characteristics. Teddy Roosevelt nearly broke your hand, but you still had reservations. Judge Norris put a cold fish in your hand, but you were his for life.

The born politician puts in your hand a hand hard or soft, warm or cold, but with a spark in it that says, "I am I, and you are you, but we are for each other." Al Smith had that sort of spark. Franklin Roosevelt had enough sparks to scorch you. Jim Farley's sparks could light a cigarette. There is a delicious spark in Herbert Lehman's hand. Truman has a spark, Taft none, Eisenhower sparks quite unconsciously.

A politician can go places with no spark, like Woodrow Wilson and Coolidge. But that is leaning heavily on accident.

Dewey's hand did not spark, any more than the hand of my old Commandant of Cadets, John J. Pershing, who for all his eminence as Supreme Commander in the First World War was never mentioned for the presidency.

As I left Dewey's suite one of the secretaries asked me if I wished to write a statement explaining why I was for Dewey, though a Democrat. Of course I was glad to write such a statement. It was published, and may have gained a few votes Dewey didn't need. He was elected by a majority so substantial as to make him master of the state and the logical Republican nominee for the presidency in 1944.

Soon after his inauguration Dewey invited me to assume the chairmanship, then vacant, of the War Council Committee against discrimination in employment.

The committee consisted of a group of public-spirited citizens, representing the various parties, races, creeds of New York. There were vacancies on the committee which I filled. My principal appointee was Louis D. Weiss, a subtle and able lawyer, chairman of the board of the New School. I needed him particularly for advice on the legal position of the committee, which looked to me very shaky. In war industries discrimination in employment on account of race, religion, or national origin was prohibited by FEPC. Our committee was authorized to hear and investigate complaints of discrimination; if we wished to issue orders, we had to refer them to the Labor Department, which might enforce them by a process of injunction. But I was informed that the Labor Department was most likely to pigeonhole such orders. Our safest reliance was on moral suasion.

We had an efficient secretary, Charles Berkeley, who had worked out and published in a small booklet a technique for integrating minority laborers, particularly Negroes, in industry. War industry concerns were suffering from a shortage of labor, and many of them welcomed an official intervention that justified them in disregarding the resistance of their employees to minority labor. In Buffalo we had a subcommittee, under Judge Searles, which had been very active in enlisting the support of both employers and unions. But the picture of committee activities, on the whole, was discouraging. Even a committee with full powers would have encountered grave difficulties in abating so ingrained an abuse as discrimination in employment. Our powers were scant and destined to disappear with the War Council upon the restoration of peace.

I reported to Governor Dewey that I meant to work out, for presentation to him and the legislature, a bill prohibiting discrimination in employment and setting up a commission to enforce the prohibition.

"All right," said Dewey. "I am personally against discrimination in any form. I believe that a majority of New Yorkers are against discrimination. Write your bill and find a way to organize majority support. If you can get up a sufficient show of support the governor will back you. If you can't show support, he won't."

I came away reflecting on the length of time it takes for a citizen to become really educated in government. Tom Dewey as private citizen would have gone all-out for an effective anti-discrimination measure, even if he were one in a vanishing minority. As governor, he could go all out for such a measure only if a force capable of developing into a majority was in sight. I had been sadly critical of Herbert Lehman for setting up a War Council Committee instead of putting through an anti-discrimination bill. Governor Lehman too had been compelled to keep an eye open for potential majorities. Now for the first time in my life I fully realized the meaning of the distinction between the private citizen and governor.

I was not discouraged, for I thought the majority could be found.

Race discrimination prevailed not only in employment but in education and housing, in hotels and restaurants and other public places. In the matter of discrimination in public places we already had a law, the deadest dead letter in the whole alphabet. I was not prepared to take on discrimination in all its forms. I wanted to begin with employment.

No law could make up for the disabilities borne by a minority through generations. Negro labor fresh from the South was likely to be qualified for nothing except occupations requiring only raw muscular strength. But among all minorities there are many qualified for jobs of superior standing. In a time of labor shortage most employers would be willing to take on such labor, if assured that this would not stir up trouble in the existing labor force. An efficiently administered anti-discrimination law would not compel an employer to take on laborers he could not use but would liberate him to take on laborers he could use.

I believed that an act banning discrimination in employment would serve as a wedge in the attack on other forms of discrimination. I meant to make provision in the act for setting up under state auspices committees of citizens in the several local communities, charged with studying all forms of discrimination and devising means to abate them.

Louis D. Weiss consented to draw up such a bill, and with the aid of William Maslow, already then one of the active foes of discrimination, he produced a masterly bill. I took a preliminary draft of it to Governor Dewey, who pronounced it admirable.

There was still much work to be done on the bill before it could be submitted to the legislature. Unfortunately Weiss fell ill. We were delayed week after week and were not ready to seek a legislative sponsor, Senator Wicks, before the closing week of the legislative session. We had no time to organize the majority opinion that we believed would back our bill.

The bill was introduced without the supporting message from Governor Dewey we had hoped for. It was destined, we knew, to die in committee.

We of the War Council Committee were deeply disappointed. We were all amateurs in practical legislative procedure, even our great lawyer, Louis D. Weiss. We assumed that Governor Dewey could have bulled the bill through if he had had a mind to do it. Weiss prepared a blistering statement condemning Governor Dewey's failure to support our measure, for all our committee to sign, if we would. I was prepared to sign it, but I thought it only fair to call up Dewey, to tell him what we meant to do.

I had a two-hour conversation with the Governor over the phone, sometimes acrimonious, but ending in an agreement. The Governor would set up a commission, with representatives of both houses and an equal number of laymen, with Irving Ives of the Senate as chairman and myself as vice-chairman, to meet through the summer and work out a satisfactory bill. We would permit no word of publicity until after the fall elections, but then we would hold hearings throughout the state, to mobilize public opinion in support of our bill. I would remain chairman of the War Council Committee and try to keep the members in line.

I had called a meeting of the War Council Committee, with the design of asking all the members to sign the attack on Dewey. I had now changed my mind: the new agreement offered everything we could have hoped for. I tried to get in touch with Weiss to explain my new position, but I could not reach him before the meeting.

I set before the committee my new view of the situation and urged the membership to remain with me. Weiss was intransigent; so was Channing Tobias, one of my most valued friends, a Negro, by the splendor of his personality and character a sufficient demonstration of the idiocy of racial discrimination.

Weiss and Tobias set me down as a compromiser, a time-server. They were my good friends, and the loss of friends is a frightful loss to me. But we were out to destroy discrimination in employment. I thought, under the agreement with Governor Dewey, we could do it. And if I had to lose friends, well—

> "Romans in Rome's quarrel
> Spared neither house nor gold,
> Nor limb nor life
> Nor son nor wife
> In the brave days of old."

But I didn't lose them.

Governor Dewey did me the honor to consult me on the membership of the temporary commission. They were persons I did not know, but they represented fairly the interests of the state. What gave me the greatest satisfaction, Dewey persuaded Charles Tuttle to serve as counsel for the commission.

Charley Tuttle is a great lawyer. For years he had appeared before Congress in support of any measure directed against discrimination. He was high-priced, but he agreed to give up his regular salary at his office—a rather astronomical item—to serve us for nothing.

At the first meeting of the temporary commission I needed to whistle to keep my spirits up. With a single exception the members of the commission deplored the fact of discrimination but thought nothing could be done about it except by way of education. That was the attitude of the chairman, Irving Ives, who had come out of the north woods, where the air is so pure you can't discriminate even against the ground hog.

I soon discovered that all but three of the twenty members had reasonably open minds. One of the three closed minds belonged to a representative of the Associated Industries, who held consistently to the position that any limitation upon the right of the employer to hire and fire according to his own sweet will would bring disaster: industries would remove to other states, where the employer's rights were respected. The second closed mind belonged to a representative of a railway union which carried in its constitution a clause limiting membership to white Caucasians. The third closed mind was my own. What I wanted had been definitely expressed in the Wicks bill: prohibition of discrimination in employment on grounds of color, race, religion, or national origin; a commission with power to investigate charges or complaints of discrimination and to issue enforcible cease-and-desist orders; provision for encouraging the organization of voluntary local committees to investigate discrimination in all its forms and to take all practicable measures for abating it.

There is little profit in debating with men of closed minds. They only repeat views already familiar. It seemed politic to me to enter into the discussion only when the lawyer members got too confident about the efficiency of education as a means of abolishing discrimination or sought to limit the function of the proposed commission to advice and conciliation. I would dwell on the paradox that the lawyers put their faith in education while the educators put their faith in law. And I would point out that dueling would have continued to exist, in spite of education, if it had not been put down by law. As for limiting the functions of the proposed commission to conciliation and advice, my comment was that there could be no charm in a smile without teeth behind it.

As the sessions of the commission proceeded we kept coming nearer to agreement. This was due mainly to the extraordinary skill of Chairman Ives as discussion leader and the consummate diplomacy of Charley Tuttle. We finally reached agreement on a draft of a bill, which we all signed, with reservations filed by the representatives of the Associated Industries and the railway union.

In essentials our draft embodied the principles of the Wicks bill. The draft departed from the Wicks bill in one particular: it provided for an appeal to the courts against the orders of the commission. This

provision was attacked, inside of our commission and by outside representatives of anti-discrimination organizations, as bad administrative
practice. It meant subjecting the expert judgment of the proposed
commission to the inexpert judgment of the courts. I felt that this
concession to the exaggerated fear of some employers could do no
harm.

After the fall elections of 1949 our commission set out on a tour.
We held public hearings in Albany, Rochester, Syracuse, and Buffalo,
and in New York and Brooklyn. To my gratification practically all the
persons wishing to be heard were for the bill. Some of them filed with
us weighty and convincing briefs that made me regret we had not had
the authors as members on our commission. We unearthed three persons who spoke against our measure, one, an obvious crackpot, the
other two of dubious sincerity. Charley Tuttle also took on the bar
associations. The New York City Bar Association, generally regarded
as dead at the top, was against us, but the others were with us. We had
with us every religious organization, Catholic, Protestant, Jewish; we
had the AFL and the CIO; we had the farmers' organizations. We had
at least ninety per cent of the organized citizenry.

It looked very plain sailing to me, and I went to Albany to enjoy
the cruise in the legislature. A scholar, to attain to an understanding of
politics, must live to be more than a hundred. I found that in the mind
of an expert in politics like Senator Ives, it was going to be hard sledding to get our bill through. For the persons who had not deigned to
appear at our hearings had gone to the individual members of the
Assembly and Senate, or to their uncles or aunts, with frightening accounts of what the bill would do to New York industry and menacing
accounts of what it would do to the particular aspiring statesman. Ives
thought we had a chance because we had the real support of Governor
Dewey.

What a political child I had been to think that the Wicks bill, presented out of the blue at the closing sessions of the legislature, could
have been put through by the arbitrary power of the Governor! Fate
owes it to me to let me live to a hundred, to finish my education
creditably.

Unexpectedly the face of events brightened. All the Democrats
in the Assembly agreed to support our bill. It was whispered that Tom
Dewey had slipped a suggestion to them, if they were unanimous for
the bill and the Republicans beat it, the Republicans would be deep
in a slippery hole. I doubted the story. Tom Dewey would go far on

the Lord's side; but this was pretty far. Anyway, the Republicans had to overmatch the Democrats, and our bill went through both houses with an appearance of almost unanimity, something far better than unanimity, which means innocuous indifference.

Discrimination in employment was scotched in New York. Several other states followed suit. Even today my brother Harry, a just judge in California, an uncommonly just state, is deep in the movement to join California to the galaxy of states that pronounce officially, "A man's a man, for a' that."

How has our law against discrimination in employment worked? Some say well, some say badly. I have met scores of Negroes in jobs they could never have had but for the law. I have met scores of others who say the law is a dead letter.

It had never been the presumption of those of us who were working for a law against discrimination that it would be possible to abolish by one act the result of hundreds of years of slavery and near slavery. We realized that when a man is unjustly discriminated against, he becomes something other than a free man shorn of his rights. He accumulates disabilities that do not disappear at once with the lifting of oppression.

We could not say to an employer: Here is a man who has been much sinned against. Give him a job. The employer's job is not philanthropy. But we could say, Here is a good man, competent as any to do your work, but not of the same color, religion, or national origin as your other employees. As an employer you are exercising a public function: to give fair treatment to all applicants for jobs. We ask you to be fair; we put before you a law asking you to be fair. Only if you are stubbornly determined not to be fair will our law show its teeth. It has teeth enough.

We had our law and a commission with power to enforce it. I waited anxiously to see what kind of commission Governor Dewey would set up. It was a body of fine men and women. They meant to administer the law efficiently. They worked hard to set up a machinery by which grievances could be heard and handled with tact and justice.

Yet I was forced, in honesty, to tell Governor Dewey I was disappointed. I have confessed, in matters pertaining to this act, that I had not lived long enough to be adequately educated. Neither had Governor Dewey. The will of the people was, so far as practicable, to integrate in our state economy the minorities that had suffered under discrimination. This was a diplomatic, creative job as well as an administrative one. Dewey's imagination never ran beyond the administrative side of the job. There was no creative diplomacy in his commission.

Numerous criticisms have been directed against the commission. There are thousands of Negroes, it is said, who have never heard of a law against discrimination and a commission to enforce it. That is probably true. There are thousands of Negroes fit only for the lowest forms of casual labor. No law, no commission, could do anything for them. But there are thousands who could be integrated in industry if they were taken in hand by a creative commission vividly alive to their plight and the plight of industry.

THIRTY-SIX

Belated University Problems

ADULT education has been for many years my chosen field of educational interest. In a static society like the French rural village or the American Indian tribe it is possible that the individual may acquire, through childhood and adolescence, all the education he will ever need in life. After all, life in such communities is visibly laid out in traditional patterns. One has only to follow the lines of the pattern to live in mental security. True, novel items of experience will intrude, requiring more than the conventional educational equipment for adjustment. And in epochs of social-political unrest, these items may become so numerous and so vital as to leave the individual in distressing bewilderment. His education has given him no tools for shaping the new materials life thrusts upon him.

What is characteristic of American life is the swiftness and extensiveness of change. This is most strikingly manifest in industry and finance. No machine in use fifty years ago is anything but junk today. The sound and efficient financial ideas of Grover Cleveland are equally junk. But it is primarily in the field of the physical sciences that change has been revolutionary. In the intellectual, esthetic, social, political, international fields, changes have been less spectacular but nevertheless profound.

I asked a distinguished lawyer whether there was anything he had learned as a Harvard undergraduate that had helped him solve the problems presented to him in recent years. Yes: he had learned when properly to wear a dinner coat and when to wear a white tie. For the rest, the educational equipment he had bought at the cost of four years and ten thousand dollars had been discarded a quarter of a century ago as obsolete mental clutter.

No one will take such a humorous statement for more than it is worth, but it is worth something. In American life a college training is just a prelude to the training that life gives. Post-college life is in itself adult education.

The education of life may be conducted efficiently, intelligently, as it is likely to be in the career of a great novelist, a great lawyer, a great physician, or it may be conducted in haphazard, tedious fashion, as it has been with most of us. It is the business of the adult educator to bring system, interest, plan, into the curriculum of life.

I have always been interested in the whole educational process, from the nursery school up, but more particularly interested in college education and professional training, as nearer my own field of higher adult education. In my birth state of Nebraska and in other western states it is the universal feeling that the state is under obligation to give every aspiring and qualified youth free access to college education. I have never departed from my faith in the western system, although I acknowledge the remarkable work done by the privately endowed colleges and universities of the East.

Geography operates everywhere to cut off access to college education. My home was about a hundred and fifty miles from the university at Lincoln. I was the first person born in the county to overcome the distance, twenty years after the university was opened, although there were three boys who had come to the county from the East who were ahead of me. Boys and girls from Lincoln and the vicinity were there by the hundred.

What was true of Nebraska then is true of all the country today. Hundreds of thousands of our youth are denied a college education, not so much because they cannot pay tuition—although that is a serious matter—but because they cannot afford the expense of living four years away from home. In New York only the boys and girls of the Greater City have free access to college education, in the municipal colleges. And alas, even here, instead of distributing college establishments as we distribute high schools, we draw students together in such masses that we administer rather than educate them.

These boys and girls are worth educating. The New School honored me by creating a number of graduate scholarships for the city institutions. I have met the succession of these scholars. Abler students are not to be found anywhere.

In upstate New York there are extensive regions where no boy or girl may enjoy college education unless he comes of a prosperous family. Thousands never realize their aspiration for college training. Therefore I was ardent for a New York State University, not to be another localized colossus like Columbia or Cornell or New York University or even the New York City colleges, but to be an organization of modest colleges scattered through the state. I dreamed of fine teaching colleges, each with five or six hundred students.

But fine teaching colleges premise fine teachers, and I have long been discontented with our conventional process of producing college teachers. We require them to equip themselves with the Ph.D. degree. And the training for that degree is training in research, which may or may not be training for teaching.

I may illustrate by the case of a one-time colleague of mine, a professor of history. He had set out to write as his doctoral thesis—involving half his time and three-fourths of his energy—a *History of Papal Revenues*. This he soon learned was too broad. He cut it down to the *History of Papal Revenues from England;* still too broad. He cut it to the *Papal Revenues from Fourteenth-Century England;* too broad. He cut it to the *Papal Revenues from England, 1334–1335*.

I do not doubt that his final monograph was a contribution to history. But I question whether the study put him in a position to meet his class glowing with the genial fire one derives from intimate association with the great historians.

I am not a critic of the conventional doctorate training. America produces about nine thousand Ph.D.s every year, of whom the majority are destined to go on into scientific research careers. For them the meticulous training in methods of scientific research is desirable. But we need teachers as well as research workers, teachers of the millions of young Americans who are not preparing for research careers, but for business, politics, the arts, the professions. What these millions need are teachers who are on fire with the spirit of advancing science, art, culture, philosophy. Such teachers are indeed to be found, but they are the rare individuals whose native spirit breaks the fetters of a miscast training.

I have never been deeply enamored of ideas, even true and beautiful, if I could do nothing about them. In this matter of education for college teachers I might speak to deaf ears and write for blind eyes. Prophets of old were content to be voices crying in the wilderness. I am no prophet but an American extrovert addicted to the notion that an idea is fertile only when married to action.

A succession of chances gave me a glimmer of hope that I might be able to plant a seed of the kind of training for college teachers I dreamed of.

Yale University had been *terra incognita* to me in my professorial life. It maintained two great economists, Arthur T. Hadley and Irving Fisher, whom one met occasionally at meetings of the American Economic Association. But Yale and Yale men seemed to maintain an air of aloofness in the *Sturm und Drang* of the main currents of university life.

Early in the 1930s I became acquainted with Yale through association with the advisory editorial committee of the *Yale Review*. I was flattered by an invitation to join this committee because I regarded the *Yale Review,* then under the editorship of Governor Wilbur Cross and his brilliant adjutant, Helen McAfee, as the most distinguished periodical in America. For several years I made pilgrimages to the editorial meetings, where I met one of the choicest groups of true intellectuals, of whom Governor Cross himself impressed me as the ideal combination of scholarship, culture, and citizenship. I was as powerfully attracted by Provost Edgar Furness, energetic, informed, blithe, modest, an ideal educator. I came to know President Charles Seymour and to observe the subtle operations of his mind, and Treasurer George Day, brother of my friend Clarence, and his brilliant wife Wilhelmine. I always looked forward eagerly to the meetings of the editorial committee. I loved the Yale campus with its noble old elms, the venerable buildings, even the new library, designed to withstand any assault by catapult or ballista, and to exclude, so far as practicable, the cheap and nasty competition of the light of day with the honest interests of the electric light and power company.

I was astonished, and delighted, when Furness suggested that I join the economics department as a professor on half-time. I wanted to accept, all the more because I got underground information that the rest of the department was against me. To them I was a journalist, an educational and intellectual adventurer. Sometimes one's unpopularity is flattering.

Of course I'd have to give half my time; but I had never felt justified in charging to the New School more than half my living expenses. I had earned the other half outside, and this had involved a good half of my time. The new claim on my time was nothing to trouble me.

What most concerned me was whether I had anything to give worth the cost to Yale. The university had already a good Department of Economics. Perhaps it was in some respects over-antique; but one must judge a department by its fruits, the students it trains, and the Yale graduate students I met were able, alive, and creative.

I was not so arrogant as to imagine I could better the graduate teaching performance.

But there was an appurtenance of the position that appealed to me powerfully. I should be director of the Division of General Studies. A graduate student might enroll with me and attain new educational liberties. If the student and I agreed that to supplement his program he needed to go afield from the established routine, if in working on a problem of labor standards he needed information to be had in the School of Medicine or the School of Law or the School of Theology, I could get him access to those schools.

The students coming under my jurisdiction would be for the most part aspirants for the Master's degree. There is something unique about the Yale Master's degree. It is not just a halfway house to the Doctor's degree. A Yale Master's costs as much time and effort as a Doctor's in many other institutions. It carries more or less unconsciously the tradition of the Master's degree of Oxford and Cambridge, the highest degree in course offered by those institutions.

Might it not be possible, working in the Division of General Studies under the Yale Master's tradition, to effect eventually a division of labor, the Master's for teaching, the Doctor's for research? The prestige of Yale, all the way to Point Barrow, is tremendous. If Yale were turning out as teachers young scholars trained like Oxford or Cambridge Masters the whole American educational world would take notice.

First catch your rabbit, the old cookbook says. You don't make unnecessary noise when you are after a rabbit. I accepted appointment as a Yale professor with enthusiasm. It was of no use to proclaim that I accepted with a view to making out of my opportunity an educational advance as much in the spirit of Yale as Yale itself.

My first year taught me how slowly elms grow in New Haven, though they grow exceeding large. It would take ten years to realize even the beginnings of my project. I had four years before the Yale retirement age of sixty-seven. What of it? I thought. After four years I'd be off the salary list, but I'd keep on for the rest of the ten at my own expense. No: Yale could not permit that. President James R. Angell on retirement had wished to continue in education, without salary. He was not permitted to do so. He was compelled to betake himself with his colossal energies to the National Broadcasting Company.

In the brief time left me before the inexorable statute of retirement would take effect I could accomplish nothing worth Yale's interest or my personal dignity. I resigned with sorrow, for my resignation meant divorce from an ardent hope and from close association with wonderful friends.

I'm not sure what animal it is that is so constituted that it can pull in its horns. Maybe it's a snail. Anyway, I pulled in my horns. I came away from Yale sadder but wiser.

Governor Dewey, in making up a Temporary Commission on a State University in 1946, included me in the list of commissioners along with college and university presidents, to help balance the constituted educational authorities and the legislators and watchdogs of the treasury.

The movement for a state university was in large part animated by the outraged feelings of the Jewish intellectual public over the intrusion into American educational life of Old World antisemitism and its institution of the *numerus clausus*. This was most glaringly in evidence in medical colleges, which pretended that in the best interest of medicine and of the Jews themselves all but a fraction should be excluded. Some six hundred medical students a year were forced to go to Scottish and other European universities, to gain access to the profession of their aspiration.

I had had many discussions with the polished gentlemen of the universities who administered the *numerus clausus,* which was a late formula for antisemitism proclaimed to be fair since it contemplated the admission of a certain percentage of Jews instead of the earlier general exclusion. Jews, they argued, could reasonably demand a place in education proportional to their numerical position in America. But the Jews were bent on academic and professional position. If they were not checked the universities and the professions would come to be Jewish, divorced from the American way of life. And this would be bad for the Jews themselves.

I could argue that in this great city of New York there are two groups that take to intellectual and professional life. One is the old American, where, perhaps not as a rule, but in large part, boys and girls grow up with the expectation of college training and perhaps professional life. The other group is the Jewish. The large Italian group has only recently come to aspire to intellectual and professional position, and the same thing is true of the Irish contingent in the population. If we should have a *numerus clausus* for Jews, why not also for the Yankee and patroon stocks?

I did not bother myself much about the *numerus clausus* in select colleges. If college is just a place where nice boys meet nice boys, with a view to helping each other get nice jobs and meeting nice sisters who would make nice wives, that is something out of my domain of interest. But medicine? One of these days I'll burst a blood vessel in my brain, especially if I keep encountering the *numerus clausus*. Some doctor will have to take charge of me. In my pathetically desperate condition will I ask, "Doctor, are you an Episcopalian or a Methodist or a Jew?" No. I will only ask, "Doctor, is there any hope for me?"

The prominent figures in the Commission on a State University were Chairman of the Board of Regents William J. Wallin, a powerful and opinionative man, a lay educator of true educational imagination and energy; State Commissioner of Education Francis T. Spaulding, a man so devoted to education that he let himself be afflicted by stomach ulcers; and a grave, wise, not very communicative expert on education, Dr. Oliver C. Carmichael, destined for Carnegie Foundation importance. Our lay and legislative members were mostly for a huge state university at Albany, to play a part like the University of California at Berkeley. Commissioner Spaulding was for a system of colleges, scattered through the state. He wanted them to be technical institutes. I too was for bringing the wealth of technology into colleges for the neglected youth who could not go to the colleges and pay tuition and the costs of living, but I did not want to exclude the excluded youth from the wide reaches of college education. I could go along with Commissioner Spaulding on setting up technical institutes, but I wanted them also to be colleges, preparing for all that college prepares for.

We could easily compromise on this issue, but we ran up against the watchdogs of the treasury. They would authorize local colleges, but at local expense. The State of New York has money, or could get money. There are a hundred localities where there should be colleges. None of them has any money.

We got the approval of the state—but no money. I think two colleges have been set up—two, out of the hundred we need.

But the spearhead of our problem was medical education. We heard the smooth and learned medical deans who set out to prove to us that in this best of all possible worlds the State of New York was turning out all the doctors the ills of humanity could use. And as for the *numerus clausus,* these elegant deans had never heard of it.

I was just an anonymous member of the commission. I joined with other anonymous members, and we put something across. There were two distressed medical colleges in New York which were trying to do an honest job but had not the means to do it—Syracuse and Long Island. I went to my friend Chancellor William P. Tolley of Syracuse and asked him if he would resent it if I tried to take Syracuse Medical over for the state university. Not at all.

We took over Syracuse and Long Island—two medical colleges that could never have a *numerus clausus*. And for fear of political action, the rest of the medical colleges of the state cut out the *numerus clausus*. They still find ways of keeping down the number of Jewish students, but they formally disavow intent to discriminate. Hypocrisy, if you will, but Brandeis used to say, hypocrisy is the dawn of virtue.

THIRTY-SEVEN

Retirement

As AN economist I have always been critical of the prevailing ideas and institutions of retirement on account of age. Thanks to the advances in medicine of the last half-century and to general hygienic and dietary improvements, we live longer, on the average; indeed, much longer. The percentage of the population of persons sixty years and over is steadily advancing.

I used to shock my college classes by stating solemnly that fifty years ago the college student looked forward to the time when he would be carrying two or three children on his shoulders, to lift him up in his zeal for work and advancement. But the college student of today must look forward to carrying around one or two old people, increasingly robust and heavy as the practice of medicine improves.

If a student objected that the burden of the time-expired population was to be carried by the state, I would ask, "Who carries the state?" If the objection was raised that pensions and annuities came out of savings in past years, voluntary or compulsory, I would reply, "The bread and beef a man eats, the clothes he wears, the fuel that keeps him warm, all come out of current production. There are no stockpiles from previous years that amount to anything, and except in the case of industrial raw materials and alcoholic beverages there never can be important stockpiles. The present population, young or old, lives out of current production. The labor of the active producers of today is carrying us all."

And some student was sure to ask, "Isn't it necessary to get the old boys out of the way to give us young fellows a chance?" I would discourse on the stupidity of a social organization that could not find jobs for all men willing and able to work, except under conditions of war or preparation for war.

Of course I always approved the maintenance of the disabled— generous maintenance. And insofar as advancing years bring disabilities—actual, not putative—pensions and annuities are justified. They are imperative in a humane state. But how serious are the disabilities of the average sexagenarian?

There are disabilities to be found in any stage of life. You never see a factory or a mine in which all the workers are equally endowed with physical strength. One worker does his job easily; another strains his muscles to do the same job. Their performance is about the same; and at the closing bell the big man strides away on his long legs, the little man trips along on his short legs, both apparently equally weary.

There is no important job I have ever seen where performance depends solely upon a man's congenital physical constitution. Everywhere performance entails a combination of physical strength, skilled adjustment, and will. The factors are combined in different proportions with different men. The result is a uniformity of performance that often strikes the literary observer as incredible.

The disabilities of advancing years have one peculiarity: they come on so gradually, as a rule, that compensating adjustments are made almost unconsciously. When I was a youth of twenty I worked some months on an agricultural college farm alongside of an old fellow of seventy. I was twice or three times as strong as he, and I was fairly skilled. But the old man would get as much done in a day as I could.

"I'll tell you, Johnnie, how it is. As you get old you take better care of your tools. A young fellow like you grinds his ax in the morning and chops away half a day. I keep a whetstone in my pocket and touch up the edge every half hour. I cut more wood than you do.

"I cut more grass than you did yesterday. You feel strong and hew away at the grass, with a will, as they say, but not with much good sense. I've adjusted my snath so the blade runs level with the ground and kisses the grass off at the roots. You hew the grass at an angle. Twice as hard work. But you got to live a long time to learn those things."

In the labor shortage of the war many industrial establishments brought back into the shop men who had been laid off for age. Those old fellows proved to be as efficient as ever. They liked the work and saw with regret the return of peace and their approaching relegation to the boring leisure of retirement.

I do not want to run a good principle into the ground. There are in life situations that require native strength and the elasticity of youth— pugilism, for example. The Romans retired their legionaries after thirty-six years of service. There was still fight in those veterans, and they were settled in compact colonies whence they could be called to the eagles in time of emergency. We retire our generals at a fairly early age in times of peace. They form a reserve to draw upon in time of war. New York pensions off its policemen after twenty years of service. A robust, highly pensioned man of forty-one is a phenomenon that must make sense politically. All that I maintain is that in the wide reaches of modern industrial and institutional life the retirement of men still fit and competent makes no economic sense at all.

Is academic teaching one of the special fields in which retirement at a specific age is desirable? Unlike the Army, education does not relegate men to the general public in order to have a reserve for an emergency. The retired professor may sometimes assume a position of leadership in the community where he establishes his final residence. He may use his leisure to carry through literary or scientific projects for which he had no time as an active professor. I might cite cases like that of Dr. Benjamin M. Duggar, who after retirement accepted a position with the Lederle Company and worked out aureomycin, a top antibiotic. There are such exceptions to the rule that retirement wastes manpower.

The accepted reasons for fixing an age of academic retirement are, first, to improve instruction by introducing younger blood, and, second, to give the younger scholars a chance to rise to higher academic positions.

At the time when Andrew Carnegie announced his plan of academic pensions American universities and colleges were finishing the first phase of the vast developments in higher education that characterized the last quarter of the nineteenth century. Small colleges were expanding into universities; wholly new universities sprang up overnight, like Johns Hopkins, Stanford, and Chicago; all the western and some of the southern states were establishing state universities. There were not enough well-trained scholars in the country to man the academic positions opening up. The institutions filled the positions as well as they could, often taking men with scholastic records that were mainly honorary. And these men were not always the worst teachers.

But it irked the younger scholars with soundly minted Ph.D.s from Germany or the rising American universities to work under men whose education was merely homespun. The Carnegie pension plan offered a humane way of ridding the universities and colleges of holdovers from more primitive educational days.

This motive long ago lost its relevancy. Today the professors of sixty are men and women who probably received as sound a training as the professor of thirty. Science has indeed made tremendous advances in the last fifty years, but the older scholars have followed the literature about as well as the younger ones.

Still, is there not a rigidity in the older minds that hinders adjustment to new ideas? The evidence on this point is very spotty and unconvincing. I know conservative, liberal, and radical sexagenarian scholars. It is a matter of temperament, and temperament has surprising capacity for persistence.

But am I not overlooking the physical disabilities of the older men, uncertain health, advancing deafness, failing eyesight? Where health is actually uncertain, retirement is, of course, indicated, perhaps at an age much earlier than the standard. But as to sensory disabilities, I can't make much of them.

You don't simply hear; you listen. Listening is a combination of sense perception and attention. So is seeing. It isn't so much your eyes that tire when you read a dull text, or your ears that tire when you hear a dull lecture. It is you who tire, holding your attention up to the experience by the neck. If you do not welcome the loss of hearing and sight as liberating you from responsibilities, you sharpen your attention as fast as the sense organ deteriorates. You are not even aware of any deterioration.

I studied trigonometry under an octogenarian. He could hear every word any of us students uttered in class. But if I met him on the campus walk and tried to say something to him, he'd put his hand up to his ear and shake his head. I thought he was a fraud, in his pretense of deafness. He wasn't. My non-mathematical talk bored him.

The only interesting and interested professor I ever knew who was really deaf was Charles Beard, and he wasn't too deaf to hear you if you said something that interested him, or better, something that made him mad.

I can't accept the disabilities argument for retiring professors at a fixed age. But there is something in the argument that this is necessary in order to give the younger men a chance. I have seen younger professors eying the department head piercingly, hoping to see signs of a weakening of his determination to hold on. And it has seemed to me that the universities and colleges could manage the matter more intelligently. Make the younger man department head; utilize the older man for survey courses in his field, for which his long experience should qualify him well.

For years I had urged the utilization of retired professors in adult education. Dr. Hans Simons, on his accession to the presidency of the New School in 1949, approved a project for offering courses by retired professors, five courses each term. My friends raised a modest fund to support the project.

The courses were moderately successful. But much more money was required to give the plan a fair trial. Yet the effort was not lost. The propaganda for the project reached many educators throughout the country and will have indefinite effects as the movement for higher adult education gains headway.

How was it possible for me, holding such views of retirement, to maintain my consistency in retiring from the presidency of the New School?

The position of president of the New School is a peculiar one, like that of the pugilist. He operates an institution that has virtually no income from endowment, and therefore he has to exert himself manfully, every year, to cover the costs in excess of tuition. He has no hard-and-fast curriculum: he has to study the interests of the public and develop a program according to his judgment. Of course he has to personalize his position. Even the best and most generous liberals are drawn closer to persons than to ideas and programs. Of practical necessity, the president of the New School has to claim the initiative for everything done in the institution and take credit for it. I obeyed the necessity, being too proud to be modest.

There is a touching incident in the life of Columbia University that would be forgotten but for my memory. Nicholas Murray Butler, in his late seventies, had neglected, for session after session, to appear at the general faculty meeting. There had been much talk among the faculty. He was retiring. One had it from a trustee. Another had it from a dean. Another had it from N.M.B.'s cook. And who was who for the succession?

One afternoon Butler marched into the faculty meeting, with solemn tread and slow. He strode to the Presidential chair, paused, turned around. "Gentlemen, look at that chair. It is *my* chair. It will be my chair till I die."

Butler stood on a mountain of achievement, moral, intellectual, financial. He had built up Columbia's endowment by hundreds of millions.

To compare the small with the great, I had never built up a perceptible endowment for the New School. I had a wonderful body of friends who would not let me down. But when I met one of them he would look at me piercingly and inquire sympathetically, "How are you?" I was fine, and my friend would give another check to the New School.

In my own opinion there was a good deal of life left in me. But I couldn't argue the point; I could only prove it; and the proof took time. In the meantime I admitted the need of finding a successor who had many more years to the good than I could have. I had a successor in mind, a member of the Graduate Faculty, Hans Simons.

Hans Simons had been director of the Institut für Politik in Berlin, essentially an institution of higher adult education. He had been active in the Briand-Streseman movement for a reconciliation of Germany and France, a movement which, if successful, would have excluded Hitler. We of America and England could have made a charter of peace and humanity out of the Briand-Streseman movement. We were dumb idiots and paid for it with lives.

But when the splendid hopes of Hans Simons were smashed, and he lived on the uneasy edge of Hitler tolerance, I got him to come to the New School. He had at first small English which he soon developed into great English, and became from coast to coast a favorite lecturer on international affairs.

Hans Simons was young, with fresh and significant mind. I wanted him for my successor.

A change, I saw, was coming in our affairs.

The New School carried a heavy debt, the result of financing its building. There was a first mortgage, a second mortgage, and a large volume of income bonds. I was not, myself, much troubled by the debt. The creditors of the School were lenient, and what we had actually to pay in interest amounted to what would have been a very modest rental if we had not undertaken a building of our own. We had managed to make some small payments on our second mortgage, for which we got in compensation a lower rate of interest. Our income bonds, still counted at par, were coming in as contributions deductible for purposes of income taxation. I foresaw increasing income taxes and an increasing rate of recovery of bonds by way of contributions.

The board was so fortunate as to enlist the interest of James Causey, a marvelously talented business organizer and reorganizer. He looked at our financial structure and held up his hands in horror. With our fantastic debt structure we were skating on thin ice toward some terrible collapse.

I did not think we were. Our creditors were not going to foreclose on us and sell our building, for they couldn't sell it at a price that would give them back their money, or any fair part of it. At the end of twenty years our bondholders could sue us and get what satisfaction they could out of that. In the meantime some tens, perhaps hundreds, of thousands in bonds would have come in as contributions.

But when the practical Jim Causey was crying wolf, the academic Alvin Johnson could not go around admonishing, "Keep your shirt on."

Causey declared that it was imperative to put us through the wringer and clear off our debts. I alone of the New School board was not convinced. And this special position of mine made me reflect. Was I the man to head the institution in the new age of steel and gold? I was only what I had always been, and I could not find in me the germs of adjustment to the new order. I proposed to Causey to put my resignation before the board.

Causey vetoed my suggestion. I was a part of the merchandise he had to sell. I could not fly the coop until the business of putting the school through the wringer was finished. His program was simple and straightforward. We were to refuse to pay interest on our mortgages. The mortgagees would then foreclose. Our building would be put up at auction. Our friends would bid it in at the modest price such a building could command in time of depression and hand it back to us, all lily-whitened of its debts and sins.

I felt very uneasy about so bold a procedure. All turned on our having friends who would fork over something like two hundred thousand dollars. In my opinion we hadn't any such friends. I was wrong.

Professor Staudinger had drawn to his class on population a brilliant and charming lady, Marian Paschal, friend and trusted secretary of Doris Duke. Marian introduced Staudinger to Doris Duke; they became good friends, for Doris Duke needed wise counsel and Hans Staudinger is about as wise a counselor as any human being is permitted to be. I too was introduced to Doris Duke, a much more serious, intelligent, and public-spirited young woman than the press made her out to be. I did not succeed in establishing a solid friendship, for Doris Duke was shy, and I was diffident.

When our building was put up on the block, Doris Duke bid it in and presented it to us. We were debt free. The New School had been saved—by a miracle. It could go forward with a deeper breath of liberty. I did not feel that it could go forward with full vigor under me.

The New School had grown into a great and complicated institution. Starting with a limited program of lectures and research in the social sciences, it had expanded in every direction until it could say that no object of genuine intellectual interest is alien to the New School. It did not expand according to any deliberate plans of mine. But I am so conceited as to say I possessed an educational green thumb. Intellectual plants grew under my hand.

The University in Exile, at the outset a refuge for exiled professors and an implantation of sound European culture in the American environment, set out on a triumphant development that raised it to the front rank of graduate faculties of political and social science. I had contemplated a dozen or twenty intelligent adults seeking guidance in special inquiries. Soon they numbered scores and are now running between four and five hundred, each with all the demands on expert instruction native to men and women who feel the creative spark.

Having realized in my academic career that the intellectual world has thousands of members who have ideas but are under the illusion that they can't write, I welcomed Gorham Munson's offer of a course on writing. Out of that course have come more than twenty books and hundreds of published articles. The demand for writing courses expanded; we annexed Don Wolfe, Hiram Hayden, Charles I. Glicksberg, and others. The present literary output is such, I'd need the multiple eyes of Argus to master it all.

I fostered courses of lectures on painting and sculpture, to find that the intelligent adult wanted also to know how paintings and sculptures are made and how he could make them. The result is a thriving department of creative art under Camilo Egas and José de Creef. Lectures on architecture led to an architectural workshop, which produced two young men who went off to a competition of housing in Stockholm and won it. Our town-planning courses fired Albert Mayer, who built the New School building, to make a town planner of himself; he is planning cities and villages in India today, with great prestige and success.

Courses in psychology and psychiatry and psychoanalysis led to an enormous development of a department for training psychologists. Adolf Lowe and Hans Staudinger created out of their expert competence in international affairs a World Institute, which executed researches of commanding importance and drew together an advisory committee consisting of many of the best business and intellectual heads in New York.

I saw opportunity in the presence in America, in exile, of Erwin Piscator, who had challenged the predominance of the great Max Reinhardt in the theatrical field in Germany. As always, I had a limited program: I wanted Piscator to give courses to show our adult students how plays are translated from the author's manuscript to the show we see on the stage. Soon Piscator expanded his work until it became a powerful and militant Dramatic Workshop, too huge and obstreperous to be lodged under the New School roof. We helped it to set up independently.

An institution with so wide a reach, with so powerful a tendency to expand in every direction, necessarily presents serious problems of administration. I had never been an administrator. My Middle-Western democratic instinct had no place for giving and taking orders, the staple of administration. My plan had always been to entrust a function to an officer and back him up. I made the Graduate Faculty autonomous. I left the Institute of World Affairs to the able direction of Lowe and Staudinger. I split the adult educational program into a School of Philosophy and a School of Political Science and put the first under Clara Mayer, the second under Hans Simons, with all powers of decision in their hands. As for my own functions, they lay largely in the field of public relations, within the institution and without. And if I ever seemed to be neglecting an issue, I had a succession of remarkably able secretaries to haul me up.

I do not think the New School ever suffered from my scheme of administration, or non-administration. I do not impute the immunity to mistakes of the school to my genius for leadership, but to miraculous luck in always having a personnel true, faithful, intelligent, and resourceful.

There was another, as I have indicated, more serious reason for my retiring. It is customary in institutions like the New School for the president to absorb all the credit that really belongs to his co-workers. That is necessary for publicity purposes. But one result is that when the years sneak up on one, the question begins to be mooted: What will happen to the institution when the head of it drops dead?

I began to hear that too often. True, I was not in the habit of dropping dead. But the question was bad medicine for the fund-raisers.

I proposed Hans Simons to Causey, as my successor. No, it wouldn't do: we couldn't have a German. German. Good God, what are national origins under the blue sky over the whole world, under the spirit of man that means somehow to make a sweet garden of the earth?

I couldn't have Simons. I sat on my job, sure that it would take an earthquake to dislodge me. Louis D. Weiss, chairman of the board, felt as strongly as I did that the school should have a new president. He rejected the idea of Simons. No German.

I went through a bad time. Candidate after candidate was presented to me. I judged them and found them wanting. Weiss, a very grand person in himself, almost went out of his head. I was playing a Gromyko game in his opinion.

Finally we agreed on Bryn J. Hovde as president. In 1945 I retired into the limbo of emeritus, only to find that I was still A. J., with all the obligations still on me that I ever had.

Bryn J. Hovde proved to be a distinguished administrator, true, human, intelligent, but not, alas, with a constitution up to his stature. He worked faithfully to do his job, but it is a terrible job for any man to carry a serious educational enterprise which has no endowment. After four years Hovde retired, to be succeeded by Hans Simons.

And so I live on, emeritus. The New School gives me a pleasant office, and I have the services of a most efficient secretary, Stefanie Ruskin. I am as devoted to the New School as ever, eager to be helpful to the school and my admired chief, Dr. Simons. In the open season I spend much of my time at my home in Nyack, where I dig the soil, plant, mow the grass, and cut out weed trees, restoring my touch with Mother Earth.

I have more leisure, and a proof of that is this exceedingly long autobiography of a common man. I dare not ask the reader, "Have I missed anything?" for he might reply, like the hearer of a very long speech, "Yes, you missed a good many excellent places to stop."

Index